What's *Social* About Social Cognition?

What's *Social* About Social Cognition?

Research on Socially Shared Cognition in Small Groups

Edited by
Judith L. Nye
Aaron M. Brower

SAGE Publications
International Educational and Professional Publisher
Thousand Oaks   London   New Delhi

For information address:

SAGE Publications, Inc.
2455 Teller Road
Thousand Oaks, California 91320
E-mail: order@sagepub.com

SAGE Publications Ltd.
6 Bonhill Street
London EC2A 4PU
United Kingdom

SAGE Publications India Pvt. Ltd.
M-32 Market
Greater Kailash I
New Delhi 110 048 India

Printed in the United States of America

Library of Congress Cataloging-in-Publication Data

Main entry under title:

What's social about social cognition?: Research on socially shared cognition in small groups / editors, Judith L. Nye and Aaron M. Brower.
p. cm.
Includes bibliographical references and index.
ISBN 0-8039-7204-0 (cloth: acid-free paper).—ISBN 0-8039-7205-9 (pbk.: acid-free paper)
1. Social groups. 2. Social perception. 3. Social psychology.
I. Nye, Judith L. II. Brower, Aaron M.
HM133.W47 1996
302.3'4—dc20   96-4479

This book is printed on acid-free paper.

99   00   01   10   9   8   7   6   5   4   3   2

Sage Production Editor: Gillian Dickens
Sage Typesetters: Yang-hee Syn Maresca & Andrea D. Swanson
Sage Cover Designer: Candice Harman

Contents

Preface

This book is based on the premise that an ideal arena for studying the social and interactional aspects of social cognition is the small group. In this volume, we present exemplar research on various aspects of social cognition conducted within a small group context. This book expands on a special issue of *Small Group Research* (May 1994) that addressed this very topic. We invited prominent researchers in social cognition and groups research to present their research dealing with the more social side of social cognition.

The book is organized into three main parts that describe central topics in the study of what's social about social cognitions. In the part titled "The Group as a Cognitive Unit: Group Beliefs, Decisions, and Products," the chapters address the delicate and potentially explosive balance between the resources and talents of individual members and the interpersonal dynamics that go on between group members. This part includes chapters that address groups as they set about their tasks: Wittenbaum and Stasser (Chapter 1) discuss their research on how groups manage and use information; Haslam, McGarty, and Turner (Chapter 2) address the bias that group members tend to hold toward the credibility and relevance of information provided by their own group members; and Moreland, Argote, and Krishnan (Chapter 3) reveal that groups can be trained to work better than individuals in constructing products.

In Part II, "Impact of the Group on Thinking About the Self and Other Group Members," the chapters focus on how self-concept and perceptions of others in the group change based on group processes. These chapters address effects on the self and others based on "real" group interactions rather than on those that are analogue or imagined. Patterson (Chapter 4) focuses on the relationship between person perceptions and interactive behavior in groups and how they affect impression formation and management. Forsyth and Kelley (Chapter 5) describe how members shift their initial "egocentric" focus to a "sociocentric" one once their group coalesces. Nye and Simonetta (Chapter 6) describe which aspects of members' perceptions of leaders change and which remain stable after group successes and failures and how both stability and change are influenced by members' leadership schemas. Johnson and Neimeyer (Chapter 7) discuss unique interaction effects on member perceptions after perceiver and target effects are teased out. Finally, Oyserman and Packer (Chapter 8) describe how individuals view themselves differently depending on the groups with which they identify, and they note that one's sense of self has an inherent social component.

The last of the three main parts, "Impact of the Group on Member Identification and Group Boundaries," includes chapters discussing how group members tend to think about their own groups in relation to members of outgroups. All three chapters note that group entitativity (Campbell, 1958) is not rigidly determined—in fact, a group's sense of "we-ness" is constantly open to change. Mullen, Rozell, and Johnson (Chapter 9) demonstrate how factors as simple as group size can affect how ingroups and outgroups are represented in the mind of the social perceiver. Gaertner, Rust, Dovidio, Bachman, and Anastasio (Chapter 10) call on the common ingroup identity model to explain the cognitive mechanisms that can contribute to the reduction of prejudice between groups. Considering the impact of temporal factors, Worchel (Chapter 11) argues that as groups change over time, group members' perceptions of ingroup and outgroups members and their habits of interacting change in predictable patterns.

These empirical pieces are bracketed by two provocative chapters on the common ground between social cognition and groups research. In the Introduction, Fiske and Goodwin point out that, although the two areas have traditionally overlooked each other's offerings, "small group research and social cognition research need each other." They suggest a number of research pursuits in which each area could address the shortcomings of the other, thus strengthening both. In the second to last chapter, Ickes and Gonzalez (Chapter 12) offer *social* (i.e., intersubjective) cognition as an alternative research paradigm. They argue that pursuing research that acknowledges the interdependence of cognitions that occurs in interaction situations may serve to enhance the overall quality and meaningfulness of social psychological research and theory. Finally, we close the book with a discussion of the 11 empirical chapters. We identify a number of the common themes within them that can help point the way to future research and thinking on the uniquely social aspects of social cognition.

One can read this book straight through, or one can use each part as an example of how different authors view similar phenomena. Because this book brings together two major areas of research, we believe it will speak to a wide audience. Within social cognition research, social psychologists have been calling for a more social emphasis on the research for some time now—our book offers research that meets this challenge. Groups researchers, on the other hand, will find that the views provided by social cognitive theories may provide coherence to what Levine and Moreland (1990) call a "badly fragmented" field (p. 586).

The empirical study of true social interactions is both devilishly complex and tantalizingly appealing. And although it may be a quixotic pursuit, it is where we feel true discoveries in academic psychology will be found. It is our sincere hope that this book can move us a step forward in this discussion.

This book was, truly, a rewarding and challenging project on which to work—not exactly heavy labor but a labor of love nonetheless. We wish to acknowledge the contributions of several people in the development of this book. Jack Demarest, Don Forsyth, and Charles Garvin provided the initial encouragement to begin this project. Jim Nageotte and Nancy Hale at Sage Publications were invaluable in bringing it to completion. Karen Carlson, Jack Husted, and Janice Stapley reviewed chapters in rough form and served as sounding boards for the project at various points along the way. Both Monmouth University and the University of Wisconsin provided much needed support at critical stages in the production of the book.

One wonderful outcome of this project has been the development of collaborative relationships among the authors contributing to this book. In addition to writing chapters, they very graciously reviewed the other chapters within their parts, which served to strengthen the overall coherence of the book. We wish to thank all of our authors for their commitment to pursuing good science while retaining their enthusiasm for capturing the complexities of real life.

Finally, we wish to dedicate this book to Richard Su and Nancy, Jacob, and Nathaniel Brower. Their continuing love and support have made all the difference in our personal and professional lives.

Judith L. Nye
Aaron M. Brower

Introduction
Social Cognition Research and Small Group Research, a West Side Story *or . . . ?*

SUSAN T. FISKE
STEPHANIE A. GOODWIN

Small group research and social cognition research need each other. Neither has dealt adequately with the other's phenomena. Recent reviews of each area bear out this simple observation of neglect, first in social cognition research: "The social perceiver . . . has been viewed as somewhat of a hermit, isolated from the social environment. Missing from much research on social cognition have been other people in a status other than that of stimulus" (Fiske &

AUTHORS' NOTE: The writing of this paper was supported by the first author's NIMH grant 41801, which also supported the second author. Correspondence may be addressed to the first author at Department of Psychology, Tobin Hall, University of Massachusetts, Amherst, MA 01003.

Taylor, 1991, p. 556). And in small group research, social cognition apparently can be utterly ignored. Nowhere in Levine and Moreland's (1990) *Annual Review of Psychology* chapter, "Progress in Small Group Research," are social cognitive theories singled out as a fruitful past or future source of stimulation for small group research. Although social cognitive approaches have been accused of being imperialistic, threatening to dominate social psychology, the *Annual Review of Psychology* chapter might lead one to judge, at the opposite extreme, that social cognition is totally irrelevant to small group research. The situation resembles that of two rival gangs each having staked out their separate turf, crossing boundaries at their peril; this perception is the source of our *West Side Story* theme.

In contrast to gang warfare, we endorse a more spontaneous and open interplay between research on social cognition and small groups, as equal parties, both with a long history within social psychology as well as a bright future. To that end, as kibitzing outsiders, we commend the research in this volume, and we will offer some additional opportunities that seem to beg for research attention. In doing this, we do not wish to blur the distinction between individual and group phenomena, which we acknowledge differ fundamentally (e.g., Ruscher, Fiske, Miki, & Van Manen, 1991; Schopler & Insko, 1992; Tajfel, 1982). Nevertheless, many intriguing points of contact do emerge.

THERE'S A PLACE FOR US

There is a central place for the phenomena of both small groups and social cognition in social psychology, which follows from what we all do and how we all define ourselves as social psychologists. The earliest and most current definitions of the field unanimously endorse the need to study interaction as well as perceptions and interpretations. Allport (1954) defined social psychology as "an attempt to understand and explain how the thought, feeling, and behavior of individuals are influenced by the actual, imagined, or implied presence of other human beings" (p. 5). Prominent in this definition are both actual interactions and cognitively mediated interactions (imagined, implied).

E. A. Ross (1908) asserted that,

> Social psychology deals only with uniformities due to *social* causes,
> i.e., to *mental contacts* or *mental interactions*. In each case, we must
> ask, "Are these human beings aligned . . . by their *interpsychology*,
> i.e., the influences they have received from one another or from a
> common human source?" . . . It is *social* only insofar as it arises out
> of the interplay of minds. (pp. 2-3)

Again, prominent in the definition is the importance of actual interaction as well as mental interaction.

According to Mead (1909, 1910), a social act is defined by one
person serving as a stimulus to a response by another person and vice
versa; such "interstimulation links them functionally together in a
common social situation" (Karpf, 1932, p. 321), making a "conversation" of social stimulation and response. This conversation is
mediated by meaning, images, symbols, and empathy.

Whether social psychology is viewed as social influences, mental
interaction, or conversation (interstimulation), each of these implies
people together, and each implies that people are interpreting each
other. These foundational definitions suggest a central place for
face-to-face interaction, as studied, for example, within small groups,
research on which has been present since the beginning of American
social psychology. For example, the index to Karpf's (1932) *American
Social Psychology* contains numerous references to the "group approach"; Dashiell's (1935) survey of experiments examining the
influence of social situations on individuals explicitly defines itself in
terms of person-to-person relationships and the effects of the group
on the individual. More recently, Levine and Moreland (1990) conclude that small group research is alive and well but living elsewhere
(in allied fields). The point is that social psychology, the study of
people's impact on each other, requires or should require the study
of person-to-person interactions of which small group research is a
prominent part.

The study of social influences, mental interaction, and conversation-
like interstimulation also requires the study of minds in social settings. The influence of others is filtered through the individual's

cognitive system. As Ross and Nisbett (1991) note, studying the impact of social situations requires studying the impact of social situations as perceived by the individual in question; they trace their idea of construing to Asch (1952), Brunswik (1956), and Lewin (1935). Lewin's (1935) concept of the life space, the situational forces perceived to be operating on the person, emphasizes subjective interpretation. So does the Brunswik (1956) lens model of social perception—the proximal cause of people's responses is their filtered perception, not the distal object. And Asch, along with Helen Block Lewis (Asch, 1940; Asch, Block, & Hertzman, 1938; Lewis, 1941), emphasized how meaning and judgment result from social standards.

To honor the equal importance of social cognitions and face-to-face interactions, we will discuss first how social cognition has dealt with face-to-face interaction, and second how small group research has dealt or might deal with social cognitive issues. In doing this, we will suggest that it is not a case of the Jets versus the Sharks (or Montagues versus Capulets) but of more constructive potential interaction.

THE RUMBLE

Rumors of discontent, even confrontation, have challenged social cognition research from early on. Over the past 15 years, the primary complaints have been three (e.g., Fiske, 1981; Manis, 1977; Taylor, 1981b; Zajonc, 1980): Social cognition research fails to deal adequately with affect; it fails to deal adequately with motivation; and it fails to deal adequately with actual interaction. The "hermit" criticism, noted in the opening paragraph, is shared by other commentators: "The focus [of cognitive psychology] has remained on the individual as a solitary and, for the most part, purely intellective being" (Levine, Resnick, & Higgins, 1993, p. 586). In a similar vein, Ickes and Gonzales (Chapter 12, this volume) endorse the need for a *social* cognition, citing the lack of affect, intersubjectivity, and naturalistic interaction.

A more formal analysis of the established paradigm for studying social cognition reveals some cause for complaint along these lines. In an inspired survey of methods in major social and personality psychology journals of the 1980s, de la Haye (1991) has documented the most common paradigms for studying interpersonal cognition. As might be expected, they are short on actual interaction, affect, and motivation.

Consider first interaction. In social cognition studies, interaction would be potentiated by the mode of presenting the target person. Only 15% of the studies involved the physical presence of the target person, with another 3% allowing audio or video presentation believed to be live, but neither set necessarily allowed interaction. In contrast, in 45% of the studies, the target person was presented in a purely verbal medium, which hardly represents interaction.

Consider next the role of affect in social cognition paradigms. To be fair, the purpose of this subfield has been to push cognitive explanations, not to study affect, but many would argue that social cognition requires affect. In any case, among the independent variables, affect is never mentioned in the de la Haye (1991) analysis. Among the dependent variables, a category called Subject's Involvement, found in 22% of the studies, includes liking, preference, social distance, and judged physical attractiveness; assumed similarity; and assumed familiarity and assumed relationship. A possibly overlapping 25% of the studies include judgments of the target, some of which are at least evaluative if not emotional in nature. And 24% of studies (again, potentially overlapping) include judgments of the target's transitory covert characteristics, such as affective states. Noncognitive dependent variables not included elsewhere are present in 24% of studies. So, at least on the dependent variable side, affect is not wholly absent. Although affect may not be represented often as full-blooded emotion (cf. Dijker & Fiske, 1993), at least some evaluative and affective judgments are clearly present. Admittedly, de la Haye omits a substantial literature on mood, but only some of it deals with mood effects on social perceptions.

The presence of motivational variables is harder to gauge. Characteristics of the situation surrounding the subject, manipulated in a full 34% of the studies, include goals, success or failure, roles, and subject-target relationship. This is not a modest proportion of motivational variables. Moreover, a clear upswing of interest in goals and motivation has appeared after a decade's hiatus. Researchers have returned to some of the pragmatic themes implicit and explicit in the founding of social psychology, following the pragmatic Jamesian idea that thinking is for doing (Fiske, 1993b). Motivation and goals anchor this enterprise. Numerous social cognition theories address different types of interaction goals with which people approach social perception (for reviews, see Fiske, 1992; Hilton & Darley, 1991; Kruglanski, 1990; Snyder, 1992; Stangor & Ford, 1992). New editions of *Social Cognition* (Fiske & Taylor, 1991) and the *Handbook of Social Cognition* (Wyer & Srull, 1994), as well as Ross and Nisbett's (1991) new book, all address goals and motivation to a greater degree than the comparable efforts a decade ago. Three edited volumes (Higgins & Sorrentino, 1990; Sorrentino & Higgins, 1986, 1996) collect a variety of theoretical and empirical advances in motivation and cognition.

In short, social cognition research stands accused of three main types of neglect: interaction, affect, and motivation. Of these, the accusation about affect is least credible: Affect has been a persistent junior partner in the enterprise from the beginning of the most recent two decades' flurry of activity. One might argue that it should have had a bigger role or that emotion (rather than evaluation and mood) should have been focal, but it is hardly fair to criticize a cognitive approach for focusing first on cognition and only secondarily on affect.

Turning to the status of motivation, it seems that there was indeed a period of neglect but that hiatus is flanked by an early interest in motivational issues, as reflected in the pragmatic origins of the enterprise, and by the current acceleration of interest in goals and motivation, as reflected in a recent upsurge of empirical and theoretical activity.

Finally, we come to the neglect of interaction. The accusation here is completely justified. Social cognition research is guilty on this count: Our subjects sit alone in the lab, like Tolman's rats in the maze, lost in thought. In this limited but important sense, social cognition is insufficiently social. The importance of neglecting social behavior should be evident. To its peril, research on attitudes historically neglected overt behavior, initially assuming that social behavior would follow directly from attitudes. A major upheaval followed reviews arguing that the typically measured attitude-behavior relation was small (e.g., Wicker, 1969). Within social cognition research, so few studies have measured the cognition-behavior relation that one cannot even argue about its size.

Would research on social cognition within small groups potentially answer these criticisms, especially the clear neglect of interaction? Not exactly. But it may help. The research represented in this volume, combining social cognition and small groups, varies on how much it deals with actual interactions. But there is clearly more social behavior reflected herein than in the usual sample of articles in the front section of the *Journal of Personality and Social Psychology*. And the odds are, the more we examine social cognition in small groups, the more we will address affect, motivation, and (especially) interaction. As the next section indicates, social cognition research has already developed some of the relevant groundwork. The section after that examines activity within small group research that does or could relate to social cognition processes.

SOMETHING'S COMING

Recent research in social cognition, as noted, is beginning to deal more actively with actual interactions and with issues related to interaction. As argued elsewhere (Fiske, 1992, 1993b), the core issues in thinking-for-doing are good-enough accuracy of perception, constructing meaning, and interaction goals. We will illustrate with special reference to issues likely to concern small group researchers.

Accuracy

Just a few years ago, the criticism was leveled that "the social perceiver is often viewed as having a somewhat lunatic disregard for external reality. This fantasizer seems to operate solely on whatever convenient fictions are in his or her own head" (Fiske & Taylor, 1991, p. 556). Some solutions are appearing to counteract this overemphasis on being in the head without reference to the stimulus world. After a considerable hiatus, accuracy has returned to the main agenda, particularly in the context of interaction.

For example, Kenny's innovative social relations model (e.g., Kenny & Albright, 1987), which assesses every person's rating of every other person except perhaps the self, seems ideally suited to small group settings. It then separates components of accuracy, for example, disentangling effects contributed by the perceiver versus the target versus their unique relationship. Small groups provide a natural laboratory for examining accuracy as defined by observer consensus because everyone observes the same behaviors, which is crucial to consensus (Kenny, 1991). As observers see more overlapping behavior, if that behavior is consistent and if they generally agree about the meaning of behavior, then acquaintance can increase consensus accuracy. Small groups also provide a context for what Swann (1984) would call circumscribed accuracy. Fairly good accuracy can be negotiated, within certain interaction contexts and with certain partners, a description that fits many small group contexts. And empathic accuracy is a central issue in any interaction (Ickes, Stinson, Bissonnette, & Garcia, 1990).

Accuracy refers not only to judgments but also to memory, on which judgments can sometimes later be based. The accuracy of memory relies on the constructive tension between prior knowledge, established by experience, and new information that may contradict it. Until recently, research on memory for people had little to say about small group settings and actual interaction. The paradigm indeed may have been the prototype, imagined by researchers outside of social cognition, as that best representing the whole subfield of social cognition. (Many social cognition researchers would take exception to this prototype.) The person memory paradigm isolated subjects reading lists of traits to form an expectancy and then reading standardized behaviors, after which they listed the behaviors they could recall. The most usual effect in this particular paradigm was a recall advantage for expectancy-inconsistent behaviors (Stangor & McMillan, 1992). However, altering the paradigm to make it more emphatically social, using factors that would apply to a small groups context, dramatically eliminates or reverses this effect. A group of targets, instead of an individual, attenuates or reverses the effect. Expanding the task beyond a single experimental setting alters the effect. Irrelevant tasks interpolated between exposure to the information and its subsequent recall similarly eliminate the inconsistency advantage. Task complications (multiple trait dimensions or task demands) have similar effects (Hamilton, Driscoll, & Worth, 1989; Stangor & Duan, 1991). Finally, receiving the information in a conversational format also eliminates the effect (Wyer, Budesheim, & Lambert, 1990; Wyer, Lambert, Budesheim, & Gruenfeld, 1992). In short, memories for people with whom one actively interacts are determined by both prior knowledge and incoming data, allowing the potential for at least good-enough accuracy. Making the paradigm more social alters the basic effects, and researchers are actively pursuing this insight.

Not only can one complicate the person memory paradigm by making targets multiple, but one can also make the perceivers multiple. Wegner (1987) proposes that groups divide up the memory tasks, enabling individuals to concentrate on smaller domains, thereby presumably remembering more. Moreland, Argote, and Krishnan (Chapter 3, this volume) argue that the development of such transactive memory systems accounts for their research findings that work groups perform better when their members are trained as a unit rather than as separate individuals. Moreover, committing people to a group makes people remember an ingroup message more accurately (Haslam, McGarty, & Turner, Chapter 2, this volume). Groups provide an interesting context for the study of accuracy and consensus about social perceptions. More important, knowing when and how groups are accurate and consensual in their social perceptions is a crucial research agenda for intergroup relations and for decision-making groups, as the next section indicates.

Meaning Making

Until recently, the major metaphor of social cognition research was the cognitive miser, beset by an overwhelming stimulus environment and hoarding scarce mental resources. One of the clearest cognitive miserly strategies is to construct or recycle coherent, compact structures (schemas) that adequately contain the challenge of messy new input. This is one form of meaning making that is actively researched (for reviews, see, e.g., Fiske & Taylor, 1991, ch. 4; Higgins & Bargh, 1987). The renewed pragmatic approach also points out that meaning can be made more elaborate when necessary to achieve particular goals. Individual-level analyses have indicated the role of traits as rich descriptors, stereotypes as associatively complex portraits, and stories as generating meaning (Fiske, 1993b). Each of these readily carries over to small group research.

If anything, shared meaning and its impact on consensus (Kenny, 1991) is even more important in interactions, dyadic or group. People communicate more effectively when they know the other's level and kind of understanding (Fussell & Krauss, 1989a, 1989b; Krauss & Fussell, 1991), and people are often not bad at estimating the other's knowledge (Fussell & Krauss, 1991). But establishing that common ground is clearly a central task of interaction.

One of the intriguing ideas to emerge from this insight is the possibility that small group processes and individual processes are parallel in some respects. For example, Ruscher and Hammer (1994) studied how dyads negotiate joint impressions of a third party. They found that studies of dyadic impression formation can use the same stimuli and parallel forms of the same measures, for example, attention as conversation time, thought content as conversation content, and linguistic structure as an indicator of psychological meaning. Dyads apparently try to achieve common ground or a shared understanding of a joint target of social perception. When that shared impression is disrupted by negative or perhaps inconsistent information, the dyad tries to adjust by spending more time discussing how impression-consistent information fits and generating exemplars of the complex of information.

The negotiation of a shared meaning structure also occurs in decision-making groups. Juries, for example, construct a shared narrative understanding of the events to be explained (Hastie & Pennington, 1991; Pennington & Hastie, 1991). The story must account for the evidence, follow rules of narrative form, and fit world knowledge. The best stories are comprehensive and coherent, thus enabling a decision. It would be useful to apply such a model to other types of decision-making groups such as personnel committees. In its extreme, rigid form, such shared meaning would suggest groupthink, research on which is integrated in a paper by Mullen, Anthony, Salas, and Driskell (1994).

Meaning making does not just occur as external social perception, not just as individuals, dyads, and groups dealing with stimuli external to the perceiving body. Patterson (Chapter 4, this volume) discusses meaning making within the group: how individuals within groups interact and form mutual impressions depending on relative attention and effort devoted to self and others. Meaning making within groups depends on expectancies, goals, and incoming information just as it does for individuals. The small group literature has long known this (see Levine & Moreland, 1990) but only borrowed sparingly from social cognition perspectives to enrich its analysis.

Meaning making also occurs between groups. This insight is represented by some chapters in this volume. Mullen, Rozell, and Johnson (Chapter 9, this volume) discuss representations of ingroup and outgroup as a function of relative group size. They suggest that smaller groups may be represented as single abstract prototypes, whereas larger groups may be represented as a series of concrete exemplars. Gaertner, Rust, Dovidio, Bachman, and Anastasio (Chapter 10, this volume) discuss how intergroup contact can create the representation of a common ingroup identity, more inclusive than the previously separate multiple outgroups. All this shows the role of representations as meaning making for intergroup relations.

Implicit in these discussions is the idea that stereotypes (as generic representations) inherently misrepresent individuals, and (as outgroup members) usually in a negative direction. An interesting alternative viewpoint is that stereotypes can serve to provide additional information beyond what is known about the individual, thereby enriching social understanding (Oakes & Turner, 1990). In a related vein, Leyens (1990) suggests that stereotypes can serve the function of smoothing interactions by providing expectancies as mutual frames of reference for interactants. These ideas, which run counter to the traditional ways of viewing stereotypes, deserve some research consideration.

In conclusion, meaning making occurs not only within individuals but also within dyads and groups and between groups. This collection of small group research showcases papers that make this point especially clear. A variety of research on meaning making suggests that the cognitive miser metatheory is less relevant than previously thought.

Goals and Control

With the reintroduction of motivation into social cognition research, a new metatheory for social perceivers is the motivated tactician (Fiske & Taylor, 1991), who has available a variety of strategies for understanding other people, choosing among them according to current goals. As noted earlier, social cognition researchers have focused more explicitly on a variety of goals, taking a pragmatic perspective that reflects longstanding concerns dating back to the origins of social psychology as a field (Fiske, 1992). The pragmatic perspective fits well with the applicability of much small group research. Studying people in applied (or applicable) settings brings home the importance of people's own goals, precisely because it is not an artificial, isolated, irrelevant, or rarefied atmosphere. Social cognition research has examined two major types of goals, and within each type are many directly relevant to small group interaction (for reviews, see Fiske, 1992; Hilton & Darley, 1991; Kruglanski, 1990; Ruble, 1994; Snyder, 1992; Stangor & Ford, 1992).

One kind of goal tends to motivate people to attempt accurate social perceptions (for a review and references, see Fiske, 1993b, pp. 172-178). Among the more interaction-oriented goals are simple instructions to be accurate, clear social norms to individuate, and personal feedback. Social relationships can encourage accuracy goals: When individuals are interdependent (either cooperatively or competitively), they attempt more accuracy in their understanding of each other. Subordinate status makes having a sense of accuracy more important to social perceivers. Accountability to third parties also makes people try to be more careful. In each case, these variables are natural phenomena within small group contexts; none of them guarantees accuracy, only greater efforts toward a sense of accuracy.

Another type of goal tends to encourage people to make rapid, good-enough decisions with less effort. Capacity-limiting conditions such as time pressure or noise make people more likely to use prior expectancies over additional information. Such contextual features are relevant to the ecology of small groups, as the next section will review. Being action oriented, preparing to interact, or being in the midst of interaction also makes people more decisive and less thorough.

All of these kinds of motives, reviewed elsewhere, support the view of the social perceiver as situated in interaction contexts, often in small groups. It would seem that the goal-oriented view of social cognition, along with work on meaning making and accuracy, all support the perspective that thinking is for doing, making this view completely consistent with a small group perspective. We turn now to areas of small group research that offer opportunities for contact with social cognition perspectives.

ONE HAND, ONE HEART?

Much small group research is applied or applicable and investigates how various characteristics and dynamics of the group influence outcomes such as group performance, interaction, and satisfaction. On the one hand, an applied approach broadens interest and distributes investigations across many topics. On the other hand, it can also inhibit the development of more general theories as investigators across domains find it more difficult to share results and to collaborate. Levine and Moreland (1990) suggest that the multidisciplinary approach to small group research has left the field "badly fragmented" (p. 586).

Our intention in this section is to build some conceptual collages, that is, to indicate areas of small group research that may be pieced together using social cognitive views as the glue. In fact, several small groups theorists are already leaning in the cognitive direction, even though much of their language belies their interest in cognitive variables. Levine and Moreland's (1990) review of the field provides a useful structure for addressing social cognition issues within this area of research. Our discussion therefore focuses on the major areas of research as presented in their review: ecology, composition, structure, conflicts, and performance.

Ecology

How individual group members perceive and think about their physical and social environments should, of course, have some bearing on the group's outcomes. Several cognitive themes emerge when one considers research in this area. First, the environment can affect group members' abilities to process information. For example, crowded and exotic environments lead group members to experience cognitive overload and to think more rigidly (Argote, Turner, & Fichman, 1988; Staw, Sandelands, & Dutton, 1981). "Overstimulation" and "cognitive load" may be mediating mechanisms for the deleterious effects of situations on social interaction and performance (Cox, Paulus, & McCain, 1984; Paulus & Nagar, 1989). Social cognition research on cognitive busyness and attribution (e.g., Gilbert, Pelham, & Krull, 1988) would lend some support to these hypotheses, yet researchers in neither field have addressed these issues adequately using both interactional group settings and cognitive measures.

The interaction environment can also influence people by altering the way information is processed (e.g., filtering of information, differential weighting of information). Certain group settings may prime individuals to interpret information in terms of their prior expectations about a particular situation (i.e., their schemas, defined as cognitive structures that organize knowledge about a particular object, person, or event).

Some background on the schema concept is necessary to understand how this construct might play a role in small group research. Schemas are thought to be hierarchical structures that include both identification information (e.g., managers in this company all wear navy suits) as well as other information acquired through direct and indirect experience (e.g., managers make important decisions). When schemas become activated, they guide the way information is attended and processed. For example, people not only prefer information that confirms their expectations, they also tend to process this information more quickly than information that does not fit their schemas.

Consider the range of schemas potentially relevant to small group contexts. One may differentiate between those that pertain to events (scripts) and those that pertain to people (person schemas). Scripts contain information about the sequencing of social events and provide templates for social interaction (e.g., what to do at a managerial meeting). Person schemas are further distinguished as (a) schemas about individuals (e.g., one's boss), (b) schemas about groups of people (e.g., bosses in general), (c) overgeneralized schemas about members of a particular group, also called stereotypes (e.g., women, Asians), and (d) schemas about people with certain personality characteristics, also called implicit personality theories (e.g., anxious people). Priming social schemas can influence the way an individual thinks and, consequently, behaves in a particular situation. If a stereotype becomes active (e.g., bosses are unapproachable), it can lead a group member to ignore or reinterpret disconfirming information about a particular target person (e.g., my boss's open door is not an invitation for discussion but an opportunity to eavesdrop on the employees). Whether or not a schema becomes primed is in part contingent on stimuli in the environment. For example, the presence of sexually explicit materials may prime sex-role stereotypes for women (Bargh & Raymond, 1995; Borgida, Rudman, & Manteufel, 1995).

The schema concept may be easily applied to research on small group environments. For example, research in job satisfaction and working conditions could perhaps use analyses of how the physical environment primes particular schemas. For example, if people in a work environment tell jokes about the management, it is likely to prime negative schemas about worker relations, which in turn could influence job satisfaction and productivity.

Similarly, research on crowded and threatening environments might build on understanding people's schemas for these situations. Research indicates that it is not the actual social or spatial density that predicts group performance, but instead, it is the individual group members' perceptions of crowding that make the difference (Paulus & Nagar, 1989). Apparently, features of the environment prime people to interpret their environment in negative or threatening ways. These issues remain to be tested.

We should also bear in mind that the relationship between perceiver and environment is not unidirectional. The environment may influence the perceiver, but the perceiver also may manipulate the environment. Research issues such as territoriality and responses to threats in small groups could be enhanced by considering the group's perceptions of control as well as its social identifications (i.e., schemas about one's own group in relationship to other group identifications).

Schemas, both those held by the individual and those shared by the group, may also play a role in the temporal ecology of the group. For example, scripts may influence group members' expectations about development of the group (e.g., whether members expect the group to dissolve or to grow over time). Similarly, schemas may influence group expectations about pace within task groups, consequently influencing performance and satisfaction within the group. Finally, research indicating that older groups become more rigid and rely less on outside information may be explained in terms of schemas and cognitive processing (Katz, 1982). As groups age, their shared scripts may be played out automatically, leading to less interaction outside the group and more rigid information processing within the group. Theories of automatic cognitive processing by individuals, such as those in Uleman and Bargh (1990), could be applied to test these ideas in group settings.

Group Composition

Given cognitive capacity limitations and the impact of schemas on processing, the composition of a group could clearly influence individual group members' perceptions, group identifications, and cognitive-processing strategies. Research suggests that as group size increases, production and satisfaction decrease. In cognitive terms, this may be related to issues of cognitive capacity. As the number of group members increases, individuals within the group have fewer resources to manage social interactions, to maintain attention, and so on. In addition, larger groups require individual members to maintain more relationships, which in turn requires more cognitive resources. Job satisfaction and productivity may suffer as a result of these factors, first, because they reduce group members' abilities to complete their tasks and fulfill their roles in the group and, second, because they may increase group members' perceived levels of stress. The context of the group composition (e.g., number of men vs. women) can also have an influence on group members' satisfaction. Social cognition research suggests that a solo (e.g., the only Asian American in a group of Anglo Americans) is more salient and, as a result, receives more attention from other group members (Taylor & Fiske, 1978). The consequences include being seen as more influential, being evaluated more extremely, and being evaluated in stereotypic terms. In a meta-analysis of studies using solo gender targets, Mullen (cited in Fiske, Bersoff, Borgida, Deaux, & Heilman, 1993) reports that these effects are quite robust. Solo effects could alter the overall interaction of the group and satisfaction levels. Heterogeneous groups may also set the stage for priming stereotypes. To the extent that salient characteristics of group members activate stereotypes, these schemas may then influence social interactions within the group.

Group Structure

The small groups literature has explored several characteristics of group structure, including status, norms, roles, and cohesion. All of these factors influence group members' cognitive processing. Schemas and scripts may define the roles and norms that guide behavior within the group. For example, group expectations or shared schemas about leaders may influence their evaluations of the leaders' behavior (Lord, 1985).

Small group research suggests that status hierarchies develop very rapidly, oftentimes within the first few minutes of interaction. The two theoretical explanations for this phenomenon, expectation states versus ethological theories, both posit a cognitive comparison process whereby individuals are sized up relative to some personal characteristic. In the case of the expectation states theories, characteristics vital to achieving the group's goals are more important in the comparison process (Berger, Rosenholtz, & Zelditch, 1980). For the ethological theorists, physical appearance and demeanor play the crucial role (Mazur, 1985). In either case, the fact that status roles develop so quickly suggests that group members rely on schemas or expectations about what these characteristics imply in order to process the information quickly. This in turn suggests some level of automatic cognitive processing. One could further predict more conflict regarding status roles within a group or more change in status hierarchies over time, to the extent that group members do or do not share the same expectations about status.

Conflicts

Several areas of small group research fall under the topic of conflict research, including communication, power, and minority-majority influence. These areas of research reflect stronger trends toward social cognition as compared to other areas of small group research.

In the area of communication, Bodenhausen, Gaelick, and Wyer's (1987) analysis of the communication process begins to address the significance of group members' cognitions. Their model, originally developed to describe communication in romantic dyads, suggests that a critical component of the communication process is each member's perception of what is being communicated. This acknowledges that people may be differentially interpreting or processing what is communicated based on their individual or shared schemas.

Power research using both social cognition and small groups paradigms is perhaps on the eve of convergence. Recently, theories of power from both views have come to the same conclusion—the nature of interdependent relationships determines who has power over whom (Cook, 1987; Deprét & Fiske, 1993). Research suggests that the nature of power relationships influences evaluations of both the powerful (Kipnis, 1984; Stevens & Fiske, 1995) as well as the powerless (Goodwin & Fiske, 1995). For example, perceivers who have outcome control, the powerful, are motivated to use both effortful and effortless attention strategies to confirm stereotypic expectations about subordinates (Goodwin & Fiske, 1995). Closely related to this issue is Nye and Simonetta's contribution on followers' perceptions of leaders (Chapter 6, this volume). Future research should extend existing theories into interactional settings to determine if these findings are stable. In addition, the study of how people respond to the exercise of power could benefit from analysis in these terms. For example, job satisfaction and productivity may be related to how group members perceive the nature of asymmetrically interdependent relationships.

Group influence research has already adopted one important cognitive theory to explain how minority-majority group members alter group opinion. Chaiken's (1987) heuristic-processing model, which posits several underlying cognitive mechanisms that determine the outcome of an influence attempt, has successfully been applied to group influence situations in laboratory settings (Chaiken & Stangor, 1987). Still, this theory remains to be tested outside the lab and in interactional settings.

Performance

The literature on group performance is heavily intertwined with many of the areas of research that have already been discussed. For example, much of the previously mentioned research has been conducted in service of understanding and improving productivity and satisfaction within groups. In addition to that already discussed, the social information processing theory of productivity (Salancik & Pfeffer, 1978) is clearly cognitive. According to this model, the route to improved productivity lies in changing perceptions of the group's task, not necessarily in changing the task itself.

Unlike some other areas of small group research, cognitive theories of leadership have been well integrated into the literature. For example, Lord's (1985) work on implicit theories of leadership addresses shared beliefs and expectations about leaders and how these factors influence perceptions of the leader. From the perspective of how leaders view others, Green and Mitchell's (1979) theory posits an automatic attributional response that affects how leaders evaluate their subordinates. Although these theories have received empirical support in laboratory settings, replication in more interactive settings is still to follow.

Finally, decision-making theorists have ventured further out into cognitive waters, as evidenced by the application of persuasion and social comparison theories as well as computer-simulated models of decision-making processes (e.g., Hastie, Penrod, & Pennington, 1983; Stasser, 1988; Stasser, Kerr, & Davis, 1989). In contrast to these quantitative approaches, qualitative approaches to decision-making research are much less cognitive. This area of research could nevertheless recognize how cognitive factors may affect qualitative features of decision making. For example, group discussions tend to be dominated not by new information but instead by shared information and by information that confirms existing expectations (Stasser, Taylor, & Hanna, 1989; Wittenbaum & Stasser, Chapter 1, this volume). This could be explained in terms of schema-driven processing biases at the group level.

GEE, OFFICER KRUPKE

We have tried to provide some context for the discussion of links between small group research and social cognition research. After noting that the two domains are both core features of the social psychology enterprise, we also noted that they rarely cite each other and even square off as adversaries to the extent that social cognition research neglects person-to-person interaction and small group research neglects cognitive processes. A change is in the air, as social cognition research becomes more concerned with the pragmatic issues of consensus and accuracy, meaning making, and interaction goals. Similarly, as the collection of chapters in this volume indicates, social cognitive analyses hold much promise for small group phenomena; we have also illustrated some possible openings for social cognition in small group settings. As social cognition researchers addressing small group researchers, we would like to close by saying, with the Jets of *West Side Story*, "We ain't no delinquents; we're misunderstood; deep down inside us, there is good."

What we all have in common, social cognition and small group researchers alike, is social psychology. Together, we need to make our shared case to a sometimes skeptical larger society, a case that rests on our common interests. To quote the Jets again: "Gee, Officer Krupke, we're down on our knees, 'cause no one wants a fella with a social disease. . . . What are we to do?"[1]

Note

1. "Gee, Officer Krupke" from *West Side Story*. Music by Leonard Bernstein, lyrics by Stephen Sondheim. Copyright © 1956, 1957 (renewed) by Leonard Bernstein and Stephen Sondheim. The Leonard Bernstein Music Publishing Company LLC, U.S. and Canadian Publisher, G. Schirmer, Inc., worldwide print rights and publisher for the rest of the world. International copyright secured. All rights reserved. Reprinted by permission.

Part
I

The Group as a Cognitive Unit:
Group Beliefs, Decisions, and Products

Management of Information in Small Groups

GWEN M. WITTENBAUM
GAROLD STASSER

A jury deliberating a high-profile criminal case, a faculty debating the merits of an educational policy, and friends deciding where to go on a weekend outing are hotbeds of cognitive activity. Members recall and communicate information, formulate arguments, attempt to influence each other, and form and reform opinions. This chapter focuses on the process of selecting information for discussion in small decision-making groups. Thus, we describe

AUTHORS' NOTE: Preparation of this chapter was supported by National Science Foundation Grant (SBR-9410584) awarded to the second author and a fellowship awarded to the first author from the National Science Foundation (DIR-9113599) to the Mershon Center Research Training Group on the Role of Cognition in Collective Political Decision Making at The Ohio State University. Correspondence concerning this chapter should be addressed to Garold Stasser, Department of Psychology, Miami University, Oxford, OH 45056. E-mail may be sent to gs4apsyf@miamiu.acs.muohio.edu.

cognition that is social to the extent that information retrieval, knowledge acquisition, and judgment occur collectively through social interaction (Larson & Christensen, 1993). Such social cognition in groups represents the "intersubjective" paradigm described by Ickes and Gonzalez (1994) whereby interacting individuals' cognitions are interdependent.

In decision-making groups, individual members often have access to different sets of information for a variety of reasons. In some contexts, members may have different roles and responsibilities. In an architectural firm, engineers are expected to know things that accountants do not. More generally, people are exposed to different media, converse with different acquaintances in social networks, and occupy different nodes in the formal and informal communication structures of organizations. As a result, people do not hold the same knowledge, and given any topic of conversation, some invariably know information that others do not. When small groups must choose some course of collective action, there are frequently attempts to equalize the relevant knowledge base through briefings, position papers, and memoranda so that members can come to a shared understanding of the issues. Often, however, groups rely on face-to-face discussion to disseminate information en route to a decision. Whatever the mode of communication, one goal in collective decision making and problem solving is to pool diverse knowledge so that the group can reach an informed decision (Hastie, 1986; Stasser, 1992).

In this chapter, we explore some of the consequences of *distributed information systems* for the pooling of information in decision-making groups (Hutchins, 1991; Radner, 1986). In a distributed information system, access to information is often not uniform across a group's members. Thus, at the onset of discussion, some information may be *unshared* in that it is available to only one member, whereas other information may be completely *shared* in that it is available to all members. Of course, other information may be partially shared in that it is possessed by more than one, but not all members. Of interest here is the process by which groups sample items for discussion when information is not evenly distributed among members.

COLLECTIVE INFORMATION SAMPLING

When information is distributed so that individual members have unique information before discussion, then group discussion can serve an educational function. Members can convey novel information to one another and, in doing so, base their collective decision on more information than is possible if any one member were to decide alone. The potential for such an *assembly effect* is a commonly invoked justification for using groups to decide issues of importance (Hastie, 1986; Stasser, 1992). However, a theme of past empirical work is that groups often omit unshared information from discussions while focusing on information that all members already know (Engel, 1992; Parks, 1991; Stasser, Taylor, & Hanna, 1989; Stasser & Titus, 1985, 1987; Stewart & Stasser, 1995). This bias may serve to help members better relate to and understand one another by forming a "common ground" (Clark & Brennan, 1991). At the same time, groups may forego the potential benefit of having diverse knowledge.

For example, Stasser, Taylor, et al. (1989) gave university students descriptions of candidates for student body president. These descriptions were constructed so that some information (shared) was read by all members of a group before discussion, whereas other information (unshared) was read by only one member. Participants then discussed the candidates in either three- or six-person groups and decided which one was best suited for the position. Overall, discussions contained about half of the shared information (46%) but only about one sixth of the unshared information (18%). Also, this difference was greater for six-person than for three-person groups.

A Collective Sampling Model

Stasser and Titus (1987) proposed a collective information sampling (CIS) model that provides one way of understanding why groups often omit unshared information from their discussions. Based on earlier formulations in the group performance literature (e.g., Lorge & Solomon, 1962; Shiflett, 1979; Steiner, 1972), the model represents the mentioning of an item of information during discussion as a *disjunctive* task: The group will fail to discuss an item only if *all* members *fail* to mention it. More specifically, the probability that the group will discuss an item, $p(D)$, is a function of the number of members who can mention it, n, and the likelihood that any one of these members will mention it, $p(M)$:

$$p(D) = 1 - [1 - p(M)]^n \tag{1}$$

(see Stasser, 1992, for a graphic display of the relationship between $p(D)$ and $p(M)$ for various levels of n). To illustrate, if each member of a six-person group mentions about 30% of the information that he or she knows before discussion, the model predicts that the probability of the group discussing a shared item is very high: $p(D_s) = 1 - [1 - .3]^6 = .88$. In contrast, a piece of unshared information can be mentioned only by the member who received it: $p(D_u) = 1 - [1 - .3]^1 = .3$. The model also allows for the possibility that information could be partially shared. In the foregoing example, if two members had access to an item, then $n = 2$ and $p(D_{ps}) = 1 - [1 - .3]^2 = .51$.

As this example illustrates, the model teaches a simple lesson: the more members who have access to an item before discussion, the more chances that item has of emerging during a group's discussion. An implication of this lesson is that pooling diverse sets of information via face-to-face discussion may be more difficult than it seems on casual reflection. Moreover, the model teaches some other lessons that counter our intuitions about information pooling via discussion. For example, if each individual brings a few items of unique information to a group's discussion, it seems that larger, as compared to smaller, groups should enjoy the advantage of having more information at their disposal. Each additional member potentially brings something new to the discussion. However, consistent with the aforementioned findings of Stasser, Taylor, et al. (1989), one implication of the CIS model is that the disparity between the likelihoods of mentioning shared and unshared items increases as group size increases. Thus, the members of large groups may collectively possess more information than members of small groups, but their discussions are more likely to be dominated by information that everyone already knows (i.e., shared information).

Notwithstanding the value of these lessons, they may be too simple for many groups and decision-making environments. The basic CIS model rests on several assumptions, including (a) shared and unshared items are equally memorable [i.e., $p(M_s) = p(M_u)$], (b) members have the same base rate of recalling and communicating information (e.g., equally talkative, equally able to retrieve items), and (c) recall among members is functionally independent (what one member recalls does not substantially alter what another is likely to recall). Thus, the model has worked well when equal-status members have comparable information loads, shared and unshared items are similar in content and task-relevance, and no cues in the decision environment allow members to distinguish shared from unshared items (e.g., Engel, 1992; Parks, 1991; Stasser, Taylor, et al., 1989; Stasser & Titus, 1985, 1987). However, these assumptions are likely to be violated in many groups. For example, members may not be equal in status, and some members may talk much more than others (Kirchmeyer, 1993; Smith-Lovin, Skvoretz, & Hudson, 1986; Stasser & Taylor, 1991). Moreover, members may have or develop impressions of how information access is distributed among members, allowing them either to focus on or avoid unshared information (Wegner, 1987; Wittenbaum, Stasser, & Merry, in press). Finally, discussion may be organized around themes (stories; Pennington & Hastie, 1986; scripts or schemas; Fiske & Goodwin, 1994), and the emergence of one theme over others may elicit the recall of some items while suppressing the recall of others. In this case, items will not be equally memorable, and the theme of discussion may enhance or suppress the mentioning of unshared information.

Therefore, the CIS model is best regarded as a *baseline* model that summarizes the anticipated effects of information distribution on discussion content when other things (such as member status and item memorability) are equal. Although such "other things" are often not equal, a baseline model can still be informative. For example, suppose that one wanted to show that task-proficient members who are experienced in working with one another (i.e., intact, expert groups) can effectively pool unshared information. Furthermore, suppose that the six members of such an intact, expert group are given a series of familiar problems to solve and that the organizational environment affords each member unique access to an important domain of information that others cannot access (unshared information). What are we to conclude if examination of the discussions of this six-person, problem-solving group reveals that they mentioned, on average over a series of similar problems, 50% of the shared and 50% of the unshared information? On the face of it, this result suggests that this expert group is not particularly sensitive to the potential advantage of pooling unshared information in the pursuit of an optimal solution to a problem; items of shared and unshared information are equally likely to emerge in their discussions. However, the CIS model suggests that discussing equal proportions of shared and unshared information can be realized only if members are, indeed, giving relatively high priority to the communication of unshared items (Stewart & Stasser, 1995). In other words, our fictitious expert group is swimming against a strong current in collective information sampling that often floods group discussions with already shared information.

Our characterization of the CIS model as a baseline model is deliberate. Whereas comparisons of obtained results with the predictions of the model are informative, the connotation of baseline implies that the impact of many interesting psychological and social variables will emerge as deviations from these predictions. It has been amply demonstrated that ad hoc groups of equal-status peers working on ill-structured (and often unfamiliar) tasks produce discussions that favor shared over unshared information as the model predicts (Engel, 1992; Parks, 1991; Stasser, Taylor, et al., 1989; Stasser & Titus, 1985, 1987; Stewart & Stasser, 1995). Thus, in the last half of this chapter, we will explore temporal, social, and task variables that go beyond the static and circumscribed sampling processes that can be adequately described by the CIS model.

Resampling Information During Discussion

One interesting feature of group discussion that goes beyond the sampling process as it is characterized in the CIS model is that groups often return to previously considered information. This resampling process is selective; some items are mentioned and never reconsidered, whereas other items may emerge repeatedly during the course of discussion. The dynamics of selective resampling are not entirely clear, but knowing what information a group hears and then reconsiders undoubtedly tells us something about how the group evaluates and uses information. At a minimum, the more times an item emerges during discussion, the more opportunities it has to impact members' opinions and to shape the emerging consensus.

At first blush, it seems that unshared information should demand the attention of the group when it is mentioned. After all, when a member communicates an unshared item, it is new to everyone else and they have not had the opportunity to consider its implications for their opinions. Moreover, because of its novelty, it should have greater potential for reshaping opinions than does information that all members knew before discussion. Burnstein and Vinokur (1977) make a similar point in their persuasive arguments theory of group polarization. They assert that group discussion polarizes opinions to the degree that members exchange novel arguments. Whereas the idea that information and argument novelty imparts influence potential is compelling, the resampling process observed in discussions adds a distinctly different hue to the picture.

Larson, Christensen, Abbott, and Franz (1995) had three-person medical teams (resident, intern, and medical student) view videotapes of a physician's initial interview with a patient and then discuss the case and agree on a diagnosis. The tapes were edited so that some information was presented to only one team member whereas other information was presented to all members. For example, in one team, the resident might learn that the patient had experienced severe headaches recently but the intern and student might not receive this information. Conversely, in another team, all three might know that she had experienced headaches. If all three members knew before discussion that the patient had experienced headaches, the team was much more likely to consider this symptom *more than once* than if only one member initially viewed a tape that contained the headache complaint. Overall, initially shared information was about twice as likely as unshared information to be repeated after it was mentioned.

Stasser, Taylor, et al. (1989) observed a similar result in groups of students who were discussing and selecting the best of three candidates for student body president. These groups were much more likely to repeat a candidate's position on an issue if it was read by all members before discussion than if it was read by only one member.

In sum, these results suggest that the fate of an item of information in a group's discussion is determined partly by the number of members who were aware of the item *before* discussion. It seems that shared information has not only a sampling advantage but also a resampling advantage over unshared information.

Hidden Profiles: When Unshared Information Matters

Lest we give the impression that discussing and rehashing shared information is necessarily a bad thing, let us consider the conditions under which the pooling of unshared information can improve the quality of group decisions. A simple example can place the importance of pooling unshared information in perspective. Consider a simplified (and somewhat contrived) version of the medical diagnosis task used by Larson et al. (1995). Suppose that there were two possible diagnoses, A and B, based on the presenting problems of the patient. Furthermore, suppose that the correct diagnosis is A and is supported by 12 symptoms. However, the case also presents 6 symptoms that suggest diagnosis B. Now contrast two different ways that this entire set of 18 symptoms might be distributed among the three members of a medical team.

In an *unbiased* distribution, half of the information supporting each diagnosis is shared and half is unshared. That is, each member receives six shared and two unshared items that support diagnosis A and three shared and one unshared items that support diagnosis B. This distribution is unbiased because each member has a nearly representative sample of the entire set of presenting symptoms. In this case, each member, based solely on what he or she knows, should favor a diagnosis of A because each has access to eight items that support A and only four that support B (assuming, to keep the example simple, that every symptom is equally diagnostic). Moreover, the team will tend to make a correct decision if they discuss primarily their shared knowledge, and discussion of unshared knowledge should only strengthen their initial impressions. In a benign world in which group members tend to have representative subsets of knowledge, discussions that focus on shared information will effectively lead to a collective decision and, at the same time, probably foster members' confidence and commitment to the group's action (Sniezek, 1992).

However, the world may not always be so benign. Stasser (1988) identified a *hidden profile* as a particularly interesting distributed information system. In a hidden profile, a superior decision alternative exists, but its superiority is hidden from individual group members. To illustrate an extreme version of a hidden profile using the previous example, suppose that all of the information supporting the A diagnosis is unshared and all of the information supporting B is shared. That is, each member receives four unshared symptoms supporting the A diagnosis and six shared symptoms supporting the B diagnosis. In this case, each member should individually favor the B diagnosis because each has access to six items that support B and only four that support A. Moreover, if discussion focuses on shared information, the team will discuss the merits of B and will not discover that the entire set of evidence points to A as the appropriate diagnosis. Pooling unshared information is critical to discovering hidden profiles when they exist. Note that it is in this pernicious world of hidden profiles that groups have a distinct advantage over individual decision makers. Here, the group can identify a superior decision that none of the members initially favored based on their individual slices of the relevant information. Note also that, in this world of hidden profiles, the tendency of discussion to sample and resample shared information has dire implications for group performance.

Stasser and Titus (1985) demonstrated that groups frequently fail to discover hidden profiles. In their study, students read descriptions of candidates for student body president and then met in groups to discuss and pick the best candidate. One of the candidates, A, had a larger number of positive attributes (positions and characteristics that were regarded as desirable by an independent sample) than the other two candidates. When students were given all of the information about the candidates, 67% of them favored A before discussion and

83% of the four-person groups chose A. However, when a hidden profile was constructed by giving each member of a four-person group only part of the information supporting A, 23% favored A before discussion and only 18% of the groups chose A. All groups collectively had access to all of the information, but those in the hidden profile conditions needed to exchange a substantial amount of their unshared information for each individual to recognize the superiority of A. Examination of postdiscussion free recall suggested that the hidden profile groups considered few of the unshared items. Other studies have documented similar hidden profile effects using decision tasks such as business investment (Hollingshead, 1993) and a homicide mystery (Stasser & Stewart, 1992; Stasser, Stewart, & Wittenbaum, 1995).

In summary, failures to pool unshared information do not necessarily lead to poor group decisions. If members possess a representative sample of decision-relevant information, discussion of shared information may be an effective way of focusing the group's attention on a manageable subset of issues and fashioning a shared understanding of the relative merits of the decision alternatives. Nonetheless, focusing on shared information runs the risk of overlooking hidden profiles. A nagging unanswered question of both theoretical and practical importance is, "How can groups detect the presence of a hidden profile without systematic and exhaustive exploration of members' unique knowledge?" Perhaps the answer to this question is one key to understanding highly proficient and efficient team decision making.

THE ECOLOGY OF INFORMATION SAMPLING

Small groups work in environments that vary in their temporal, social, and task characteristics. Such environmental variations undoubtedly impact members' use of information in anticipation of and during group interaction. Research to date has investigated how members use information over time; how expert roles, member status, and leadership impact information sampling; and how task demands influence the use of information in anticipation of and during group discussion.

Although we are considering temporal, social, and task environments separately for the purpose of clarity, we note at the outset that these three factors likely interact and are mutually dependent.

Temporal Environments

There are always implicit time limits for discussion; groups do not discuss an issue indefinitely, and they do not ordinarily consider all of the information that is available before terminating their discussions. Moreover, the duration of discussion may be foreshortened by environmental pressures and social dynamics. Impending events may require quick decisions, members may have competing demands on their time, or a consensus may emerge early, lessening the felt need to prolong discussion. Whatever the reasons for brief discussions, it is obvious that short discussions will elicit less information than long discussions (although groups may compensate somewhat for severe time limits by increasing the pace of their discussions; see, e.g., Karau & Kelly, 1992). Of interest here is how the content of discussion may differ qualitatively between short and long discussions. Staw, Sandelands, and Dutton (1981) suggested that groups, like individuals, may restrict their scope of attention to information and become more rigid in their approach to problems under severe time pressure. One implication is that time pressure may promote the discussion of salient and widely shared information, thereby discouraging the introduction of novel ideas. Another implication is that groups may quickly determine the dominant views within the group (e.g., via straw polls) and then focus the remaining time on the most popular positions.

Larson, Foster-Fishman, and Keys (1994) argued that there are systematic temporal patterns in the mix of shared and unshared information introduced in discussion. They extended the CIS model to capture the temporal effects of information sampling throughout the course of discussion. Basically, their extended model predicts that the sampling advantage to shared information should erode as discussion progresses because the pool of unconsidered shared items will gradually be depleted, leaving predominantly unshared items for the group to discuss. Thus, the marked tendency for discussions to include shared but not unshared information may characterize brief discussions or the early portions of long discussions. However, unshared information may dominate in the later portions of long discussions. In support of this temporal prediction, Larson et al. (1995) observed that the first symptom mentioned by their medical diagnosis teams was almost certain to be a symptom that all three members had received earlier. However, as discussion progressed, the likelihood of mentioning shared symptoms gradually decreased: The 10th symptom mentioned during discussions was about equally likely to be shared or unshared information, and subsequently mentioned items became increasingly more likely to be unshared items.

As Larson and his colleagues noted, these temporal effects may not be all good news for the information-pooling capacity of face-to-face discussions. First, their groups were very familiar with the task and probably highly motivated to perform well because they were composed of resident physicians, interns, and medical students in a training hospital. Thus, they were adept at processing and recalling information and sufficiently invested in the problem to consider large amounts of information before agreeing on a diagnosis. Not all groups benefit from such a concentration of ability and highly motivated performance from all members. Second, they noted that many kinds of judgments are susceptible to a primacy effect. Information considered early has more impact on judgments, opinions, and preferences than information considered later (Wyer, 1988). Thus, even when discussions are sufficiently prolonged to sample extensively unshared information, the shared information that dominates in the early going may still have a disproportionate influence on the emerging consensus within a group.

As a glimmer of hope, Larson et al.'s (1994) findings suggest that the bias toward discussing shared information may be most pronounced in newly formed groups. In such groups, conformity pressures are high and members are motivated to emphasize similarities with fellow group members in order to build cohesion and group loyalty (Worchel, Coutant-Sassic, & Grossman, 1992). Given that groups studied in the laboratory are generally ad hoc and short lived, the laboratory-based research investigating information sampling may overestimate the degree to which shared information dominates the discussions of long-lasting, intact groups.

Social Environments

Expert Roles. Groups are often composed of members with heterogeneous expertise so that the group can benefit from a larger knowledge pool than any individual member possesses. Such a group advantage may not be realized unless members understand how expertise is distributed among themselves. Several researchers have noted the importance both of having diverse expertise represented and of members' mutually recognizing their complementary expertise for effective group performance (Liang, Moreland, & Argote, 1995; Libby, Trotman, & Zimmer, 1987; Littlepage & Silbiger, 1992). Moreover, in his theory of transactive memory, Wegner (1987) proposed that groups can function as effective memory units when their members learn about each others' domains of expertise. When new information is encountered, members presume that it will be remembered by their partner who has special skills, interests, or knowledge in that domain. By coordinating their management of information, the group collectively can take advantage of the unique knowledge possessed by individual members. Larson and Christensen (1993) also noted the importance of knowledge about members' likely task-relevant information, or "meta-knowledge," in the group problem-solving process. The group's total pool of meta-knowledge consists of the group's "meta-knowledge base"—an important determinant of effective problem solving and decision making. That is, in order for groups to successfully complete their tasks, it may be crucial for members to have a sense of their own and other members' expertise in order to coordinate effectively their information search, storage, retrieval, and management of information.

The available empirical evidence is consistent with this reasoning. Stasser et al. (1995) gave participants a homicide mystery to read and later discuss in three-person groups to decide on the guilty suspect. Groups who were explicitly informed at the onset of discussion who among them had access to unique information in specific domains (expert role assignment) mentioned more unshared information than groups who were not informed about the distribution of unique information. In addition, groups in which expert roles were assigned reached the correct decision more often than groups without expert role assignment and with the same frequency as groups whose members held all shared information before discussion. However, merely forewarning members of their own expertise domain before reading the case information (forewarned) did not increase the sampling of unshared information or improve the groups' decisions relative to those groups who were not forewarned about their unique expertise (no forewarning). Therefore, it seems critical to know not only one's own expertise domain but also the domains in which other members possess expertise. However, both role assignment and forewarning increased the repetition of unshared information. It may be that in order for members to emphasize unshared information after it is mentioned, they must feel confident about their recall accuracy. Hinsz (1990) reported that members with more confidence in their recall accuracy needed less social support to persuade the group to adopt their recall as correct. Because unshared information cannot be socially validated by others (i.e., confirmed as accurate by other members), the contributing member must be able to convince others that the recall is accurate, and likewise, others must feel confident in the credibility of the source.

Stewart and Stasser (1995) investigated the impact of known expertise on the management and validation of information in collective recall and decision-making groups. Three-person groups discussed political candidates twice: once to recall collectively candidate information and once to choose the best candidate. Those groups whose members were assigned expert roles at the onset of the first discussion (expert role assignment) mentioned more unshared information during both the collective recall and the decision tasks than did groups who were not assigned expert roles. Like previous research, these results highlight the importance of mutually recognized expertise in the facilitation of unshared information use. Moreover, when expertise was assigned, virtually all of the unshared information mentioned orally during collective recall was included on groups' collectively endorsed written recall. In contrast, when expertise was not assigned, groups omitted from their written accounts some of the unshared information that was mentioned during the recall task. In addition, individual members, after both discussions, completed a recognition recall task. On this task, more of the unshared candidate information mentioned during discussion was correctly recognized when expertise was assigned than when it was not. Both the comparison of the oral and written group recall and the performance on the individual recognition task suggest that expert role assignment serves as a form of social validation for the recall of unshared information. Recognized experts who recall uniquely known information in their domain of expertise may be judged as accurate and credible, and as such, their unshared information is accepted and retained by others to a greater degree than when members' expertise is not recognized.

Status. Group members often differ in their *status*—the degree of ascribed prestige, power, or competence. Ascribed status can be based on members' task-relevant resources (e.g., access to important information), skills and interests relative to the group's task (e.g., prior experience on a similar task as the group's), and diffuse status characteristics (e.g., age, gender, race) (Berger, Fisek, Norman, & Zelditch, 1977). Status has been shown to impact the influence and decision-making processes in groups. Kirchler and Davis (1986) demonstrated that decision-making groups were more likely to choose the higher status member's preference over lower status members' preference as the group's decision. In addition, gender differences in mixed-sex task groups may be the result of status differences between men and women, where men are ascribed higher status than women (Ridgeway & Diekema, 1992). When the only salient status cue is members' gender, women in mixed-sex interactions participate less, engage in less active-task behaviors, are interrupted more, and are less influential than men (Dovidio, Brown, Heltman, Ellyson, & Keating, 1988; Eagly, 1983; Kelly, Wildman, & Urey, 1982; Moreland & Levine, 1992b; Piliavin & Martin, 1978; Pugh & Wahrman, 1983; Smith-Lovin & Brody, 1989; Wood & Karten, 1986).

Given that status has been shown to impact participation, influence, and task behavior of small groups, it is likely that member status would also affect information sampling in decision-making groups. For example, status differences due to the possession of additional task experience have been shown to affect information sampling. Participants in Wittenbaum's (1996) study read the curriculum vitae of two hypothetical candidates applying for the job of assistant professor and later discussed and chose the better candidate of the two in four-person groups. Before reading the vitae, two members of the group had worked on a similar personnel selection task (experienced members) and the other two members had worked on an unrelated brainstorming task (inexperienced members). Unexpectedly, inexperienced members contributed more information during discussion than did experienced members. Nonetheless, inexperienced members exhibited a pattern of information sampling reminiscent of past findings (Stasser, Taylor, et al., 1989); they mentioned more shared than unshared information. In contrast, experienced members showed no such sampling bias. Moreover, deviating from past findings, experienced members repeated more unshared than shared information, but inexperienced members showed no repetition bias. In sum, experienced, as compared to inexperienced, members were less prone to favor shared information in mentioning and repeating information.

The fact that inexperienced members contributed more information overall seems counterintuitive. However, these findings make more sense in light of the fact that inexperienced members apparently needed to support their preferences more actively than did experienced members to get them adopted by the group. Interestingly, the inexperienced members persuaded their groups to adopt their preferences about half of the time: 54% of the groups chose the candidate supported by the inexperienced members. When the inexperienced members prevailed, they contributed much more information than did the experienced members. In contrast, when the experienced members prevailed, they did not contribute more than the inexperienced members. Thus, it seems that inexperienced members had to work harder to win by contributing more information, particularly commonly known information, than did experienced members.

These results suggest that experienced and inexperienced members managed information differently. Although their additional experience was minimal (one previous exposure to a similar task), the experienced members may have developed greater real or perceived task competence or appreciated more the value of unshared information in determining the better job candidate. One interesting possibility is that felt competence may be a key factor in promoting the use of unshared information—information that is to some degree "risky" because its accuracy and relevance cannot be validated by others. The added confidence felt by group members with assigned expertise (Stasser et al., 1995; Stewart & Stasser, 1995) or with additional task experience may encourage their use of unshared information.

Leadership. Group leaders may play an active role in the management and use of information. For example, leaders may be in an especially advantageous position to increase the group's meta-knowledge base (Larson & Christensen, 1993). By determining who in the group possesses expertise in particular areas, the leader may coordinate the retrieval of information among members. In this way, active leadership may facilitate the use of unshared information and its impact on the group's decision-making efficacy.

Larson et al.'s (1995) study investigating information sampling in trained, three-person, medical decision-making groups found support for the notion that leadership facilitates the use of members' uniquely known information. Recall that each group in this study contained a resident, an intern, and a 3rd-year medical student. Compared to the intern and student, the resident possessed more task experience and expertise, higher status, and received higher pay for completing the study. Results revealed a leadership effect: Residents repeated more shared and unshared information than did interns and medical students. Moreover, the probability of the resident repeating unshared information that he or she did not originally possess increased over the course of the groups' discussions. The authors inferred that repetitions were the leaders' way of ensuring that information received adequate attention and was fully considered in determining the correct diagnosis. Prior research has shown that unshared information can fall by the wayside because it is less likely to be repeated than shared information (Stasser, Taylor, et al., 1989). However, Larson et al.'s (1995) results suggest that leaders may accept the responsibility for keeping unshared information alive by repeating it, particularly toward the end of discussion.

The finding that leaders are more likely than others to repeat unshared information is congruent with the recent research examining the influence of expert roles and member status on information sampling. Recall that groups repeated more unshared information when expert roles were assigned (Stasser et al., 1995; Stewart & Stasser, 1995), and experienced members repeated more unshared than shared information (Wittenbaum, 1996). Like both expert and experienced members, leaders may feel especially confident in their recall of unshared information, and at the same time, other members may be more likely to ascribe importance to unshared information if a leader emphasizes it. Leaders, perhaps because of their higher status and perceived competence, may have the social credit to risk using uniquely known information and may provide the necessary social validation of others' contributed unshared information. Consistent with Hollander's (1958, 1964) notion of "idiosyncrasy credit," leaders may earn status among followers that gives them the credit to risk innovative actions such as emphasizing unshared information. Larson et al.'s (1995) findings are consistent with the idea that the use of unshared information may be viewed as risky and thus only "advantaged" and confident members may afford to use it.

Task Environments

Task Demands. Groups work on a variety of tasks, including problem solving, decision making, idea generation, and collective recall. The demands placed on members often differ depending on the nature of the task and the collective goal to be accomplished. For example, tasks vary in the degree to which they possess a demonstrably correct solution (Laughlin, 1980). *Intellective tasks* consist of problem-solving tasks for which a correct answer exists, and *judg-*

mental tasks involve aesthetic or evaluative judgments that cannot be considered correct or incorrect. Stasser and Stewart (1992) applied the logic of task demonstrability to the study of hidden profile effects. They reasoned that, if groups think their task involves a problem to be solved (intellective), they may engage in a comprehensive information search in order to find the right answer. In contrast, if groups think their task involves making a judgment, they may discuss only enough information to reach a consensus. In their study, participants reviewed case materials for a homicide mystery in order to discuss the case and either determine the guilty suspect (solve set) or decide which suspect was most likely to have committed the crime (as they may lack sufficient evidence to solve the case; judge set). Task set impacted the sampling of information and group decisions. Solve groups mentioned and repeated more unshared information than judge groups. Moreover, solve groups chose the guilty suspect more often than judge groups, who were no more likely than individual members before discussion to choose the best answer. Thus, inducing group members to think that their task had a demonstrably correct solution led them to engage in a more complete review of the information, resulting in more unshared information being recalled and emphasized. This finding optimistically suggests that members' *construal* of the group's task as intellective (a problem to be solved) can ameliorate the discussion advantage of shared information and consequent ill-informed decisions.

Stasser and Stewart (1992) described the poorer decisions of judge set groups as the result of inadequate information pooling. That is, they assumed a direct correspondence between the information that groups discussed and the quality of group decisions. Because groups tend to discuss more shared than unshared information on average, shared information is likely to impact group decisions to a greater extent than unshared information, resulting in suboptimal decisions in hidden profile situations. Gigone and Hastie (1993) proposed that shared information can impact group decisions in another way: through individual members' prior judgments. Shared information affects the judgments of every group member before discussion, and these individual judgments then influence the group's decision. Conversely, unshared information only affects the judgment of single members, and thus its impact, via member preferences, on the group's decision is muted. Gigone and Hastie designed a study to test this *common knowledge effect*—the phenomenon whereby an item of information has a greater impact on a group's judgment because it impacts a greater number of members' judgments before discussion. Participants in their study collectively estimated the grades (e.g., B-, C+, A) obtained by 32 stimulus targets in an introductory psychology course. For each target, each member first individually reviewed four of six possible cues about the target (SAT score, high school GPA, target-rated class enjoyment, other course workload, class attendance, and anxiety), estimated the target's class grade, and then discussed the same target in a three-person group to reach a consensus on the estimated grade. The results were generally suppor-tive of the common knowledge effect: When cues were shared, they had a greater impact on groups' decisions than when cues were unshared. Moreover, groups discussed cues more when they were shared than when they were unshared. However, the impact of shared cues on group judgments was apparently unaffected by what infor-mation was actually discussed. Group judgments could be predicted from members' prediscussion judgments that, in turn, were impacted disproportionately by shared cues. Knowing what cues were actually discussed added nothing to the prediction of group judgments.

This research demonstrates a group task for which information sampling may have little or no influence on the group's decision. Because there was an underlying response continuum, Gigone and Hastie's task allowed members to aggregate easily their prediscussion judgments to obtain a collective judgment without necessarily dis-cussing the justifications for their prediscussion judgments. That is, if the three members' prediscussion judgments for a target were B, C-, and C+, they could "average" their judgments to arrive at the grade C+ as the group judgment. Such an averaging process is not possible when a task presents discrete, unordered decision alterna-tives (as for the political candidate task or homicide mystery task used by Stasser and colleagues). For example, if each member of a three-person group favors a different suspect in the mystery task, there is no obvious way for them to aggregate their initial preferences to obtain a group choice. Therefore, they may be forced to consider information and generate arguments for one position over another in search of a consensus, thus allowing information discussed to impact the group decision to a greater degree.

In summary, Gigone and Hastie's common knowledge effect suggests two implications for information pooling. First, to the degree that a task provides a simple heuristic for aggregating members' preferences, the apparent need for extensive discussion may be reduced, thereby diminishing discussion's impact on group judgment. Second, the disproportionate impact of shared information on group decisions may predate discussion and be difficult to ameliorate through discussion. Both of these possibilities do not bode well for the information-pooling efficacy of face-to-face discussion and the ability of groups to discover hidden profiles when they exist.

Tacit Coordination. When group members work together on a task, they must coordinate their actions in order to perform the task effectively. Such coordination is often tacit in that members do not explicitly discuss strategies for how to go about completing the task. *Tacit coordination* can be understood as the synchronization of group member actions based on unspoken assumptions about what others in the group are likely to do. Although coordination can be explicit, prior research suggests it is often tacit. Hackman and Morris (1975) found that groups rarely discussed their strategies for performing the group's task. Also, Gersick (1988) noted that interaction patterns are established very quickly during the initial stages of discussion. She assumed that the speed with which these patterns developed indicated that they were the result of processes operating before the group convened, such as members' expectations about each other, the task, and the context. Wegner (1987) proposed that members develop expectations about the expertise domains of group members and assume that others will take responsibility for remembering information falling in their area of expertise. So, instead of explicit discussion of how to approach the task, it seems that members quickly coordinate their actions by developing expectations about others' likely actions based on others' presumed areas of expertise.

Wittenbaum et al. (in press) conducted research to examine directly the formation of members' expectations about others' likely behavior (based on implicit or explicit cues about others' expertise) and the use of these expectations to guide their own behavior. Given that coordination is defined relative to something to be accomplished, Wittenbaum et al. also investigated whether members are sensitive to variations in task demands when coordinating their actions. Participants in their study read political candidate statements in anticipation of discussing the candidates in small groups. Anticipated task demands were varied by telling some participants that their group would decide on the best candidate and telling others that their group would collectively recall information about the candidates. Before reading the candidate information, participants read biographical sketches that were ostensibly completed by the other members of their group. In lieu of group interaction, participants unexpectedly were asked to recall individually the candidate information. When participants anticipated a group decision, they remembered more information that was associated with others' presumed areas of expertise, whereas when they anticipated collective recall, they remembered more information that was *not* associated with others' presumed areas of expertise. Thus, when anticipating a group decision, group members focused on information that they thought would be commonly known, possibly in order to facilitate reaching a consensus. When anticipating collective recall, members focused on information that they thought others would tend to ignore. By avoiding duplication of others' expected recall, the group could maximize its collective recall output. In sum, members selectively attended to information depending on their assessment of task demands and their perception of the group's social environment.

A limitation of this study is that it assessed the information that members recalled before discussion but did not assess actual discussion content. It is not a foregone conclusion that discussion content would mirror the content of members' recall prior to discussion. It is possible that efforts at the individual level to duplicate others' expected recall would result in more shared or commonly known information being discussed by the group, whereas efforts at the individual level to supplement others' expected recall would result in more unshared or diverse information being discussed by the group. However, the bulk of research reviewed in the chapter has demonstrated that group discussion, other things being equal, enhances the recall of commonly known information. Thus, efforts at the individual level to duplicate others' expected task efforts may be enhanced, whereas efforts to supplement others' expected task efforts may be attenuated. Investigating the relation between members' management of information in anticipation of small group interaction and their eventual information use during interaction is a potentially fruitful avenue for future research.

FUTURE DIRECTIONS

Interest in groups as information processors emerged recently (Larson & Christensen, 1993), and many questions regarding information management in small groups still remain unanswered. Recent directions in this area have moved toward understanding the psychological underpinnings of information management, such as how expert roles, status, leadership, and perceptions of the task influence information sharing. Future directions will likely continue along these lines, incorporating social cognition, motivation, and organizational factors into the theoretical framework and extending beyond the limited sampling processes described by the CIS model.

The research examining status, expert roles, and leadership suggests that *social perception* may play a key role in determining what information members share and how others react to that information. Members who are perceived to be highly competent due to their membership in particular social and demographic groups, knowledge in a unique niche, or occupational role may feel the needed confidence from self and others to emphasize unshared information. Indeed, unshared information communicated by a presumably low competent member may be assigned less importance or dismissed by others compared to identical information communicated by a presumably competent member. However, unshared information may not be limited to communication by high status members but may be used by low status members as an *impression management* tool to bolster their status. A member who communicates unique information may be perceived as more competent, as better prepared for the task, and as having access to valuable sources of information (e.g., connections with important people outside of the group). How the information is acquired probably influences the impact that unshared information has in the group and the reactions it evokes from others. In previous research, information was given to group members by the experimenter. Thus, the information that members possessed could not be an indication of information acquisition skill or important connections. In sum, it may prove fruitful to examine (a) how information is interpreted and reacted to by others depending on the contributing member and (b) how members may manage their impressions through their management of information.

Most of the research reviewed in this chapter investigated information sampling in ad hoc groups—groups whose members were previously unacquainted before the study. Relatively little is known about the management of information in *intact groups*—groups whose members have a history of working together and work on tasks that have personal relevance and importance. Consideration of intact groups suggests several dynamics that may be largely absent in ad hoc groups. First, intact groups, because they work together over time, may have a better sense of members' areas of expertise, thus increasing the group's meta-knowledge base. Also, their anticipation of future group interaction may influence the sharing of information. Second, many organizational teams are composed such that members' areas of expertise are made explicit by roles or titles. This meta-knowledge of the group's expertise composition may also facilitate the use of members' unique pools of knowledge. Third, long-standing groups experience turnover in membership. Because these new members (i.e., "newcomers"; Moreland & Levine, 1989) lack experience with the group, they may show similar patterns of information sharing as inexperienced members in Wittenbaum's (1996) study, whereas "oldtimers," who have been in the group for a longer period, may behave like experienced members. Fourth, in intact groups, a natural leader may emerge over time, and this leader may facilitate unshared information use (as in Larson et al., 1995). Finally, most groups work in a larger social context consisting of an organizational firm, government agency, or community and engage in activities external to the group that affect performance (Ancona & Caldwell, 1992). In such groups, the amount and type of information discussed can be influenced by outsiders in the firm or community with a stake in the group decision. These suggestions emphasize the point made by Worchel et al. (1992): It is important to study groups in a social context that "includes their history, their expectations for the future, their structure, their purpose, and their relationship with other groups" (p. 183).

Intact groups often work in environments in which "hot dynamics," such as power, motives, threat, and intergroup competition, are operating. Because the research to date has focused on relatively benign factors (e.g., group size, expert roles, task demonstrability), we do not know how groups manage information under conditions in which some members can control the need satisfaction of other members, member motives differ from collective goals, the group is threatened by an external source, or the group faces competition for scarce resources. Any condition that enhances perceived threat or intergroup competition may suppress unshared information use due to groups' tendency to exhibit automatically well-learned, habitual behaviors under threat (Staw et al., 1981). Likewise, groups composed of members with mixed motives or unequal power may suppress the sharing of information. In these cases, members may use information strategically in order to attain individual goals or maintain power over others. If reaching a particular decision serves the selfish interests of one member, that member may actively withhold from others information that may compromise his or her interests. Such situations may be particularly common in political decision-making groups in which members are accountable (i.e., need to justify their judgments) to constituencies (Tetlock, 1992). In this way, group members may not just passively mention information but actively manage it in order to attain a particular personal or collective outcome. Thus, it is important to understand members' individual and collective goals in order to determine whether sharing uniquely known information is in members' or groups' best interest. Future research building on the aforementioned suggestions will likely broaden our understanding of how members select and manage information in small groups.

.

2

Salient Group Memberships and Persuasion
The Role of Social Identity in the Validation of Beliefs

S. ALEXANDER HASLAM
CRAIG McGARTY
JOHN C. TURNER

A s other contributors to this volume note, failure to take into account the *distinct* nature of social cognition has been quite widespread in social psychological research. In large part, this can be seen to have arisen from the relatively straightforward borrowing (or extension) of paradigms and theories from the nonsocial (i.e., experimental cognitive) domain over the past two or three decades. Nonetheless, over that time a number of social psychologists have moved consistently against this individualistic trend (e.g., Pepitone, 1981; Steiner, 1974; Tajfel, 1979). In this vein, social identity theorists (Tajfel & Turner, 1979, 1986; see also Hogg & Abrams, 1988; Hogg & Turner, 1987; Turner, 1982; Turner & Oakes, 1986) have presented an analysis of the psychological substrates of intergroup behavior that incorporates an appreciation of the distinct role of the group in determining individual cognition and behavior. These ideas, and the central concept of social identity, were subsequently developed in self-categorization theory (Turner, 1985; Turner, Hogg, Oakes, Reicher, & Wetherell, 1987) in an attempt to provide *inter alia* a nonindividualistic analysis of social influence. As Turner and Oakes (1986) note, such a development appeared warranted in light of abundant evidence that "the psychological group appears to be at the beginning, not the end of the influence process . . . its precondition and not its product" (p. 244).

This chapter represents an attempt to explore and test some of the ideas arising from this particular theoretical approach to issues of social cognition and social influence. It starts by briefly reviewing some of the traditional perspectives on these issues, most of which have sought conceptually to isolate group life from the process of "true" influence and persuasion. An alternative position advocated by self-categorization theory is then presented. This asserts that influence and persuasion represent social forms of action that are mediated by perceptions of shared group membership (or social categorical identity). In particular, it is argued that people are more likely to be persuaded and positively influenced by others with whom they recognize a shared identity. The theory proposes that these others are persuasive because their psychological equivalence to self is seen to qualify them to validate self-relevant aspects of reality. In other words, we come to believe what others tell us when we categorize them as similar to us in relevant ways, and we cease to believe them when we categorize them as different. These ideas are tested in two studies that manipulate the categorical identity of a constant source as well as subjects' recognition of their relationship to that source. Based on this research, we conclude that the contribution of groups to the persuasion process is far from peripheral or unthinking but rather is absolutely central to these and other related forms of rational cognitive activity.

SOCIAL INFLUENCE AND PERSUASION: TRADITIONAL DUAL PROCESS MODELS

A historical survey of research into persuasive communication and social influence reveals a consistent tendency to treat these very much as separate areas of inquiry. This separation can be revealed by a cursory examination of the reference lists of the chapters of introductory social psychology textbooks on persuasion (or attitude change) and social influence. Indeed, we would go so far as to argue that there has been a gulf between the study of social influence and the study of persuasion that has rarely been bridged.

The existence of the divergence between approaches to the two areas is all the more remarkable in view of the fact that the mainstream social psychological approaches in each area can be seen to share similar assumptions. In particular, both social influence and persuasion researchers have conventionally adopted what Turner (1991) refers to as a *dual-process model* of influence. Dual-process models postulate that there are two distinct routes to persuasion or social influence. In each case, one type of influence is seen as a true, real, long-term change of opinions involving thought and genuine acceptance of the new view. The other type of influence is seen as relatively unthinking and impressionistic. It is understood to constitute short-term compliance with the source of a communication that involves attention to cues or behaviors rather than factual arguments.

Examples of such dualism in the social influence domain are found in the distinctions between physical and social reality testing (Festinger, 1950), informational and normative influence (Deutsch & Gerard, 1955, a treatment that represents the clearest early statement of a dual-process model), informational and effect dependence (Jones & Gerard, 1967), internalization and identification (Kelman, 1961), and conversion and compliance behavior (Moscovici, 1980). Within the persuasion domain, a similar distinction exists between central and peripheral route processing (Petty & Cacioppo, 1981, 1986) and systematic and heuristic processing (Chaiken, 1980, 1987). The important differences between the approaches do not conceal the similarities in the nature of the dichotomy in each case. Although it is true that in both Chaiken's (1987) and Petty and Cacioppo's (1986) persuasion models the theorists see both routes to relate to true cognitive change in opinions, these can still be seen very much as dual-process models. This is because in each case the former type of influence is held to be more valid than the latter due either to the veridicality (or stability and depth) of the opinion change or to the objectivity (depth of processing) of the process by which influence is achieved. The distinction between the two modes of the dual-process model suggests a difference in validity in both process and the anticipated (i.e., anticipated by the theorist) content of the new opinions. That is, because the first kind of process is held to be more objective, new beliefs derived by this route are considered more likely to be accurate (i.e., congruent with objective reality).

A further point, made originally by Turner (1985) in the social influence domain but also by Mackie, Worth, and Asuncion (1990) and Turner (1991) with respect to persuasion research, is that there is a clear link between the type of process believed to be occurring and the role that the social context (i.e., other people) is believed to play in these processes. In short, there is an asymmetry such that group memberships tend to be associated with *unthinking* influence. For example, in Petty and Cacioppo's (1986) elaboration likelihood model, group member-ships are seen to be persuasive by the peripheral route. That is, the group membership of a source is believed to function as a cue that leads to superficial rather than systematic, thoughtful (elaborated) processing of the message. Such cues can be contrasted with the content of (or arguments contained within) a message. In the elaboration likelihood model, it is only these objective persuasive qualities of messages that are deemed to lead to persuasion.

This analysis of influence follows directly from Festinger's (1950) theory of informal social communication. In this theory, there are two modes of reality testing by which we validate our opinions (and in Festinger's [1954] social comparison theory, our abilities): the physical and social means. Physical reality testing is objective and is the method to which perceivers first resort. In the absence of available physical means to test the validity of our opinions, we turn to social means (i.e., social reality testing). In the theory, these social means are secondary and inferior. As Mackie et al. (1990) argue, the elaboration likelihood model adopts an approach that is very close to Festinger's (1950) insofar as group-mediated communication is seen to be less objective and involves less extensive content-related processing.

However, given the critical role of the informational content of messages in the elaboration likelihood model, it is surprising to note that there is no statement within the theory of what actually makes an argument persuasive. This is despite the explicit recognition by Petty and Cacioppo (1986, p. 132) and other writers that this is the biggest unsolved problem in the study of persuasion (for empirical purposes these theorists simply define an argument to be persuasive when the majority of a subject population find it persuasive). Thus, according to the elaboration likelihood model, group-mediated opinion change is held to be inconsistent with the objective qualities that make messages persuasive, but there is no independent statement within the theory of what these objective qualities are. At the very least, then, it appears that there are some important blind spots in the model's treatment of group-based persuasion that need to be explored more fully (bearing in mind that this was not the level at which the model was originally pitched).

SELF-CATEGORIZATION THEORY: A SINGLE PROCESS MODEL

As noted, the purpose of this chapter is to explore ideas that have developed out of Turner's critique of the dual-process model as presented in self-categorization theory (Turner, 1985; Turner et al., 1987; see also Turner, 1982). This theory is a general theory of social behavior based on the critical assumption that the self-concept is both flexible (context dependent) and hierarchically organized. Under this view, social cognition and the social context are interdependent. More specifically, there is assumed to be an interplay between how we view other people and what we think, such that the way we interact with other people (and the impact they have on us) varies as a consequence of the group memberships we perceive them to have.

Thus, the process of persuasion involves more than just the processing of factual information, because the way we process information is profoundly mediated by our group memberships and associated perceptions of social reality.

This view, and evidence that social influence is intimately bound up with issues of social categorization and the group memberships of a message's source and its recipient, has recently been presented by a number of researchers. Experiments by Mackie et al. (1990), van Knippenberg and Wilke (1992), and Wilder (1990) all suggest that message persuasiveness is an *emergent* (rather than a pregiven) property dependent in part on the ingroup-outgroup status of its source. Thus, in Mackie et al.'s (1990) first study, strong messages from an ingroup that challenged subjects' prior beliefs about the worth of standardized student testing were more persuasive than the same messages from an outgroup (M response shift = 1.29, 0.32, respectively). Moreover, a second study demonstrated that this effect was contingent on the message being perceived as relevant to ingroup membership. This basic finding was reproduced by Mackie, Gastardo-Conaco, and Skelly (1992), who also found that when subjects were aware of a group's position on an issue before processing its message, the quality of the message (weak or strong) had little impact on persuasion and attitude change as this was largely predicted by the source's ingroup-outgroup status. Elaborating on similar results, Wilder (1990) also found that messages from a collection of outgroup members were relatively unpersuasive only when biographical information bearing on the homogeneity of that collection reinforced perception of the separate sources as distinctly different *groups*. That is, messages from both an outgroup and an ingroup were relatively influential when the subjects were encouraged to see the sources as individuals (Ms = 5.30, 5.20, respectively), but when seen as homogeneous groups, the outgroup was much less influential than the ingroup (Ms = 3.90, 4.95).

The first application of self-categorization theory to the analysis of social influence was in the realm of group polarization (see Turner, 1987; Wetherell, 1987). The theory proposes that this phenomenon (the tendency for discussion to make a group's responses more extreme than the average of prediscussion individual responses) can be explained as a group-based process of social influence involving conformity to an extremist ingroup norm or prototype. It is argued that group polarization is a common occurrence because this prototype (which simultaneously maximizes similarities within the ingroup and differences between the ingroup and salient outgroups) is typically more extreme than the average position of individual group members. Consistent with this analysis, empirical studies suggest that when contextual factors encourage individuals to categorize themselves in terms of a shared ingroup membership, their behavior (e.g., expressed beliefs) converges toward the prototypical ingroup position (Hogg, Turner, & Davidson, 1990; McGarty, Turner, Hogg, Davidson, & Wetherell, 1992; Spears, Lea, & Lee, 1990; Turner, 1991; Turner, Wetherell, & Hogg, 1989).

The role of social categorization in the influence process has also been investigated in studies of minority influence seeking to explain the ability of dissenting groups to induce significant attitude and belief change in a larger population. Here again, evidence suggests that the persuasiveness of a minority depends *inter alia* on it being (a) categorized as a group (i.e., with its members presenting a consistent and consensual message; Moscovici, Lage, & Naffrechoux, 1969; Nemeth, Wachtler, & Endicott, 1977; cf. Wilder, 1990) and (b) categorized as an ingroup rather than an outgroup (Maass, Clark, & Haberkorn, 1982; Martin, 1988a, 1988b; Mugny & Papastamou, 1982; for a review, see Turner, 1991, pp. 96-98). This analysis has recently been elaborated from the perspective of self-categorization theory by David and Turner (1992). Among other things, in an initial set of studies (David & Turner, in press), they found that messages from an ingroup (whether a minority or a majority) produced substantially more influence (defined as attitude change in the direction of the message) than messages from outgroups and that the impact of the ingroup minority was especially marked on measures of delayed and private influence.

Detailed statements of self-categorization theory and its application to the analysis of social influence are presented elsewhere, so we will confine ourselves here to some particularly pertinent points (in particular, see Turner, 1991; Turner & Oakes, 1989). In simple terms, the theory postulates that at different times we perceive ourselves as unique individuals and at other times as members of groups and that these two are equally valid expressions of self. That is, it is proposed that our *social identities* (deriving from the groups we perceive ourselves to be members of in particular contexts) are as true and basic to self as personal identity (derived from views of oneself as a unique individual) and that the extent to which we define ourselves at either the personal or social level is both flexible (context dependent) and functionally antagonistic. For example, if in a particular situation we define ourselves in terms of group memberships such as "male" or "Australian," this means that at that time we perceive ourselves as sharing identity with other members of these social categories and less as unique individuals. The theory acknowledges the possibility of more than two levels of identity (referred to as *levels of abstraction*), not just the personal and social. It is this flexible change in self-perception that provides the cornerstone of the theory. Crucially for the study of social influence, the group level of abstraction is the level at which individuals tend to regard themselves as relatively *interchangeable* (in terms of perceptions and beliefs) with other members of an ingroup social category (Turner, 1982).

The mechanism by which these self-definitions are selectively deployed is central to the predictions of the theory. The extent to which a categorization is applied at a particular level is referred to as its *salience* (Oakes, 1987). Importantly, salience relates not just to the general relevance of a group membership but refers to a selective change in self-perception whereby people *actually define themselves* as unique individuals or as members of groups in a given setting. When they define themselves as members of a group (i.e., when their social identity is salient), they perceive themselves to be interchangeable with members of that group and distinct from members of other groups.

Self-categorization theory has been applied to many processes in social psychology, in particular, social stereotyping, social judgment, crowd behavior, and small group processes, but one of its most extensive applications to date has been the explanation of social influence. In this regard, the most important aspect of the theory is that it rejects dichotomies of the type presented by dual-process models that suggest there are two processes of influence, one of which is more valid than the other. On the contrary, the theory maintains that there is one process that can have different (but interdependent) individual and social *phases*. As Festinger (1950) maintained, we are motivated to have valid opinions about the world, and to the extent that we believe our opinions correspond to objective underlying conditions, they can be said to have subjective validity. However, there is no sense in which we have direct access to the objective underlying conditions: Some of the most famous experiments in social psychology (e.g., Asch, 1951) indicate that even the most seemingly direct (or "physical") forms of an individual's knowledge (e.g., that a line is of a certain length) are structured by that person's place within a particular social system of belief. The social context is influential in this process because when people's social identity is salient and they see themselves as interchangeable with other ingroup members, they regard those others as valid sources of information about those conditions. Here they both expect, and are actively motivated to engage in processes of mutual influence so as to achieve, agreement with other ingroup members. In terms of self-categorization theory, then, group memberships are valid psychological components of the individual that, among other things, provide the basis both (a) for validation (and invalidation) of individual cognitions and (b) the emergence of ingroup consensus.

From this perspective, persuasion is an embodiment of the social influence process and

> is believed to originate in the need of people to reach agreement with others perceived as interchangeable in respect of relevant attributes (psychological ingroup members in the given situation) about the same stimulus situation in order to validate their responses as correct, appropriate, desirable (reflecting the requirements of the objective situation rather than subjective biases and errors). (Turner, 1987, p. 72)

It follows too that the persuasiveness of a person's arguments will vary as a function of the degree of relative ingroup support for that person's position with respect to a currently salient frame of reference.

So in the context of an election campaign, for example, the arguments and policies of one party will be more persuasive for a supporter of that party than those presented by an opposing party. The theory's explanation of this difference is that agreement with one's own political party both derives from and contributes to social consensus in the ingroup. Such a consensus is persuasive because in reflecting the views of people who are similar to self and share the same perspective (rather than the views and perspective of those different from self), it is held to be more informative about underlying reality.

EMPIRICAL INVESTIGATION

In order to investigate this analysis of the role of group memberships in the persuasion process, we conducted a series of experimental studies (McGarty, Haslam, Hutchinson, & Turner, 1994). In broad terms, the objective of these studies was to test the idea that the persuasiveness of information is not simply a function of its content but rather is mediated by the social categorical status of an informational source relative to the perceiver. We also sought to examine more critically the exact role of the group in this process: seeking to question the dual-process argument that this is associated with a distinct and inferior form of information processing.

In our first experiment, we sought to conduct preliminary tests of arguments derived from self-categorization theory. There are several aspects of the theory that require direct tests in ways that can be linked with previous research on persuasion (see van Knippenberg & Wilke's, 1992, treatment of prototypicality). One of the most important of these aspects is the salience mechanism. As previous researchers have found, we would expect that ingroups would be more persuasive than outgroups, but further to this, we would also expect that when group memberships are salient (i.e., functioning psychologically to define individuals' self-concepts), this would increase the relative persuasive superiority of ingroups over outgroups. This is because under these conditions ingroup members should be more likely to be seen as interchangeable and outgroup members as

noninterchangeable with self. The early research on group membership salience and social influence (Charters & Newcomb, 1952;
Festinger, 1947; Kelley, 1955) suggests that salience effects will be
stronger when subjects openly express identification with or commitment to the ingroup (as does the social judgment involvement theory;
Sherif, Sherif, & Nebergall, 1965). Self-categorization theory predicts much the same effects, but the analysis is somewhat different.
Even though merely mentioning a social categorization may be sufficient to make it salient for some people, we cannot expect salience
effects unless the salience manipulation involves people identifying
themselves with the group (i.e., perceiving themselves in social categorical terms). In other words, a psychological change is necessary so
that commitment to a group produces perceived interchangeability
with ingroup members and rejection of outgroup members as currently different from self.

Experiment 1

Our first experiment adopted a methodology similar to that used
by Mackie et al. (1990) in that subjects were presented with a
persuasive communication (on brain damage) that was attributed to
either an ingroup or outgroup speaker. The group membership was
varied by presenting the speaker as a member of one of two groups,
which were defined in terms of their attitudinal positions. Salience
was manipulated by asking half the subjects to express their acceptance or rejection of the stance of the (female) speaker's group before
they were exposed to her message. Accordingly, subjects were randomly assigned to one of four conditions arranged in a 2 (in-
group/outgroup) × 2 (low/high salience) between-subjects design.

The central dependent measure in which we were interested here
was subjects' agreement with this message. We used this measure to
gauge persuasion, rather than the perceived persuasiveness of the
message or the speaker, as the latter may only reflect the impressions
subjects form rather than any actual change in their attitudes. Furthermore, there are reasons to believe that people are often unwilling
to admit (or are unaware of) attitude change (as found, e.g., by

Braver, Linder, Corwin, & Cialdini, 1977). In this study, then, we hypothesized that the difference in agreement with the messages of ingroup and outgroup speakers should be greatest when the social categorization (and the extent of shared categorical identity between source and subject) was salient.

Subjects were given a questionnaire and asked to read its front page, which presented a description of the speaker. They were then shown a 5-minute videotaped communication on the causes and consequences of brain damage. The speaker of this message (an actor) suggested that brain damage was a great burden on society and (in very general terms) that the government should be taking more action to prevent it. The message included three major causes of brain damage: road accidents, alcohol abuse, and the combination of these two (i.e., drinking and driving).

The group membership of the speaker was manipulated by describing her as a member of the general public who was also either (a) a member of a group that wanted to improve road safety or (b) a member of a group that wanted to outlaw the sale and consumption of alcohol. We expected that students would identify with the first group and reject the second (i.e., that the former would constitute a psychological ingroup and the latter an outgroup). The salience of the intergroup context was increased for half the subjects by asking them whether they agreed or disagreed with the position associated with the speaker's attitude group. The question was of the form:

> Before watching the video . . ., we would like to know whether or not *you* are in favour of improving road safety (outlawing the sale and consumption of alcohol). Indicate this by placing an "X" beside one of the responses below:
>
> _____ Yes, I am in favour of improving road safety (outlawing the sale and consumption of alcohol).
> _____ No, I am not in favour of improving road safety (outlawing the sale and consumption of alcohol).
>
> (The words in parentheses denote alternative wordings in the outgroup salient condition.)

The subsequent response sheet asked subjects to rate (on 11-point scales from 0 to 10) (a) the persuasiveness of the speaker's message, (b) how much they agreed with the message, (c) how pleasant they thought the speaker was, (d) how interested they were in the experiment, (e) how well informed they thought the speaker was, (f) whether they agreed that road safety should be improved, and (g) whether they agreed that the sale and consumption of alcohol should be outlawed.

There were no differences between groups in the extent to which subjects favored improving road safety (mean for the entire sample = 8.8), but in the high salience conditions, subjects were less likely to be in favor of banning alcohol (F (1,125) = 4.01, $p < .05$, Ms low salience: 1.5; high salience: 0.8). Overall, though, we can conclude (as we had anticipated) that the sample was strongly in favor of improving road safety and strongly opposed to banning alcohol.

Analysis of responses on the primary measure of interest, subjects' agreement with the speaker's message, revealed a main effect for group membership such that subjects were more likely to agree with the message when it came from an ingroup source (F (1,125) = 11.1, $p < .001$) and a main effect for salience such that subjects were less likely to agree with the message when salience was high (F (1,125) = 4.1, $p < .05$). However, these main effects were qualified substantially by the predicted group × salience interaction (F (1,125) = 4.1, $p < .05$), indicating that the ingroup-outgroup difference was only observed under conditions of high salience (low salience: outgroup vs. ingroup Ms = 6.4 vs. 6.9; high salience: outgroup vs. ingroup Ms = 4.7 vs. 6.9).

These results thus supported our primary hypothesis in that they demonstrated an ingroup-outgroup difference in persuasion *only* when the social categorization was salient. In other words, subjects perceived the ingroup target's message to be superior to that from the outgroup target only when they explicitly acknowledged the extent of shared identity between them and this source. These results, therefore, provide support for predictions derived from self-categorization theory, although it should be noted that the theory suggests that the salience of relative social identity-based interchangeability should increase the persuasiveness of the ingroup speaker as well as reduce that of the outgroup source. Here though, the observed pattern points to a reduction in the persuasiveness of the outgroup member when group membership was made salient, but not to an increase in the persuasiveness of the ingroup speaker.

One possible interpretation of this failure of salience to enhance the persuasiveness of the ingroup message is that it arose from a ceiling effect due to the already very high levels of agreement in the ingroup conditions. Given that our manipulation of salience was close to one of involvement in the issue, it is also the case that the pattern of results here is consistent with the argument presented by social judgment-involvement theory (Sherif et al., 1965) that increasing involvement increases the size of the latitude of rejection without changing the latitude of acceptance. However, it should be noted that the absence of effects on the posttest interest measure suggests that differences in involvement per se were not implicated in the effects here (cf. Haslam & Turner, 1992). Finally, it is also possible to argue that effects in the high salience conditions reflected the extent to which subjects had to cognitively elaborate on the speaker's message. That is, in the high salience condition, subjects may have felt the need to justify their rejection of the outgroup speaker's arguments more than they needed to justify acceptance of them in the ingroup condition. The important feature of this alternative account is that it suggests that group-based rejection of a message may be more cognitively demanding than acceptance—an argument that can clearly be reconciled with the claim that group-based (positive) influence is a relatively thoughtless process (cf. Petty & Cacioppo, 1986).

In relation to the possibility of reconciling these data with a dual-process analysis, it is interesting to note, however, that in this study the lack of persuasiveness of the outgroup speaker was not associated with derogation of the outgroup. Subjects were less likely to agree with the outgroup when the social categorization was salient, but responses on additional measures indicated that they did not actually perceive the outgroup speaker to be any less persuasive or less well informed. Importantly, the results thus suggest that the greater persuasive power of ingroups is not dependent on relative derogation of outgroups. Moreover, in this study, it was also the case that subjects in ingroup conditions typically found themselves in the position of agreeing with the message but not actually liking the speaker or the way she presented the message. Our results therefore indicate that subjects can be sensitive to peripheral cues from both ingroup and outgroup speakers and that they can react negatively to these cues without them necessarily affecting their agreement with the message. In contrast to the elaboration likelihood model, this implies that the effect of salient group memberships on the actual (rather than perceived) persuasiveness of a message is unrelated to the effect of peripheral cues.

These points notwithstanding, it was clearly the case that we needed to conduct a follow-up study to investigate in more detail the mechanisms by which the salience of group membership increased the relative persuasiveness of ingroups (or the relative unpersuasiveness of outgroups). More specifically, we needed to resolve some of the ambiguity concerning exactly whether acceptance of the ingroup message in high salience conditions was a thoughtful process or not. In a second study, we thus decided to investigate the effects of salience and the source's social category membership not only on agreement but also on the depth of processing of her message.

Experiment 2

In this study, we included additional measures in order to assess the elaboration of the message produced by the various conditions in our first experiment. As has already been noted, the elaboration likelihood model suggests that groups are persuasive by the peripheral route (i.e., they involve persuasion without detailed processing). In order to explore these ideas, this experiment included a thought-listing task and other measures of the extent to which the speaker's message was being processed in a thoughtful and detailed way. In contrast to the prevailing orthodoxy (and the argument that a lack of cognitive elaboration was responsible for the failure of high salience to enhance agreement with the ingroup message in Experiment 1), we expected a difference such that *more* thoughtful and detailed processing would be associated with salient ingroup messages than salient outgroup messages.

The other novel feature included in this study was an indirect manipulation of salience. Rather than having subjects express their agreement or disagreement with the attitudinal position of the speaker's group, subjects were simply told that they were going to see two messages—one from an ingroup speaker and one from an outgroup speaker. In fact, they saw only one message (either ingroup or outgroup). This indirect manipulation of salience was a weak manipulation because it did not require explicit commitment to a position. As Turner (1975) notes, merely making subjects aware of a social categorization does not necessarily lead them to perceive themselves in terms of that categorization. That is, it would not necessarily lead to a change in level of abstraction whereby the subjects perceive themselves to be relatively interchangeable with fellow ingroup members. We therefore predicted that the indirect salience manipulation would have weaker effects than the direct manipulation. The study thus had a 2 (ingroup/outgroup) × 3 (no salience, indirect salience, direct salience) design with subjects randomly assigned to experimental conditions. The manipulation of ingroup-outgroup status was identical to that used in Experiment 1—in the ingroup conditions subjects were told that the target was a member of a group that wanted to improve road safety and in outgroup conditions they were told that her group wanted to ban the sale and consumption of alcohol.

The posttest questions included the questions asked in Experiment 1 and three additional measures used by Mackie et al. (1990). These questions (which were again responded to on 11-point scales) were: (a) How strong and valid do you think the arguments the speaker used to support her position were? (b) How objective do you think the speaker was? and (c) How important is the issue of preventing brain damage to you? Having responded to these questions, the subjects were asked to complete the thought-listing task. Following Mackie et al. (1990), this was introduced as follows:

> Finally, please list any and all thoughts you had while listening to the speaker's message; these can include anything related to what the speaker said in the message, the speaker and the speaker's

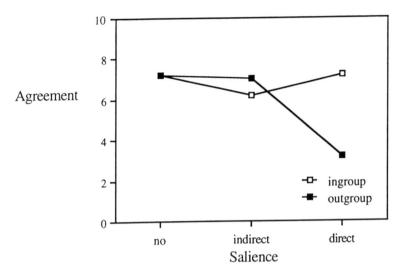

Figure 2.1. The Effects of Speaker's Group and Salience on Agreement in Experiment 2

> personality, the topic of the message, the context in which the speaker spoke, or anything else you might have been thinking about during the message presentation, including totally unrelated things. (p. 814)

Manipulation checks again confirmed the success of the basic ingroup-outgroup manipulation. In general, the subjects were in favor of improving road safety ($M = 8.4$, $sd = 2.1$) and opposed to banning alcohol ($M = 1.9$, $sd = 2.5$). As in our first experiment, analysis of subjects' agreement with the speaker's message revealed a group main effect such that subjects were more likely to agree with an ingroup than an outgroup speaker ($F (1,84) = 5.1$, $p < .05$) and a condition effect such that subjects were less likely to agree in the direct salience conditions ($F (2,84) = 6.4$, $p < .01$). However, as predicted, these effects were again qualified by the group × salience interaction ($F (2,84) = 7.6$, $p < .001$). As Figure 2.1 shows, only in the direct salience condition did subjects agree more with the ingroup than the outgroup source.

From the analysis of subjects' other responses, only two effects emerged, both for the group factor, showing that subjects who saw the speaker as an ingroup member perceived her to be more objective ($F (1,84) = 7.6, p < .01$) and to be more pleasant ($F (1,84) = 4.9, p < .05$). It is worth noting that although the group × salience interaction for the speaker's pleasantness was not significant, the trend was in the opposite direction in the direct salience cell (M (ingroup) = 4.3 vs. M (outgroup) = 4.5)—in other words, the greater persuasiveness of the speaker in this condition was *not* associated with her being perceived as more pleasant.

Following Mackie et al. (1990), after a process of independent blind coding, reactions to the thought-listing task were classified as accurate recall of the speaker's argument, as favorable or unfavorable reactions to the speaker, and as favorable or unfavorable reactions to the message or issue. The results revealed a group main effect ($F (1,84) = 4.7, p < .05$) and a group × salience interaction ($F (2,84) = 3.9, p < .05$) for the number of the speaker's arguments accurately recalled. Consistent with predictions, as can be seen in Figure 2.2, this interaction was based on the fact that subjects recalled more arguments in the ingroup condition than in the outgroup condition but *only* when group memberships were made directly salient ($Ms = 1.0$ vs. 0.2). In the no salience condition ($Ms = 0.1$ vs. 0.3) and in the indirect salience condition ($Ms = 0.6$ vs. 0.3), multiple comparisons indicated that there were no differences in recall of ingroup and outgroup messages.

Analysis of subjects' reactions to the speaker revealed a highly significant tendency for there to be more unfavorable than favorable reactions ($Ms = 1.9$ vs. 0.1, $F (1,84) = 104.8, p < .001$) and a salience main effect ($F (2,84) = 3.8, p < .05$), indicating that there were fewer reactions to the speaker in the direct salience condition (M (direct) = 0.7, M (nonsalient) = 1.3, M (indirect) = 1.1). There was also a within-subjects effect for favorableness of the reactions to message content (M (unfavorable) = 1.8, M (favorable) = 0.7, $F (1,84) = 24.8, p < .001$).

Beyond standard analyses of variance, the design of this study also allowed us to conduct a partial test of the idea that elaboration

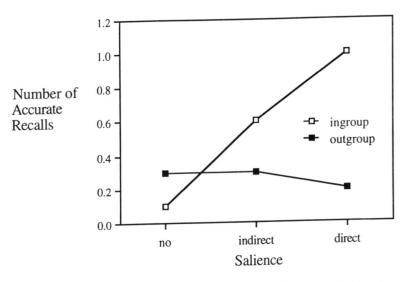

Figure 2.2. The Effects of Speaker's Group and Salience on the Number of Arguments Accurately Recalled in Experiment 2

of arguments mediated the effect of group membership salience on persuasion. Because group membership only affected persuasion in the direct salience condition, it was only meaningful to look for the mediational effect in this condition. This analysis indicated that the increased generation of arguments did not appear to mediate the relationship between group membership salience and agreement but that group membership salience and elaboration were related to agreement independently. However, for a number of reasons (including the order in which measures were obtained and lack of knowledge about the reliability of the thought-listing measure), these results need to be considered with some caution.

Overall though, the results of this second study again supported self-categorization theory's analysis of persuasion. The persuasive superiority of ingroups over outgroups was only observed when the social categorization was salient and when subjects were committed to group memberships (thereby replicating the findings of Experiment 1). These findings are consistent with the proposition that in order for group memberships to have an impact it is not sufficient for people merely to be aware of the social categorization—instead, they must see the social categorization as directly relevant to self in order for it to affect social perception (Turner, 1975). Having said this, it was again apparent that under conditions of social category salience, agreement was decreased for an outgroup member but not increased for an ingroup member (see Figure 2.2; cf. Wilder, 1990). This points to a consistent pattern across the two experiments such that salience led to a rejection of the outgroup speaker rather than increased agreement with the ingroup speaker. Although this particular pattern does not provide the strongest possible support for self-categorization theory (although unlike other theories, it does predict the observed interaction), it should be noted that (a) ceiling effects may again have played a role here and (b) the pattern of responses on the thought-listing task suggest that this failure of the salience manipulation to increase agreement with the ingroup was *not* a product of a lack of cognitive elaboration (as the "no need for justification" analysis of the results to Experiment 1 might suggest).

GENERAL DISCUSSION

Given that findings from both the above studies establish the importance of salient group memberships in persuasion, it is pertinent, as we noted earlier, to ask *how* group membership salience affects persuasiveness. The current results indicate that salience produces an ingroup-outgroup difference in persuasion and an independent difference in the number of arguments recalled. As well as this, the ingroup speaker was perceived to be more objective than the outgroup source.

In contrast to the conventional view that these effects are simply the manifestations of an ethnocentric and irrational bias, we would argue that there are subjectively good reasons for these differences between ingroups and outgroups. An outgroup message is not seen as compelling because the opinions (a) are discrepant from one's own and (b) emanate from a source not perceived to be informative about underlying reality because it is noninterchangeable with self and hence associated with a conflicting (or irrelevant) perspective. To the extent that people believe a source is not informative about (their own) reality (and hence, from their perspective, is nonobjective), they are less likely to perceive that source's arguments as persuasive and will attend to them less. However, because ingroup members *are* informative about a relevant social consensus (which is believed to match objective reality), their arguments will be seen as persuasive and will therefore be attended to.

Following this analysis, the present results, together with those of Mackie et al. (1990), therefore suggest that the elaboration likelihood model's dichotomy between central and peripheral route processing does not relate to the differences between ingroups and outgroups that we have found here. Put simply, persuasion by the ingroup does not have the characteristics ascribed to the peripheral route under conditions in which group memberships are salient. That is, salient group memberships do not appear to be peripheral cues that serve as an *alternative* to deep and thoughtful processing of the message. The evidence here in fact demonstrates quite clearly that when group memberships are relevant to the judgment, they can lead to thoughtful processing of an ingroup message. We would therefore argue that the results challenge any dual-process analysis that seeks to represent cognitions about objective reality and the impact of social context as being mutually exclusive. These two are not normally opposed features within an individual's mind; instead, social context is a part of objective reality and is understood to be informative about it.

Findings consistent with this point have previously been demonstrated in the study of the effects of agreement and disagreement on uncertainty using visual stimuli. In particular, McGarty, Turner, Oakes, and Haslam (1993) demonstrated that when good stimulus information was available, agreement with an ingroup source increased confidence but disagreement did not necessarily reduce it. These results appeared to indicate, then, that disagreement initiated a process of uncertainty reduction whereby perceivers sought to bring their own perceptions into line with the feedback of others with whom they expected to agree.

Both these and the current results suggest that individuals seek to understand the world around them in cooperation with relevant others. Indeed, we would argue that the intersubjective nature of definition of the self in terms of social identity (based on the recognition of what one shares with other ingroup category members) provides not only a common perspective on reality but also the basis for the coordination of cognition and behavior through mutual influence, and hence leads to the development of *shared* beliefs, norms, and values (cf. Ickes & Gonzalez, 1994). This process of consensus development is shown particularly clearly in the emergence of social stereotypes—in many respects the paradigm case of shared cognitions (Gardner, 1993; Oakes, Haslam, & Turner, 1994; Stangor & Lange, 1993). And important for the present argument, our own research into the psychological determinants of stereotype consensus suggests quite strongly that the emergence of shared cognitions is premised on (and structured by) shared identification rather than simply shared experience (Haslam et al., in press; see also Haslam, in press).

The analysis we are presenting here, then, does not cast the individual as subordinate to the social context but instead presents an analysis that sees the individual as working in sympathy with this context. Yet although we are led to conclude that the elaboration likelihood model and other dual-process models need to encompass a reconceptualization of the role of salient (and psychologically real) group memberships in persuasion, such theories seem to deal with nonsalient group memberships quite adequately. We would agree, therefore, that group memberships can function as peripheral cues in the manner that Petty and Cacioppo (1986) have specified but believe that this is the case only under conditions of low salience. In these circumstances, group memberships are not psychologically effective (i.e., people are seeing themselves and others as individuals rather than as members of groups). Here, then, a nonsalient group membership is a peripheral cue that observers may use rather than process the message deeply. Indeed, in such a situation, the group membership functions more as an individual characteristic of the source (like attractiveness) because a lower (personal) level of abstraction is salient. In Experiment 2, the clearest evidence of this is that the total number of elaborations about the speaker (most of which were negative statements about her personal attributes) was higher in the indirect salience and nonsalient conditions. Thus, it was in the cells in which there was *no* ingroup-outgroup difference in the strength of influence that subjects were attending to peripheral cues.

It is also worth noting that similar evidence of fluidity in the generation of elaborations about a message emerging as a consequence of changes in patterns of social identification has recently been reported by David and Turner (1992, Study 7). They found that in contexts in which a former outgroup became recategorized as an ingroup (as a result of changes in comparative context), the message it presented stimulated significantly more novel and divergent thinking. That is, subjects were more likely to generate additional arguments to elaborate on those contained by the source's message in situations that defined the subjects and the source as sharing a common social identity (as feminists in comparison to nonfeminists, rather than as separate feminist subgroups). Consistent with the present results, this finding (which is used by the authors to explain the commonly observed creativity that exposure to a minority group's arguments can engender; Nemeth & Kwan, 1985; Nemeth & Wachtler, 1983; Volpato, Maass, Mucchi-Faina, & Vitti, 1990) again suggests that under appropriate conditions, group-based processing of ingroup messages encourages rather than undermines cognitive activity. Indeed, the current studies supplement a body of research in the area of minority influence, which suggests that, far from precluding deep processing, groups and group conflict can actually be the catalyst for elaborated thinking and intellectual development (Moscovici & Facheaux, 1972).

CONCLUSION

As detailed in the introduction to this chapter, previous researchers have suggested that group-based influence is unthinking and prejudicial because of the evaluative differences associated with group judgments. It has been suggested that group-based influence may be attributed to the peripheral route because perceivers respond negatively to sources of messages on the basis of prior stereotypic beliefs. There is ample evidence of such intergroup differences in evaluation, but the present research suggests that what is crucial for the ingroup to be a superior source of influence to the outgroup is the belief that the ingroup is a more valid source of information than the outgroup, not that it is necessarily better in other ways. So, for example, we might see charity workers as being better people (in a moral sense) than social psychologists, but we are more likely to regard the views of social psychologists as informative about some aspects of reality. In a similar manner, results of our second study showed that the outgroup speaker was disparaged in terms of her objectivity but not necessarily in superficial ways that were irrelevant to the message (relative to the ingroup speaker). Thus, even though there was an ingroup-outgroup difference in perceived pleasantness, this effect did not occur in the direct salience cell in which differences in level of agreement were most pronounced (where the perceived pleasantness of the outgroup speaker was slightly higher than that of the ingroup speaker).

Consistent with previous research, these results suggest a process whereby the group membership of a speaker affects the amount of persuasion produced by a message (cf. Mackie et al., 1990; Wilder, 1990). However, it is important to stress that the process envisaged by self-categorization theory involves an interaction between individual cognition and the social context that is highly selective and context dependent (see Turner, Oakes, Haslam, & McGarty, 1994). Salient group memberships can function as cues to the cogency of arguments, but on the other hand, we can also accept or reject group memberships on the basis of the arguments expressed by group members in particular settings (especially where these arguments have already been evaluated on the basis of preexisting social consensuses). Experiment 2 shows the first of these processes, where group memberships influenced the persuasiveness of arguments, and the first process is apparent in other studies that we have conducted to test the argument that the very perception of shared group membership is structured by a process of categorization in context. Indeed, a distinctive feature of self-categorization theory is that it predicts that the *very same* person can be persuasive or unpersuasive depending on the way he or she is categorized in a given context. For example, it follows from the principle of metacontrast (one of the primary determinants of category salience; Oakes, 1987; Turner, 1985) that an outgroup member who is perceived to be uninformative about reality in one context will be recategorized as an ingroup member and become informative about reality in a context that includes others who are more different from self (David & Turner, in press; Gaertner, Mann, Murrell, & Dovidio, 1989; Haslam & Turner, 1992; see also Gaertner, Rust, Dovidio, Bachman, & Anastasio, Chapter 10, this volume). So for instance, a social psychologist may categorize a developmental psychologist as an outgroup member at a funding meeting in the psychology department and find their arguments unpersuasive (because they are not motivated—or expecting—to agree with that person), but the same person presenting the same arguments may be quite persuasive at a funding meeting involving both psychologists and physicists. Evidence consistent with this point has been reported by David and Turner (1992). Among other things, they found that different subgroups of feminists who were uninfluenced by each others' messages in narrow contexts, including messages from only those feminists subgroups, became mutually influential in broad contexts that also incorporated messages from antifeminists.

The findings from this research thus suggest that there is a persuasive difference between ingroups and outgroups that goes beyond the argument that ingroups are persuasive because they are perceived to be independent and outgroups are not persuasive because they are seen as homogeneous (Wilder, 1990). The results do not disconfirm this perspective; indeed, the argument is highly plausible when it is considered that such varied perceptions are outcomes of the categorization process. Our recasting of Wilder's (1990) findings suggests, however, that homogeneous outgroups are relatively unpersuasive, not because they are homogeneous per se but because perceived homogeneity bears on the categorization of them as groups (by affecting the comparative *fit* of individuals into social categories as predicted under the metacontrast principle). Put another way, heterogeneous outgroups are not more persuasive because their heterogeneity reflects their members' independence but because that heterogeneity serves to undermine reality-based categorization of them as outgroups in the first place.

Accordingly, we do not believe that the relative heterogeneity of groups is the first link in the causal chain that leads to the persuasive superiority of salient ingroups over outgroups. Among other things, this is because when social categorizations are highly salient we would actually expect *equal* homogeneity within groups rather than relative outgroup homogeneity. This point has been confirmed in much of our own recent research that demonstrates that when ingroups and outgroups are judged under equivalent conditions (in particular, when both are judged in an intergroup context on normatively fitting dimensions), ingroups and outgroups will be perceived to be equally and highly homogeneous (Doosje, Spears, Haslam, Koomen, & Oakes, 1995; Haslam, Oakes, Turner, & McGarty, 1995; for a review, see Haslam, Oakes, Turner, & McGarty, 1996).

It also follows from self-categorization theory that we would expect the perceived homogeneity of ingroup members to become increasingly high to the extent that conditions render their social identity more salient. Recent support for this view was provided by a field study that reported the emergence of a shared self-definition accompanied by increasing ingroup homogeneity in small groups participating in a 26-day Outward Bound course (Oakes, Haslam, Morrison, & Grace, 1995). Furthermore, we would anticipate that when ingroup identity becomes salient, there may even be evidence of a relative ingroup homogeneity effect on key ingroup-defining value dimensions. It may, for example, be highly desirable for an ingroup to be completely uniform in some circumstances (as in the case of a political party prior to a general election), whereas at the same time uniformity may be seen as undesirable in the outgroup. This is likely to be particularly true for minority groups and other groups actively engaged in intergroup conflict (as expressed in the rallying cry "united we stand, divided we fall"). Empirical confirmation of this point is provided by Simon's extensive investigations of the homogeneity judgments made by members of minority groups (e.g., Simon, 1992; Simon & Brown, 1987) and Kelly's (1989) study of the same behavior on the part of political party members.

These issues of interpretation aside, the most important conclusion of the research presented in this chapter is that salient group memberships do not appear to affect the persuasiveness of messages in ways that would suggest processing of those messages by the peripheral route. Instead, our findings can be seen as consistent with arguments (a) that group memberships are *central* to the persuasion process in providing a subjectively valid means of engaging in reality testing and (b) that this process is not characterized by a lack of cognitive activity but rather is the manifestation of a rational and relatively elaborated thinking process. On this basis, we would suggest that the central-peripheral dichotomy has the same flaws as those shared by other similar dichotomies in the social influence literature in tending to downplay the significance and rationality of group-based influence.

In the final analysis, then, we would argue that it is a mistake to dismiss the contribution of groups to the persuasion process by characterizing them as sources of influence that preclude valid cognitive activity and lead inexorably to faulty and biased perception. On the contrary, we believe that if groups and group life did not impact on cognition it would be impossible to achieve meaningful and properly coordinated social action. Moreover, we would argue that it is precisely because they do have this impact that social cognition is distinctly social (Tajfel, 1979; Turner & Oakes, 1986). Social movements and social consensuses, for example, clearly achieve their force—and, indeed, only come about—through the ability of groups (both large and small) to structure and regulate individual cognitive activity in an ongoing and dynamic manner.

As other contributors to this volume note, it is an awareness of this intersubjective coordination of psychological activity and an identification of its social psychological underpinnings that have been most conspicuously absent from previous social cognitive theorizing (Ickes & Gonzalez, Chapter 12, this volume; Moreland, Argote, & Krishnan, Chapter 3, this volume; Worchel, Chapter 11, this volume; see also Haslam, in press; McGarty & Turner, 1992). The present chapter demonstrates how shared social identity plays a role in this coordination by providing at the same time both a common perspective and a basis for mutual influence. Based on this and other related research (see Turner et al., 1994) and in contrast to the analysis presented in most other theories of persuasion, it is thus our conviction that the way forward lies not in denying but in reaffirming the meaningful contribution that group memberships make to individual cognition.

3

Socially Shared Cognition at Work
Transactive Memory and Group Performance

RICHARD L. MORELAND
LINDA ARGOTE
RANJANI KRISHNAN

A recent review by Moreland, Hogg, and Hains (1994) of social psychological research revealed a resurgence of interest in studying small groups. Much of that resurgence was due to new theoretical approaches for analyzing group behavior. One approach that was especially influential involved analyses incorporating social cognition. Fiske and Goodwin (Introduction, this volume) have argued that valuable insights into many group phenomena can occur when the cognitive processes associated with group membership are studied. Similar claims have been made by other observers as well (e.g., Goethals, 1987; Messick & Mackie, 1989).

There are two general ways in which such cognitive processes could be studied (Ickes & Gonzalez, Chapter 12, this volume). Most researchers focus on cognition about groups, studying such phenomena as self-categorization (Brewer, 1991), outgroup homogeneity effects (Judd, Ryan, & Park, 1991), the group attribution error (Allison &

Messick, 1985), and so on. Their work explores how *individuals* process information about groups and their members (including themselves). A few researchers, however, focus on more complex phenomena involving cognition by groups. Their work explores how *groups* process information for their members. Information processing by groups requires *socially shared cognition,* that is, collaboration among members who seek to encode, interpret, and recall information together rather than apart. Although little is yet known about socially shared cognition, it has captured considerable attention (see Klimoski & Mohammed, 1994; Larson & Christensen, 1993; Resnick, Levine, & Teasley, 1991) and seems likely to generate much new research.

WORK GROUP CULTURES

One intriguing phenomenon that arises from socially shared cognition is culture. Psychologists are accustomed to analyzing culture at the societal level (Markus & Kitayama, 1991; Triandis, 1989) or within large organizations (Schein, 1990; Trice & Beyer, 1984), but small groups can develop cultures as well. Evidence for such cultures can be found in research on families (Wolin & Bennett, 1984), sports teams (Fine, 1979), and work groups (Rentsch, 1990). Cultural analyses of work groups have been especially popular. In a recent review of this research, Levine and Moreland (1991) suggested that every group of workers develops its own unique culture. Of course, the culture of a particular group may be weak, depending on such factors as the age of the group, the homogeneity and stability of its composition, the levels of process and outcome interdependence among members, and the group's cohesion. And even if a work group's culture is strong, it may be tacit, sensitive, or dynamic and thus difficult to study. Nevertheless, cultural analyses of work groups are possible and can reveal aspects of group dynamics that might otherwise be overlooked.

What, exactly, is the "culture" of a work group? According to Levine and Moreland (1991), it consists of two related elements, namely socially shared knowledge and a set of customs. Cultural knowledge can focus on the group, its members, or the work that

---

Knowledge About the Group

➤ What are our norms?
➤ How successful are we?
➤ Who are our allies/enemies?

Knowledge About Group Members

➤ How do I fit in?
➤ What are the cliques?
➤ Who is good at what?

Knowledge About Work

➤ What are our working conditions?
➤ Why do we work?
➤ How is performance evaluated?

Figure 3.1. Cultural Knowledge in Work Groups: Examples of Questions for Which Workers Seek Common Answers

they perform (cf. Cannon-Bowers, 1993). Some examples of knowledge related to each of these foci are provided in Figure 3.1. The examples are phrased as questions that often concern a work group's members. Their concern is what drives the development of culture, which provides group members with the answers to such questions. Customs, which include routines (Gersick & Hackman, 1990), accounts (Orr, 1990), jargon (Truzzi & Easto, 1972), rituals (Vaught & Smith, 1980), and symbols (Riemer, 1977), embody this cultural knowledge and thus serve (often in subtle ways) to communicate and validate it.

Although the questions shown in Figure 3.1 may seem simple, answering them often involves complex cognitive/social processes. Consider, for example, how workers evaluate their group's success. Success implies some standard, which may be objective (e.g., meeting production goals, avoiding accidents) or subjective. Subjective standards include temporal and social comparisons (Levine & Moreland, 1987); the latter comparisons may focus on various outgroups. To evaluate their group's success, members must thus agree about which standards to use and how they should be applied. It may also be necessary to reconcile their own evaluation of the group with evaluations by outsiders. Even after a final evaluation is made, other questions may soon arise, such as why the group is succeeding or failing (Leary & Forsyth, 1987) and how it might be improved. Discovering the cliques within a group can also be difficult for workers (Krackhardt, 1990), who may be reluctant to provide one another with direct information about who they like or dislike within the group. Indirect information about cliques can be gathered through observations of social behavior, but members must agree about which behaviors are important and how they should be interpreted. And once again, further questions are likely to arise, such as how certain people became friends or enemies and whether their feelings toward one another are likely to change. Finally, workers may also struggle to explain why they work. Intrinsic and extrinsic motivators must be identified, assessed, weighted, and combined. These activities often require considerable discussion among group members (Salancik & Pfeffer, 1978).

Our own research has focused on a question asked by many members of work groups: Who is good at what? Workers are not clones—every member offers the group a unique set of abilities, skills, and knowledge that may be relevant to a variety of tasks. Although self-deception can occur, many workers seem to have an accurate sense of their own competence (Shrauger & Osberg, 1981). Evaluating the competence of other group members, however, can be difficult. Claims of personal competence by coworkers cannot always be trusted because they may reflect efforts at impression management (Gardner, 1992). Accepting coworkers' evaluations of one another's competence can be risky as well because these "secondhand" evaluations are often based on limited information (Gilovich, 1987) and may reflect more subtle impression management efforts by the people who provide them (Cialdini, 1989). The best approach for evaluating competence may be to observe how well each group member actually performs various tasks. But even this method has its drawbacks. For example, opportunities for displaying some kinds of abilities, skills, or knowledge may be rare, and even when they do occur, such opportunities may not be distributed equally among group members. Various biases, such as racism or sexism, may also distort evaluations of competence, causing some co-workers to seem better or worse than they really are (Ridgeway, 1991).

Given these and other problems regarding evaluations of competence, why should the members of a work group worry about who is good at what? We believe that such knowledge is valuable because it can improve the group's performance in several ways. First, when group members know who is good at what, they can plan their work more sensibly, assigning tasks to the people who will perform them best. As a result, the group can make optimal use of its human resources. Second, coordination among workers is likely to improve when they know who is good at what. Familiarity with one another's strengths and weaknesses helps workers to *anticipate* behavior rather than merely *react* to it. Even when tasks have not been assigned to particular people, workers can thus interact more smoothly and efficiently. Finally, unexpected problems can be solved more quickly and easily when workers know who is good at what (Moreland & Levine, 1992a). Such knowledge allows workers to match problems with the people most likely to solve them. Those people can then be asked for help, or the problems can simply be turned over to them.

If these claims seem unconvincing, then just imagine a work group whose members knew nothing about who was good at what. In such a group, sensible planning would be impossible. Tasks might be assigned to workers at random or, worse yet, on the basis of such irrelevant cues as appearance or demeanor. Or the group might fail to plan its work at all, simply allowing people to work on whatever tasks they liked best (cf. Hackman & Morris, 1975; Weingart, 1992). It would be lucky indeed if any of these options led to optimal use of the group's resources. Coordination would probably suffer as well, as confused workers struggle to make sense out of one another's behavior, and problems might become more troublesome, as unqualified workers try (or are asked) to solve them.

Do work groups really perform better when their members know who is good at what? The available evidence (e.g., Bottger, 1984; Libby, Trotman, & Zimmer, 1987; Littlepage & Silbiger, 1992; Stasser, Stewart, & Wittenbaum, 1995; Yetton & Bottger, 1982), drawn mostly from laboratory research on the recognition of expertise in decision-making groups, suggests that they do. Libby and his colleagues (Libby, Trotman, & Zimmer, 1987), for example, asked groups of bank loan officers to review the financial profiles of various companies and predict whether each company would go bankrupt. The subjects performed this task twice, first individually and then in groups. The companies were real (but disguised), so their actual outcomes were known, allowing the accuracy of all these predictions to be assessed. The ability of groups to recognize expertise was measured in two ways. First, each group was asked, after all the predictions were made, to identify its best member. The relative accuracy of that person's individual predictions, versus those of the other group members, was then evaluated to see how much better than his colleagues he really was. Second, the relationship between each person's relative accuracy and his influence on the group (how often he and the group made the same predictions) was evaluated to see how much better than his colleagues the most influential person was. Analyses of group performance showed that both diversity in group members' expertise and the ability of groups to recognize expertise were associated with more accurate group predictions.

Littlepage and Silbiger (1992) asked groups of college students to take trivia tests on such topics as geography, sports, and entertainment. After answering each test question, groups were asked to assign it a point value, indicating their confidence in the answer. It was thus possible to measure not only the actual expertise of a group (the number of questions answered correctly) but also its ability to recognize expertise. That ability was measured by first calculating the total number of points a group earned and then dividing that sum by the total number of points that could have been earned if the group had assigned the largest possible values to the questions that it answered correctly. Analyses of these data showed that the ability to recognize expertise was associated with better group performance, even when actual expertise was taken into account.

Finally, Stasser et al. (1995) provided groups of college students with clues to a hypothetical murder and then asked them to discover who (among several suspects) committed the crime. Within each group, some clues were distributed to everyone, whereas other clues were distributed in ways that provided every member with expertise on a different suspect. The latter clues were critical for solving the crime. Every group was informed that its members might receive different sets of clues. Information about exactly who knew what, however, varied from one group to another. In some groups, but not others, each member was privately informed about his or her own area of expertise. And in some groups, but not others, everyone's area of expertise was publicly announced. Simply informing group members about their own expertise had little impact on group performance, but announcing everyone's expertise helped group members to discuss more of the critical clues and thereby solve the crime.

TRANSACTIVE MEMORY SYSTEMS

A key factor in the performance of many work groups is the ability to remember information relevant to their tasks. Once again, knowing who is good at what, or more narrowly, who *knows* what, could be helpful. Although memory is usually viewed as a cognitive process that occurs within individual minds, some psychologists (e.g., Clark & Stephenson, 1989; Walsh & Ungson, 1991; Wegner, 1987) have become interested in the cognitive/social process of collective memory. One of the most intriguing analyses of such memory was offered by Wegner (1987). Wegner noted that few people rely exclusively on their own memories, which are limited and often faulty. Instead, most people supplement their own memories with external aids. These memory aids include both objects (e.g., address and appointment books, lists of uncompleted projects) and other people (e.g., friends, spouses, coworkers). Wegner was especially interested in the use of people as memory aids. He argued that in many groups, a *transactive memory system* develops for the purpose of ensuring that important information is not forgotten. Such a system combines the knowledge possessed by particular group members with a shared awareness of who knows what. So when group members need information, but either cannot recall it themselves or are uncertain about the accuracy of their own memories, they can turn to one another for help. A transactive memory system thus provides access to more and better information than any single group member could remember alone. Although research on transactive memory systems is scarce and limited to couples (see Wegner, 1987; Wegner, Erber, & Raymond, 1991; Wegner, Giuliano, & Hertel, 1985), the available evidence suggests that such systems may be both common and useful in groups.

Transactive memory systems should be very helpful for work groups, especially groups that perform complex tasks requiring considerable knowledge. When are such systems likely to develop? If transactive memory systems are viewed as cultural phenomena, then many of the factors associated with stronger group cultures may be important. These factors, which were mentioned earlier, include the age of a work group, the homogeneity and stability of its composition, the levels of process and outcome interdependence among workers, and the group's cohesion. Our research has focused on the role of *shared experience* (which incorporates several of these factors) in both the development and operation of transactive memory systems. As people work together on group tasks, they not only acquire more information about those tasks themselves, but also discover whatever relevant information other group members possess. When these two kinds of information are combined, a transactive memory system becomes available for use by the group.

If transactive memory systems are helpful to work groups, and shared experience is indeed important for the development of those systems, then a group's performance should improve as its members spend more time together working at similar or related tasks. This claim has two general implications for the management of work groups. First, managers should try to minimize changes in a group's composition (due to absenteeism, leaves, transfers, or turnover) because the arrival of newcomers and/or departure of oldtimers from the group can seriously disrupt its transactive memory system. Although no one has studied this phenomenon directly, several studies suggest that groups do learn to make better use of their members' knowledge over time (e.g., Larson, Foster-Fishman, & Keys, 1994; Watson, Kumar, & Michaelsen, 1993; Watson, Michaelson, & Sharp, 1991), especially if their composition remains stable.

Argote (1993), for example, reviewed research on group learning and found some evidence of "learning curves" similar to those displayed by individuals. Over time, a group's task performance improves, but at a decreasing rate (Leavitt, 1951; Perlmutter & De Montmollin, 1952). Argote argued that group learning may reflect learning by individual group members, changes in the group's structure or dynamics that improve productivity, or the adoption of useful methods developed by other groups to perform the same task. This analysis suggests that turnover should disrupt group learning because (a) newcomers generally know less than oldtimers about performing the group's task and (b) newcomers and oldtimers are often unfamiliar with one another's abilities and interests. A recent experiment by Argote, Insko, Yovetich, and Romero (1995), in which laboratory groups spent several consecutive work periods producing origami objects of varying complexity, showed that turnover indeed disrupts group learning and that its impact grows worse as time passes. Moreover, training newcomers in origami skills before they entered those groups did not weaken that impact. This finding suggests that turnover was harmful primarily because newcomers and oldtimers were unfamiliar with one another and thus had difficulty working together effectively. A similar experiment by Devadas and Argote (1995), in which much of the damage caused by turnover was averted by strengthening group structure (assigning specific roles to members and prescribing work procedures), suggests the same conclusion.

Research by Goodman and his colleagues (see Goodman & Shah, 1992) on how "familiarity" affects workers in coal-mining crews also seems relevant to this issue. In coal mines, familiarity might involve equipment, terrain, or personnel. Changes in any of these factors should decrease familiarity and thus be harmful. This is just what Goodman and his colleagues found after analyzing archival data from several mines. In one study (Goodman & Garber, 1988), familiarity was associated with fewer accidents among pairs of crew members who worked very closely together (e.g., roof bolters and bolter helpers). Although familiarity with terrain had somewhat more impact than personnel familiarity, the latter factor was clearly important, especially when groups worked in less familiar terrain. In a later study (Goodman & Leyden, 1991), familiarity was associated with higher levels of crew productivity, even after other labor, technology, and environment factors were taken into account. Once again, personnel familiarity had less impact than familiarity with terrain—perhaps crews adjust more easily to changes in personnel than to changes in terrain. However, changes in personnel were clearly harmful, and the fact that some of the effects of familiarity on productivity were mediated by labor (but not technology or environment) factors provided further evidence for the importance of such changes.

Our claim about the benefits of shared experience has another general implication for the management of work groups, namely that managers should train the members of such groups together rather than apart. Most organizations emphasize individual learning in their training programs. Participants in those programs work on their own, under the guidance of instructors, to learn how various tasks should be performed. The fact that they may later perform those tasks in groups is largely ignored. Some training programs do include group activities, of course, but these often focus on general topics such as leadership or cooperation (Oddou, 1987; Silberman, 1990; Tetrault, Schriesheim, & Neider, 1988) that are relevant to any group. Specific knowledge about the actual groups that workers will later form or join is seldom provided. In particular, few workers learn much about who knows what within those groups. As a result, transactive memory systems develop more slowly and operate less efficiently than they could if group members were trained together. Training the members of a work group together rather than apart would not only provide each person with the information needed to perform tasks well, but also help him or her to learn what everyone else in the group knows about those tasks.

Some organizations have recently begun to train work group members together rather than apart. General Motors, at its Saturn automobile manufacturing plant, has received considerable publicity in this regard, but other examples can also be found, such as the U.S. Army's unit personnel replacement system (Griffith, 1989) and efforts by several airlines to provide team training for cockpit crews (Oberle, 1990). Although enthusiastic claims have been made about these innovative training programs, convincing evidence regarding their benefits is scarce. Few researchers have actually compared the performance of work groups whose members were trained together versus apart (see Dyer, 1985, for a review), and the results of those studies are mixed. Some studies (e.g., George, 1967) have shown that group training is superior to individual training, whereas others (e.g., Briggs & Naylor, 1965) have shown that group training is inferior. Several studies (e.g., Laughlin & Sweeney, 1977) showed no difference at all between the two forms of training. These divergent findings are puzzling, and their interpretation is further clouded by methodological problems and a general lack of theory. Clearly, further research is needed to determine whether group or individual training yields better group performance.

We have embarked on a program of research designed to explore this issue. Our research involves laboratory experiments in which groups of subjects are trained to perform a complex task. Various types of training, focusing on either groups or individuals, are provided and their effects on group performance are compared. Several hypotheses are tested, but our two general predictions are that (a) group performance improves when group members are trained together rather than apart and (b) the benefits of group training are due to the development and operation of transactive memory systems.

OUR FIRST EXPERIMENT

Our first experiment (Liang, Moreland, & Argote, 1995) was performed at Carnegie Mellon University, where 90 students enrolled in undergraduate business courses served as subjects. These subjects were randomly assigned to small work groups, each containing three persons of the same sex. We chose a task that simulated the type of work found in many manufacturing organizations. Every group was asked to assemble the AM portion of an AM/FM radio using materials from kits. Each kit included a circuit board and dozens of mechanical and electronic components. The circuit board contained prepunched holes marked with special symbols indicating where different components should be placed. To assemble a radio, the subjects had to insert each component into the circuit board at the proper place and then wire all of the components together in the proper manner.

Two types of training were provided for this difficult task. Half of the groups were randomly assigned to a group training condition, whereas the other half were assigned to an individual training condition. The training *format* differed across these conditions. In the group training condition, members of the same group were trained together, whereas in the individual training condition, they were trained apart. The *content* of training, however, did not differ across conditions—the same trainer presented the same information to everyone in similar ways. If group performance on a task like this depends solely on the knowledge of individual group members, then training them together or apart should not matter. But if group performance depends partly on transactive memory, which allows group members to use one another's knowledge as well, then training them together should be advantageous, because it helps a transactive memory system to develop.

The experiment was carried out in two sessions, each lasting for about an hour. The first session focused on training, whereas the second session (which occurred about one week later) focused on testing. In the group training condition, the members of each group participated in both sessions together. But in the individual training condition, each person participated in his or her own training session, and group members did not meet or work together until the testing session.

When subjects arrived for the training session, they were told that our research examined how training affects work group performance. An overview of the experiment was then provided so that everyone knew what to expect. Every subject realized that at the next (testing) session, he or she would be working in a group whose performance would be evaluated. Subjects in the group training condition expected to remain in their current work group, but subjects in the individual training condition did not know who their coworkers might be. To provide an incentive for good performance, cash awards were offered for members of the best work groups.

The actual training began with a demonstration by the experimenter of how the radio's components should be inserted into the circuit board and wired together. Subjects were allowed to ask questions during this demonstration, which lasted for about 15 minutes. They were then given up to 30 minutes to assemble a single radio themselves, again asking questions if necessary. Finally, the experimenter examined the radio carefully, identified any errors that the subjects made, and explained how those errors could be corrected.

When groups arrived for the testing session, they were first given a memory test. Each group had 7 minutes to recall (without access to any materials or instructions) how a radio should be assembled. Group members collaborated at this task and recorded whatever they could remember together on a single sheet of paper. Each group was then given up to 30 minutes to actually assemble a radio, without consulting its recall sheet or receiving any help from the experimenter. The subjects were told to work as quickly as possible, but also to make as few errors as possible. Every group's activities were recorded on videotape. Finally, each subject completed a brief questionnaire that provided background information about that person and measured his or her beliefs about the group and its task.

We analyzed three measures of group performance, namely (a) how well each group recalled the procedure for assembling a radio, (b) how quickly each group assembled its radio, and (c) how many assembly errors that radio contained. Groups in the two training conditions assembled their radios at about the same speed. However, there were significant differences between conditions in both procedural recall and assembly errors. These differences are shown in Figure 3.2. As we expected, groups whose members were trained together rather than apart recalled more about how a radio should be assembled, and produced radios containing fewer assembly errors.

Videotapes of the groups allowed us to explore several factors that could have produced these effects. Two judges, one of whom was blind to the research hypotheses and to each group's condition, were given a list of specific behaviors exemplifying each factor. They were then asked to watch each videotape carefully, keeping those behaviors in mind, and make an overall rating of the group on each factor. Intraclass correlations, computed for each factor, indicated that these ratings were made reliably.

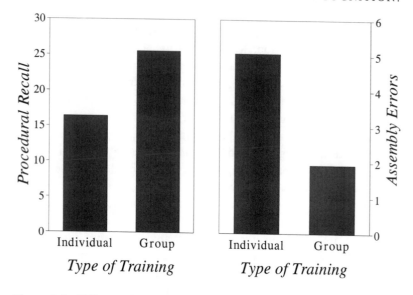

Figure 3.2. Effects of Group and Individual Training on Procedural Recall (Left) and Assembly Errors (Right) in the First Experiment

We were especially interested in three factors that may reflect the operation of transactive memory systems. The first factor was *memory differentiation,* or the tendency for group members to specialize in recalling different aspects of assembling the radio. One person, for example, might remember where certain components should be inserted into the circuit board, whereas another one remembered how those components should be wired together. The second factor was *task coordination,* or the ability of group members to work together smoothly while assembling the radio. In groups with stronger transactive memory systems, there should be less confusion, fewer misunderstandings, and greater cooperation. Finally, the third factor was *task credibility,* or how much group members trusted one another's knowledge about the radio. In groups with stronger transactive memory systems, there should be less need to claim expertise, better acceptance of any procedural suggestions, and less criticism of work by others. Scores on these three factors were highly correlated with one another, as might be expected if they measured the same underlying phenomenon. We thus created a composite index of transactive memory activity by averaging together each group's scores on these factors.

Three other factors were also coded from the videotapes. These factors seemed relevant to group performance, and might have varied across training conditions, but were not assumed to measure any single underlying phenomenon. The first factor was *task motivation,* or how eager group members were to win the prize by assembling their radio quickly and correctly. Group members whose motivation is stronger should express more enthusiasm for the task, encourage one another more often, and work harder. The second factor was *group cohesion,* or the level of interpersonal attraction among group members. Members of more cohesive groups should sit closer together, speak more warmly to one another, and so on. Finally, the third factor was *social identity,* or the tendency for subjects to think about themselves as group members rather than individuals. This was the only factor not evaluated through ratings. Instead, the judges counted how often personal pronouns (e.g., "I") and collective pronouns (e.g., "We") were used while the members of each group assembled their radio. The ratio of collective pronouns to all pronouns used was then computed and served as a measure of social identity (cf. Cialdini et al., 1976; Veroff, Sutherland, Chadiha, & Ortega, 1993).

We expected stronger transactive memory systems to develop in groups whose members were trained together rather than apart, and that is what we found. Scores on all three transactive memory factors (memory differentiation, task coordination, task credibility) and on the composite index of transactive memory were significantly higher in the group training condition. Only one of the other three factors differed significantly across training conditions. Whether group members were trained together or apart had little impact on task motivation or group cohesion scores, but higher social identity scores were earned by groups whose members were trained together.

Group training clearly produced better group performance and stronger transactive memory systems. Are those findings connected? We believed that the effects of group training on group performance were *mediated* by transactive memory systems. To explore that issue, a series of multiple regression analyses was performed (Baron & Kenny, 1986). The goal of those analyses, as shown in Figure 3.3, was to separate the direct and indirect (mediated) effects of training methods on group performance. If the direct effects (Path C) are weak while the indirect effects (Paths A and B) are strong, then that would provide evidence for mediation. Our measure of group performance for these analyses was assembly errors—training methods did not affect how quickly the groups assembled their radios, and the effects of training methods on procedural recall occurred before transactive memory was measured. We began by regressing assembly errors on training methods (coded as a dummy variable). The overall effects of training methods were significant and accounted for 42% of the variance. We then regressed transactive memory (using scores from the composite index) on training methods. The effects of training methods on transactive memory (Path A) were also significant and accounted for 70% of the variance. Finally, we regressed assembly errors on training methods and transactive memory simultaneously. The effects of transactive memory on assembly errors (Path B) were significant, but the effects of training methods (Path C) were not. Together, training methods and transactive memory accounted for 57% of the variance in assembly errors.

These results suggest that the impact of group training on group performance was indeed mediated by transactive memory systems, because when differences among groups in the strength of those systems were taken into account, training methods no longer mattered. Although we did not expect social identity to play a similar role, analogous regression analyses involving that factor were also performed. The results provided no evidence of mediation—when differences among groups in social identity were taken into account, the effects of training methods on group performance remained significant.

Our first experiment provided clear evidence that a work group's performance can be improved by training its members together rather than apart. As we expected, groups whose members were trained together recalled more about how to assemble their radios and made fewer errors while assembling those radios. We also expected and found stronger transactive memory systems in groups whose members

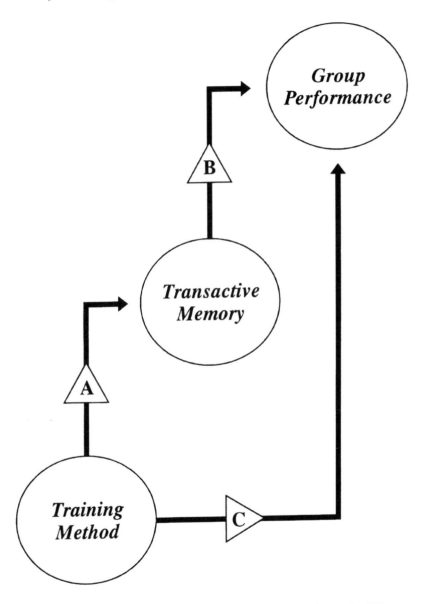

Figure 3.3. Testing Whether Transactive Memory Mediates the Effects of Training Methods on Group Performance

were trained together. The members of those groups, while working on their radios, were more likely to (a) recall different aspects of the procedure, (b) coordinate their activities, and (c) trust one another's expertise. These findings represent the first evidence that transactive memory systems can develop in work groups, as Wegner (1987) claimed. Finally, we found that transactive memory mediates the effects of group training on group performance. When differences in the strength of their transactive memory systems are taken into account, groups whose members were trained together perform no better than groups whose members were trained apart.

OUR SECOND EXPERIMENT

Although these initial results were encouraging, several important issues remained unresolved. A second experiment (Moreland & Wingert, 1995) was thus performed. The subjects for this experiment were 186 students enrolled in undergraduate psychology courses at the University of Pittsburgh. Many of the procedures for this experiment were identical to those described earlier. Once again, subjects were randomly assigned to small work groups, each containing three persons of the same sex. These groups were then randomly assigned to group or individual training conditions. The task and materials remained the same, and each group again participated in training and testing sessions, which lasted for about an hour each and were held one week apart. The training sessions for this experiment were changed slightly for groups in the individual training conditions. Rather than participating in separate training sessions, the members of these groups were trained in the same room at the same time but were not allowed to talk with one another or to observe one another while assembling the radios. This simplified the experiment and made the experiences of subjects in the group and individual training conditions more comparable. Another minor procedural change, which affected groups in every training condition, involved the testing sessions. At the beginning of those sessions, all of the subjects completed brief questionnaires (to be described later in more detail) that measured feelings and thoughts about their groups. The general format (including time limits) for both the training and testing sessions was otherwise unchanged. During the training sessions, group members again watched a demonstration of how to assemble a radio and then practiced assembling one themselves with guidance and feedback from the experimenter. During the testing sessions, groups again recalled how to assemble a radio and then assembled one entirely on their own, working as quickly and accurately as possible. All of the groups were again videotaped while they worked.

One simple, but important, goal for this experiment was to replicate our initial results. The same individual and group training conditions were thus re-created so that their effects on group performance could be reexamined. Our first experiment showed that group training led to better performance and that this advantage was due to the development of transactive memory systems. Similar results were expected from our second experiment.

A second goal for this experiment was to evaluate alternative explanations for the improvement in group performance associated with group training. For example, group training allows group development to occur. Newly formed groups suffer from many problems (e.g., anxiety about acceptance, interpersonal conflicts, uncertainty about norms) that can impair their performance (LaCoursiere, 1980; Tuckman, 1965). Training the members of a work group together provides them with extra time and opportunities to solve such problems. Perhaps the performance advantages of group training are due more to group development than to transactive memory. Several results from the first experiment challenged this conclusion—neither group cohesion nor social identity (both potential indexes of group development) mediated the effects of group training on group performance, and although questionnaire responses revealed that the members of a few groups were acquainted before the experiment began, those groups (which were probably more developed) did not perform especially well. Nevertheless, the role of group development in group training seemed to deserve a closer examination.

Strategic learning is another alternative explanation for improved performance by work groups whose members were trained together rather than apart. Working together creates coordination problems, some of which can be solved through simple, generic strategies that do not require much information about who knows what. These strategies include building commitment to the group and its task, organizing task activities, and maintaining harmony among group members. Perhaps the performance advantages of group training are due more to the acquisition of these strategies than to transactive memory. What people may learn during such training is how to perform the task well in any group, rather than in a specific group. None of the results from the first experiment really challenged this conclusion, so the role of strategic learning in group training clearly deserved a closer examination as well.

To evaluate the contributions of group development and strategic learning to the performance advantages of group training, we added two new conditions to our second experiment. One new condition was identical to the individual training condition, except for the addition of a brief team-building exercise that was designed to encourage group development. This exercise, adapted from McGrath (1993), occurred at the end of the training session after subjects finished working on their radios. Group members were seated at a round table and given 10 minutes to develop a quiz that could be used by the university to evaluate juniors and seniors who wanted to become "mentors" for freshmen during fall orientation sessions. Six multiple-choice questions were required, two on each of three topic areas (history and traditions, rules and regulations, locations of buildings and services). Three alternative answers were required for each question, with the correct answer marked on the quiz. The other new condition was identical to the group training condition, except that all of the groups were scrambled between their training and testing sessions. That is, the subjects were reassigned to new groups in ways that separated people who were trained together. When each of these groups began its testing session, its members were thus strangers to one another. The subjects were not told that this scrambling would occur until the end of their training sessions.

The team-building condition was meant to encourage group development, without providing subjects the information (who knows what?) needed to produce a transactive memory system. The reassignment condition was meant to disable existing transactive memory systems by making them irrelevant, leaving strategic learning as the primary benefit of group training. Insofar as group development and strategic learning each contribute to the performance advantages of group training, performance by groups in these two new conditions should be good. But what if transactive memory systems mediate the effects of group training on group performance, as the results from our first experiment indicated? Groups in the team-building condition lack transactive memory systems, whereas groups in the reassignment condition have transactive memory systems that are no longer useful. As a result, the performance of the groups in these two new conditions should be poor.

A final goal for this experiment was to explore the impact of turnover on transactive memory systems. One benefit of such systems is that no one needs to know everything—each person can rely on the knowledge of others to some extent, so long as everyone agrees about who knows what. But what if someone leaves the group, taking away some valuable knowledge that no one else possesses? Other members of the group may feel regret, because they could have acquired that knowledge themselves, but chose not to do so, and frustration, because they know where that knowledge resides, but no longer have access to it. And, of course, the group's performance may suffer on any tasks requiring that knowledge. In our experiment, these problems could arise among groups in the reassignment condition. Those groups experienced sudden and dramatic turnover after their training sessions. When the members of those groups later began their testing sessions, working with strangers whose knowledge about assembling radios was largely unknown, some of them probably wished they had learned more about the task, wanted to recontact old coworkers and ask task-related questions, or wondered whether such questions could be answered by their new coworkers. How harmful is all this for group performance? We hoped that groups in the reassignment condition might help to answer that question.

Our first data analyses focused on the brief questionnaire that subjects completed at the beginning of their testing sessions. The purpose of that questionnaire was to evaluate how the various training conditions affected subjects' feelings and thoughts about their groups. The questionnaire contained 10 questions that subjects answered by making ratings on 7-point scales. Some of the questions (e.g., "Does this work group seem more like one group or three separate individuals?") assessed feelings related to group development, whereas others (e.g., "How much do you think the other members of this work group know about your skills at assembling the radio?") assessed thoughts related to transactive memory. Scores within each set of questions were highly correlated, so they were averaged together, first within and then across subjects, to create two composite indexes for each group. Scores on the group development index were significantly higher in the group training and team-building conditions than in the individual training or reassignment conditions. And scores on the transactive memory index were significantly higher in the group training condition than in the individual training, team-building, or reassignment conditions. The two new conditions thus seemed to affect groups as we hoped they would: The team-building condition encouraged group development, without producing transactive memory systems, while the reassignment condition disabled such systems by making them irrelevant.

Our next set of analyses focused on group performance, measured in the same three ways described earlier. As in the first experiment, we found that groups trained in different ways assembled their radios at about the same speed. There were, however, significant differences among conditions in both procedural recall and assembly errors. These differences are shown in Figures 3.4 and 3.5. As we expected, group training led to better performance outcomes than did any of the other training methods, which did not differ from one another.

Videotapes of the groups were again viewed by two judges, one of whom was blind to the research hypotheses and to each group's condition. As before, these judges were given a list of specific behaviors exemplifying various factors. Three of those factors (memory differentiation, task coordination, and task credibility) reflected the operation of transactive memory systems, whereas the others (task motivation, group cohesion, and social identity) did not. The judges watched each

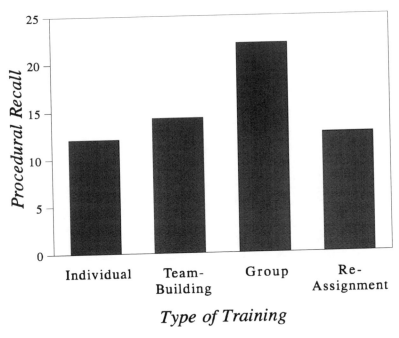

Figure 3.4. Effects of Various Training Methods on Procedural Recall in the Second Experiment

videotape and made an overall rating of the group on each factor. Once again, intraclass correlations indicated that these ratings were made reliably. Scores on the transactive memory factors were highly correlated, so we again created a composite index by averaging each group's scores on those factors. As we expected, scores on that transactive memory index were significantly higher in the group training condition than they were in the other three conditions, which did not differ from one another. Among the remaining factors, only social identity differed significantly across conditions. Social identity scores were higher in the group training and team-building conditions than in the individual training or reassignment conditions.

Were the effects of training methods on group performance mediated by transactive memory systems? Once again, we explored that issue using multiple regression analyses, following the logic of

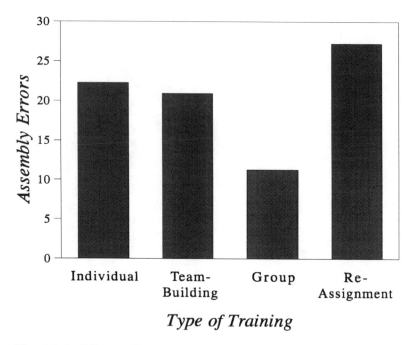

Figure 3.5. Effects of Various Training Methods on Assembly Errors in the Second Experiment

Figure 3.3. Assembly errors served again as our measure of group performance for these analyses, but the four training conditions were now coded as three dummy variables, using a scheme (Cohen & Cohen, 1983) that contrasted the group training condition with the other three conditions. We began, as before, by regressing assembly errors on training methods. The effects of training methods were significant and accounted for 27% of the variance. We then regressed transactive memory on training methods. The effects of training methods were also significant and accounted for 37% of the variance. Finally, we regressed assembly errors on training methods and transactive memory simultaneously. The effects of transactive memory on assembly errors were significant, but the effects of training methods were not. Together, training methods and transactive memory accounted for 47% of the variance in assembly errors.

Social identity could have mediated some of the effects of training methods on group performance, but an analogous set of regression analyses involving that factor revealed no evidence of such mediation. When differences among groups in social identity were taken into account, group training still produced significantly better performance outcomes than any other form of training.

As we noted earlier, this experiment was designed with several goals in mind. One goal, to replicate the results from our first experiment, was clearly achieved. Once again, group training produced better performance than did individual training, and this advantage was due to the development of transactive memory systems. We also wanted to evaluate the contributions of group development and strategic learning to the performance advantages of group training. Those contributions appeared to be minimal, although further research is needed before any final conclusions are drawn. During the training sessions, groups in one condition participated in a team-building exercise that encouraged their development, whereas groups in another condition learned generic strategies for coping with coordination problems. However, few of the groups in either condition had strong transactive memory systems. Groups in the team-building condition lacked the information required for such systems, and groups in the reassignment condition had their systems disabled through membership changes. Without stronger transactive memory systems, neither group development nor strategic learning was sufficient to improve group performance. Groups in both the new conditions performed worse than those in the group training condition and no better than those in the individual training condition. Their poor performance can be attributed to weak transactive memory systems, because training methods no longer affected group performance when differences in the strength of those systems were taken into account. Finally, this experiment also provided a glimpse of how turnover can influence the operation of transactive memory systems. Groups in the reassignment condition experienced sudden and dramatic turnover, which probably created confusion and dismay among their members and thereby harmed their performance. Yet the damage was less serious than it might have been. Although these groups performed poorly, their performance was no worse than that of groups in the individual training or team-building conditions. Perhaps if work groups were forewarned about turnover (so they could prepare for it), or if fewer group members were lost all at once, then serious disruptions in the operation of transactive memory systems could be avoided. Further research, again, is needed on this issue.

WHAT NOW?

We are currently working on a third experiment, whose primary goal is to prove that group training really does help workers to learn who knows what. In the experiments just described, such knowledge was never measured directly. Videotape measures of several behaviors that reflect the operation of transactive memory systems were examined, but the systems themselves were not assessed. Our third experiment, like the others, involves small groups of college students who are first trained to assemble radios and then tested to see how well they can perform that task. The effects of group and individual training are compared, much as they were in the earlier experiments. However, there is one critical difference: The subjects expect to work in groups during their testing sessions, and groups are in fact scheduled for those sessions, but all of the testing is actually done at the individual rather than the group level. When they arrive for their testing session, the members of each group are first asked to complete questionnaires that measure (in various ways) their beliefs about each person's abilities, skills, and knowledge. Then, working alone, each subject is asked to recall the procedure for assembling a radio and to actually assemble a radio as quickly and accurately as possible. This procedure allows us to assess the actual abilities, skills, and knowledge of every group member, which can then be compared with the subjects' beliefs about such matters, as revealed by the questionnaires. Our general prediction is that more accurate beliefs will be found in groups whose members are trained together rather than apart. The experiment will also allow us to explore other issues, such as whether group training encourages social loafing or free riding (Karau &

Williams, 1993; Shepperd, 1993). Group training makes it unnecessary for everyone to learn everything about a task; people can specialize in ways that reflect their talents. But group training also allows some people to learn nothing about a task, if they believe that the group can succeed without them. Although group performance is better when workers are trained together, individual performance may thus be worse.

There are, naturally, many other issues that we plan to explore as our program of research progresses. One set of issues involves the kinds of work experiences that help transactive memory systems to develop. Task experiences are presumably more valuable than social experiences, but even the latter may be helpful if accurate information about relative competence (across workers and tasks) is conveyed. Task experiences may not be necessary at all, if (for example) the manager of a newly formed work group provides its members with information about their abilities, skills, and knowledge, or the workers are led to provide such information themselves. And what happens to work groups whose tasks change—to what extent are transactive memory systems generalizable? Another set of issues involves factors that might moderate the effects of group training on work group performance. Such factors include characteristics of the group, its task, and the work setting (see Liang et al., 1995). For example, training the members of a work group together rather than apart may be especially helpful when (a) the group's composition is heterogeneous, (b) its task requires coordinated effort, or (c) the work setting is stressful. In all of these situations, a transactive memory system is likely to improve group performance, which otherwise might be poor. A final set of issues involves the potential risks of group training. These risks, some of which we have already noted, include social loafing/free riding, the development of group norms that inhibit productivity, and susceptibility to the harmful effects of turnover. Whether the risks of group training ever outweigh its benefits, and how those risks can be minimized or avoided altogether, are questions that we hope to answer.

Our research program focuses on who knows what within work groups, but other cultural features of such groups seem interesting and important as well. Workers seek collective answers to many questions about themselves, their groups, and the work that they perform (see Figure 3.1). As time passes and shared experiences accumulate, these questions are gradually answered. The resulting knowledge is incorporated into the group's culture and expressed through a variety of customs. Social scientists from several disciplines are now exploring work group cultures, often with intriguing results. Rentsch (1990), for example, has found that different work groups within an organization may interpret the same events in quite different ways. As a result, the impact of a particular event, such as reengineering the organization, can vary considerably from one work group to another. And the role that shared interpretations of events may play in coordinating activities within work groups has been analyzed by Weick and Roberts (1993), who argued that dangerous mistakes can be made when workers ignore or disagree about their task interdependence. Clearly, there is a growing interest in studying work group cultures, not only because of the potential practical value of such research, but also because of the theoretical insights that it may provide.

One of those insights is that cognition can indeed be a group, as well as an individual activity. People often collaborate in the processing of information about matters that concern them. What's surprising is not that such collaboration occurs, but that so few social psychologists (who claim social influence as their domain) acknowledge or investigate it. Social psychology is, ironically, a science that emphasizes individual behavior. Several observers (e.g., Forgas, 1983b; Pepitone, 1981; Steiner, 1986) have commented on this troubling issue, and their comments, which are both thoughtful and emotional, include a variety of predictions about the future. No one can be sure what the future holds, but as we noted earlier, there does seem to be a resurgence of interest among social psychologists in studying small groups, and some of that research involves socially shared cognition. Our own research, along with much of the other research described in this book, shows that group members can process information together, that some of their activities in this regard can be studied scientifically, and that evidence about such activities can clarify important aspects of group life.

Part

II

Impact of the Group on Thinking About
the Self and Other Group Members

4

Social Behavior and Social Cognition
A Parallel Process Approach

The study of interaction behavior has long been an important topic in social psychological research. In the past 30 years, the systematic study of the nonverbal components of interaction has facilitated an understanding of some of the subtleties of social behavior. During the same period, another important topic in social psychological research—social cognition—has helped to fuel the broader cognitive revolution in psychology. Although social cognition is clearly relevant for understanding interaction behavior, research in the two areas has developed relatively independently. In fact, Fiske and Taylor (1991) noted that, although much of the research in person perception assumes an important link between interaction and social cognition, advances in this area have been quite modest.

AUTHOR'S NOTE: Requests for reprints should be addressed to the author at the Department of Psychology, University of Missouri-St. Louis, 8001 Natural Bridge Rd., St. Louis, MO 63121.

The purpose of this chapter is to describe a perspective on the social behavior-social cognition linkage and show its relevance for the study of interaction in small groups. On the behavioral side, the specific focus will be on nonverbal exchange, that is, the give-and-take in patterns of nonverbal behavior. On the social cognition side, the focus will be on person perception processes. In laying the groundwork for this integrative perspective, I will first provide a broad overview of theory on both nonverbal exchange and person perception. Next, I will outline a theoretical framework for linking behavioral and cognitive processes into a common dynamic system. Finally, a paradigm for studying the behavior-social cognition linkage will be briefly discussed.

THEORIES OF NONVERBAL EXCHANGE

A number of different theories have evolved to explain patterns of nonverbal interaction in groups. Although the vast majority of the empirical research and the theories themselves focus on dyads, the underlying dynamics may be extended to larger groups. In general, theories have focused on compensatory and reciprocal patterns of nonverbal involvement among interactants.

Compensatory adjustments refer to a kind of homeostatic change in response to a partner's initial behavior. For example, if a member of a group approaches his two partners at a very close distance, the targets of this approach might turn away from and avoid gazing toward the intruder. Presumably, such adjustments serve to "compensate" for the close approach and make the recipients of the intrusion more comfortable. Reciprocal adjustments refer to matching or reciprocating the initial behavior. For example, the close approach just described might, under some circumstances such as celebrating good fortune, lead to smiling at and touching the approaching individual. Thus, the overall level of nonverbal involvement is reciprocated or increased by the partners.[1]

Communalities and Differences Among Theories

Although the early theories (e.g., Argyle & Dean, 1965; Burgoon, 1978; Cappella & Greene, 1982; Patterson, 1976) proposed different mediating mechanisms to explain compensation and reciprocation patterns in interaction, they all share two important communalities. First, the models are all reactive in nature; that is, they seek to explain the nonverbal adjustments of one person given initial changes in a partner's behavior. Consequently, these theories do not address the origin of specific exchanges in interaction but only reactions to prior patterns of behavior. Furthermore, such reactive mechanisms overlook the role of scripted sequences in interactions, such as those involved in greetings and departures. In such instances, individuals are probably guided as much by their knowledge of the script sequence as they are by "reacting" to the immediately preceding behavior of the partner.

Second, all of the models are affect driven. That is, the proximate determinant of an individual's behavioral adjustment is the valence of the affect resulting from the partner's behavior. A common prediction in all of the models is that positive affect precipitates reciprocation and negative affect compensation. For example, if the recipient of a close approach, touch, and gaze feels increased attraction toward the partner, reciprocation is predicted. This might be manifested by increased gaze and smiling. Conversely, if the same pattern produces anxiety or discomfort, compensation is predicted. In such a case, compensation might be manifested by decreased gaze and turning away from the partner.

A simple affect-driven mediating process cannot, however, account for those instances in which affect is inconsistent with overt behavior. For example, "acting friendly" (close approach, high level of gaze, and smiling) toward a disliked superior is a strategic pattern that does not reflect underlying affect. Similarly, acting disinterested in someone you really like is also a strategic pattern that does not reflect underlying affect. In an attempt to address the limitations of existing theories, I proposed a functional model of nonverbal exchange (Patterson, 1982, 1983). Particularly important in the functional model was the distinction between relatively spontaneous affect-driven behavior and more managed or deliberate behavior. Spontaneous patterns might be mediated by affect, but managed patterns would not. Specifically, such managed patterns would be goal oriented or strategic, and consequentiy, behavior patterns might be independent of affect.

Although the functional model incorporates the reactive, affect-based adjustments characteristic of earlier models, it also recognizes the importance of more deliberate, strategic patterns of nonverbal behavior. Furthermore, cognitive processes play a broader role in the functional model in affecting scripted behavior, expectancies, and the naive perception of the function of the interaction. In addition, instead of focusing only on the directional adjustments (e.g., compensation or reciprocation) characteristic of the other models, the functional approach focuses on the stability of sequences in the course of interaction. Unexpected or extreme behavior triggers instability, arousal change, and a need to make sense of the situation. Finally, in contrast to the predictions of the affect-based models, compensation and reciprocation patterns may be either affect driven (i.e., relatively spontaneous) or strategic in nature (i.e., relatively deliberate and managed).

Limitations of Nonverbal Exchange Theories

It is clear from this brief overview that cognitions play an important role in understanding nonverbal exchange. Whether they take the form of expectancies, emotional labeling, scripts, or attributions about the partner and interaction, cognitions are critical mediators in explaining nonverbal adjustments in interaction. Nevertheless, because social cognitions are enlisted as mediators in these theories, their role is a limited, episodic one. That is, in these theories, social cognitions merit attention only to the extent that they can offer an "explanation" for subsequent social behavior.

Of course, social cognitions take the form of more than just episodic reactions to a partner's behavior. An individual's own behavior may be the stimulus for social cognitions that focus on the direct perception of self (Bem, 1972) and on metaperspective judgments, that is, judging the partner's perception of self (Kenny & DePaulo,

1993). In any case, the relationship between a person's social cognitions and social behavior is a dynamic one, affected by available cognitive resources and the relative automaticity of the cognitive and behavioral processes. This kind of complexity has been ignored in the various models of nonverbal exchange. In the next section, the complementary side of social interaction (i.e., person perception) will be examined. In turn, this will provide the foundation for an integrative perspective on social behavior and social cognition.

AN OVERVIEW OF PERSON PERCEPTION THEORIES

It is not my intention, nor is it possible, to review an extensive field like person perception in this paper. Instead, in this section, I will briefly examine different theoretical approaches to person perception in laying the groundwork for an integration of the behavioral and cognitive aspects of interaction. Three relatively distinct approaches are identified, including (a) information-processing models, (b) behavior-focused attribution models, and (c) the ecological model.

Information-Processing Models

Many of the existing theories describe the manner in which information is processed once the input is available to the perceiver (e.g., Anderson, 1981; Brewer, 1988; Fiske & Neuberg, 1990; Smith & Zárate, 1992; Wyer & Srull, 1986). Most information-processing models employ both category-based and integration mechanisms in explaining the development of judgments about a target. Categorization occurs when physical characteristics of a target cue useful social categories (e.g., gender, race, age, or occupation). In contrast, the integration mechanism starts with the identification of specific attributes and then combines them, leading to an overall judgment. The categorization process is typically primary, and integration occurs only when categorization does not yield a satisfactory solution or when there is sufficient incentive to invest additional effort in validating initial judgments.

Behavior-Based Trait Attribution

In contrast to the emphasis on static characteristics in the information-processing approach, the specific aim of these attribution models is to describe how inferences are made about a target's behavior. Trope (1986) proposed a two-stage model of dispositional inference that included behavior identification in the first stage, followed by a higher order process of inferring traits or dispositions. Gilbert and his colleagues (Gilbert, Pelham, & Krull, 1988) modified Trope's model with the addition of a third stage that permitted the correction of dispositional inferences with situational information.

Initial inferences do not, however, always take the form of dispositional attributions. Krull (1993) suggested that, as the perceiver's inferential goals emphasize the importance of external determinants of behavior, the initial stage of inference may change from dispositional to situational. Furthermore, many non-Western (collectivistic) cultures may be more likely to make situational attributions for behavior than are Western (individualistic) cultures (Smith & Bond, 1994, pp. 104-106).

As one moves through the multiple stages of inference, the processes become less automatic and require greater cognitive effort. Consequently, when cognitive resources are limited, correction for an inappropriate initial inference, whether dispositional or situational in nature, becomes more difficult.

Although the information-processing and trait attribution approaches differ in the kind of judgments they seek to explain, they do share an important communality. That is, both approaches assume that person perception is primarily a product of social inference, in contrast to the third approach.

Ecological Model

McArthur and Baron's (1983) ecological perspective is a conceptual extension of Gibson's (1979) ecological theory of object perception to the area of person perception. This model assumes that the important information in social perception does *not* involve trait inferences regarding the characteristics or behavior of target individuals but, rather, involves how the perceiver might relate to the target. Furthermore, this approach assumes that much of the important information about individuals is readily available in their appearance characteristics and movement patterns. Thus, person perception is usually direct and not the product of social inference (Berry, 1990).

An example of an important physical characteristic that apparently triggers such direct perceptions is facial babyishness (large eyes, small chin, and a disproportionately large forehead). A baby-faced appearance typically leads to judgments that the target is approachable and nonthreatening (Berry & McArthur, 1985). The ecological model assumes that the origin of such judgments lies in their adaptive value in relating to infants who are dependent on the nurturance of others. In general, McArthur and Baron (1983) assume that perceivers are more concerned about what the target person can do for (or to) them than they are about making abstract inferences about the target's traits.

Limitations of Person Perception Theories

In contrast to the theories of nonverbal exchange, the emphasis in person perception theories is clearly on the perceiver's social cognition processes and not on the perceiver's behavioral processes. Furthermore, the empirical research on person perception has been criticized for focusing too much on the passive perceiver, that is, a thinker and processor of information but not really an interactant (Funder, 1987; Swann, 1984). There are signs in recent years, however, of a renewed appreciation of the pragmatic link of social cognition to interactive behavior (Fiske, 1992). An example is the Gilbert et al. (1988) trait attribution model that addresses the effects of cognitive demand (including that associated with behavior management) on person perception.

The three approaches described here engage relatively distinct processes in explaining person perception. In addressing the comparable variety in theories of object perception, Neisser (1992) suggested that both Gibson's ecological theory and more conventional theories of matching inputs to representations are all correct, but they are correct about different perceptual systems. Similarly, the theoretical approaches discussed here might be viewed as complementary, rather than competing, explanations for social perception. Thus, a more comprehensive understanding of person perception may well include the conditional activation of these distinct processes. In the next section, the relationship between the behavioral and cognitive processes in interaction will be examined.

SOCIAL BEHAVIOR AND SOCIAL COGNITION

Although the theoretical explanations of the behavioral and person perception processes in interaction have developed relatively independently, the two processes are clearly related. That is, interactants are simultaneously initiating their own behavior and forming impressions about their partners, and consequently, these two processes affect one another. In addition, because the cognitive resources needed for individuals' judgments of others and for the management and monitoring of their own behavior come from a common, finite pool, applying resources to one process necessarily limits the resources available for the other process. In the next section, the interdependence of the behavioral and person perception sides of interaction will be elaborated in a parallel process framework.

Overview of the Parallel Process Approach

In this approach, the parallel person perception and behavioral processes are shaped by the coordinated influence of the determinants, the social environment, and the cognitive-affective mediators. Figure 4.1 provides an illustration of the linkages among variables across the related stages of this model (see Patterson, 1995, for a more developed description). First, determinant factors in the form of biology, culture, gender, and personality are primary influences in the choice of social environments and in shaping habitual patterns of social behavior (e.g., Fridlund, 1994; E. T. Hall, 1966; J. A. Hall, 1984) and social cognition (see Zebrowitz, 1990). Next, self- and setting-

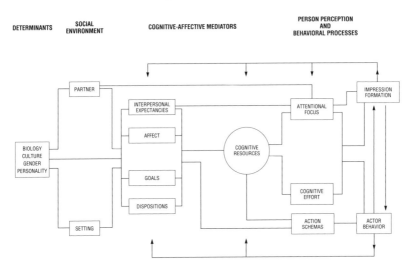

Figure 4.1. A Diagram of the Parallel Process Framework for Social Behavior and Social Cognition

selection processes constrain the context for interaction and promote increased homogeneity among group members (Barker, 1968; Wicker, 1979). Within a specific social environment, the cognitive-affective mediators (expectancies, goals, affect, dispositions, and cognitive resources) influence (a) the initiation of action schemas and (b) the application of attention resources and cognitive effort in the behavioral and person perception tracks. Thus, individuals are initiating the behavioral expression of feelings, intentions, scripts, or other reactions while at the same time making judgments from the appearance characteristics and behavior of their partners.

It should be emphasized that both the behavioral and person perception processes vary from being spontaneous and automatic to deliberate and managed. For example, behavior that is "mindless" (Langer, 1989) or guided by scripts is initiated relatively automatically, with little or no investment of cognitive resources. In contrast, some strategic behavior requires a considerable investment of cognitive resources for the monitoring and control of behavior (Patterson, 1994). On the person perception side, Bargh (1989) has suggested that there are different levels or varieties of automaticity, depending on the intention, awareness, efficiency, and control involved in attending to and processing social information.

Because the available cognitive resources serve simultaneous behavioral and person perception processes, the effectiveness of both processes may depend on the distribution of those resources. Nevertheless, more resources are not always better. Behavioral and person perception processes that operate well in a relatively automatic fashion are not likely to be more effective if greater thought is given to them. This relationship between the cognitive demands of simultaneous behavioral and person perception tracks is at the heart of the parallel process approach. Next, the dynamic relationship between the behavioral and person perception processes will be discussed, starting with the cognitive-affective mediators.

Dynamics of the Parallel Processes

Consistent with earlier discussions of the behavioral (Patterson, 1991) and the social cognition sides (Fiske, 1992) of interaction, it is assumed that these parallel processes are adaptive in nature. That is, they operate in a coordinated fashion in the service of different functions. The proximate determinants of the parallel processes are discussed next.

Cognitive-Affective Mediators. The cognitive and affective mediators develop from the combined influence of actor and partner characteristics as constrained by the setting. Included among the cognitive and affective mediators are dispositions, goals, affect, interpersonal expectancies, and cognitive resources. Each of these mediators can also affect the activation of the other mediators. First, dispositions refer to the states of an actor precipitated in a specific social environment, that is, in interacting with a particular partner in a specific situation. The more obvious dispositions are related to personality.

Second, the importance of goals is consistent with the adaptive, functional perspective of this model. Earlier discussions of the functions of nonverbal behavior have emphasized the behavioral expression of different functions (Patterson, 1982, 1983), but the comple-mentary person perception processes are also critical for achieving specific goals in interaction. Specific goals affect not only the general distribution of cognitive resources but also the type of information noticed and the depth of processing information about a partner (Neuberg & Fiske, 1987). For example, when a person is particularly concerned about making a good impression in a difficult situation, attention and effort are required not only for behavior management but also for evaluating the effectiveness of the impression manage-ment. In such a case, an individual will have more focused, practical concerns in judging a partner and not be so interested in making global trait attributions (Swann, 1984).

Third, *affect* in interactions is influenced by the individual's momentary dispositions and goals, relationship to the partner, setting constraints, and the partner's behavior. Although patterns of nonver-bal behavior can be independent of affect, the theories of nonverbal exchange reviewed earlier posit a central role for affect in mediating relatively reactive patterns of nonverbal exchange (e.g., Argyle & Dean, 1965; Burgoon, 1978; Cappella & Greene, 1982; Patterson, 1976). In a similar manner, affect is important in forming judgments of others (e.g., Fiske & Taylor, 1991, chap. 10; Higgins & Sorrentino, 1990; Isen, 1984).

Next, the effects of *interpersonal expectancies* are especially salient in the interdependence of behavioral and person perception processes. An actor's expectancies about a target often precede and even determine, indirectly, the very behavior that the actor later judges. Although such self-fulfilling prophecies (Rosenthal, 1974; Snyder & Swann, 1978) often have important effects on both person perception and behavioral processes, Jussim (1991) suggests that some effects that look like self-fulfilling prophecies are really accu-rate perceptions of social reality. That is, when subtle appearance or behavioral cues reflect underlying dispositions, the perception of such cues represents accuracy in judgment, not a self-fulfilling prophecy.

Finally, *cognitive resources* refer to the total cognitive capacity available for attending to, processing, and managing encoding and person perception operations in social situations. Although increased motivation can temporarily increase cognitive resources, over time a cost is likely to be exacted (Humphrey & Revelle, 1984). Even when resources are concentrated on the immediate social situation, they can be variously distributed toward the self, the partner, the setting, or the topic of conversation. Nevertheless, it is *not* the case that directing more resources toward a particular process necessarily improves the behavioral or person perception outcome. In the following section, the specific effects of the cognitive-affective mediators on the development of these parallel processes are discussed.

Behavioral and Person Perception Processes. The effects of the social environment and the cognitive-affective mediators on the parallel tracks may be seen in the investment of *attention* and *cognitive effort* in the behavioral and person perception processes (see the right side of Figure 4.1). Furthermore, to the extent that *action schemas* structure behavioral options, then fewer cognitive resources are needed for behavior management. On the person perception side, automatic judgments produced by appearance, nonverbal, and vocal cues require a minimum of cognitive resources (Gilbert et al., 1988; McArthur & Baron, 1983). In contrast, the processing of verbal input and adjusting initial inferences usually require a larger investment of cognitive resources.

Social behavior and social cognition may be viewed as adaptive, complementary processes in relating to others. For example, if an individual is particularly concerned about making a good impression on the boss, more resources will be invested in monitoring and managing behavior than in a casual interaction with an acquaintance. Furthermore, the focus of person perception track will probably be on reading the boss's reaction to the individual's behavior (i.e., metaperspective judgment) rather than on simply trying to make dispositional inferences about the boss (i.e., a direct perspective judgment). In such a case, metaperspective judgments constitute the means to evaluate the efficacy of the impression management attempt.

Although the behavioral and person perception processes draw on common cognitive resources, the effects of limited resources are selective and not necessarily negative. In fact, it is likely that increased attention to automatic or scripted behavioral sequences reduces their effectiveness (Vallacher & Wegner, 1987). Similarly, as Gilbert and Krull (1988) report, the application of cognitive resources to otherwise effective automatic judgments can reduce accuracy (see also Wilson & Schooler, 1991).

An Example in Small Group Interaction. The dynamic relationship between behavioral and person perception processes might be seen in the following example. Suppose that Tom, a socially anxious person (dispositional characteristic), is meeting with a group of coworkers that he wants to impress (goal). Tom expects that his coworkers will be critical, and consequently, he is pessimistic about his chances of conveying a favorable impression (negative expectancy and affect). Because of his anxiety, his goal, and his negative affect, Tom's behavioral management concerns will engage most of his attention and cognitive effort. Furthermore, Tom is not likely to have effective action schemas to employ in impression management.

The overall picture is one of excessive self-focus and monitoring in the service of behavior management. As a result, Tom has fewer resources that might be applied to the person perception side of the interaction (and to a skillful presentation of the content side of his case). Thus, impressions that require greater cognitive processing (i.e., social inference processes) will suffer more, whereas the more automatic impressions (i.e., automatic judgments) will be relatively unaffected. In particular, appearance cues, vocal behavior, and non-verbal behavior are likely to be processed in a more automatic and efficient manner than is the verbal behavior of the partner (Gilbert & Krull, 1988; McArthur & Baron, 1983).

In contrast, a less anxious, self-confident individual with an effective impression management schema will require fewer cognitive resources for behavior management. In turn, such a person will have an advantage in forming impressions of his partners, particularly if the partners' verbal behavior is most relevant. Furthermore, a less anxious person is likely to gaze more at interaction partners (Daly, 1978) and approach them at closer distances (Patterson, 1977). Greater nonverbal involvement with partners, particularly increased gaze, facilitates the gathering of information about partners and forming more accurate impressions (Ickes, Stinson, Bissonnette, & Garcia, 1990).

Finally, it should be noted that impression formation and behavior outcomes also feed back to influence the antecedents and the cognitive mediators (see the right half of Figure 4.1). In the next section, an example of the impression formation-behavior management interdependence will be described in the context of a paradigm for studying these related aspects of interaction.

A PARADIGM FOR THE STUDY OF BEHAVIOR AND PERSON PERCEPTION IN INTERACTION

Initial Study

The paradigm described here is derived from a published study of the effect of impression management difficulty on accuracy in judging a partner's reactions in an interaction (Patterson, Churchill, Farag, & Borden, 1991/1992). Prior to the interaction, one subject was randomly chosen to receive the impression management manipulation—either create a positive and favorable impression or a modest and unfavorable impression. Forty-six pairs of subjects were run in a 2 (favorable or unfavorable impression) × 2 (male or female dyad) design. We assumed that the unfavorable impression subjects would experience greater cognitive demand because the management of their behavior was less scripted than that of the favorable impression subjects. As a result, we predicted that unfavorable impression subjects would be less accurate in judging their partners than would favorable impression subjects.

In this study, two unacquainted subjects engaged in an interaction focused around questions related to college and career plans and personal interests. Subjects took turns asking the questions of one another until all of the questions were completed. The interactions averaged about 4.5 minutes, with a range from a little over 2 minutes to about 25 minutes. Immediately following the interaction, subjects returned to their original rooms and completed a set of ratings on (a) how he or she felt during the interaction, (b) how the partner felt (direct perspective), and (c) how the partner thought the subject felt during the interaction (metaperspective). Finally, subjects were asked to recall the partner's name and any other descriptive characteristics. Interactions were unobtrusively videotaped, with debriefing following the completion of the experiment.

Two different accuracy scores were computed for each actor-subject, that is, the subject who received the impression management instruction. Direct perspective accuracy was operationalized as the correlation between the actors' ratings of how the target felt and the targets' ratings of how they felt. Metaperspective accuracy was the correlation between the actors' ratings of how they thought their partners judged them (i.e., the actors) and the targets' own ratings of the actors. Such correlations between actor and target ratings represent unbiased measures of person perception accuracy (Cronbach, 1955; Snodgrass, 1985). The two accuracy correlations were transformed to z-scores for analysis.[2]

In brief, the results showed that the unfavorable impression management subjects were less accurate in their metaperspective judgments than were the favorable impression subjects. Furthermore, additional analyses suggested that it was unlikely that actor-subjects' moods, as reflected in their own self-ratings, were responsible for the accuracy difference. Duration of the interactions was not a factor in the differences either. The significantly lower recall of partner characteristics by unfavorable than favorable impression subjects was consistent with unfavorable impression subjects experiencing greater cognitive demand than did favorable impression subjects.

Future Directions

Although the results of the Patterson et al. (1991/1992) study are consistent with the parallel process model, the study was not designed as a test of the model. To examine the critical balance between the simultaneous cognitive demands of person perception and behavior management, those demands must be experimentally manipulated, and subsequently, social behavior, thought focus, and person perception accuracy all have to be assessed. Furthermore, the type of partner judgments required may well affect accuracy. For example, judgments of extraversion are made quite accurately on the basis of minimal physical appearance information—probably physical attractiveness (Kenny, Horner, Kashy, & Chu, 1992). In such a case, accuracy should be high even when few resources are applied to the person perception track because the perception of physical attractiveness is relatively automatic.

In addition, by manipulating increased attention toward the more automatic behavioral and cognitive reactions, the predicted decrement in effectiveness in social behavior and accuracy in social judgments may be examined. This might be accomplished by giving low-level action identification instructions (e.g., smile, increase gaze, and nod) for high-level action identification sequences such as "making a good impression" (Ritts & Patterson, in press). Finally, the role of important personality moderators should be investigated. A particularly interesting one is social anxiety, because anxious individuals behave less effectively in social situations and devote a disproportionate amount of cognitive resources to self-focused concerns.

The procedures described in the Patterson et al. (1991/1992) study can be easily modified to provide additional opportunities for studying the link between interaction behavior and person perception processes. For example, if a two-camera system were used, with one camera behind each interactant, measuring gaze duration would provide an estimate of the amount of useful visual information that the actor-perceiver actually noticed about the partner. It seems likely that the amount of visual information that registers would be an important determinant of person perception accuracy. Of course, the qualifier here is that the target, like the actor, may be managing his or her behavior to create a particular impression. Then we have to consider the skill of the target in impression management and the skill of the actor in reading such attempts.

Another measurement option is the application of the thought-listing procedure after subjects have completed the interaction (Ickes, Robertson, Tooke, & Teng, 1986; Ickes, Stinson, et al., 1990). In the postsession period, subjects play back the videotape of the interaction and stop the tape wherever they recall a particular thought from the interaction. The reported thoughts can then be scored in terms of focus (partner, self, situation, miscellaneous) and valence (negative, positive, neutral). The focus and valence of thoughts can, in turn, be examined with respect to self- and partner ratings, interactants' behavior, and person perception accuracy. An obvious prediction is that increased accuracy is related to more partner-focused thoughts and fewer self-focused thoughts. In conclusion, these suggestions provide some alternatives for pursuing the important relationship between cognitive and behavioral processes in interaction.

CONCLUSIONS

Although research and theory on interaction behavior and person perception have developed relatively independently, a balanced un-derstanding of social interaction requires attention to the behavior-cognition interface. The framework described in this chapter provides a means of conceptualizing the behavior-cognition linkage within a dynamic system driven by common cognitive resources and pro-cesses. The primary advantage of this framework is that it relates distinct, yet complementary, impression formation processes to si-multaneous behavior processes in interaction. As a result, this ap-proach facilitates an integration of previously separate research areas.

A second advantage of this approach is that it suggests a new direction for research on person perception, consistent with the criticism that the traditional paradigm of person perception research has limited external validity (Funder, 1987; Swann, 1984). That is, greater emphasis should be placed on studying active perceivers in the context of social interaction rather than focusing on passive perceivers who simply attend to stimulus presentations and make judgments. Furthermore, the framework and research paradigms described here extend the "cognitive busyness" approach of Gilbert and his colleagues (Gilbert & Krull, 1988; Gilbert et al., 1988) from interaction analogs to live interactions, with all of their complexity for both actors and their partners. In this way, actor-perceivers' cognitive and behavior patterns may be simultaneously examined.

A third benefit of this approach is the potential for extending the cognitive dynamics proposed here beyond behavior management and impression formation to fundamental group processes, like problem solving and decision making. Given finite cognitive resources to manage these different aspects of group interaction, investing substantial resources in any one area necessarily limits the resources available in other areas. It should be noted, however, that an investment of more resources in a given process does not necessarily ensure increased effectiveness. For example, the application of substantial cognitive resources in the service of behavior management, especially in the case of excessive self-focused attention, may not enhance self-presentation. At the same time, those resources would not be available for person perception processes.

The specific research paradigm described in this chapter was used on dyadic interactions, but it can also be applied to larger groups. Practically, however, the logistics for adequately recording the relevant behaviors become more complicated as group size increases. Two or more video cameras would be necessary to obtain a relatively comprehensive record of interactants' behavior, especially for gaze direction. Multiple camera perspectives would also facilitate the video-cueing procedure for the thought listing after the interaction. That is, the best perspective for cueing subjects regarding their earlier thoughts would probably be one that approximated their visual regard during the interaction.

In summary, the theoretical framework presented and the related research paradigm provide an alternative means of studying interactive behavior and person perception in groups. Thus, in place of the typical approach of isolating these processes for the sake of experimental control, this perspective emphasizes the utility of studying the social behavior-social cognition interface.

Notes

1. See Burgoon, Dillman, and Stern (1993) for a critical analysis of compensation and reciprocation patterns of nonverbal communication.

2. Kenny (1991) is more cautious in interpreting consensus as indicative of accuracy. He states that consensus is neither a necessary nor sufficient condition for accuracy, although the two issues are related. It should also be noted that Kenny's (Kenny & Albright, 1987) social relations analysis focuses on consensus among peer group members judging a common target and not on perceiver-target consensus, as in the present chapter.

5

Heuristic-Based Biases in Estimations of Personal Contributions to Collective Endeavors

DONELSON R. FORSYTH
KARL N. KELLEY

Current theories of motivation and self-regulation argue that individuals, after they have completed a task, expend considerable mental energy reviewing their efforts and outcomes. They gather and weigh information about their performance and determine whether they met their personal and social standards. They review the strategies they used to accomplish their tasks and determine whether these strategies require revision. They also plan their future undertakings, ever mindful of the long-term goals they have set for themselves (Karoly, 1993).

Just as individuals carry out extensive cognitive appraisals of their successes and failures, so group members devote significant

AUTHORS' NOTE: Thanks are extended to Ray Archer and several anonymous reviewers who provided useful suggestions for improving earlier drafts. Correspondence should be addressed to Don Forsyth at jforsyth@cabell.vcu.edu.

cognitive resources to the analysis and comprehension of collective endeavors. This appraisal, however, is complicated by the collaborative nature of group activities. Group members must identify the factors that contributed to each member's performance, assign credit and blame, and make decisions regarding rewards, power, and status. The members must also calibrate their chances of succeeding in the future given the resources of the members and set in motion changes in the group's composition, structures, and strategies if the analysis indicates that their future outcomes are in jeopardy (Ickes & Gonzalez, 1994; Wegner, 1987; Zander, 1985).

This chapter examines one aspect of this postperformance cognitive analysis: retrospective estimations of personal contributions to group endeavors. In a variety of work and interpersonal settings, the group's product is determined, in large part, by the quality and quantity of various members' individual contributions to the collective goals. The nature of these contributions is rarely a matter of objective record, however, and as a consequence, individuals' after-the-fact estimations of their responsibility for a group endeavor do not always reflect their actual contributions. As noted below, allocations of responsibility in groups can be biased in two ways: They can promote the individual (*self-serving bias*), or they can promote the group (*group-serving bias*).

ALLOCATING RESPONSIBILITY IN GROUPS

All groups are not created equal. One policy group may formulate an effective plan for dealing with a problem, but another may create a plan that ends in disaster. The committee may strive to consider all issues, but it may also fall prey to groupthink (Janis, 1982). For every team that triumphs, there is a team that is triumphed over.

How do group members allocate responsibility for group endeavors that end in success or failure? Past research suggests that group members often display both a self-serving bias and a group-serving bias. The self-serving, or egocentric, bias is said to occur whenever group members attribute positive outcomes to internal, personal factors while blaming negative outcomes on external, situational factors—including other group members (Leary & Forsyth, 1987). When trying to recall a turning point in a team sport, athletes usually point to something they did rather than the contributions of others (Brawley, 1984). Students who worked closely with a professor on a joint project give, on average, more than 80% of the credit to themselves rather than their mentor (Ross & Sicoly, 1979). Clinicians credit their good work when the client responds positively but blame the client when the therapy session goes poorly (Roberts & McCready, 1987). In organizations, subordinates blame negative performance appraisals on their boss, the poor working conditions, or unfair standards but credit their own hard work when they receive a positive review (Giola & Sims, 1985).

Results obtained in laboratory settings parallel these findings, with members of successful groups usually taking more personal responsibility for the group's performance than do members of failure groups. They also tend to attribute their performance to internal factors (e.g., ability) following a group success and external factors (e.g., task difficulty) following group failure (e.g., Forsyth & Schlenker, 1977; Medow & Zander, 1965; Miller & Schlenker, 1985; Mullen & Riordan, 1988; Mynatt & Sherman, 1975; Norvell & Forsyth, 1984; Schlenker, 1975; Schlenker & Miller, 1977a, 1977b; Schlenker, Soraci, & McCarthy, 1976; Wolosin, Sherman, & Till, 1973; Wortman, Costanzo, & Witt, 1973; Zaccaro, Peterson, & Walker, 1987).

Group members' postperformance analyses can also be group-serving, or sociocentric, with group members emphasizing the entire group's responsibility after success and the group's blamelessness after failure. Rather than allocating responsibility in ways that make them appear in a favorable light compared to other group members, they instead formulate appraisals that protect the group as a whole. After success, members may praise the entire group for its good work with such comments as "we all did well" or "our hard work really paid off." Similarly, after failure, members may join together in blaming outside forces and absolving one another of blame. Indeed, some studies have shown that members of successful groups attribute more responsibility to the "average" member and the group as a whole than do members of failing groups (Forsyth & Schlenker, 1977; Schlenker et al., 1976). In addition, the more positive the group's performance on the task, the more likely the group members will (a) emphasize the validity of the feedback (Forsyth & Schlenker, 1977; Schlenker et al., 1976), (b) stress the importance of success on the particular task (Forsyth & Schlenker, 1977; Zander, 1971), (c) express commitment to the group (Zander, 1971), (d) emphasize their membership in the group (Cialdini et al., 1976), (e) accurately recall their group's score (Dustin, 1966; Zander, 1971), and (f) exaggerate the degree of consensus present in the group (Schlenker & Miller, 1977b).

ALLOCATION ASYMMETRIES: BIASES OR ERRORS?

Why are group members' responsibility allocations after success and failure asymmetrical, stressing internal causes after success but external causes after failure? Paralleling analyses of individuals' reactions to their personal successes and failures, two basic theoretical models have been offered to account for allocation biases that occur at the group level. The first is a "hot," motivational model that assumes that individuals' need to view themselves positively distorts their interpretation of their responsibility for good and bad outcomes. When deciding who deserves the credit for a team's victory or who does the most for the group, members can increase their feelings of self-worth by thinking "me" (Leary & Forsyth, 1987). Hence, the tendency is generally referred to as the self-serving bias.

The motivational model can also account for group-serving tendencies. As social identity theory notes, because the self includes both a personal component and a collective component, group members' sense of self-worth prospers when their groups are well respected or admired by others (Luhtanen & Crocker, 1992; Turner, Hogg, Oakes, Reicher, & Wetherell, 1987). Individuals who join prestigious groups generally feel more satisfied with themselves and their attributes (Brown & Lohr, 1987). Studies of "birg"ing, or

Basking in Reflected Glory, suggest that when people draw attention to their membership in successful groups, their sense of self-esteem tends to increase (Cialdini et al., 1976; Hirt, Zillmann, Erickson, & Kennedy, 1992). Individuals can also enhance their level of self-esteem by derogating members of other groups and by blaming their group's failures on external causes (Crocker & Luhtanen, 1990; Deaux, 1993).

Self- and group-serving biases, however, may also be produced by "cold," cognitive factors. Individuals may strive to be objective in their allocations, but perceptual and cognitive processes may nonetheless lead them to make errors. A heuristic model of information processing suggests that individuals likely base their estimates of responsibility for collective endeavors on the information that they have readily available. As Kahneman and Tversky (1973) note, this availability heuristic works well when individuals' memories are accurate, but the sheer ease of recall or ability to imagine events biases one's estimates. The risks associated with air travel, for example, are often considered to be greater than the risks associated with automobile travel simply because air crashes are vivid events that are readily available to people when they are formulating their risk assessments (Lichtenstein, Fischhoff, & Phillips, 1982).

The availability heuristic can be used to explain self-serving tendencies in group performance settings. In such settings, members have more information about their own contributions than other's contributions, so they are more likely to encode this information and spend more cognitive resources reviewing it (Ross & Sicoly, 1979). One's various contributions to the group effort, however, are not equally memorable. Evidence indicates that, in a variety of performance settings, individuals tend to assume that their efforts will result in success rather than failure (Miller & Ross, 1975); in the absence of evidence to the contrary, they have unrealistically positive expectations about their future outcomes (Weinstein, 1982). Therefore, when individuals review their achievements, their expectation-confirming successes and positive achievements are more easily recalled than their expectation-disconfirming failures and deficiencies (Vreven & Nuttin, 1976).

BIAS OR ERROR? AN EMPIRICAL ANSWER

We examined group members' allocations of responsibility after a competitive task in an attempt to compare the motivated, self-esteem maintenance explanation with the cognitive approach. Members of groups worked on a task that paralleled the structure of the tasks many naturally occurring groups face. Subjects were assigned to one of two groups. After completing a preliminary group discussion task, the groups were seated facing one another. Then, in round-robin order, each member was given a problem to solve. Each time a subject answered, he or she was given feedback publicly. Some subjects were told that they incorrectly answered many problems, others were told they answered most correctly, and others received a mixture of success and failure feedback. At the end of the testing period, subjects were given information about their group's performance. Moreover, all rewards in the situation were based on the group's performance rather than on individual performance.

After the groups received their feedback, the subjects were moved to separate tables where they completed two types of measures of responsibility. One type of item was drawn from procedures developed by Schlenker (Schlenker, 1975; Schlenker & Miller, 1977a; Schlenker et al., 1976): Subjects rated their responsibility and other group members' responsibility on independent rating scales. The second type of responsibility measure was based on one used by Wolosin, Sherman, and Till (1973). Subjects were asked to divide 100 "responsibility points" among the three group members. These two types of items allowed us to differentiate more clearly between responsibility allocated to the self and responsibility allocated to the other group members. When individuals are asked to allocate responsibility points, they must give some people less responsibility if they give others more responsibility. Separate items that ask subjects to rate each group member's responsibility, in contrast, do not force subjects to allocate responsibility in a compensatory fashion.

A self-esteem maintenance approach argues that the group members should avoid the blame for the group's failure and seek out credit for the group's success. Indeed, their need to bolster their self-esteem should be greatest when their personal performance was of poor quality, so those who personally failed should be particularly biased. A heuristic-based approach, however, argues that only individuals who performed well will take the credit for success and avoid the blame for failure.

A cognitive approach maintains that the label *self-serving bias* is something of a misnomer because individuals internalize their successes but externalize their failures only because they generally expect to succeed rather than fail. If, for example, people assume that their personal performance when working as part of a group is adequate, how will they react when the group fails? If the tackle on a football team knows that he played well, if the leader assumes that she organized the group adequately, and the assembly line workers know they did their part, then how can a failure by the group be explained? The answer is by attributing responsibility to factors other than oneself. Conversely, if the group succeeds, these individuals should feel responsible because their group's outcome is inconsistent with their own personal performance. Individuals who know that their personal performance was inadequate, however, should take more responsibility for the group's failure rather than its success.

METHODS

Each group included six same-sex subjects, who were randomly split into two groups of three members each. Any subjects who knew each other were dismissed and replaced with additional subjects. The sessions were conducted by two experimenters, one man and one woman. A total of 96 women and 54 men participated in hourlong sessions (9 men and 16 women in each cell of the balanced factorial design).

Group members thought the study was an investigation of their ability to work together to solve problems that required creativity, communication, and raw intellect. They were encouraged to work as efficiently as possible, and they were told that as a reward the group with the better score would be entered in a raffle with a prize of $50. The losing team would not be able to enter the raffle.

The two groups then worked separately on a group consensus task. Subjects, in face-to-face discussion, decided on the ranking of 15 objects in terms of their usefulness when surviving in the wilderness. When this task was completed (15 minutes), the two groups moved to two separate rectangular tables. They then were told that they would be shown a series of slides containing multiple choice and fill-in-the-blank questions drawn from an intelligence test. Each member of the group would be asked a question, and only that individual could answer. They were told that only correct answers would earn the group points and that some questions were worth more than others.

One of the experimenters then guided the two groups as members answered the 48 questions. These questions were designed so that subjects couldn't identify the correct answer without assistance from the experimenters. For example, a fill-in question asked "The overabundance caused a ____," and options included "surfeit," "satiety," and "glut." Similarly, one of the analogy questions asked "Elbow is to fulcrum as biceps is to: weight, balance, or force." These questions were sufficiently difficult or ambiguous that subjects could be given arbitrary feedback about their performance. During the performance phase, the subject stated his or her answer aloud, and then the second experimenter announced if the answer was correct, partially correct, or incorrect. This *individual performance* information was contrived so that within each three-person group, one individual was given a random sequence of primarily positive feedback (5 correct, 2 partially correct, 1 incorrect), one received a randomized sequence of mixed feedback (3 correct, 3 partially correct, 2 incorrect), and one was given negative feedback (1 correct, 2 partially correct, 5 incorrect).

Group performance was manipulated immediately after the completion of the group test. The second experimenter stated, "I know you would like to find out if you qualified for the raffle, so if you give us a few minutes we can tell you." After a delay, the groups were told "I've got good news for Group 1 [2] and bad news for Group 2 [1]. Both groups did fairly well, but Group 1 [2] wins. Their Group

Ability Quotient was 112, while Group 2's [1's] score was 88." The members of the successful group completed raffle ticket forms.

Subjects, after being told whether their group succeeded or failed, were moved to individual tables and given a questionnaire that measured the effectiveness of the manipulations, feelings of satisfaction with and responsibility for personal and group performance, and emotional reactions to the experience. Written instructions stated that their answers were confidential, and they were told to seal their form in an envelope when they were finished.

The critical items on the questionnaire asked individuals to allocate responsibility to themselves and to the other group members. Two 9-point questions asked "How responsible are you personally for your group's performance?" and "How responsible are the other group members (excluding yourself) for the group's performance?" The endpoints on the accompanying rating scales were labeled "very responsible" (9) and "not very responsible" (1). A third question asked subjects to divide 100 points among the three members of their group, "giving more points to the more responsible member." This item explicitly stated that the total should equal 100, but some subjects allocated more than 100 points. A group debriefing session was held immediately after the questionnaires were completed.

RESULTS

Subjects' responses were examined in a series of 3 (individual performance: success, failure, and mixed) × 2 (group performance: success and failure) × 2 (sex: male and female) analyses of variance. When appropriate, post hoc tests were conducted using Tukey HSD at the $p < .05$ level.

Reactions to the Feedback

Subjects rated both their personal and group performance on 9-point scales with the endpoints marked "very well" (9) and "very poorly" (1). The individual performance main effect was significant on

TABLE 5.1
The Effect of Group Performance Feedback on
Ratings of Performance, Satisfaction, Responsibility, and Affect

	Group Performance		F-ratio	p-value
	Success	Failure		
Personal performance	6.0	5.2	10.63	< .01
Group performance	7.2	5.3	63.80	< .001
Satisfaction (own)	5.9	5.2	7.86	< .01
Satisfaction (group)	7.6	5.2	58.43	< .001
Responsibility (own)	5.8	5.5	1.20	ns
Responsibility (group)	6.6	5.6	18.36	< .001
Percentage of personal responsibility	36.5	32.6	3.34	< .07
Percentage of others' responsibility	72.4	70.9	0.16	ns
Negative affectivity	1.6	2.0	9.04	< .001
Positive affectivity	3.6	2.8	20.98	< .001
Arousal	2.6	2.5	0.32	ns
Calm	3.2	3.1	0.78	ns

NOTE: $df = 1, 138$.

the item "How well did you personally do on the test?": $F(1,138) = 48.71$, $p < .0001$. Successful subjects rated their scores more positively than failure subjects, and the mixed performance group fell intermediate but significantly different from the others; the means were 6.6, 6.1, and 4.2. Moreover, even though this question focused on personal performance, the group performance main effect was also significant. As shown in Table 5.1, people who were members of successful groups felt their personal performance was better than did members of failure groups.

The manipulation of group performance was also successful, as the significant group performance main effect on the item "How well did your group do on the test?" shown in Table 5.1 indicates. People in failure groups rated their group's efforts more negatively than those in the successful groups. No other effect was significant for this item.

Subjects' ratings of their satisfaction also confirm the effectiveness of the manipulations. The group performance main effect was significant on items that asked subjects to rate their satisfaction with their personal performance and their group performance on 9-point

scales with endpoints marked "very satisfied" (9) and "very dissatis-
fied" (1). As Table 5.1 indicates, people in successful groups were
more satisfied with their personal performance and their group's
performance relative to individuals in failing groups.

The main effect of individual performance was also significant:
F (2,138) = 51.83 and 27.81, respectively, ps < .0001. People who
failed felt less satisfied with their personal performance than those
who received mixed feedback, and they in turn were less satisfied
with their performance than those who received positive feedback;
the means were 4.1, 5.9, and 6.6, respectively. Similarly, those who
failed, relative to those who succeeded or received mixed performance feedback, reported less satisfaction with their group's performance; the means were 6.2, 6.7, and 6.8, respectively.

Responsibility Allocations

Analysis of responses to the item "How responsible are you
personally for your group's performance?" revealed an individual
performance main effect qualifying interaction of individual performance and group performance: F (2,138) = 5.35, p < .01. The
means shown in Figure 5.1 reveal a self-serving pattern but only
among individuals who succeeded on their portion of the group's
task. Individuals whose personal performance was mixed or failing
showed no bias. In fact, individuals who failed on the task were more
likely to deny themselves responsibility for a group success. However,
people who performed poorly in a losing effort took no more
responsibility for the failure than did people who performed very
well; they evidenced no self-blame. People who performed well in
failing groups, in contrast, took less responsibility for their group's
outcome than did people who performed well in successful groups.

As Table 5.1 indicates, the main effect of group performance was
significant for allocations of responsibility to the other group members. Instead of denying the other group members' responsibility for
success and blaming them for failure, subjects displayed the opposite
tendency: They gave more responsibility to their group members
when the group succeeded rather than failed.

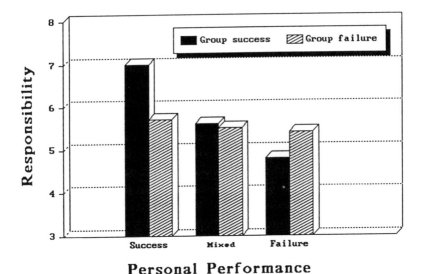

Personal Performance

Figure 5.1. The Impact of Individual Performance Feedback and Group Performance Feedback on Attribution of Personal Responsibility

Subjects divided 100 responsibility points among the members of the group, including themselves. For self- allocations, the group performance main effect approached significance (see Table 5.1); subjects tended to take less responsibility after a group failure. The individual performance main effect was also significant, however: F $(2,138) = 4.31, p < .05$. Subjects gave themselves an average 38.5% of the responsibility when they performed well, 34.3% when their performance was mixed, and only 30.7% of the responsibility when they failed (all means differed, $p < .05$).

Because all subjects did not enter responsibility allocations that totaled 100, responsibility points allocated to the other group members were summed and analyzed. The individual performance main effect was significant: F $(2,138) = 3.22, p < .05$. The means for the successful, mixed, and failure subjects were, respectively, 66.2, 71.2, and 77.7; all differed at the $p < .05$ level. These effects were not qualified by any higher order interactions.

Affective Reactions

Subjects completed a checklist on which they indicated the degree to which they experienced 32 affective reactions, the 7-point scale ranging from "extremely" (9) to "not at all" (1). These 32 items were averaged to yield 4 general affective scales: negative affectivity (e.g., distressed, sad), positive affectivity (satisfied, happy), arousal (tense, excited), and calm (calm, tranquil) (Redstrom, Kelley, Forsyth, & Noel, 1986). Internal consistencies for the scales were adequate (Cronbach's alpha > .82). The main effect of group performance was significant for negative affectivity and positive affectivity. As Table 5.1 indicates, individuals in successful groups felt more positive and less negative than did members of failure groups. The only other effects that reached significance on these affective items involved sex as a variable. These sex differences are discussed in the next section.

Sex Differences

Even though a priori hypotheses pertaining to sex differences were not posited, men and women responded differently to individual performance feedback across a number of dependent measures. The two-way interaction of individual performance and sex was significant on both satisfaction with one's personal performance and satisfaction with the group's performance items; Fs (2,138) = 6.39, 4.00, respectively, $ps < .05$. As Table 5.2 indicates, women who failed reported feeling significantly less satisfied with their own performance and their group's performance. Although men who failed were less satisfied than men who succeeded, women who failed were less satisfied than all other women and men. When rating their satisfaction with their group's score, women who failed were less satisfied than women whose performance was mixed.

The interaction of individual performance and sex also emerged for ratings of personal responsibility: F (2,138) = 3.67, $p < .05$. The

TABLE 5.2

The Impact of Personal Performance on Reactions of Men and Women

Measure	Sex	*Personal Performance*		
		Success	*Neutral*	*Failure*
Satisfaction (own)				
	Males	6.3$_{ab}$	5.6$_{bc}$	4.9$_c$
	Females	6.9$_a$	6.2$_{ab}$	3.4$_d$
Satisfaction (group)				
	Males	6.6$_{ab}$	6.2$_{ab}$	6.8$_{ab}$
	Females	6.8$_{ab}$	7.2$_a$	5.9$_b$
Responsibility (own)				
	Males	5.9$_{ab}$	6.1$_{ab}$	5.6$_{bc}$
	Females	6.6$_a$	5.3$_{bc}$	4.8$_c$
Responsibility (group)				
	Males	5.5$_c$	6.2$_{abc}$	6.5$_{ab}$
	Females	6.7$_a$	6.1$_{abc}$	5.7$_{bc}$
Positive affect				
	Males	3.4$_a$	3.2$_a$	3.5$_a$
	Females	3.5$_a$	3.4$_a$	2.5$_b$
Aroused affect				
	Males	2.4$_{ab}$	2.6$_{ab}$	2.8$_a$
	Females	2.9$_a$	2.7$_a$	2.0$_b$

NOTE: Means without a single letter subscript in common differ at the $p < .05$ level by Tukey's HSD test.

means in Table 5.2 again suggest that the interaction was produced by the extreme reaction of women who personally failed. They took less responsibility than women who succeeded and less responsibility than men who succeeded or men who received mixed scores. Men's responses were not significantly influenced by their personal performance.

The individual performance and sex interaction for ratings of others' responsibility were significant: $F (2,138) = 5.87$, $p < .01$. Women who succeeded gave more responsibility to others relative to women who failed (see Table 5.2). Men displayed the opposite response; successful men gave less responsibility to others relative to men who failed.

Last, the two-way interaction of individual performance and sex emerged in subjects' ratings of their positive affectivity: $F (2,138) = 4.97$, $p < .01$. Women who failed had lower positive affect when compared to all other subjects (see Table 5.2). This same effect emerged in subjects' ratings of their arousal: $F (2,138) = 3.59, p < .05$. Women who failed reported the lowest level of arousal when they failed, whereas men reported the lowest level of arousal when they succeeded. Last, only the main effect of sex emerged as significant in ratings of degree of calm: $F (1,137) = 7.78, p < .01$. The mean was 3.6 for men and 2.9 for women.

DISCUSSION AND CONCLUSIONS

Self-serving patterns of responsibility allocations following collective endeavors can take at least three forms: (a) Members of successful groups take more responsibility for the group's performance in comparison to members of failure groups; (b) members of successful groups take more responsibility than they give other group members; and (c) members of failure groups can take less responsibility than they give to other members (Leary & Forsyth, 1987). In the current study, only the first type emerged and even then only when group members had succeeded on their individual portion of the task.

These findings are more consistent with a cognitive rather than a motivational interpretation of reactions to success and failure (Tetlock & Levi, 1982; Tetlock & Manstead, 1985). A motivated-bias approach argues that if group members blamed themselves for their groups' failures, then their sense of self-confidence and self-worth would be undermined. Therefore, individuals externalize failure by blaming external factors or other group members, whereas they internalize success by crediting their personal abilities and efforts (Schlenker & Miller, 1977a). A cognitive, information-processing approach offers a contrasting view. It suggests that people are more likely to attribute expected than unexpected outcomes to themselves. To the extent that most people assume things generally go well, they accept more responsibility for group success than group failure. Because the typically observed asymmetry emerged only when group members had performed successfully on their individual portion of the task, these findings support a cognitive interpretation. Individuals who did not do well on their portion of the task showed, if anything, a tendency to take more responsibility for failure than success. Moreover, irrespective of their own personal performance, when subjects estimated the other members' responsibility on a separate measure that was dissociated from estimates of their personal responsibility, people gave more responsibility to their group members when the group succeeded rather than failed. This willingness to credit the group more after success than failure suggests that responsibility allocations are as much group-serving as they are self-serving (Forsyth, Berger, & Mitchell, 1981).

Why were group members so group-serving in the current investigation? One explanation suggests that the use of two groups in each session rather than one heightened subjects' desire to protect and enhance their group. Prior laboratory studies usually used only a single group that succeeded or failed at a collective endeavor. The current study, in contrast, always included two groups in competition with one another, setting the stage for social categorization based on membership (Turner et al., 1987). Social identity theory suggests that such a situation may prompt group members to devalue the qualities of the outgroup while simultaneously overestimating the positive attributes of their own group. Therefore, the group-serving tendencies in evidence in their responsibility allocations may reflect this ingroup-outgroup bias (Hunter, Stringer, & Coleman, 1993; McKeever, Joseph, & McCormack, 1993).

Group members were not, however, altogether accurate in their perceptions of the performance and responsibility. The group's performance influenced people's ratings of their own individual performance, even though they were given explicit, individualized feedback after each response. People who performed very badly nonetheless felt better about their personal performance when their group succeeded rather than failed. They also felt more satisfied with their personal efforts when their group succeeded, irrespective of their own contribution to that collective enterprise. Also, individuals who were members of failure groups avoided responsibility for that failure. The individual who performed very poorly on the task took no more of the blame for the group's failure than the individual who performed very well. People in failing groups also gave slightly more responsibility to other group members than they gave themselves.

These findings suggest that self-serving and group-serving tendencies are not necessarily mutually exclusive processes. Members of a failing group can maintain that they had little to do with the group's actions but at the same time point out that the group, as a whole, is blameless as well. When their group prospers, in contrast, they can credit the entire team but also highlight their own personal contributions to the team effort. Thus, performing tasks in groups offers clear advantages to the individual. When the group does well, the mediocre performer can take pride in his or her group's work and share in the group's success. Moreover, the top performer in the group can magnanimously share the credit with others but also claim the lion's share for himself or herself. When the group fails, however, responsibility can be diffused throughout the entire group, and no one individual need bear the brunt of the blame. In this research, at least, little scapegoating was noted: Even individuals who were very successful did not blame their incompetent coworkers for the group's failure.

Additional research is required to explore two significant questions unanswered in the current effort. First, additional work is needed to explore the interpersonal implications of responsibility allocations in collective endeavors. In the current work, individuals' claims of responsibility were kept private. In many settings, however, one claims responsibility or avoids blame publicly. Whereas members may be publicly gracious after group performance, privately they may formulate self-serving estimates of their own performance to protect their personal sense of self-worth. Responsibility allocations may be shaped as much by self-presentational concerns as by cognitive processes or the need to enhance self-esteem (Miller & Schlenker, 1985; Norvell & Forsyth, 1984; Schlenker, Weigold, & Hallam, 1990; Taylor & Tyler, 1986).

Second, the unexpected reaction of women who failed requires further study. None of the subjects responded positively to personal failure, but women's reactions were particularly negative. Women who received negative feedback were less satisfied with their own score and their group's score. They took less personal responsibility than women who succeeded, but they also allocated less responsibility to the other members of their groups. They also had lower positive affect and were less aroused in comparison to others. These responses suggest that, in general, women who failed felt less involved in the group experience than women who received positive personal performance scores and men in general.

This sex difference may be due to differences in women's attributional tendencies. Women, in some cases, take less responsibility for their performance outcomes. Significantly, however, in most cases this effect occurs following success rather than failure (Frieze, Whitley, Hanusa, & McHugh, 1982). Alternatively, the effect may be due to women's greater involvement in their groups. If they were more involved, then failure of the groups may have been personally threatening. They therefore responded more negatively to the failure experience. Also, although men who failed in the group were able to use the group as a shield to protect them from the esteem-damaging implications of their poor performance, women did not seem so facile in their use of the group for egocentric purposes. This possibility, however, is admittedly speculative and requires further study (Eagly, 1995).

6

Followers' Perceptions
of Group Leaders
The Impact of Recognition-Based
and Inference-Based Processes

JUDITH L. NYE
LEO G. SIMONETTA

And when we think we lead, we are most led.
—Lord Byron (1881, p. 433)

According to Hollander (1985), leadership can be viewed as a reciprocal process in which leaders influence, and are influenced by, group members. Rather than assume that leaders simply exert authority over their followers, this transactional model recognizes that both leaders and followers must adjust to the changing demands of their group members and the group situation. A leader's effectiveness depends on the reciprocal relationships among three elements: the leader, the followers, and the situation. In short,

124

leaders are individuals who possess the skills to satisfy the needs of their followers and of the situation and must answer to their followers when they fall short of fulfilling those needs (Bass, 1981; Hollander, 1985; Lord & Maher, 1991).

One of the important components in this transactional process that has often been overlooked by leadership researchers is the perceptions of followers (Kouzes & Posner, 1990; Lord & Maher, 1991). Followers know what they want in a leader. Research suggests that most people have well-defined, implicit theories about leadership and the appropriate behaviors involved in the process (Calder, 1977; Eden & Leviatan, 1975). Therefore, personal theories of leadership in the minds of followers can play an important role in whether or not a leader will be effective. Regardless of the skills or power an individual brings to a group situation, he or she is not a leader unless recognized as such by the group members (Kouzes & Posner, 1990; Lord & Maher, 1991). Leadership, Lord and Maher (1991) argue, is "the process of being perceived by others as a leader" (p. 11).

This chapter addresses some of the cognitive processes that are believed to influence followers' perceptions of their leaders. We present two studies that explore both the preconceptions followers bring into the group situation and the behavioral data they use when evaluating leaders. Congruent with previous research, our findings suggest that these cognitive processes play a substantial role in the social dynamics occurring between followers and their leaders.

What goes on in the mind of a follower? Drawing on information-processing models of cognition, Lord (Lord, 1985; Lord & Maher, 1991) argues that the follower interprets leadership situations just as any social perceiver would interpret a social event, using the same

AUTHORS' NOTE: Address correspondence to Judith L. Nye, Department of Psychology, Monmouth University, West Long Branch, NJ 07764 (Internet: nye@mondec.monmouth.edu).

Study 1 was supported, in part, by a Grant-in-Aid for Creativity award from Monmouth University. We wish to thank Nick Angiulo, Duane Dalesandry, Joy Knight, Michael Riehl, and Laurna Townsend for their assistance with data collection for Study 1. Special thanks go to Valerie Arnone, Kristina Larsen, Melissa Minelli, Terrance Ruppel, Kristen Springer, Debra F. Stueber, and Thomas Wiltsey for their work in developing and carrying out Study 2.

social-cognitive processes. However, these processes that underlie both social cognition in general and the leadership perceptions of followers specifically are quite complex. At first glance, the social perceiver presents a paradox. When it comes to understanding our social world, we are capable of thorough, deliberate examination of that world (controlled processing). Yet at times we fail to make use of these cognitive abilities, relying instead on habit and preconceived beliefs to guide our processing (automatic processing; Shiffrin & Schneider, 1977). Controlled cognitive processes tend to be effort-intensive, requiring almost all of our attention to pursue, whereas automatic processes are second nature to us and can be easily pursued while we are focused on other things. Most processing of social information employs a combination of the two extremes: Automatic processes usually work quite well in simplifying the social world and reducing cognitive processing demands; however, the social perceiver is free to switch to more controlled processes when necessary (Fiske & Taylor, 1991; Gilbert, Krull, & Pelham, 1988; Gilbert, Pelham, & Krull, 1988; Markus & Zajonc, 1985).

These automatic processes rely on underlying knowledge structures, or schemas: bundles of already existing knowledge that can be used as frameworks for organizing and interpreting new information (Fiske & Taylor, 1991; Galambos, Abelson, & Black, 1986; Markus & Zajonc, 1985). Schemas play an important role in understanding the social world, operating as the framework necessary for organizing and interpreting social events (Markus & Zajonc, 1985). Leadership perception, like other forms of social information processing, relies on schemas (Lord & Maher, 1991).

LEADERSHIP PERCEPTIONS

A recent model of leadership perceptions, developed by Robert Lord, recognizes the importance of schemas to social perception and social perceiver's capacity for pursuing both controlled and automatic processes. Based on past research (Butterfield & Bartol, 1977; Calder, 1977; Lord, Binning, Rush, & Thomas, 1978), Lord and his associates (Lord, Foti, & DeVader, 1984; Lord & Maher, 1990, 1991) point out that leadership perception, like other forms of social perception, tends toward the automatic end of the continuum. As social beings, we have interacted with and thought about leaders all of our lives. Although we may have seemed totally absorbed in the tasks at hand, we have also developed a vast store of information and impressions about the events and behaviors of leadership. In addition, we have had many opportunities to engage in more deliberate thinking about leaders. We may employ more controlled processes, for example, when we listen to a political commentator discuss the relative merits of two candidates or argue with a colleague over whether a manager should be promoted to a higher position. Processes from both extremes in cognitive processing contribute to the social perceiver's perceptions of leaders.

Lord outlines a general theory of leadership perceptions that encompasses two separate models of perceptual processes: recognition models and inferential models. Recognition-based processes occur when the perceiver uses the target's attributes and behaviors as cues that the target is a leader, whereas inference-based processes rely on outcomes of the target's behavior (i.e., group success or failure) to make attributions about leadership. Both processes are equally likely to impact leadership perceptions depending on the available evidence (Lord et al., 1984; Lord & Maher, 1990, 1991).

Recognition-Based Processes

The recognition-based processes occur during everyday interactions with leaders and discussions with others about leaders. In either case, the social perceiver notices relevant behaviors or traits and compares them to personal ideas about leadership. These personal ideas are often called *implicit leadership theories,* personal definitions of effective and ineffective leader behaviors and abilities (Calder, 1977; Eden & Leviatan, 1975; Rush, Thomas, & Lord, 1977). Such theories are a variation of "implicit personality theories" (Bruner & Tagiuri, 1954; Cronbach, 1958), knowledge structures consisting of what the perceiver believes to be the attributes of other people and the connections between these perceived attributes. Evidence suggests that individuals draw automatically from implicit leadership theories whenever they are in any situation of leadership evaluation (Calder, 1977; Eden & Leviatan, 1975; Lord & Maher, 1991).

Lord has proposed a leadership categorization theory (Lord et al., 1984; Lord & Maher, 1990, 1991) to explain these recognition-based perceptions of leaders, based on Eleanor Rosch's (1978) theory of how humans categorize the objects and events of their world. This view suggests that people develop category systems to provide themselves with maximum information about their world with the least amount of cognitive work, thus managing complex social information-processing demands (Lord, 1985; Lord et al., 1984; Phillips, 1984; Phillips & Lord, 1982).

Rather than worry about specific boundaries between categories, one category is distinguished from another by its prototype (a cognitive summary of the most typical features of the category), and incoming stimuli are categorized in terms of how well they match the category prototypes. Thus, categorization of incoming stimuli is decided in terms of prototypes using a "family resemblance" criterion: a new instance is considered a member of a given category if it is similar to the category prototype. The social perceiver creates a conceptual prototype of the ideal leader, and then a simple comparison between the target person and the prototype decides whether the target should be categorized as leader or nonleader (Lord, 1985; Lord, Foti, & Phillips, 1982). For example, an individual in a group may assume that effective leaders concern themselves with completing group tasks while maintaining a positive emotional climate within the group. This individual judges the leaders he or she observes according to these beliefs. If a leader engages in these actions, the follower will attribute leadership ability to that leader (Bartol & Butterfield, 1976; Calder, 1977; Lord, 1985).

There is evidence that individuals differ in their criteria for effective leadership, developing different leadership prototypes. For example, Nye and Forsyth (1991) found that participants endorsed differing prototypes for effective leadership and that their prototypes affected their perceptions of stimulus leaders. Leaders whose behavior more closely matched the participants' prototypes (assessed on a pretest before exposure to leaders) tended to be rated as more effective and collegial than leaders who did not. These results are not surprising: Because implicit theories of leadership appear to develop out of personal experience with leaders (Calder, 1977; Eden & Leviatan, 1975), individuals with differing experiences should develop differing leadership prototypes.

Inference-Based Processes

Turning to inference-based processes in Lord's theory, he suggests that these processes center on people's belief that the main function of leaders is to help groups succeed in meeting their goals. Because effective leadership tends to be viewed as the cause of good performance, people often infer effective leadership when group performance is good. Thus, outcome information provides important, salient evidence of a leader's capabilities. Drawing from the classic literature on attribution theory (Kelley, 1973), Lord argues that the social perceiver makes leadership inferences based on knowledge of successful task or organizational performance. Learning that a group has been successful lends itself to attributions of capable leadership.

Several investigators (Larson, 1982; Larson, Lingle, & Scerbo, 1984; Lord, 1985; Phillips, 1984) have noted this *performance cue effect* on raters' perceptions of leaders. For example, Larson et al. (1984) found this effect when they told half of their participants that a stimulus group performed well and the other half that the group performed poorly. In the stimulus videotape, the leader exhibited behaviors from both the Consideration and the Initiating Structure dimensions of the Leadership Behavior Description Questionnaire (LBDQ; Stogdill, 1963). Larson et al. (1984) found that the performance cues influenced participants' responses: Cues of good performance resulted in attributions of more behaviors from both LBDQ dimensions than did cues of bad performance. Baron and Hershey (1988) would argue that participants' responses reflect a natural human tendency to over-rely on outcome information, thereby confusing evaluations of behavior with evaluations of the consequences of the behavior.

Lord's model also accommodates the social perceiver's tendency toward more controlled processing when making leadership inferences. Sometimes the social situation is rather complex with several factors leading to a group's success or failure. It is the responsibility of the social perceiver to sift through what may be conflicting information to make leadership inferences. For example, Lord cites Kelley's (1972) principles of *discounting* and *augmentation* as important moderators of the attribution process. The social perceiver tends to discount the causal impact of the actor when alternative potential causes are present, perceiving the actor as a less plausible explanation for the outcome. By the same token, when a given outcome occurs in spite of inhibiting factors, this fact serves to strengthen, or augment, perceptions that the actor was a causal agent. Phillips and Lord (1981) tested Kelley's (1972) principles when they manipulated alternative explanations for groups' successes or failures. They varied the ability and motivation of groups working with their stimulus leaders and then looked at subsequent leadership perceptions. They created an augmentation effect with highly able and motivated stimulus groups who performed poorly and low ability/poorly motivated groups who performed well. They created a discounting effect with stimulus groups possessing skills and motivation levels that corresponded to group performance. In doing so, Phillips and Lord (1981) found that the ordinarily strong impact of performance cues were diminished in discounting conditions: Leaders were simply not perceived as causal factors. Performance cue effects on perceptions of leaders, however, remained strong in conditions of augmentation.

OVERVIEW OF STUDY 1 AND STUDY 2

The research presented in this chapter is based on many of the assumptions of Lord's theory of leadership perceptions. However, we have attempted to go beyond Lord's program of research on two counts. First, we have chosen to explore the notion that individuals hold differing leadership prototypes based on their experiences with leaders. Lord and his colleagues have not directly assessed individual differences in leadership prototypes, although they acknowledge that these differences should exist (Lord & Maher, 1991). We tested whether identifying these individual differences provides more predictive power. We examined whether judgments of leaders are affected by how well the leader matches any given perceiver's leadership prototype. In both studies presented here, we pretested participants for their leadership prototypes and then compared these prototypes with the actual behaviors of the stimulus leader, creating an index of prototype match. We then tested whether participants' judgments of leaders were affected by how well the leader matched their individual prototypes.

Our research differs from Lord's work on a second point. Whereas Lord's theory makes predictions about group members' perceptions of leaders, his research typically uses outside *observers'* perceptions of leaders. In his studies, participants observe group interactions, making judgments of group leaders without actually participating in the groups in question. Lord generalizes his findings to perceptions of group members. However, do followers' perceptions regarding leaders parallel the perceptions of observers? We have attempted to address this very question in the second study presented. We tested the assumptions of Lord's theory in an actual group situation in which the participants were followers/partners of the leaders they were rating.

STUDY 1

In the first study, we addressed the impact of three variables on perceptions of leadership: group performance information, the behavioral match between implicit leadership theories and stimulus leaders, and sex of leader. Participants were pretested for their leadership prototypes and then exposed to what they thought was an actual group participating in a problem-solving exercise. After exposure to the stimulus group, participants were provided with varying information about how well the groups performed and then allowed to record their perceptions of the group and its leader.

We expected a number of reactions from participants. First, leaders whose groups performed well would be judged as more effective and collegial than leaders whose groups performed poorly. Presumably, the cues provided by the performance information allow the social perceiver to make judgments about leaders using inference-based processes, attributing good group performance to good leadership and poor group performance to poor leadership. Second, leaders whose behaviors more completely matched participants' prototypes would be judged as more effective and collegial than leaders whose behaviors did not match as well. Thus, recognition-based processes should impact perceptions of stimulus leaders. Moving to possible interactions between performance information and leadership prototypes, we expected that when participants were provided with information that "agreed," or followed, a logical pattern of expectations, they would have no difficulty forming clear judgments of the leaders. However, when the information provided to participants did not follow a logical pattern of expectations (e.g., leaders' characteristics matched participants' prototypes but groups were unsuccessful), we expected that participants would make judgments consistent with their leadership prototypes.

Method

Materials

Stimulus Materials. The stimulus group was presented to participants in the form of a 15-minute audiotape/color slide presentation. The stimulus group consisted of the leader and four other group members. They worked from a prepared script (adapted from Brown & Geis, 1984) outlining the leader's behavior, the overall tone of the group interaction, and the sequence of action. This script portrayed a group of graduate students involved in a problem-solving discussion in which they attempted to solve Hall's (1971) "Lost on the Moon" group decision problem: They were to imagine that their spaceship had crash-landed on the moon, and they must rank-order a list of 15 items in terms of their survival value.

There were two versions of slides and audiotape. In both cases, the four group members remained the same (two males and two females); however, one version portrayed the group led by a male and the other version portrayed the group led by a female. Leaders carried out their responsibilities using a slightly task-oriented, slightly socioemotional-oriented style of leadership. Behavioral consistency between male and female leaders was achieved through careful staging of actors during photographing of the slides and editing of the audiotapes.

Prototype Assessment. Individual differences in participants' leadership prototypes were assessed using the Systematic Multiple Level Observation of Groups (SYMLOG) "General Behavior Descriptions" checklist developed by Bales (Bales, Cohen, & Williamson, 1979). SYMLOG consists of 26 adjective phrases that tap three dimensions of interpersonal behavior: dominance/submission, friendly/unfriendly, and instrumentally controlled/emotionally expressive. Participants were instructed to think about the characteristics that they felt "a good leader would have (a leader in a business or a small organization, not a political leader)" and then describe this leader using the SYMLOG adjectives.

This measure was intended to allow an estimate of how well the stimulus leaders matched participants' prototypes for effective leadership. Presumably, the degree of matching that occurs between participants' prototypes and stimulus leader behavior partially determines whether participants categorize stimulus leaders as effective leaders.

Dependent Measure. After exposure to performance information, participants responded to a series of questions about their perceptions and evaluations of the stimulus leader and group. This final questionnaire contained a number of items pertaining to the leader's effectiveness and collegiality, as well as items referring to participants' perceptions of the stimulus group. All items were followed by 9-point scales with appropriate alternatives for the item.

Design and Procedure

This study used a 2 (sex of leader: male vs. female) × 3 (group performance feedback: good, poor, control) between-subjects factorial design. Performance information was provided on a cover sheet before presentation of the dependent measure. Participants in the good performance information condition learned that their group correctly ordered 11 of the 15 items included in their exercise and that out of the 21 groups that participated, their group was ranked 3rd by independent evaluators (Grade: A). Participants in the poor performance information condition learned that their group correctly ordered only 4 of the 15 items included in their exercise and that their group was ranked 19th by evaluators (Grade: C). Participants in the control condition learned that their group correctly ordered 11 of the 15 items in their exercise; however, no information was provided regarding their ranking by evaluators.

Participants were 68 male and 98 female undergraduate students recruited to participate from their psychology classes; their ages ranged from 18 to 40 years. They were tested in groups of 2 to 15 people. After the experimenter briefly explained the nature of their task, participants signed informed consent forms and completed the prototype assessment instrument. Stimulus groups were presented using an audiotape player and slide projector. In addition, printed transcripts of the audiotape were provided so that participants could follow the action more easily and accurately.

In viewing the stimulus groups as they worked toward attaining their assigned goals, participants had the opportunity to observe their patterns of interaction and the specific behaviors of group members, especially the group leader. After viewing the presentation, participants were given the opportunity to evaluate the group leader on a final questionnaire.

Estimation of Prototype Match

To provide an estimate of how well stimulus leaders matched participants' actual leadership prototypes, it was first necessary to employ independent judges. These judges were 234 students from a research participant pool who were trained to use the SYMLOG measure to rate the stimulus leader's behavior. They viewed the slides, listened to the audiotapes, read the stimulus transcripts, and then documented the stimulus leader's actual behavior on a SYMLOG questionnaire.

To ensure that judges fully understood the measure they were completing, they were provided with definition sheets that explained every SYMLOG item fully, providing definitions for each term, and then put the entire item into context in a sentence or brief paragraph. Rather than expecting judges to respond to all 26 items, the SYMLOG questionnaire was split in half with each judge responding to only 13 items. There were 109 judges that responded to one set of items and 125 judges that responded to the other set of items. Judges were instructed to "answer how often you believe the leader showed each of the following behaviors." Consistent with the scoring guidelines for the SYMLOG questionnaire, they responded on 3-point scales: "not often" (1), "sometimes" (2), and "often" (3).

Because judges answered using a nominal scale, mode scores were used to determine the judges' estimation of the stimulus leader's behavior. For the most part, judges' ratings of the stimulus leader's behavior were fairly consistent. On the 26 SYMLOG items, judges' ratings of stimulus leaders agreed with the mode score from 41% to 100% of the time (average agreement overall: 77%), with half of the items achieving agreement scores of over 80%. The judges' average responses were combined to yield scores on the three SYMLOG dimensions, indicating that the stimulus leader's behavior was slightly dominant, very friendly, and somewhat instrumentally controlled (specifically, U-3, P-14, F-7 on the SYMLOG questionnaire). Given this information, we were able to pinpoint the stimulus leader in the three-dimensional space conceptualized by Bales (Bales et al., 1979) and compare him or her with each participant's individual prototype via euclidean distance. This comparison yielded a new predictor for data analyses: *prototype match*.

Not surprisingly, stimulus leaders were not a perfect match to participants' prototypes. Participants' responses to the SYMLOG premeasure revealed that they generally favored slightly dominant rather than submissive leaders, friendly rather than unfriendly leaders, and slightly controlled rather than emotionally expressive leaders (mean responses were U-4.3, P-10.5, and F-5.4). Thus, the stimulus leader was less dominant and more friendly and controlled than the average participant's prototypical leader.

Results and Discussion

Participants' Perceptions of Stimulus Leaders

Participants responded to 10 items on the final questionnaire pertaining to their perceptions of the stimulus leaders. These items were written to tap into two aspects of leader perceptions: leader effectiveness (competence, capabilities, etc.) and leader collegiality (participants' liking for the leader, desire to work for leader, etc.). However, to confirm the existence of this structure, participants' responses to the 10 items were submitted to factor analysis using the maximum-likelihood method of extraction followed by varimax rotation. The Kaiser-Meyer-Olkin measure of sampling adequacy (Kaiser, 1970, 1974) was .88, indicating that the correlation matrix was appropriate for factor analysis. Two factors emerged from this analysis and together they accounted for 53% of the total variance. Initial eigen values reveal the appropriateness of a two-factor model: Factor 1 (5.09), Factor 2 (1.10), Factor 3 (.79), and Factor 4 (.71). The pattern of factor loadings confirmed the implicit division of the questionnaire items pertaining to perceptions of stimulus leaders. However, one item was dropped from subsequent analyses because it did not load highly on either dimension. All remaining items failed to violate the assumptions of normality as outlined by Tabachnick and Fidell (1989).

Following the pattern of factor loadings, the six effectiveness items were combined to form an aggregate effectiveness score, and the three collegiality items were combined to form an aggregate collegiality score. These scores were submitted to stepwise multiple regression analyses that included performance information, proto-

TABLE 6.1
Summary of Multiple Regression Analyses Addressing
Performance Information Effects on Ratings
of Leader Effectiveness and Collegiality, Study 1

Item	*b*	*SE B*	β	*t*	*p*
Effectiveness aggregate score	3.21	0.90	0.23	3.58	.0005
Effective behavior?	0.51	0.19	0.20	2.66	.0087
Effective in work world?	0.56	0.20	0.22	2.85	.005
Competent?	0.76	0.19	0.30	4.03	.0001
Effective leadership style?	0.65	0.17	0.29	3.85	.0002
Collegiality aggregate score	1.74	0.43	0.30	4.02	.0001
Like this leader?	0.67	0.15	0.32	4.39	.0001
Work for this leader?	0.63	0.19	0.25	3.26	.0013

type match, and sex of leader as predictors. Using simple effects coding, the three performance information conditions were coded into two predictors and the sex of leader conditions were coded into one predictor. In addition, all possible two-way interactions were examined by creating interaction predictors and including them in the analyses. No sex of leader effects were revealed in the initial analyses, so this predictor was dropped from subsequent analyses. Only the effects that were found to be significant in the aggregate analyses were subjected to individual MRC analyses and are discussed here.

Analysis of the effectiveness aggregate score revealed only one significant effect: performance information (specifically, the predictor comparing good performance with bad performance conditions), $R^2 = .07$, $F (1,164) = 12.82$, $p = .0005$. This effect was significant univariately on four items (see Table 6.1). Not surprisingly, stimulus leaders whose groups performed well were perceived to be significantly more effective than leaders in the poor performance condition.

Turning to perceptions of collegiality, analysis of this aggregate score once again revealed a significant effect for performance information, $R^2 = .09$, $F (1,164) = 16.19$, $p = .0001$. This effect reached univariate significance on two items (see Table 6.1). Here again, participants responded with the expected pattern of perceptions, with good performance information yielding significantly higher collegiality ratings than poor performance information. Thus, the most striking finding of Study 1 is the effect of group performance information on participants' perceptions of stimulus leaders. Participants' leadership prototypes and sex of the stimulus leader were not significant factors here.

Thus, performance information, provided after participants' exposure to stimulus groups, profoundly influenced their perceptions of leader effectiveness and collegiality. Participants sat side by side viewing the same group interaction stimulus. Nevertheless, their leadership attributions were quite different once they learned the final group outcome. Participants' written responses regarding the stimulus leaders reflect the power of performance cues in perceptions of the leaders. For example, one participant in the good performance condition wrote, "Obviously, his good leadership qualities paid off because they did so well in the test. His performance as a leader reflects on the grade they got." Participants in the bad performance condition responded quite differently: "Chris showed his incompetence by not giving any intellectual input in the problem-solving session." These findings offer support for Lord's (Lord & Maher, 1990, 1991) argument that inference-based processes affect perceptions of leaders.

Surprisingly, the impact of prototypes on leader perceptions was not evident. We predicted that stimulus leaders who more closely match individuals' prototypes for good leadership would receive higher ratings than those who did not. This was not the case. These findings do not support Lord's (Lord & Maher, 1990, 1991) expectation that recognition-based processes impact perceptions of leaders.

Perceptions Regarding Group Members

Three items on the final questionnaire pertained to participants' perceptions of the stimulus group, asking questions such as "How satisfied do you think the group members were with their performance?" Analysis of an aggregate of these items revealed two effects, a significant main effect for prototype match and an interaction between performance information and prototype match, $R^2 =$

.22, F (1,163) = 23.0, p < .0001. The main effect for prototype match reached significance on two of the group items. On the item "How satisfied do you think the group members were with their performance?" participants attributed greater satisfaction to groups whose leaders more closely matched their own leadership prototypes (b = −.15, SE B = .06, β = −.18, t = −2.39, p < .05). The same pattern of responses was revealed on the item "In your opinion, how well did these individuals work together as a group?" (b = −.09, SE B = .04, β = −.17, t = −2.27, p < .05).

This main effect was qualified by a two-way interaction between prototype match and performance information (predictor comparing good performance with poor performance). The interaction achieved significance in the analyses of two of the group items, "In your opinion, how effective was this group at arriving at a good solution to their problem?" (b = .14, SE B = .02, β = .49, t = 7.19, p < .0001) and "In your opinion, how well did these individuals work together as a group?" (b = .08, SE B = .02, β = .31, t = 4.19, p < .0001). Both items yielded similar patterns of response. Plotting the simple regression lines[1] for the second item (see Figure 6.1), it becomes evident that all groups received rather high ratings in situations in which their leaders closely matched participants' leadership proto-types. As the prototype match became more distant, however, the poor performing groups were rated as significantly less collaborative than the groups who performed well. Interestingly, groups in the good perform-ance condition were rated slightly higher as the prototype match became more distant. These findings are somewhat surprising because partici-pants were asked to record their perceptions of everyone in the group *except* the leader. We did not expect leadership prototypes to be a factor in perceptions of the group. However, participants may have per-ceived the leaders as conceptually inseparable from their groups. As one participant wrote, "The group members were not very responsi-ble for the group performance because they knew that in the end only one opinion would be important, which is the leader's opinion. Another [sic] words no matter what they thought the leader had the final word." Certainly, both effects involving prototype match offer some support for the argument that participants' leadership prototypes

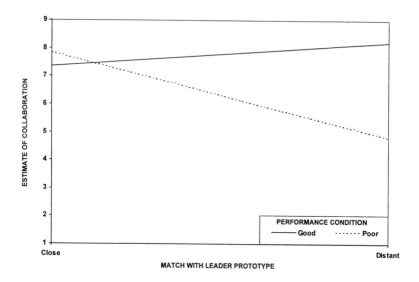

Figure 6.1. Regression Lines Depicting Significant Interaction Between Performance Feedback and Leader Prototype Match on the Item "In your opinion, how well did these individuals work together as a group?"

have an impact on their judgments. If this influence exists, however, it appears to be more subtle than anticipated.

STUDY 2

In the special issue of *Small Group Research* on social cognition research conducted in group settings (Nye & Brower, 1994), a number of authors point out the importance of pursuing social cognition research in true interaction situations (e.g., Fiske & Goodwin, 1994; Ickes & Gonzalez, 1994). Inspired by the example set by the research presented in the special issue, Study 2 was designed to draw participants into the leadership perception equation. That is, participants were not merely passive observers making judgments about prerecorded stimulus leaders. They were active participants in the group with a more personal stake in the outcome. We reasoned that participants would be less likely to rely on performance information when judging their leaders because they would actually share responsibility for group outcomes with their leader. Therefore, Study 2 is an attempt to test some of the assumptions of Lord's theory in a truly interactive situation. This experiment is a new step in the first author's program of research, and we are reporting on a study that is currently in progress.

This experiment is somewhat similar to one reported by Phillips and Lord (1981) that tested the effects of performance cues on causal attributions under conditions of discounting and augmenting (Kelley, 1972). However, their participants were observers, whereas we tested the reactions of actual group members. We brought small groups of participants into the laboratory to compete on a series of problems, creating the conditions of discounting and augmenting by sabotaging the materials in half of the groups.

Once again, we expected to find clear evidence of performance cue effects, with participants in successful groups attributing more responsibility to the leader than participants in the unsuccessful groups. Sabotaged materials, however, would force participants into more controlled inference-based processing. In this case, the responsibility of the leader for group performance would be likely to fluctuate: Successful groups would assign more responsibility to the leaders because they led the group to success in spite of setbacks (augmenting), and unsuccessful groups would assign less responsibility to the leaders because no one could avoid failure under the circumstances (discounting). Finally, following the assumptions of Lord's theory (Lord & Maher, 1991), we expected participants' attributions of responsibility to be moderated by leadership prototypes, with participants who failed defending the leaders who matched their leadership prototypes.

Method

Participants and Materials

Participants were 58 students (11 male, 47 female) from the first author's social psychology courses recruited to participate in a group interaction exercise. Their leadership prototypes were assessed the week before the experiment using the SYMLOG questionnaire (Bales et al., 1979). Respondents were instructed to "Try to create an image of good student leadership qualities and then answer this questionnaire with that image in mind."

For the group interaction task, we created a two-page package of problems designed to require the group's full attention and collaborative efforts to complete. For example, one problem read, "If you have a 7-quart jar A and a 4-quart jar B, how can you obtain exactly 10 quarts of water?" Groups attempted to complete a total of nine problems during the 20-minute group interaction period.

The dependent measure was a questionnaire fashioned after one developed by Phillips and Lord (1981). This questionnaire asked respondents to record their attributions about the causal roles that the leader, group members other than the leader (including themselves), and they themselves played in the group's success or failure. Several dimensions of responsibility (e.g., ability, guidance) were addressed on this measure.

Leader Training

Two female confederates were trained to lead these groups through the nine problems following a carefully constructed script. Participants were told that these confederates were members of the first author's upper-level leadership course who were brought into the group situation for added interest. Although leaders contributed several solutions to the exercises, care was taken to keep them from appearing to know all of the answers. Instead, leaders appeared to focus their attention on structuring the group and drawing the answers out of group members. Leaders were trained to behave as somewhat dominant and instrumentally controlled leaders (5-U, 6-F) but were also rather friendly (12-P). Because this study is still in progress and leader behavior will not be coded by judges until data collection is complete, we determined the leaders' SYMLOG scores by how they were trained to behave. All group sessions were videotaped, and a review of these tapes by the first author suggests that both leaders behaved well within their roles. Once again, leader behavior was compared with each participant's individual prototype, yielding a "prototype match" predictor for analyses.

Design and Procedure

Groups (ranging in size from three to six members) were randomly assigned within constraints to conditions of a 2 (group performance information: success vs. failure) × 2 (material sabotage: sabotage vs. no sabotage) between-subjects factorial design. Each experimental session included two groups who competed against each other. During each session, one group succeeded and the other failed, and one group's materials were sabotaged whereas the other's materials were not sabotaged. A total of 12 groups were run—three groups assigned to each of the four cells of the factorial.

Participants were brought into a reception area and immediately separated into their groups on opposite sides of the room. After completing informed consent forms, group members were then introduced to their leaders and their group task was explained to them. At this point, they were told that the two groups would be competing against each other, and to add to the spirit of competition, the winning group would be entered into a $50 raffle (in actuality, all groups were entered into the raffle, and the money was awarded the following week).

Participants accompanied their leaders to their laboratory rooms, where they worked for 20 minutes to complete as many problems as possible. All group sessions were videotaped to allow subsequent coding of leaders' behaviors for prototype match.

The groups expected to complete their work with only one interruption, when the experimenter entered the room briefly to deliver the materials for one of the exercises. Groups assigned to the no sabotage condition completed their work without incident. Groups assigned to the sabotage condition, however, soon discovered that the second page of their exercise handout was missing (the second page was a duplicate of the first page). They alerted the experimenter to the problem when she entered the laboratory to deliver additional materials. She feigned surprise and dismay, left the laboratory briefly, and then returned with the second page of the exercises. To add to the disruption of the sabotaged sessions, the second page was poorly photocopied and difficult to read, causing the group to lose considerable time for completing the exercises. To avoid having participants discount the leader's role completely in the sabotage conditions, the leader's script called for her to "persuade" the experimenter to add 5 minutes to the group's time to complete their exercises.

Although leaders were prepared to respond to the four possible experimental conditions, during the experiment they were blind to their group's assigned condition. They did not know whether they would be sabotaged until the group discovered the missing second page, and they did not know whether their group would succeed until the bogus performance feedback was delivered.

After 20 minutes (or after 25 minutes in the sabotage condition), the group's timer sounded, and the experimenter entered the room to stop the interaction. Groups were given a brief questionnaire to complete while the experimenter tallied their scores. After a short period of time, the experimenter slipped a package under the laboratory door. This package contained the group performance feedback, which the leader related to the group, and the dependent measure, which participants were asked to complete. Once all group members had completed the final questionnaire, the experimenter entered the room, thanked them for participating, and answered their questions.

Groups were fully debriefed the next week when they met again in their classes. During this time, they were introduced to the leaders, the finer points of the experiment were discussed, and their questions were answered. The $50 prize was distributed to the members of the group that won the raffle.

Results and Discussion

Perceptions of Stimulus Leaders

The dependent measure asked participants to generate attributions for their group's performance. For example, items addressing the leader's responsibility asked whether leader ability, effort, guidance, and structuring were important causes of their group's performance. Similar items addressed the causal role that the group as a whole and the participants themselves played in the group outcome. Because this study is still in progress and the data are incomplete, only analyses based on aggregate scores for these attributional loci are presented here.

Participants' responses to the questionnaire items addressing the responsibility of the leader were combined to form an aggregate leader score and subjected to stepwise multiple regression using the following predictors: performance information, sabotage, prototype match, and all possible two-way interactions. Categorical predictors were coded using simple effects coding. This analysis revealed significant effects for three of the predictors (performance information, sabotage, and the interaction between the two), $R^2 = .34$, $F (3,53) = 9.03$, $p = .0001$.

As predicted, participants in the successful groups attributed significantly more responsibility to their leaders than did participants in the groups that failed ($b = 4.92$, $SE B = 1.41$, $\beta = 0.39$, $t = 3.49$, $p = .001$). For the lucky leaders whose groups succeeded, this attribution should have enhanced their standing in the minds of their followers. Drawing on the assumptions of attribution theory (Kelley, 1973), Lord and Maher (1991) suggest that perceiving the leader as more responsible for group success reinforces the overall perception of leadership capability. Heider (1958a) referred to this tendency as the "suasion of success": "Success convinces us of the worth of a person even if the success is largely due to chance circumstances" (p. 5).

The second main effect revealed that participants in the sabotaged materials condition attributed significantly less responsibility to their leaders than did those participants in the nonsabotaged materials condition ($b = 4.07$, $SE B = 1.41$, $\beta = 0.33$, $t = 2.89$, $p < .01$). Both main effects were qualified by the significant two-way interaction between performance information and sabotage ($b = -3.27$, $SE B = 1.41$, $\beta = -0.26$, $t = -2.32$, $p < .05$).

As shown in Figure 6.2, participants showed a tendency to defend their leader in the failure conditions, assigning them less responsibility

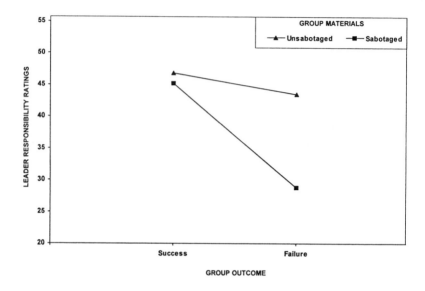

Figure 6.2. Ratings of Leader Responsibility for Group Performance, by Group Outcome and Treatment of Group Materials

for the group's poor performance. This defensive tendency, however, was particularly pronounced in the cases of leaders whose group materials were sabotaged, suggesting that discounting was affecting leadership attributions. However, leaders whose groups were successful in spite of sabotaged materials were not seen as more responsible than the other successful leaders, suggesting that augmentation was not affecting leadership attributions. Although not completely consistent with the predictions, our findings correspond with those of Phillips and Lord (1981), who also documented evidence of discounting but not augmentation in observer's perceptions of leaders. Thus, we have found additional support for Lord's (Lord & Maher, 1990, 1991) argument that more controlled inferential processing impacts perceptions of leaders. Rather than simply assigning blame for failure, participants recognized the odds against group success and made their attributions accordingly.

Contrary to expectations, there were no significant effects due to prototype matching. Once again, participants' implicit leadership

TABLE 6.2

Interaction Between Performance Information and Sabotaged Materials
on Participants' Responsibility Ratings of Self and the Group, Study 2

Predictor	Group Outcome		Analysis Summary
	Success	Failure	
Ratings of self			$b = -3.74, SE\ B = 1.16$
Sabotaged materials	41.09$_b$	31.67$_a$	$\beta = -0.40, t = -3.21, p < .005$
Unsabotaged materials	37.64$_b$	42.65$_b$	
Ratings of the group			$b = -3.28, SE\ B = 1.21$
Sabotaged materials	45.18$_b$	34.13$_a$	$\beta = -0.34, t = -2.72, p < .005$
Unsabotaged materials	41.21$_b$	43.41$_b$	

NOTE: The greater the mean, the more responsibility attributed to self or the group. Means without a single letter common subscript differ significantly at $p < .005$, according to Duncan's multiple range test.

theories, as measured by the SYMLOG instrument, failed to impact participants' perceptions of their group leaders. This finding contradicts Lord's theory (Lord & Maher, 1990, 1991). However, these results are consistent with those of Study 1 in which perceptions of leaders' effectiveness and collegiality were not significantly influenced by participants' leadership prototypes.

Perceptions Regarding Group Members

Moving away from attributions regarding leaders' responsibility, participants also responded to questionnaire items addressing their own responsibility and the responsibility of the rest of the group for the group's performance. These items were combined to form two aggregate scores and analyzed using stepwise multiple regression. In both cases, only one significant effect emerged: the interaction between performance information and sabotaged materials. Turning first to participants' ratings of their own responsibility for group outcome ($R^2 = .16$, $F(1,55) = 10.33$, $p = .005$; see Table 6.2), whether or not group materials were sabotaged appeared to be the deciding factor here. Participants were significantly less likely to blame themselves for group failure when group materials had been sabotaged. Participants' attributions of responsibility to their fellow group members were remarkably similar to their attributions for self, $R^2 = .12$, $F (1,55) = 7.38$, $p < .01$.

GENERAL DISCUSSION

The findings of both studies lend support to Lord's (Lord, 1985; Lord et al., 1978; Lord & Maher, 1990, 1991) argument that inference-based processes play a significant role in the perception of leaders. In our studies, varying performance information created differences in the participants' perceptions of leadership behavior when, objectively, there were none. These differences in perceptions suggest a clear outcome bias on the part of participants, in which actual behaviors were essentially ignored and only performance information was used to make judgments. The findings of Study 2, which required actual group members to evaluate their group leader, suggest that Lord's assumptions hold true in actual group interaction situations. In this study, followers' perceptions of their leaders were shaped by group success and failure, paralleling the well-documented effect of performance information on independent observers' perceptions (Larson, 1982; Larson et al., 1984; Phillips, 1984; Phillips & Lord, 1981). In addition, followers' perceptions after failure of the group were moderated by discounting information (i.e., sabotage of group materials), supporting Lord's claim that social perceivers engage in both automatic and controlled thinking as they evaluate leaders (Lord & Maher, 1990, 1991).

The transactional model of leadership (Hollander, 1985) would suggest that this influence of performance information has serious implications for the leadership situation in terms of the perceptions of followers (as well as superiors). Leaders must satisfy the needs—as well as the biases—of the followers and other participants in the leadership situation. In a world that is predominantly results oriented, one of these needs is likely to be that leaders provide positive outcomes. Leaders who bring about positive results for their followers are valued, regardless of the actual quality or nature of their leadership. Apparently Nietzsche was correct when he asserted that "success was always the greatest liar" (Klages, 1926, p. 86).

Turning to the recognition-based processes suggested by Lord (Lord, 1985; Lord & Maher, 1990, 1991), we expected that participants' implicit leadership theories, as represented by leadership prototypes, would influence participants' perceptions of stimulus leaders. Unfortunately, we did not find substantial evidence in either study that recognition-based processes were operating. Lord suggests that both inference- and recognition-based processes are equally likely to have an impact on leadership perceptions. The results of our studies, which varied both processes simultaneously, suggest that inference-based processes have far more influence.

There are a number of possible explanations for our not finding clear evidence of recognition-based processes in leadership perceptions. First, we did not test the effects of these processes in the manner typically pursued by Lord and his associates (Fraser & Lord, 1983; Lord, 1985; Lord et al., 1984). Operating on the assumption that individuals hold differing implicit theories (due, in part, to their differing experience with leaders; Calder, 1977; Eden & Leviatan, 1975; Lord & Maher, 1991), we attempted to measure participants' leadership prototypes before exposing them to the stimulus leaders. It is possible that the SYMLOG instrument was not a valid measure for these prototypes. However, in responding to this measure, the participants showed distinct patterns in their endorsement of leadership behaviors, suggesting that the SYMLOG measure was sensitive to at least some components of participants' implicit leadership theories. In addition, this measure has been used satisfactorily by Nye and Forsyth (1991) to tease out recognition-based differences in leadership perceptions. Still, in future studies, an additional instrument will be devised to measure participants' prototypes.

Secondly, the participants' implicit leadership theories may have been operating too well, causing them to recognize only those behaviors that matched their prototypes. Unfortunately, the merits of this possibility cannot be assessed because neither study included measures of participants' accuracy of recall for actual leader behaviors. Lord (1985) notes that in processing social information, the perceiver relies heavily on schemas and prototypes for directing attention and recalling observed behaviors. In the process, the perceiver may fail to recognize the differences between what is being viewed and what is expected to be viewed. Given this tendency, the perceiver may recall behaviors that were never actually exhibited by the stimulus leader. Whether this process is purposeful or not, Hanson (1980) pointed out that perceivers often make attributions that confirm already existing beliefs. This explanation would account for the rather positive ratings received by all leaders in both studies. Essentially, they would have matched to some degree participants' prototypes regardless of their behavior. However, participants' written responses in Study 1 do not necessarily support this alternative. For example, one participant in the good performance condition wrote, "I thought he was kind of weak," which suggests that participants may have recognized when leaders did not fit their prototype.

A final possible explanation for the apparent lack of prototype effects in either study is that performance information may have overshadowed the effects of the implicit theories. Perhaps the overwhelming evidence supplied by the positive and negative performance information caused participants to suspend judgment based on other factors. Chaplin, John, and Goldberg (1988) note that in processing social information and making judgments, the number of attributes that individuals use may vary. In some cases, multiple attributes are necessary to make a satisfactory judgment; they give the example of requiring several bits of evidence to determine whether an animal is a mammal, including having fur, bearing live young, and being warm-blooded. For other cases, however, only a single attribute may be sufficient to judge; for example, the number of calories in a given food may be sufficient criteria for judging its appropriateness for food to eat when dieting. In the case of evaluating leaders, outcome information might well be seen as irrefutable evidence of the leaders' strengths and weaknesses—participants would have no reason to process any further (Calder, 1977; Lord et al., 1978; Pfeffer, 1977). This possibility was tested in Study 1, where a control condition was built into the design. Participants' responses in this condition, however, were not significantly different from those of participants in the poor performance condition. In short, control condition participants showed no greater tendency to rely on their prototypes to evaluate stimulus leaders than did participants who received clear performance information.

Looking to the future, we are encouraged by the preliminary results of Study 2. They suggest that Lord's (Lord & Maher, 1990, 1991) assumptions about inference-based processes hold up when tested in actual interaction situations. Not just observers but group members themselves clearly take outcome information into account when evaluating their leaders. These findings represent a step forward in testing Lord's theory, a path that should continue to be pursued.

The small group may be the ideal setting for exploring Lord's (Lord & Maher, 1990, 1991) controlled recognition-based processes. In addition to providing close contact with the leader, small groups offer considerable opportunity for members to exchange information and impressions about their leaders. Thus, small groups provide a setting in which prototype matching can occur at both extremes of the automatic-controlled processes continuum: through information collected during individual contact with the leader and through socially shared information from other group members. Some researchers have already addressed the impact of social "consensus" information on perceptions of leaders. For example, Brown and Geis (1984) found that participants took group members' nonverbal reactions into account when judging stimulus leaders. Their evaluations of leadership quality were consistent with the implied emotional reactions of group members.

Moving beyond ad hoc groups, Lord's theory should be tested on the perceptions of followers in long-term groups. In the present studies, participants were apparently overly swayed by outcome information; however, in both cases the groups involved were clearly artificial. Because the availability of information suitable for leadership evaluation was strictly limited, the outcome information provided in both experiments may have been unusually salient to participants. We wonder whether this outcome bias would hold true in ongoing group situations. Lord and Maher (1991) hint that, under these conditions, the scales may be tipped in favor of recognition-based processes. As groups have greater opportunity to interact, leaders' traits and behaviors may become more salient. Over time, followers can share their leaders' triumphs and work together to recover from group failures. Studying followers' perceptions in ongoing group situations would allow researchers to see whether followers truly draw on their prototypes when evaluating leaders.

Presently, our most immediate research concern is to complete data collection for Study 2. Although our initial findings are interesting, we require additional data to fully test the hypotheses. Of particular interest will be testing the potential three-way interaction between outcome information, material sabotage, and prototype match. In addition, to date, only perceptions regarding female group leaders have been assessed. We are interested in seeing participants' reactions to male leaders. An extensive body of research (Bass, 1981; Brown, 1979; Deaux, 1984; Lord & Maher, 1991) suggests that participants will react more positively to male leaders. For example, Nye and Forsyth (1991) found subtle differences in participants' perceptions of male and female stimulus leaders. Both male and female leaders were perceived to be effective; however, some participants judged the female leader to be less collegial than the male leader, displaying a reluctance to work with her. Similar biases may become evident once data collection for Study 2 has been completed.

Continued research pursuing Lord's theory promises to help balance the traditional tendency in leadership research to focus on the influence of the leader (Bass, 1981; Hollander, 1985). More and more, researchers are beginning to recognize the importance of the other participants in the leadership equation (Hollander, 1985; Kouzes & Posner, 1990; Lord, 1985; Lord & Maher, 1990; Lord, Phillips, & Rush, 1980; Nye & Forsyth, 1991). For example, Geis and her associates (Geis, 1983; Geis, Boston, & Hoffman, 1985; Geis, Carter, & Butler, 1982) repeatedly emphasized the importance of leader recognition in leadership effectiveness. "Leadership, like achievement, is socially defined: It requires not only a good performance, but also social recognition of its value" (Geis et al., 1985, p. 636). This point is consistent with the transactional view of leadership, which suggests that group members' perceptions and acceptance of their leaders can have important effects on how leaders are able to carry out their responsibilities (Hollander, 1985; Lord & Maher, 1990). In short, "leadership is in the eye of the follower" (Kouzes & Posner, 1990, p. 29).

Note

1. Cohen and Cohen (1983) and Aiken and West (1991) recommend this method for interpreting significant interactions involving one dichotomous and one continuous variable. We have determined separate regression lines for each of the two performance information conditions and compared the slopes for each.

Perceptual Sets and Stimulus Values
The Social Relations Model
in Group Psychotherapy

MARIANNE E. JOHNSON
ROBERT A. NEIMEYER

As Fiske and Goodwin point out in the Introduction to this volume, social psychology has been concerned from its very beginning—in theory, at least—with such cognitive phenomena as the "interplay of minds" and the "interstimulation" of individuals in social contexts. Yet they also note that, ironically, most social psychological research on groups has been unsophisticated about contemporary developments in social cognition, just as re-

AUTHORS' NOTE: This study began while the first author was funded by Social Sciences and Humanities Research Council of Canada Doctoral Fellowships 452-85-1089 and 453-8S0309. Project data were collected by the second author and his colleagues with the support of NIMH grant 5-RP1-MH40477-02. Finally, the completion of the present study was funded by the Manitoba Mental Health Research Foundation Grant #2526. Thanks are due to each of these funding sources, as well as to Andrew Cook, Neharika Vohra, and Dano Demare for their work with data analysis and to Jim Nickels for his invaluable input.

154

search in social cognition has failed to deal adequately with actual interaction. This inattention to naturalistic interaction and intersubjectivity, in combination with the marginalization of affect in the majority of studies, has resulted in a social cognitive research literature that is only trivially "social" insofar as it ignores the dynamics of interdependence among people engaged in a meaningful social process (Ickes & Gonzalez, Chapter 12, this volume).

Our goal in this chapter is to help redress these limitations in much of the existing literature in social cognition by analyzing patterns of interpersonal perception in one emotionally significant naturalistic setting, namely, group psychotherapy. By applying a promising social cognitive model for delineating the sources of interdependent perceptions among group members, we hope to clarify the extent to which such interpersonal processes are driven by characteristics of the perceivers, targets, and their unique relationships to one another in the larger group context. Moreover, by comparing these sources of variance in interpersonal judgments to group member self-ratings and social adjustment, we will attempt to link the emergent social phenomena of interpersonal perceptions to individual characteristics of the group members. We will conclude by discussing the potential of promoting more conceptual and methodological exchange between the fields of social cognition and group therapy research, each of which could enrich the other.

THE SOCIAL RELATIONS MODEL

Until recently, empirical social cognitive research on groups was impeded not only by the individualistic bias of social cognitive theories but also by the constraints of available statistical techniques, which assumed independence among data being analyzed. In the traditional ANOVA design, for example, interactants can serve as subjects or objects of social perception but not both (Marcus & Kashy, 1995). Thus, if only for analytic reasons, it is unsurprising that the prototypical social cognitive study involves an isolated subject sitting alone in a cubicle and responding to trial exposures of contrived social stimuli rather than a more complex design assessing the inter-dependence of social cognition in interacting dyads or groups (Ickes & Gonzalez, Chapter 12, this volume).

However, the past decade has seen the development of powerful new conceptual and statistical models for analyzing the nonindependent observations endemic to naturalistic interaction. One such procedure is the social relations model (SRM) (Kenny & LaVoie, 1984; Malloy & Kenny, 1986), which takes into account each individual's contribution to the social process, the interdependent nature of their interaction, and the uniqueness of their dyadic relationship. This model distinguishes between two levels of analysis: (a) the individual level, which includes both how one characteristically responds to others (called the actor or *perceiver* effect) and how one tends to be perceived by others (the target or *partner* effect) and (b) the relational level, which assesses how one person uniquely relates to the other person (the *dyadic* effect). For example, Alex's liking of Bob will be affected by how much Alex tends to like others in general, how much Bob tends to be liked by others in general, and, controlling for these individual differences, how much Alex's liking for Bob is unique to their relationship.[1] Any or all of these effects may account for the rating of an interpersonal variable.

One reason for the relative rarity of analyses using the SRM is that the procedure imposes stringent design requirements in order to model the various kinds of nonindependence that arise in interaction settings, requirements that are rarely met by studies in any area of social psychology or small group research. Estimation of these effects is achieved by variance partitioning, which requires a group design with at least four persons per group, completing ratings on a mini-mum of two occasions. Moreover, to obtain stable estimates of social relations parameters, a minimum of six groups with four to eight members each is required (Kenny, 1990a). Data to be analyzed (e.g., eye contact among group members or interpersonal perceptions) are then collected using a suitable methodology (e.g., behavioral obser-vations or intermember ratings) using a round-robin design, wherein all subjects respond to all other subjects in the group, in effect serving as both actor or perceiver and partner in all possible dyads. Descrip-tions of the multivariate round-robin analysis of variance are found in Warner, Kenny, and Stoto (1979) and Kenny and LaVoie (1984).

Studies of interpersonal perception that fail to use the social relations model can produce equivocal results by relying on such measures as simple correlations between ratings of liking completed by acquaintances. For example, in a study of attraction between college students, the reciprocity hypothesis that "liking begets liking" was not supported when attraction ratings were simply intercorrelated ($r = .196$), but when ratings were partitioned using the SRM, the reciprocity hypothesis received strong support (Kenny & Nasby, 1980). Although perceiver and partner effects approached significance, the dyadic effect was highly significant, and the correlation of dyadic effects (an estimate of unique dyadic reciprocity) was .617. This demonstrates how small and inconsistent correlations between interpersonal variables may be due to a confounding of the individual and dyadic levels of analysis that conceals distinctive dyadic effects and that fails to separate either from effects attributable to random error. The methodology and statistics to model these sources of variance were not easily available until the development of the SRM.

Depending on the intent of the study, investigators may be interested in the separate contributions of perceivers, their partners, or the unique relationship between pairs of individuals (i.e., the dyadic effect). For example, researchers in group therapy might be concerned with the degree to which a particular client's perceptions of others are driven by the client's own rigid perceptual system, as formulated by such concepts as transference, projection, or cognitive distortion within various psychotherapeutic traditions. Within the SRM, a tendency toward an *assimilation* bias of this kind would be reflected in a large perceiver effect (Marcus & Holahan, 1994). On the other hand, social psychologists interested in group stereotyping might focus on the degree to which agreement emerges within an ethnically diverse group of subjects about the characteristics of each member. Such a *consensus* effect would be registered as a high percentage of variance attributed to the partner. As a final illustration, psychologists studying the development of interpersonal attraction or friendship formation might be particularly concerned with the unique *dyadic* interaction between specific pairs of interactants once their individual perceptual sets and general stimulus values were controlled. Again, the dyadic effect within the SRM would provide uncontaminated data relevant to such a research question. Of course, because the SRM simultaneously estimates the variance attributed to all of these sources, hybrid hypotheses that examine their interrelationship can also be addressed. For example, if one were interested in the phenomenon of interpersonal feedback in psychotherapy groups, one could examine the variance in feedback attributable to senders (actors) and receivers (partners) and then correlate these effects to see whether members who gave the most feedback also received the most feedback from others (Marcus & Kashy, 1995). In summary, the SRM provides a sophisticated conceptual and statistical model that permits the analysis of interdependent responses within small groups in a way that enhances their amenability to social cognitive analysis.

To date, the SRM has been applied to a limited range of social psychological problems, with an emphasis on interpersonal percep-tions among group members. Although the pattern is not entirely clear, the significance of the perceiver, partner, and dyadic compo-nents appears to depend on the type of variables being studied and the degree of acquaintanceship between subjects. In earlier literature reviews (Kenny & LaVoie, 1984; Malloy & Kenny, 1986) as well as more recent studies, significant perceiver effects are reported for ratings of attraction in short-term acquaintances, self-disclosure on low-intimacy topics and in limited acquaintance dyads, and dominance or submission among group members. Significant partner effects are found for vari-ables such as friendliness, physical attractiveness, openness and intelli-gence, and nonverbal expressiveness (Marcus & Holahan, 1994; Miller & Kenny, 1986; Reno & Kenny, 1992).

Although the great majority of SRM research has been with nonclinical samples, the model naturally applies to group psychother-apy. Studies by Wright and Ingraham with graduate students in experiential training groups reported significant actor effects for anxiety and questioning (Ingraham & Wright, 1986, 1987), partner effects for attraction (Wright, Ingraham, & Blackmer, 1985), and both effects for self-disclosure (Ingraham & Wright, 1986). For one affiliation measure, only dyadic effects were significant (Wright & Ingraham, 1986). Similarly, in one of the few clinical studies, Ingraham and Wright (1987) found only dyadic effects for anxiety in a six-member therapy group in which clients were well acquainted. On the other hand, Marcus and Holahan (1994), with a larger sample of group therapy clients completing ratings early in therapy, reported significant perceiver and partner effects for each of the dimensions of Kiesler's (1983) interpersonal circle (dominance, hostility, submissiveness, and friendliness). However, their assessment of these dimensions at a single point in time prevented them from examining the degree to which such ratings were responsive to the unique "chemistry" of particular dyads. In general then, the SRM offers a promising model for elucidating some of the more subtle dynamics of group process, one that could have particular relevance to the study of group therapy.

BACKGROUND TO THE PRESENT STUDY

In response to the call for social cognitive analyses of naturalistic interaction within small groups, we undertook an analysis of interpersonal perceptions within multiple group therapies at two points in time, thereby providing the first such analysis with a clinical sample meeting the full design requirements of the social relations model. Moreover, by focusing on group therapies whose adult members shared the experience of sexual victimization in childhood, we sought to ensure that the study would meet the criterion of emotionally meaningful interaction among members—in this case, about some of the most intimate particulars of the group members' lives. In summary, we hoped to demonstrate the methodological feasibility of SRM analysis of data of equal relevance to both social and clinical researchers.

Before reviewing the clinical literature of most direct relevance to this study, one additional methodological factor deserves at least brief consideration. As Ickes and Gonzalez (see Chapter 12, this volume) point out, "The assessment of cognitive responses [in a way that respects their interdependence in social groups] is not a trivial task." Among the approaches they cite as appropriate to this task is Kelly's role construct repertory grid or *repgrid* (Fransella & Bannister, 1977; Neimeyer, 1993), a technique for measuring interpersonal construing that has been extensively applied in both the social and clinical areas (Mancuso & Shaw, 1988; Winter, 1992). In particular, a long line of research on the acquaintance process from a personal construct perspective has successfully adapted repertory grids to analyze the convergence of interpersonal perceptions among interactants and its role in relationship growth or decline (Harter, Neimeyer, & Alexander, 1989; Neimeyer & Mitchell, 1988; Neimeyer & Neimeyer, 1981, 1983, 1985, 1986; Neimeyer, Neimeyer, & Landfield, 1983; see Neimeyer, Brooks, & Baker, 1996, for a review and extension of this literature). In these applications, interactants in naturally occurring settings (e.g., college dormitories), existing groups (e.g., families), or experimentally constructed contexts (e.g., "getting acquainted" groups) complete repertory grids using a set of personal or provided construct dimensions (e.g., friendly vs. aloof; understands me vs. misunderstands me) on which each group member, including the self, is individually rated at one or more points in time. If such grids incorporate identical constructs for all members of the group, if the group includes four or more members, and if all group members are rated at two or more points in time, then these data are ideally suited for analysis using the social relations model. We therefore applied the SRM to round-robin repertory grid ratings of participants in group therapy for incest survivors.

Group Psychotherapy With Incest Survivors

Sexual abuse during childhood, particularly incest, is associated with long-term problems, including depression, anxiety, poor self-esteem, interpersonal difficulties, sexual dysfunction, revictimization, and substance abuse (Browne & Finkelhor, 1986; Harter, Alexander, & Neimeyer, 1988). Given the interpersonal difficulties of many adult survivors seeking treatment, group therapy is often recommended (Courtois, 1988). Alexander, Neimeyer, Follette, Moore, and Harter (1989) conducted the first systematic investigation of the efficacy of time-limited group psychotherapy with incest survivors, comparing two forms of time-limited (10 sessions) group psychotherapy with a wait-list control group. One therapy approach was the Interpersonal

Transaction format with weekly round-robin discussions of incest-related topics (Neimeyer, 1988), whereas the other was a process format based on Courtois's (1988) clinical work with incest survivors and Yalom's (1985) interpersonal model of group therapy. Clients were recruited through the media; exclusion criteria included high suicide risk, psychosis, and severe substance abuse; and 65 adult female incest survivors were randomly assigned to a therapy or control condition. There were eight therapy groups, four of each type, each led by two female cotherapists. Psychological functioning was assessed at intake, termination, and a 6-month follow-up. After sessions 2 and 9, clients rated self, each group member, and each therapist using a repertory grid that included 10 interpersonal dimensions important to group therapy (Neimeyer, Harter, & Alexander, 1991; see Table 7.1). Although both group formats seemed to possess some unique advantages (Alexander, Neimeyer, & Follette, 1991), outcome data demonstrated that both treatments were generally more effective than the wait-list control in alleviating depression and distress, gains that were maintained at follow-up (Alexander et al., 1989). To complement this emphasis on outcome, Neimeyer et al. (1991) examined the role of process variables derived from interpersonal perceptions of the 49 treatment subjects during therapy. Because analyses suggested that the two group formats were not significantly different, they were collapsed for further analysis. Controlling for pretherapy status, more negative and extreme perceptions of other group members and therapists (especially in the early weeks of therapy) were associated with poorer outcome on a variety of measures. A comprehensive review of this multifaceted research program has recently been provided by Harter and Neimeyer (1995).

A Social Relations Model Analysis of Group Psychotherapy

To assess the contribution of perceiver, partner, and dyadic effects to interpersonal ratings made by clients on the repertory grid during group therapy, we analyzed client ratings of each other after the second and ninth sessions using the SRM. To understand these findings within the context of client functioning, we then correlated

TABLE 7.1

Means, Standard Deviations,
and Factor Loadings for Group Grid Items ($N = 49$)

| Group Grid Item | Raw Scores | | Factor Loadings | | |
	Mean	SD	Nur-turant	Depend-able	With-drawn
Dominant/*Submissive*	5.81	3.05	.040	−.396	.811
Shows feelings/*Hides feelings*	5.24	3.18	−.323	.105	.788
Depend on others/					
Others depend on	7.86	3.02	.077	.807	.025
Good/Poor relationship with men	6.21	3.40	−.611	−.376	.135
Attacking/*Comforting*	9.55	2.45	.740	.015	.242
Intelligent/Unintelligent	2.99	1.80	−.691	−.253	.310
Sincere/Insincere	2.81	1.76	−.730	.071	.367
Mentally ill/*Mentally stable*	10.07	2.33	.646	.391	−.070
Cold/*Warm*	10.03	2.32	.703	−.051	−.156
Vulnerable/*Not vulnerable*	6.23	3.42	.101	.798	−.168

NOTE: Italics indicate direction of loading for factor analysis. Range for Group Grid ratings is from 1 to 13 with 7 being the 0 point on the original rating system from −6 to +6.

significant rater and ratee effects with client self-ratings on the repgrid as well as with pretherapy measures of symptomatic functioning, social adjustment, and self-esteem. Our main hypothesis was that individual characteristics of the rater and ratee as assessed by the perceiver and partner effects, respectively, would account for significant proportions of the rating variance in addition to that accounted for by the unique relationships between clients. In addition, we were interested in the degree to which assimilation and consensus effects—in particular interpersonal ratings—would be related to self-ratings of individual members on various measures of social adjustment.

METHOD

Subjects

Forty-nine women completed the group therapy treatments. As reported in Neimeyer et al. (1991, p. 151), their average age was 36 years (*SD* = 8.4), and they averaged 13.7 years of education (*SD* = 3.08). In terms of marital status, 39% were single, 39% married, and 22% divorced. Racially, 69% were white, 27% black, and 4% Hispanic. On average, the sexual abuse experienced by these women lasted 7.2 years (*SD* = 5.4), with onset of the abuse occurring prior to age 6 for a third of the subjects, between ages 6 and 11 for half, and during adolescence for the remainder. Types of abuse included fondling only (35%), oral/genital contact (18%), and sexual intercourse (47%). Abusers were natural father (63%), stepfather (27%), and other male relative (10%). Thus, the typical group member was in her 30s with a long and severe pattern of abuse by a father figure that began at an early age. With reference to the present study, because SRM analyses cannot handle missing data (Kenny, 1990b) and because some interpersonal ratings were incomplete, sample size ranged from 40 to 46, with 4 to 7 subjects per group, depending on the interpersonal variable.

Measures

The *Social Adjustment Scale* (SAS) is based on a semistructured interview assessing a number of areas, including work, social activities, family and marital relationships, and parental roles (Weissman & Paykel, 1974). Trained raters viewed videotapes of structured pretherapy interviews with group members and assigned each a global rating of social adjustment ranging from 1 (excellent adjustment) to 7 (very severe maladjustment) with very high interrater reliability (Cronbach's alpha = .90).

The *Global Severity Index* (GSI) is an overall index of psychological disturbance derived from the Symptom Checklist-90-Revised, a 90-item, self-report inventory assessing current symptomatology and using a 5-point rating scale from 0 ("not at all") to 4 ("extremely"). Internal consistency and test-retest reliability are good to excellent (Derogatis, 1983). Higher scores represent greater disturbance.

The *Self-Ideal Discrepancy* (SID) score provides a measure of self-esteem based on an adaptation of the repertory grid (Harter et al., 1988; see Fransella & Bannister, 1977, and Neimeyer, 1993, for an introduction to grid technique). Subjects used a 13-point rating scale ranging from −6 to +6 to rate self and ideal self on the self-grid, which consisted of 10 standardized, bipolar interpersonal constructs drawn from the clinical literature on incest (e.g., attractive vs. unattractive, weak vs. strong, dominant vs. submissive). Negativity of self-concept was operationalized as the euclidean distance score between the self and ideal self ratings, with higher scores indicating poorer self-concept.

The *Group Grid* is also an adaptation of the role construct repertory grid. Perceptions of self and others are rated on 10 standardized, bipolar constructs representing interpersonal dimensions pertinent to group therapy (see Table 7.1) using a 13-point scale ranging from −6 to +6 (Neimeyer et al., 1991). In the present study, this measure was factor analyzed as described below to yield interpretable clusters of interpersonal perceptions that were then subjected to SRM analysis.

Procedure

After completing the SAS, GSI, and SID[2], subjects were randomly assigned to one of eight groups in the treatment conditions with some constraints due to scheduling. After sessions 2 and 9 (referred to as Time 1 and Time 2) of the 10-session therapy groups, each subject rated herself and all other clients in her group on the Group Grid.

Principal components analysis of the Group Grid items was used to identify coherent factors within the grid to be subjected to further analysis. The SRM analysis of each factor score is a multivariate round-robin analysis of variance computed by the FORTRAN program called SOREMO (Kenny, 1990b). Each effect (perceiver, partner, and dyad or relationship) was estimated by the group, and the mean of these estimates was tested for its difference from zero using degrees of freedom equal to N minus the number of groups minus one. Only effect estimates accounting for a significant proportion of the variance can be interpreted in subsequent correlations with other measures. The SOREMO program was also used to compute partial correlations (with group effects partialled out) of the effect estimates with self- and pretherapy ratings; significance tests used a conservative two-tailed t-test with degrees of freedom as noted above.

RESULTS

Because group members' perceptions of one another were largely favorable, Group Grid ratings showed extreme skewness and kurtosis. Scores were converted from a bipolar to a unipolar scale (i.e., with ratings ranging from 1 to 13), and log transformation yielded a more approximately normal distribution. The optimal factor solution, based on session 2 ratings, contained three factors accounting for 64% of the total variance. As can be seen in Table 7.1, items loaded .60 or higher on one factor and did not overlap with other factors. The three factors were labeled *Nurturant* (with six items accounting for 30% of total variance), *Dependable* (with two items accounting for 18% of the variance), and *Withdrawn* (with two items accounting for 16% of the variance). Factor scores were computed with items loading significantly (greater than .60) on the given factor using standardized factor loadings and log transformed scores.

The results of the SRM analyses for the three relationship factors at Time 1 and Time 2 are presented in Table 7.2. Nine of the 12 perceiver and partner effects were significant. Fewer significant effects were found early (after session 2) as compared to later (after session 9) in therapy. Early in therapy, the only significant perceiver effect was for the Nurturant factor, whereas the partner effect was significant for Dependable and Withdrawn. Thus, subjects appeared to have a characteristic style (or rater bias) in their perceptions of others as nurturant but not as dependable or withdrawn. These results also suggest that subjects had a characteristic social stimulus value (a ratee bias) in how others perceived their dependability and withdrawal but not their nurturance. However, several sessions later, perceiver *and* partner effects were significant for all three relationship factors, suggesting that near the end of therapy perceptual sets had been established in how each client viewed others and how each was viewed by other clients.

As shown in Table 7.2, the relationship component for Time 1 and Time 2 includes the dyadic effect and error variance. Estimation of the dyadic effect requires repeated ratings to assess the stable relationship variance (shown under the "Dyadic" effect column). As

TABLE 7.2
Perceiver, Partner, and Dyadic Components for SRM Analyses

Factor	Perceiver	Partner	Relationship[a]	Dyadic[bc]
Nurturant[d]				
Time 1	.465*	.098	.437	
				.140*
Time 2	.389*	.082*	.529	
Dependable[e]				
Time 1	.145	.317*	.538	
				.117*
Time 2	.275*	.335*	.389	
Withdrawn[f]				
Time 1	.221	.433*	.347	
				.023
Time 2	.161*	.409*	.431	

a. Includes error variance.
b. Stable variance without error across Time 1 and Time 2.
c. $df = 7$.
d. $df = 31$.
e. $df = 35$.
f. $df = 37$.
*$p < .05$, one-tailed.

indicated in the table, a significant dyadic effect emerged for the Nurturant and Dependable dimensions, after the variance attributable to perceiver and partner effects (or rater and ratee bias) was taken into account. This suggests that despite perceptual sets and stimulus values characteristic of individual clients, the unique interpersonal relationships occurring within dyads of group members influenced perceptions of one another's dependability and nurturance during the group interaction.

Table 7.3 presents correlations of significant perceiver and partner effects with self-ratings on the repertory grid-based interpersonal factors and pretherapy measures. Looking first at the correlations between ratings of self and others on the interpersonal factors, the perceiver effect for Nurturant significantly correlated with self-ratings at Time 1 and Time 2, but the partner effect (Time 2 only) did not. Conversely, for Dependable and Withdrawn, the partner

TABLE 7.3

Correlation of Significant Perceiver and Partner Components
With Self-Ratings and Pretherapy Functioning

			Pretherapy Measures		
Relationship Factor	*Time*	*Self-Rating*	*SAS*	*SID*	*GSI*
Nurturant[a]					
Perceiver	Time 1	.65*	.09	.15	-.02
Partner	Time 2	.41*	.17	.57**	.07
—	Time 2	.45	-.09	-.38	.02
Dependable[b]					
Perceiver	—				
Partner	Time 2	.15	.26	.05	-.09
	Time 1	.46*	-.45*	-.30	-.17
	Time 2	.42*	-.39*	-.34	-.30
Withdrawn[c]					
Perceiver	—				
Partner	Time 2	.01	-.31	-.54**	-.24
	Time 1	.41*	.44*	.13	-.15
	Time 2	.53*	.32	.20	.05

NOTE: — indicates no entry as effect estimate nonsignificant.
a. $df = 31$.
b. $df = 35$.
c. $df = 37$.
*$p < .05$, two-tailed; **$p < .01$, two-tailed.

effect rather than the perceiver effect significantly correlated with self-ratings, early and late in therapy. Thus, for Nurturance, perception of self is congruent with one's perception of others, whereas for Dependable and Withdrawn, perception of self corresponds not with one's perceptions of others but rather with others' perceptions of oneself.

Referring now to pretherapy status in Table 7.3, the SAS significantly correlated with partner effects for Dependable (Time 1 and Time 2) and Withdrawn (Time 1 only) but not Nurturant and did not correlate with any of the perceiver effects. The correlation was negative with Dependable, such that the greater their social maladjustment prior to therapy, the less clients were perceived as dependable by other group members both early and late in therapy. The correlation was positive with Withdrawn such that greater maladjustment prior to therapy was associated with more withdrawn ratings early in therapy, but this correlation was not significant later in therapy. It may be important to note that the SAS is rated by trained clinical raters, unlike the client-rated SID and GSI.

The SID correlated significantly at Time 2 with the perceiver effects for Nurturant and Withdrawn but not Dependable. Thus, the lower a client's self-esteem prior to entering therapy, the more she perceived others as nurturant and the less she viewed others as withdrawn when therapy was coming to an end. Early in therapy, the correlation was not significant for Nurturant. The GSI did not correlate significantly with effects for any relationship factor.

DISCUSSION

Consistent with SRM research (Malloy & Kenny, 1986; Marcus & Holahan, 1994), the results of this study support the main hypothesis that perceiver and partner effects account for significant proportions of the variance when clients in group therapy rate their relationships with other participants in their group. However, our findings also indicate the presence of a significant dyadic effect on relationship ratings once these more individualistic factors are taken into account. Thus, to the extent that perceptions of other group participants are predictive of outcomes in group therapy (Neimeyer et al., 1991), the present findings are important in demonstrating that such perceptions are attributable to both individual and relational factors.

In addition, a very interesting differential pattern emerged in connection with the three distinguishable dimensions of interpersonal judgment derived from the repertory grid: Nurturant, Dependable, and Withdrawn. In general, perceptions of nurturance, to a greater extent than perceptions of dependability or withdrawal, tended to be "in the eye of the beholder." This was reflected in the unusually large percentage of variance associated with the perceiver effect for nurturance, which was two to three times larger than is typical in SRM analyses (Marcus & Holahan, 1994). Reinforcing this conclusion is the fact that these perceiver effects on the Nurturant factor correlated only with self-ratings rather than ratings by external observers, further suggesting that they are relatively "subjective" dimensions of judgment. In contrast, ratings of dependability and withdrawal were characterized by much smaller perceiver effects, instead being characterized by substantial partner effects and reliable relationships to independent expert ratings of social maladjustment. In combination, these results suggest that, at least in the context of these group therapies, perceptions—of how comforting, sincere, or nurturant other members are—are driven substantially by the perceptual set of individual members, moderated to some extent by their idiosyncratic interactions with particular partners. On the other hand, perceptions of dependability and withdrawal (submissiveness and tendency to hide feelings) are more "objectively" determined by members' ingroup behavior in the sense that substantial consensus exists concerning ratings of group members on these dimensions. Interestingly, the stimulus value of particular members on the latter factors also converge with clinical ratings of social adjustment, with members who are least dependable and most withdrawn in the eyes of the group being those who judges considered most dysfunctional in a range of social relationships.

Although these results are provocative, a few limitations of this study need to be acknowledged for the benefit of future investigators who attempt to replicate or extend our work. Because of the focus of the original research on which our analysis was based (i.e., the process and outcome of group therapy for incest survivors), the sample was all female, spanning a range of traditional psychiatric diagnoses (particularly including mood disorders, anxiety disorders, and borderline conditions). These unique characteristics of the sample obviously constrain generalization of our results to populations that differ substantially from the women who participated in the current study. At a methodological level, the measure of interpersonal perceptions, the Group Grid, requires further validation in spite of the promising performance of repertory grids in numerous studies of group psychotherapy (Winter, 1992). For this reason, as well as the complications introduced into a factor analysis with bipolar items, the relationship factors identified in our study (i.e., nurturance, dependability, and withdrawal) should be considered preliminary. In addition, the relationship measure assesses interpersonal perceptions, not behaviors per se. Replication with other psychometrically developed measures such as the self-report and observer-coded forms for the Structural Analysis of Social Behavior (Benjamin, 1974)[3] or the Impact Message Inventory (Kiesler, 1983) would further facilitate the articulation of the SRM findings with interpersonal theory. Finally, repertory grid ratings were completed after the second and ninth sessions of therapy. Although even this degree of attention to changing psychotherapy process is rare in round-robin studies of psychotherapy groups, important changes in perceptions and relationships very likely occurred between these two assessment points that were not detectable in the present study. In terms of the SRM, the dyadic effect is estimated through stability within dyadic ratings across time, and ratings after two successive sessions are likely to provide a more sensitive assessment of dyadic effects (Kenny & LaVoie, 1984). For this reason, our findings may represent a conservative estimate of the variance in group member ratings attributable to the unique relationship between interactants.

These limitations notwithstanding, as one of the very few applications of the SRM to a "real" client sample in group psychotherapy, the implications of this study are both sobering and exciting. They are sobering because of the demonstration that relationship ratings reflect individual differences in group members' perceptual sets and stimulus values, in addition to genuinely relational features of their interaction, but they are also exciting because of the potential of the SRM to allow a more detailed and accurate assessment of interpersonal perception and its association with self-perception and clinical symptomatology.

THE SOCIAL RELATIONS MODEL AND GROUP THERAPY RESEARCH: A TWO-WAY STREET IN SEARCH OF TRAFFIC

Having demonstrated the application of the social relations model to research in group therapy, we will close by considering some potential advantages of promoting a greater interchange between these two largely nonoverlapping literatures. In our view, conceptual exchange between researchers in the two fields, and particularly collaboration in the study of group therapy process and outcome, could be helpful in advancing the research agendas of both areas. For convenience, we will summarize these under a series of headings indicating advantages of this joint effort to one or both fields of investigation.

"Real-World" Relevance

For social cognition researchers concerned with the constraints of laboratory-based studies of minimal or entirely hypothetical social "encounters," group therapy provides an emotionally meaningful (and often emotionally intense) interactive context to study. Although the laboratory offers obvious advantages in terms of experimental control over relevant variables, generalization of effects to the group therapy setting would enhance the external validity of such studies. For example, laboratory-based research might suggest that experimental induction of depressive mood results in greater attribution of negative or critical opinions to a hypothetical target or confederate, whereas the induction of positive mood reverses this attribution bias. Evaluating this effect in the context of an actual or analogue therapy group (e.g., by manipulating mood and then conducting ratings of group members using the SRM) should result in significant differences in the magnitude of perceiver effects for positive and negative attributions under the two mood conditions. Of course, any studies of this kind must be conducted with careful attention to the ethical demands of working with potentially vulnerable individuals, particularly in a clinical setting. But extension of social cognitive findings to group therapy directly addresses the expressed need of social cognitive theorists to study interdependent processes in meaningful naturalistic contexts.

Rater Bias in Psychotherapy Research

In psychotherapy research, the issue of bias by the client and/or therapist in rating their relationship has received little systematic attention. The difference between the client and therapist perspectives (as well as observer) has been recognized (e.g., Orlinsky &

Howard, 1986), but the contributions of individual and dyadic factors as delineated by the SRM have not been addressed. However, the SRM perspective provides a better understanding of the extent to which ratings made by group participants reflect their individual perceptual sets, normative judgments about particular group members, or factors unique to the interaction of specific dyads. Unfortunately, given the requirement of rating multiple partners, the SRM can only be applied to research on group, as opposed to individual, psychotherapy. However, the SRM analysis of interpersonal ratings in group therapy could have important implications for research investigating similar interpersonal constructs in individual psychotherapy.

Interpersonal Rigidity in Group Therapy

Virtually all schools of psychotherapy emphasize the role of rigid perceptual tendencies overdetermined by past experience (whether formulated as transference, projection, or cognitive distortion) that are relatively insensitive to the nuances of particular relationships. Likewise, many therapy traditions seek to identify maladaptive interpersonal patterns (e.g., submissiveness, hostility) and examine their relationship to psychopathology. As a nomothetic technique, the SRM cannot detect individual differences in such assimilation or consensus biases among group members, but it can be useful in identifying what dimensions of group perception or interaction are most likely to be driven by rigid individual response sets or how such sets might change across the course of several sessions of interaction or under different formats of therapy. Furthermore, correlating actor/perceiver and partner effects with methodologically independent measures of self-schemas or psychological adjustment can elucidate the subtle interconnection of interpersonal behavior, self-perception, impression formation, and psychological functioning, which is the focus of considerable contemporary interest (Safran, 1990; Strupp & Binder, 1984).

Just as perceiver and partner effects may provide an index of interpersonal rigidity, the SRM estimation of the dyadic effect may provide a measure of interpersonal flexibility (i.e., the ability to relate uniquely to different individuals). If so, then one might predict that such flexibility in responses among group members might be associated with favorable therapy outcome. This and related hypotheses linking process to outcome deserve attention in future research.

Social Cognitive Factors in Interpersonal Attraction

Cognitively oriented theories of the development of interpersonal relationships often posit similarity or convergence of partners' cognitive structures (Duck, 1977) or perceptions of others (Neimeyer et al., 1996) as one important determinant of interpersonal attraction. The pursuit of such hypotheses using the SRM in the context of group therapy could permit investigators to examine the degree to which groups having higher degrees of consensus also are typified by higher mutual attraction, cohesion, or related group processes among their members. For its own part, the field of group therapy might offer specific group structures that could optimize the implementation of SRM designs. For example, use of an Interpersonal Transaction group format (Neimeyer, 1988), which regulates the frequency, duration, and topical content of round-robin dyadic interactions within a small group without sacrificing the reality of face-to-face interactions, represents an ideal context for the implementation of the SRM, whether the focus is on the dynamics of attraction or any other measure of interdependent behavior among participants.

CONCLUSION

A consistent theme running throughout the current volume is that research in social cognition and in small group behavior potentially have much to offer to one another and that a rapprochement of these curiously insular fields is long overdue. In keeping with this perspective, we have sought to illustrate the advantages of applying one particular social cognitive approach—the social relations model—to an emotionally significant context of relevance to both group theorists and clinicians, namely, group psychotherapy. By examining patterns of mutual repertory grid ratings of group members in a way that modeled, rather than eliminated, various sources of nonindependence among them, we were able to clarify the extent to which particular dimensions of social appraisal in such groups were most susceptible to the influence of the perceptual sets of group members, their normative stimulus values, and the unique relational nuances of particular dyads. Moreover, our preliminary comparison of these sources of variation to methodologically independent self-ratings and clinical judgments suggests that such perceiver and partner effects might meaningfully relate to client self-concept and social maladjustment, at least within the sample of incest survivors that were the focus of our study.

In conclusion, our experience in using the SRM to deepen and clarify the statistically and conceptually challenging study of group process has persuaded us that it has considerable potential for research into group therapy, just as the domain of group therapy may be uniquely amenable to social cognitive analysis. We hope that other investigators will join us in cultivating this terrain and promoting the cross-fertilization of both perspectives.

Notes

1. The rating of liking also includes a constant for the group as well as an error term. The structural model for the rating of liking (X_{ijk}) is then as follows: $X_{ijk} = C + a_i + b_j + ab_{ij} + e_{ijk}$, where C represents the group constant, a_i the actor effect, b_j the partner effect, ab_{ij} the dyadic effect, and e_{ijk} the error term for occasion k.

2. To avoid unnecessary loss of data, missing values for one SAS and one GSI (two different subjects) were replaced by estimates based on the multiple regression for each measure using the posttherapy score as the predictor and the pretherapy score as the criterion.

3. In a study using the SRM based on the SASB, preliminary findings also have shown significant actor and partner effects (Johnson, 1993). Although the measure is both psychometrically and theoretically rigorous, the sample on which the study was based was not a clinical one.

Social Cognition and Self-Concept
A Socially Contextualized Model of Identity

DAPHNA OYSERMAN
MARTIN J. PACKER

"To grow up in Pendleton, New York, is to know oneself distinctly marginal; wherever the fountainheads of significance, . . . they are surely not here, nor are they even within easy driving distance."

—Oates (1995), on Timothy James McVeigh,
chief suspect in the recent bombing
in Oklahoma City, Oklahoma

W hat is social about social cognition? Our answer to this question is twofold: the identity of the cognizer and the process whereby this identity is constructed and maintained. In the above quote, Oates implies that we define ourselves in terms of what is possible given where we are located in time and space. Psychologists have tended to study the social thinker in isolation and to take for granted the nature of this thinker. Even developmental psychologists like Piaget have assumed both an underlying

175

"epistemic subject" unchanged by the course of development, and that development is an individual cognitive process. In this way, psychologists have neglected the ways in which cognition has a social character and the social origins of the individual thinker. In a word, they have essentialized the individual (Harre & Gillett, 1994). Following Erez and Earley (1993, p. vii), we will argue that although a sense of self is universal, its definition is shaped according to cultural values and perspectives. Although the examples we will use come primarily from the universe of children, youth, and adolescence researchers in an array of applied fields have called for attention to the intersubjective construction of self and behavior (e.g., Amaro, 1995).

In this chapter, we shall describe identity construction as a social and intersubjective process. A sense of self is produced and reproduced in face-to-face, here-and-now interactions, which are themselves embedded in specific social contexts and more general cultural-historical epochs. The ways in which social cognition is at its core an intersubjective phenomenon that cannot be accomplished alone are highlighted when one looks at the social cognizer not in isolation but in social context, especially the social context of the small group. We suggest that this intersubjectivity can be reduced analytically to the activity of individuals only at the cost of misunderstanding and conceptual confusion. Whereas individual thinking is essentially epistemological, the small group accomplishes a social practice that is ontological. It establishes a practically grasped and shared sense of reality. It is this reality that forms the scaffolding of individual cognition.

Small group processes constitute identity; they provide the basis for the kinds of person, the sorts of self, and the forms of agency that are acknowledged. In this manner, possible ways of being in the world are provided by society and its institutions. To say this is not to say that these possibilities are simply taken up and acted out. Rather, identity is established in small social groups—groups such as the family, the peer group, the classroom, and the work group. The possible positions one can adopt are provided by a social process of defining a moral space in which forms of interaction, dialogue, and exchange can take place. We become selves within these contexts, acquiring knowledge about how to be, what counts, and what has meaning. We organize and make sense of ourselves and attempt to become competent members of society within an unfolding series of face-to-face, here-and-now interactions (Ochs & Schieffelin, 1983).

In this chapter, we focus on the ways in which self-concept is a process of social cognitions, organized and given meaning within contexts. We will use as illustrations primarily our own work with youth in two Michigan communities, in Detroit and in a small industrial town half an hour from Detroit. We will argue that the meaning of even seemingly simple and everyday activities such as "going to school" are context dependent and therefore contain a socially negotiated meaning.

THE SOCIAL FIELD

Our central claim is that the small group provides the proximal context in which possible modes of identity are made available. The social interactions of the small group amount to an ontological process: the process that establishes a practically grasped, shared sense of reality—a social field. This social field provides the basis for the recognition of particular kinds of person and corresponding kinds of agency and knowledge. We suggest that this level of intersubjective phenomena has gone largely unobserved because it has been reduced analytically to the activity of individuals. The cost of this reduction has been misunderstanding and conceptual confusion.

Whereas the activity of the individual is essentially cognitive, the practical activity of the small group is ontological. Identity is established in small social groups, groups such as the family, the peer group, and the school classroom. "Local moral worlds provide sites for the experience of solidarity and community, which are crucial for the construction of identity" (Shaw, 1994, p. 113).

SEMIOTIC MEDIATION

A social field and the interactions that take place within it have a reciprocal relationship. Interactions (typically) sustain and reproduce the field, but at the same time, the field constrains and directs the course and character of these interactions. This section will discuss the various semiotic devices whereby fields are reproduced and identities defined.

A variety of semiotic practices sustains a social field and defines the identities within it. Mach (1993) argues that distinctions between "us" and "them" underlie identity (social identity theory makes similar distinctions, e.g., Tajfel & Turner, 1986; Turner, Hogg, Oakes, Reicher, & Wetherell, 1987). Contextual cues, in both speech and action, signal identity and afford understanding by positioning the individual in the local community, allowing the other to infer goals and motives on the basis of the social identity that has been indicated. Interchange within a social group typically assigns a label to group members with different identities, attributes membership to the group or a position within the group, and often makes reference to an implicit contrast with other positions or groups. Such contrasts typically carry moral weight. Attention to such interchanges makes it clear that "viewed semantically, the shape and form of identities derive as much from the interpretations ascribed by others to selves as by the meanings persons, as selves, themselves send" (Shaw, 1994, p. 112). Shaw describes the "semiotic mediation" by which identity is constructed, using the semiotic resources of the distinct moral community.

Identity is thus more than a semantic cognitive representation; it is a style, a manner, and a way of being in the world. To maintain the self, it is important to engage in activities and rituals—collective, habitual, and routine activities characterized by predefined, sanctioned ways of behaving. Bodily discipline is an important aspect of this: movement, standing, sitting, singing, and speaking at specified times and in assigned places. These provide the occasion for acquiring what Bourdieu (1980/1990) calls a bodily "hexus." On an individual level, positions are meaning making; at a group level, they are the frameworks that allow individuals from the same social context to be ⁻⁻dict or make sense of social interactions with one another press). Behavior is understood in terms of the ent positions that can be taken; the importance of these positions is assumed and one's own and others' behaviors are understood in their terms. Thus, one's own and others' behaviors seem familiar and sensible.

When individuals who have internalized divergent social positions interact, this sense of familiarity may be missing. Individuals may assume goals or orientations as common when they are in fact not held by the other, leading to misinterpretation or misunderstanding of the other. In such circumstances, individuals may understand what the other is doing and what is intended but will be fundamentally unconvinced by the other's behavior or rationale because the premises on which it is built are not shared.

HERE-AND-NOW SITUATIONS, SOCIAL CONTEXTS, AND HISTORICAL-CULTURAL FRAMES

The local social field and the social distinctions of the group relations within it are themselves shaped by the forms of the larger social system. This system sets limits on the local worlds people can construct and the forms of identity these worlds sustain. We propose that any understanding and analysis of the construction of identity must not stop at the social group but be considered at least at three levels: the specific here-and-now situation, the social contexts within which the situation is embedded, and the "times"—the political-historical epoch and cultural milieu.

The self can be understood "through" each of these levels. At each level, both social-cognitive and more hermeneutic understanding can be applied. Thus, self can be understood as constructed of properties or, more hermeneutically, in terms of the background that is playing a constitutive role. The cognitive focuses on the self that *is* within a context; the hermeneutic better captures the dynamic relationships between the person and contextual structures.

The first level is that of the situation: the here and now of the concrete circumstances that a person finds himself or herself in. This level includes attention to the project the person is engaged in, deliberately chosen or not and reflected on or not. Hermeneutically, understanding of the self at the level of the situation is a matter of recognizing situational constraints and the manner in which one is engaged with these constraints. In cognitive terms, the first level focuses on identifying one's mood, goals, and plans in the situation. For example, if "the first day of school" is the situation, one might understand oneself as being happy and as wanting to fit in or be accepted. Or one might understand that the situation calls for behaving according to a certain protocol and not knowing what the protocol is, being "engaged" in a way that covers anxiety with joking and foolishness. Whereas the social cognitive perspective focuses on the individual, the hermeneutic widens the focus to include the situation.

The next level has to do with the more enduring contexts within which the situation is embedded. For youth, central contexts are likely to be family, school, neighborhood, and peer group. What one is trying to "be" in a given situation, the ways one can be engaged in the situation are likely to be importantly delimited by the contexts within which the situation occurs. These can be termed the *positions* one can take in a context.

The third level, that of the wider historical context, deals with the time in which one lives. Examples of the importance of this level of context come, for example, from the smaller effect of gender on outcomes in more as compared to less recent research on gender effects. Similarly, the particular ways of being a self that are possible for a 6th-grade black girl in a Tuscaloosa, Alabama, school in 1940 differ from those possible for a 6th-grade black girl in a Bronx, New York, school in 1995. Here-and-now, face-to-face situations are embedded in contexts that are embedded in epochs. Whereas a cognitive perspective focuses on the traits, characteristics, goals, and emotions of the individual and the ways these are afforded or constrained by situations, the hermeneutic perspective asks which characteristics, goals, and emotions are plausible and possible in the here and now, in chronic situations of one's daily existence, and in the times in which one lives. In this way, the selves we construct and aspire to become are fully and completely social.

SOCIALLY CONTEXTUALIZED POSITIONS

One's self-concept is a social construction. The language and symbols used to construct it are socially negotiated. It is organized in terms of socially salient values, attitudes, and meanings, and it is used to make sense of behaviors, aptitudes, and tendencies that have socially negotiated meaning and value. The self-concept can be thought of as a microcosm of one's cultural world, the universe within which meanings are constructed and their supporting practices distributed (Markus & Kitayama, 1994). These meanings and practices are largely taken for granted and "go without saying" (Holland & Quinn, 1987)—though they are the building blocks of self-definition, we may not notice them (e.g., Krull & Erickson, 1995). It is hardly surprising that this transparency of context has served to preserve our professional focus on the essentialized individual (Moscovici, 1993).

Yet it is clear that we "live" a culture. Core cultural ideals are given life in the practices, norms, and institutions of everyday life. For instance, the Euro-American middle-class cultural ideal of the individual as an autonomous, separate entity is maintained via schooling and caretaking practices that emphasize a link between feeling good and standing out, being better than the rest (Markus & Kitayama, 1994). Middle-class classrooms set up a "good" student position that invokes these ideals. Similarly, Willis (1977/1981), in his classic essay, describes how working-class cultural ideals of masculinity and femininity are transmitted via peer, family, and neighborhood practices that view academic achievement as "mind work," as opposed to masculinity that is defined by "male" labor, work that involves physical exertion and some degree of risk or danger. Although not yet in the labor market, youth take up positions in their peer group and school that symbolize their future positions in the working-class community. For example, Willis (1977/1981) describes the symbolic importance to youth of openly defying school rules—it is not breaking the rules but breaking them publicly that makes a difference. These examples suggest that there may be a match or mismatch between the positions or ways of being that are made central in one context—for example, school—and the positions or ways of being that are central in another context—for example, the home or peer group. Being defined in one context may limit the positions one can take up and the ways one can self-define in another.

The interdependence between collective reality—the seemingly external, public, political, and corporate—and individual reality—the seemingly internal personal, private, and corporeal—is structured by the positions accessible in one's face-to-face social contexts (Markus & Kitayama, 1994). Individuals must make sense of themselves in terms of their own immediate reality. This reality is composed of immediate social settings (e.g., home, school), which in turn are made up of and shaped by a variety of sociopsychological processes such as linguistic conventions, socialization practices, and social scripts (e.g., Deaux & Major, 1987). These processes are themselves consti- tuted by a particular historical-political context and the "imagined communities" of race, class, nationality, and so on (Anderson, 1991). Yet it is within the specific and recurrent interpersonal environments one inhabits, one's local world, that individuals must make sense of themselves—learn who one is and what is possible for the self (Shweder & Sullivan, 1990). We have sketched these themes out schematically in Figures 8.1, 8.2, and 8.3, using as an example the social world of a school child. Figure 8.1 depicts the embeddedness of face-to-face interactions in one's everyday social contexts and the embeddedness of these contexts in larger ethnic, racial, gender, and historical contexts. Broader contexts imbue meaning, structure pos- sibilities, and create the scaffolding of face-to-face interactions. It is within face-to-face interactions, however, that identity is negotiated and maintained. In the particular example portrayed, a face-to-face school situation that overlaps with peer contexts, and family contexts in some ways, is portrayed. In the particular situation, two ways of being are made salient and are socially scaffolded. Figure 8.2 portrays the ways in which who we are, our sense of self, is constructed across contexts that vary in the positions, or ways of being, that are relevant within their confines. Thus, what is expressed in a situation is a function of both the situation and the individual (for a similar perspective, see Mischel, 1995).

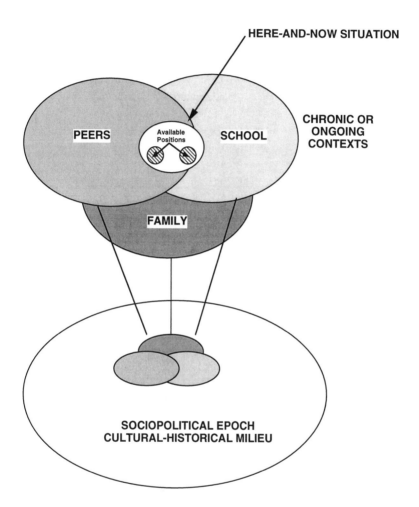

Figure 8.1. Levels of Social Context

Figure 8.3 outlines the ways in which this process results in both a stable and a dynamic or shifting sense of self. It is of note that especially dramatic shifts in situation and context are likely to produce the most discontinuity in self-concept as individuals struggle to learn and relearn how to be a self with new repertoires of positions.

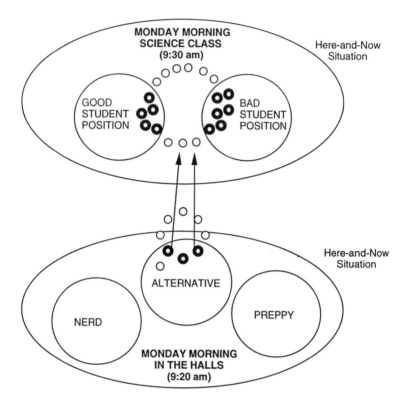

Figure 8.2. Instantiations of Self in Position

Of course, construals of social situations are personalized and therefore diverse. Yet there are commonalities across individual differences because these are powerfully afforded and constrained by situational realities. The positions one can take in a situation are limited. Attention is drawn to those positions that are central in one's context, and one's possible engagement in terms of these positions is operationalized in a language that makes sense in one's context (e.g., Markus & Kitayama, 1994; Rhee, Uleman, Lee, & Roman, 1995). These positions are organized within the moral space of one's here-and-now interactions and form the lexicon through which selves are conceptualized. The self, constructed and reconstructed within and

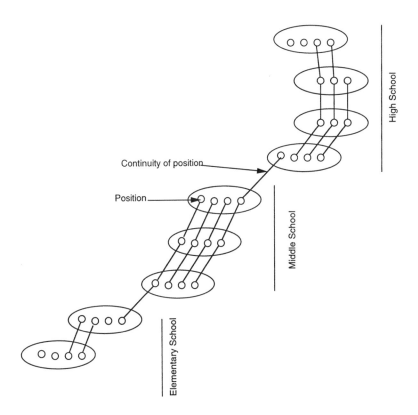

Figure 8.3. The Self Defined in Positions Set Up Within Here-and-Now
Situations Across Time

across face-to-face interactions, is clearly not a random or accidental
conglomeration of observations made by the self and others as to
one's emotions, skills, characteristics, and attributes, nor is it a
"complete set" of all possible self-relevant descriptors (e.g., Markus
& Kunda, 1986; Mischel, 1995). Instead, individuals focus on, value,
and delineate certain pieces of reality, those that are operationalized
by the possible positions or ways of being in context.

   Situationally salient positions delineate what a self is and what it
is supposed to do—its goals or purposes. These in turn afford certain
forms of self-content and certain sources of self-knowledge while

constraining others. Sources of self-knowledge are also goal linked; appropriate sources of information and feedback about the self are contextually defined (Nuttin, 1984). The self is not merely a conglomerate of content. As a cognitive structure and information-processing agent (Markus, 1977), the self functions to organize our experiences and motivate action (Cantor & Zirkel, 1990; Markus & Wurf, 1987; Oyserman, Gant, & Ager, 1995; Oyserman & Markus, 1993). Thus, as Taylor (1989) writes, "To know who you [are] is to be oriented in moral space, a space in which questions arise about what is good or bad, what is worth doing and what is not, what has meaning and importance for you, and what is trivial and secondary" (p. 28). Typically, psychologists describing identity as a social process have focused on identity as an ongoing negotiation in the tradition of symbolic interactionism (Stryker, 1987). Yet the question of levels of contextual embeddedness, the ways in which identity is negotiated from a relatively short list of relevant possibilities in a given situation and the ways that these situations might interact with one another, has been insufficiently studied, particularly in the life period of adolescence. In the following section, we will outline this process for adolescents.

IDENTITY CONSTRUCTION IN ADOLESCENCE

In Western industrialized societies, adolescence is described as a time of identity negotiation. Youths are said to be "in search of" themselves, "discovering" themselves or alternatively "making something" of themselves. Possible identities are to be tried on and the likelihood of actually being such a self is socially negotiated (Cantor & Zirkel, 1990; Stryker, 1987). Past identities and one's skills and abilities are melded to become plausible and at least reasonably satisfying adult selves (Cantor, Norem, Niedenthal, Langston, & Brower, 1987; Curry, Trew, Turner, & Hunter, 1994).

Although providing some important insights, this "identity negotiation" model does not pay enough attention to context. By focusing on interpersonal negotiation, larger issues of context are given short shrift. The ways in which sociocultural context scaffolds and informs what can be negotiated interpersonally is not taken into account. Negotiation-based models overlook the ways in which context colors interactions. Once a set of positions becomes salient, identity construction must take these into account even when they are not in the best interest of the individual. The rapidly expanding literature on stereotyping, for example, suggests that power differentials set up situations in which the powerless are likely to be stereotyped, that is, made sense of in terms of a small and intransient set of possible positions (Fiske, 1993a). In addition, others in one's own context purvey messages about which characteristics of the self are valued and important; they are resources, providing experiences of success and competence in the roles that are culturally represented as key to adult status and attainments (Crane, 1991; Ogbu, 1991; Oyserman et al., 1995; Oyserman & Markus, 1993). It is within particular contexts that youth are provided with educational, economic, and other resources, sometimes termed "cultural capital," a capital that is context relevant (Lamont & Lareau, 1988; Ogbu, 1991).

Furthermore, by implying that all identities may be equally negotiated and minimizing the effect of contextually relevant opportunities on the identity construction process, the identity negotiation model typically ignores the fact that for many youth, the self one could be as an adult is rapidly bounded by an increasingly detailed and limited array of plausible alternatives given past and current attainments and resources available in one's sociocultural context (Oyserman et al., 1995; Oyserman & Markus, 1993). Thus, though sometimes conceptualized as a psychosocial moratorium in which a limitless array of identities are "tried on," adolescence seems to involve a general restriction of alternatives for many youth. Their contexts simply do not define many positions for them to attain.

This is particularly likely to be the case for urban, working-class, or minority youth embedded in contexts that do not afford visions of oneself as succeeding in school. If youth come to view school success as unlikely, they are likely to lose interest and become less involved in school (e.g., Steele, Spencer, & Aronson, 1995). Yet in U.S. society, school success is clearly a gatekeeper for adult possibilities and resources. Furthermore, normative nonschool-related contexts are not easy to come by in these settings; youth who disengage from school are left with peer and family contexts only. There are positions one can take up in these contexts even when the context of school is reduced in centrality, for example, being a good son or daughter, being a friend, or being accepted. Yet when positions within the family context are not reinforced by school context and positions in the peer context are not constrained by positions in the school context, then more involvement in risky or deviant behaviors is likely (Cernkovich & Giordano, 1992; Freedman-Doan, Arbreton, Harold, & Eccles, 1993; Harter, 1990; Henggeler, 1991; Jessor, Donovan, & Costa, 1992; Oyserman, 1993). Perhaps this is because in our society, without the context of school, the parent-family context alone does not provide access to positions that scaffold the transition to adult roles other than parenthood. Similarly, without the constraining influence of the school context on the ways positions can be operationalized in the peer context, being accepted can focus on involvement in delinquent activities. This process has less to do with the specific interpersonal negotiations through which identities are tried out, confirmed, or reframed than with the limitations of the positions that can be taken up in these social contexts. Furthermore, recent work in cognitive development suggests that without a relatively wide open space or array of possible positions, it may be extremely difficult for youth to develop the cognitive skills necessary to strategize attainment of more long-term and abstract possible selves (e.g., Kuhn, 1995). Thus, youths attempt to create a sense of who they can be now and as adults, given what they understand a person—a man or a woman—can be in their everyday contexts. If the positions available in these contexts are limited, so are their possible selves.

By taking a more contextualized perspective, we propose to make sense of identity as a process of symbolic construction. The individual and the social groups within which he or she is embedded use symbols and devices that have meaning in a particular context to construct who one is and who one could be. Symbols and devices operationalize contextually relevant positions, and it is attainment of these positions that is negotiated interpersonally. Identity then is not wholly "inside" the person; it is a continuous, social production (Harre & Gillett, 1994). For example, in an Ann Arbor middle school, there are "nerds," "preps," and "alternatives." These positions define who one can be in the peer context at school; as such they require others. They are social at their core. One Ann Arbor teen describes the process by which 6th graders need to "learn" these possible positions: "In 6th grade you watch and copy." Possible positions vary in terms of dress, music, contact with members of the opposite sex, relations with one another, and connectedness with school. They require others who are conversant in the symbols and devices through which attainment of a position can be conveyed. Thus, being an alternative requires others; clothes signal attitudes ("We wear shirts other kids wouldn't, like bowling alley shirts or our father's old corduroys" and "We get good grades but don't care about it as much as the 'nerds' ") and also something about parent-child relations ("Alternatives have a life—we get together with our friends on weekends and half days. Nerds don't have time because they are too busy with schoolwork and extra lessons like music. Their parents don't let them be with friends") (quotes from a 13-year-old middle school female). Without the cooperation of others in establishing meaning, the clothing would merely appear to be a somewhat sloppy version of the general teen garb. Youth can dress like a group member and try to take up a position but not be accepted as such ("He dresses like a prep but he is a nerd").

SELF AS SOCIALLY STRUCTURED

We propose that within social contexts, here-and-now, face-to-face situations set up moral spaces or positions that operationalize the relevant ways of being in that situation. These positions function as common denominators that structure the engagement of individuals in the situation such that there will be some important commonalities in the selves created by those living in these contexts. An understanding or appreciation of the social representations that structure the self and give it its particular shape or nature, the goals of selfhood, and what one is to be doing to be a self all flow from the

positions available in one's here-and-now situations (Markus &
Kitayama, 1991; Oyserman, 1993; Stryker, 1987). In this framework,
the self is viewed as the nexus of social representations derived from
the social contexts within which the individual is embedded (Oyserman & Markus, 1993). By setting up representations of what it is to
be a "good person," each of these contexts makes some claim on the
person, structures a set of practices and ideas, and, most important
perhaps, organizes and gives meaning to the "reality" we perceive,
the issues we see as having meaning (Holland & Quinn, 1987;
Markus & Kitayama, 1994; White, 1992). Although we understand
ourselves within the possibilities set up by the contexts in which we
are situated and it is within these contexts that we forge a sense of
ourselves, this structuration is not necessarily experienced as such.
Through a series of discrete and ongoing interactions, we accommodate, take into account, and organize in terms of even those social
representations that are detrimental, oppressing, or limiting (Showers, 1992). Thus, an African American from Chicago describes going
to school and the meaning of going to school ("making it"):

> I've always liked going to school but in our neighborhood there
> were a lot of thugs and a lot of gang-bangers. Most of the gang-
> bangers now are drug dealers. . . . In the area where I was staying,
> I had been around some of the gang-bangers or I had cousins or
> uncles who were a part of the gangs and had been in them for a
> while. Thugs are gang-bangers; niggers that try to bully you, take
> your money and lunch, beat you up for no reason. . . . They beat
> you up and stuff like that. And that was kind of hard because I
> always had to have the fear of getting jumped on; running back and
> forth, running here and there, trying to find my way through this
> stuff, trying to get over and make it. (Johnson, 1995, pp. 14-15)

Whereas simply "going to school" may not be part of the good
student position in all contexts, it is clear that going to school in this
context meant a choice and an effortful behavioral sequence and
likely was part of the good student position in this context.

Individuals live in contexts that provide both congruent (cross-
contextual) and incongruent (context variable) messages about how

to be a self, who to compare oneself to, the meaning and likelihood of success, and so on. Within a series of specific face-to-face, here-and-now situations, possible positions or ways of being are delineated and individuals must take these positions into account in defining who they are and what is possible for them (for a similar argument, see Farr, 1987). Thus, a Latina adolescent may become engaged at the age of 14 because it is normative in her neighborhood culture but at the same time value education and hope to become a psychiatrist. The contradictions between these must be dealt with in the terms laid out by the contexts and interchanges she herself is a part of (Pastor, McCormick, & Fine, in press).

SELF-CONCEPT IN CONTEXT

The self is an organized locus of contextually anchored understandings of how to be a person, and it functions as an individualized orienting, mediating, interpretive framework giving shape to what people notice, think about, feel, and are motivated to do. What we do is due to the sense we make of our context and the positions available in this context. In the previous example, early engagement is understood as a sign of respect and serious intentions on the part of the male, and good girls are understood to become engaged young; thus, young adolescents, whatever their aspirations, feel constrained to accommodate to cultural framing. Another example of the ways contexts set up the possible positions of males and females is set out in high relief in the following description by an adolescent male of sexual relations.

> You can talk to a girl a couple of hours and, you know, wind up in bed with her. You can talk to a chick. You got it . . . most guys feel like, "This is a piece; I'm going to go ahead and get it." They don't really think, "Well, is she pregnant? Do she want to be pregnant?" I feel that . . . either she is burning, meaning that she has some kind of venereal disease, or she is pregnant already and she is trying to get a scapegoat or she want to get pregnant because she thinks you got some money. (Johnson, 1995, p. 18)

In this inner-city Chicago context, girls are at once objectified ("This is a piece") and also feared (". . . because she thinks you got some money"). Adolescent females will need to take these positions (being a desired object, being threatening) into account in making sense of the responses of young males to them. Whether they choose to define themselves in opposition to or in terms of these positions, they cannot be simply ignored because it is in terms of these positions that young males make sense of young females. When sexualized and negative images of women are consistently part of one's face-to-face situation, it may be difficult or impossible to negotiate shared reality with an alternative, that is, a more positive self-defining position (e.g., Deaux, 1995).

In the domain of school and schooling, what it means to be a good student depends on the moral space or positions in one's here-and-now situations. The specific content of these positions can differ broadly with important consequences. If being a good student is conceived of in terms of being independent and creative and having innate abilities, one will experience school differently and be motivated to behave differently than if being a good student is conceived of in terms of acceptance of hierarchy, attaining preestablished standards, and the importance of perseverance. But where do these positions come from? They are structured, we will argue, in the specific circumstances of one's contexts.

CONTEXT DELIMITED

Until now we have focused on the specific interchanges in the unfolding "situation" of one's daily life. It is also possible to look across situations at the contexts of gender, race, ethnicity, culture, and socioeconomic class and the situations likely to be encountered by individuals in these contexts. Authors studying adolescence have often noted the importance of understanding the ways these contexts operate on individuals. Thus, "the findings of race, ethnic and gender differences are so ubiquitous that the case has been made that the effects of other distal or proximate variables depend on these" (Day,

1992, p. 750). It is the interplay between and among contexts within a particular historical era that delineates the self as a complex social cognizer. Thus, we define ourselves in terms made relevant by standards, mores, values, and goals of larger society and the interplay between these and the standards, mores, values, and goals of the groups to which we belong (e.g., Hogan, 1989). To the extent that we perceive ourselves and are perceived by others as belonging to groups in addition to or instead of the implied larger societal group (of middle class, white, and male), then the mores, standards, and values of larger society recede in relevance as the unique standards, values, and mores of these groups become more salient. What stands out, what is relevant and processed in a context, is that which has bearing on these standards and mores (e.g., Schneider & Yongsook, 1990). Contextual meanings may be congruent or incongruent to the mores of larger society; mores may also be complementary. It has been argued, for example, that certain understandings of homosexuals, women, and people of color are required by working-class men in defining themselves as working- class men (Fine, 1995). More broadly, women and men occupy positions that afford and constrain certain ways of being. Eagly (1995) summarizes the ways in which men and women are conceptualized, showing that men are defined in terms of their agency and women in terms of their nurturance. According to her analysis, what is critical about being a woman is that one is not a man: Maleness implicates power, and femaleness implicates lack of power. Other research reviewed by Deaux (1995) suggests that one of the most consistent female stereotypes is one that defines females in sexual terms and excludes work-relevant terms. Women may choose to self-define as not nurturant or as agentic, but this self-concept must take into account the vocabulary others will use in making sense of them. This process occurs both as males define females and as females define themselves. "People signal their [subject] position through their identification with a particular local moral world—a community whose symbolic boundaries are largely determined by the shared subject of its members in relation to other status groups" (Shaw, 1994, p. 111).

Looking at race, we can see a similar process. For example, in contemporary America, it is likely that blacks interacting with non-blacks must take race into account in defining themselves because race is defined as important, as having meaning, and as providing information in the larger societal context (e.g., Dole, 1995; Eisenman, 1995). Early theorizing focused on the presumed "master status" of some social roles such that one may be considered black first and anything else second (Becker, 1963). Judd (1993) recently found that blacks are viewed as athletic, musical, fun-loving, religious, violent, loud, uneducated, and irresponsible by whites. One may choose to use this vocabulary to self-define or attempt to define in terms of the "vocabulary" used to define whites (independent, ambitious, intelligent, self-centered, uptight, greedy, racist, and wealthy). In either case, however, this template or grid must be taken into account. The social representation of blackness produces a vocabulary, a prism, or a lens through which the self is viewed. Allen, Thornton, and Watkins (in press) provide another example of how this process works. They show that both blacks and whites describe blacks as religious, musical, pleasure-loving, lazy, and superstitious. To this representational rubric, blacks add some unique African American representations of blackness: intelligent, athletic, loud, with rhythm, and sportsmanlike. Steele, Spencer, and Aronson (1995) describe the stereotype vulnerability of African Americans, arguing that academically competent blacks underperform on average when their membership in this social category is made salient. Moving to the next level of contextual complexity, we can ask how the interplay between race and gender or race and class (or race, class, and gender) impacts on these rubrics. We propose that individuals do not simply draw information from each context in an additive fashion but rather that contexts structure meanings interactively. Thus, because blacks vary in socioeconomic status, markers of "being" black are likely to differ within blacks as a group. To the extent that larger society assumes a middle-class stance, being black and middle-class may be less distinctive than being black and poor. However, because blacks are disproportionately likely to be poor, both social representations about poverty and the self-definitional meaning of poverty are likely to color the ways in which blacks represent themselves as a group. Following theories of distinctiveness-based identity and social categorization (e.g., Nelson & Miller, 1995), middle-class blacks may view blacks as more indistinguishable from larger society than will poor blacks. In fact, Allen, Thornton, and Watkins (in press) did find that higher socioeconomic status (SES) African Americans have fewer positive and negative images of African Americans, viewing them as more indistinguishable from the majority, whereas those with lower SES are more likely to view African Americans as distinct from the larger group.

Through this process, gender, socioeconomic class, race-ethnicity, and the interplay among them infuse meaning into the everyday contexts of school, peer group, and family. Thus, being female, working-class, or white each sets up likely ways of engaging in the moral space of one's here-and-now social situations. The moral space organized by small groups in here-and-now situations affords certain engagements and constrains others; individuals must both define in terms of what they are and also in terms of what they are not in spite of expectations that they will be. In this vein, we have hypothesized that in urban contexts, a triadic structure of ethnic identity may be vital in facilitating engagement with school and schooling. Specifically, we have hypothesized that youth who (a) conceptualize themselves in terms of connectedness with the black community, (b) have identified ways in which being African American may be negatively stereotyped or result in obstacles to advancement, and (c) view school as part of being African American will be better equipped to keep trying to do well in school, will view school success as self-defining, and will therefore perform better and persist longer at school-related tasks (Oyserman et al., 1995). This triadic structure of identity takes into account cultural traditions of communal helping, family aid and connectedness, the legacy of racism (Asante, 1987, 1988; Martin & Martin, 1985), and cultural imperatives based on the Protestant work ethic to be independent, successful, achieving, and self-focused (Katz & Hass, 1988). Making sense of the self in terms of connectedness and awareness of racism and viewing school achievement as part of being African American may therefore be vital in promoting engagement in school (Oyserman et al., 1995). Our empirical research that these components of identity do promote persistence and performance in school, particularly for females (Oyserman & Burks, 1995; Oyserman et al., 1995). In this sequence of studies, our data suggest that for males, ethnic identity per se does not predict school persistence. Rather, it is the future-oriented element of the self-concept, the content of one's possible selves, that seems to make a difference. Thus, especially for males, it appears central that school success be viewed as possible and plausible and that self-relevant strategies for avoiding problems in school be articulated. Unanswered in these initial studies is the question "What does it mean to be a good student, and how is this position articulated in here-and-now situations?" To explore this issue, we have engaged in an ethnographic study of a predominantly blue-collar community in Michigan, half an hour from Detroit. Because the town has only one middle school where we conducted our research, we do not name the town because to do so would be to violate the anonymity of the participants. Our fieldwork in the middle school suggests that in this context, students and teachers hold positions represented in terms of kinds of authority and responsibility. Teachers have authority and responsibility to give directions and maintain order; students have responsibility to be silent, obedient, sit in place, and follow directions. "Doing your job" is a central phrase used to describe the good student role. The "job" most commonly is what the teacher defines it to be so that accomplishments are viewed as fulfilling obligations. It seems that this process sets up a continuation of a working-class ethic among youth as they move toward adulthood (Harvey, 1990). Good students are not defined in terms of learning, knowing, and having initiative but rather in terms of completing externally organized tasks, following rules, and not interfering.

CLASSROOM AS CONTEXT

Schools help reproduce the social order by teaching youth knowledge and skills but also by introducing them to the values of society (Carnoy & Levin, 1985; Fine, 1995). It has become apparent that schools are institutions in which identities are constructed and in which youth come to adopt particular ways to be, not just things to know. Because school as a context structures a large part of youth's everyday experiences, whether they choose to attend or not, school frames responses to basic questions such as, "Who am I?" "What do I care about?" and "What do I expect in the future?" Identities are formed both in relation to the social group of peers—the nerds, the preps, and the alternatives—and in relation to teachers, as we will describe below. Parents, churches, and other social contexts may serve to focus youth's attention on school, highlighting or defusing the centrality of this context for other life domains.

The school classroom provides an important group setting in which identity is constructed. It involves participation and member-ship in a specific community and, hence, familiarity with positions relevant to this community, shared practices, and a normative. For example, school can emphasize mental labor as opposed to manual labor, allowing for the practice of one and devaluating the other.

Yet clearly, the positions set up by the school are not equally accepted by all students. School positions focus on what is valued, what it means to be a "good" student, and what it means to be a "bad" student. In essence, if all students focused equally on attaining a good student position, everyone would be a nerd. The fact that there are additional groups reflects the additional postures and attitudes to-ward schooling—and the positions that can be taken up with regard to school. Youth bring with them the positions established in their peer contexts and apply these to the positions set up by the school. Some ways of being that are viewed as good student and some viewed as bad student are carried from peer context to school and influence youth's stance or the positions they can take up. Thus, the alternatives position is that of nonconformist in the peer context; some of the behaviors that symbolize this may be viewed as bad student behaviors in the context of school—talking loudly, dying hair, wearing unusual clothing—even though the alternatives accept school, view school as important, and aspire to some portions of the good student position. To understand the normative framework of the classroom, we fo-cused on the explicit reference to norms and values made by the sixth-grade teachers in the beginning of the school year. We chose to focus on entry into sixth grade as it involves entry into middle school; as a transition time, it would likely provide articulation of frame as it is not yet routine or assumed. At entry into middle school, the teacher must draw the students' attention to what counts as violation of the frame. We found that "doing" versus "not doing your job" seems key to the classroom's moral space. The teacher makes this explicit by illuminating the concept: "People are sitting here not doing their job." Doing your job seems to entail both positive actions and avoidance of negative actions. On the one hand it means taking notes, having responsibility to team, providing information, giving the teacher attention, doing what a teacher tells you to do, walking quietly in the corridors, and so on. On the other hand it means not having an attitude, not getting on someone's case ("that's my job," says the teacher), not forgetting to bring books to class ("that's your job"), not being tardy, not using bad language, not wasting time ("You wasted a minute of your passing time"), not being "rude" (i.e., talking while others talk), and not socializing. Although most frequently ways of being a student are defined in terms of positive and negative actions, sometimes, good and bad student roles are defined more globally. The teacher says, "Finishing books is wonderful," "It's in your best interest to read," and "Use this time wisely" ("Don't waste time, spend it wisely") and emphasizes keeping up the class's reputation as compared with another teacher. Being a good student is framed as doing your job in this predominantly blue-collar industrial town where employment has traditionally focused on the auto assembly plant. And doing your job translates into doing what the teacher tells you is your job, even though teachers try to transfer ownership of the job to students. "Someone read our mission—what our job is going to be" (sixth-grade teacher, middle school, small town half an hour from Detroit). Possible positions for youth in the normative framework of the classroom can be organized in terms of two central dimensions, or axes. The first focuses on doing your job versus wasting time and being rude. The second focuses on the locus of responsibility—internal, "you are responsible for your own work," versus external, "Do I need to tell you what to do?" At the start of the year, most violations of the normative frame seem to be occasions when a youth does not do what he or she has been told to do. The teacher has made it clear that he or she expects that youth will come to do their job without needing to be told; the responsibility will become theirs. Though sometimes youth are viewed as being deliberately bad—choosing the bad student role—teachers frame youth behaviors mostly in terms of not yet grasping their responsibilities and a need for external (teacher-located) responsibility. When a student is viewed as deliberately breaking rules or deliberately not bringing books to class, he or she is treated differently, that is, afforded different ways of being.

Thus, in a community organized around one stable employment base—automobile production—studentness invokes doing your job in a way that connects youth with work on the assembly line. The stability of this representation once created is illuminated by the fact that the automobile plant on which local job structure was based announced its closing 3 years ago. In the wake of this, the school received funding to engage in systemwide change, to refocus the goals of education. The reform efforts require changing the social representation of studentness specifically and being from the town more generally, not just in the classroom but more pervasively, in each of the contexts in which the here-and-now situation of the classroom is embedded—the school, the family, the peer group, and the community and region. When the positions available in the family and peer group do not mesh well with those of school or when the school seeks to define new positions, it is likely that the engagement of students with school will be problematic. Youth cannot merely bring with them their at-home ways of being; school-relevant positions may not translate well from school to the world outside school either. Our fieldwork suggests that parents have not experienced school as being relevant to their jobs or their lives after school. This working-class expectation that schooling is a phase to be gotten through rather than a preparation for the world of work means that students acting consistently and coherently within this expectation would not come to value schooling or the learning and knowledge to be gained in this framework. The closing of the automobile assembly plant means that the community can no longer safely expect reasonably well-paid and stable employment independent of schooling. The goal of the current school initiative is to develop a way of integrating schooling with the transition to adulthood and the world of work.

CONCLUSION

The account we developed is one in which identity is not a fixed property of an individual but a temporal accomplishment that must be constructed and reconstructed. It is an ongoing effort to grasp and bring together what one knows of one's past skills and attributes, one's present characteristics and abilities, one's plausible future, and one's hopes and fears with regard to the self one might become (Cantor, 1994; Oyserman & Markus, 1993). This effort engenders a series of relatively concrete and discrete strategic moves as well as a repertoire of strategies to be tried and retried in one's ongoing efforts to create and maintain a self (Sanderson & Cantor, 1995). Very concretely, identity is what one has and who one is. It is the bringing together of one's past with one's current circumstances to project and anticipate some kind of comprehensible and plausible possible future and organize one's behaviors toward this possible self (Oyserman & Markus, 1993). Identity is situational, relational, and libidinal, "forged through a certain temporal unification of the past and future with the present before me" (Jameson, quoted in Harvey, 1990, p. 53). To the extent that personally meaningful projects are to be pursued over time, this self must be constructed and reconstructed with a focus on the possibility of engaging in activities that "make" or "create" the self one is striving to become (Cantor, 1994).

Identity is both highly personal, an individually crafted achievement, and also a social construction or culturally assigned social representation. The two identities, the sociocultural side and the psychological, must both be taken into account. Thus, identity is always both "outside in" and "inside out." It is the way we are defined by other people and the way we define ourselves through our actions and symbolic interactions (e.g., Aronson, Cooper, & Blanton, 1995). In addition, the very issues of concern, the qualities and characteristics that are important and therefore self-defining, are social constructs. Views, values, goals, and patterns of reciprocity are sociocultural constructions that, in many ways, "come with the territory" or are built into context. Being a teen involves different behaviors, beliefs, and motivations among the Baining of New Britain, Papua, New Guinea, than it does for a middle-class white American teen in Ann Arbor, Michigan (see Fajans, 1985). Even in the American context, what it means to be a teen and what teens can do and be is an evolving and hotly contested issue. Thus we ask, "Is work good or bad?" (Bachman, Johnson, & O'Malley, 1982) and "What about sexuality?" (Harter, 1990).

In our previous studies with youth in Detroit, we have found that youth who have a "balanced" vision of themselves in the domain of school—youth who view both doing well and also doing poorly in school as possibly self-defining (Oyserman & Markus, 1990)—youth who believe that they are trying to become like the positive possible self and avoid the negative one (Oyserman & Saltz, 1993), and youth who have strategies to avoid failure in this domain (Oyserman & Burks, 1995) are likely to be less involved in delinquent activities and perform better in school. Yet the specific content of these identities, what it means to be a good student, will differ by context.

Thus, identity can be thought of as a social cognitive process and structure. Striving to answer the "Who am I?" question makes key and central both certain end states and certain ways of being or self-processes. One's sense of self, which focuses one's attention, information processing, and motivational resources, may scaffold and organize the sense we make of our everyday lives and behavioral opportunities. Thus, if being a good student is central to who I am and if I view school success as a plausible possible self and school failure as something to be avoided, this social identity may color or organize how I am in the world—the goals I seek to pursue, the information I seek in interactions with others, and so on (Oyserman et al., 1995). We have sought to address the varied ways that being a good student might be a plausible or implausible self-definition for youths in contemporary, and particularly urban, settings and in this way explore the self as a social cognitive process.

Part

III

Impact of the Group on Member
Identification and Group Boundaries

The Phenomenology of Being in a Group
Complexity Approaches to Operationalizing Cognitive Representation

BRIAN MULLEN
DREW ROZELL
CRAIG JOHNSON

In men we various ruling passions find;
In women, two almost divide the kind;
Those, only fixed, they first or last obey,
The love of pleasure and the love of sway.

—Alexander Pope (1735)

Gentlemen of the old régime in the South used to say: "A woman's name should appear in print but twice—when she marries and when she dies."

—Arthur W. Calhoun (1918)

A s illustrated in the epigrams presented above, the members of one group can, and often are, thought about by members of another group with relatively low complexity. This tendency to employ cognitive representations of varying degrees of complexity for social groups, and the mechanisms which guide these cognitive representations, are the focus of this chapter. We begin by considering two broad classes of cognitive representations used for social groups: prototype representations and exemplar representations. The use of these modes of cognitive representation is shown to vary as a function of the salience of the target group, as often gauged by the relative size of that group. Next, ethnophaulisms, or ethnic slurs, are considered as indictators of cognitive representations of social groups. The complexity of the ethnophaulisms for a given group are shown to vary as a function of relative group size, in archival historical data as well as in experimental data. We conclude with a consideration of the validity of these complexity approaches to operationalizing cognitive representation, and discuss the implications of this perspective.

Cognitive Representations of Groups. In their *Annual Review* chapter on intergroup relations, Messick and Mackie (1989) proposed that the distinctive cognitive tone of recent research on group membership will fruitfully augment traditional approaches. Consistent with this proposal, recent theoretical models have attempted to explain intergroup perception phenomena in terms of the cognitive representations formed for the ingroup and the outgroup. These theoretical models include Fiske and Neuberg's (1990) continuum model, Gaertner, Mann, Dovidio, Murrell, and Pomare's (1990) recategorization model, Kraus, Ryan, Judd, Hastie, and Park's (1993) mental frequency distribution model, Mullen's (1991) phenomenology of being in a group model, and Smith and Zárate's (1990) exemplar model.

All of these models describe different conditions under which people will engage in prototype or exemplar cognitive representations

AUTHORS' NOTE: Portions of this chapter were presented as the invited address at the 1992 annual meeting of the British Psychological Society, Northern Ireland Branch, Virginia, Co. Cavan, Ireland, at the 1992 annual meeting of the Society for Experimental Social Psychology, San Antonio, TX, and as an invited address at the 1995 meeting of the Eastern Psychological Association, Boston, MA. Address correspondence to Brian Mullen, Department of Psychology, Syracuse University, Syracuse, NY 13210.

of the ingroup and the outgroup. The distinction between prototype representations and exemplar representations was highlighted by Medin, Altom, and Murphy (1984):

> According to prototype models, a category is represented as the "central tendency" of the category members along each of the component attribute dimensions. This category representation in terms of average or typical attributes is referred to as a prototype. . . . Exemplar models of categorization differ sharply from the prototype models in their assumption that category judgements are based on retrieval of information about specific category members rather than on summary information about typical attributes. (p. 334)

Thus, the various theoretical models of intergroup perception (cited above) have attempted to explain the conditions under which people will employ different cognitive representations for a social group. Specifically, these theories have attempted to elucidate how groups are represented in terms of retrieval of information about specific group members (exemplar representations), or in terms of summary information about the typical group member (prototype representations). Prototype and exemplar models have in the past been treated as mutually exclusive. However, recent evidence indicates that both prototype representations and exemplar representations can contribute to the handling of information about category members, both for nonsocial information tasks (e.g., Medin, 1989; Medin et al., 1984) and for social information tasks (e.g., Fiske & Neuberg, 1990; Smith & Zárate, 1990).

Consistent with this proposal, Mullen (1991) presented the results of several meta-analytic integrations of research domains at the interface between social cognition and group processes. The basic theme in Mullen (1991) is that the proportionate sizes of the ingroup and the outgroup exert a central effect on fundamental cognitive mechanisms, which in turn converge to determine what it is like to be a member of this group or that group.

According to this model of the phenomenology of being in a group, proportionate group sizes influence the salience of the ingroup and the outgroup: The larger group recedes as less salient and the smaller group emerges as more salient. Salience in turn determines whether prototype or exemplar cognitive representations will be used for the ingroup and the outgroup: The less salient group is represented more by exemplar representations and the more salient group is represented more by prototype representations[1] (see Mullen, 1991, for a discussion of evidence for this model). This model of the phenomenology of being in a group is aptly illustrated in the following passage from a recent popular science fiction novel. In this Star Trek tale, Captain James Kirk's cognitive representations of Vulcans are affected by the immediate social context:

> There were a surprising number of non-Vulcans in attendance, but no more than about a thousand all told, in a place that could hold fifteen thousand easily. Vulcans filled the rest of those seats, silently, and Jim found himself suffering from the ridiculous feeling that he was being stared at. . . . As he chatted with them he was once again rather delighted that Vulcans were in fact different from one another. A lot of people had the idea that Vulcans were all tall, dark, and slender, men and women alike. But though a large percentage of them did indeed fit into those parameters, there were also short Vulcans, blond Vulcans, and even a redhead over by one of the tables. . . . "They look like people," Jim thought, and then had to laugh at the idea. (Duane, 1988, p. 233).

In much of the Star Trek mythology, the lone Vulcan target of Human cognitive representations (Mr. Spock) embodies the rare minority of one. This would elicit a prototype representation of the social category Vulcans, as illustrated on the left side of Figure 9.1: The social category of Vulcans is represented by summary information about the most typical group member. This prototype representation sets the stage for various intergroup perception phenomena, including ingroup bias (e.g., Mullen, Brown, & Smith, 1992), perceptions of relative heterogeneity (e.g., Mullen & Hu, 1989), and the cross-racial facial identification effect (Anthony, Copper, & Mullen, 1992). However, in the passage quoted above, the Vulcan targets of Human cognitive representations are the vast majority. This would elicit an exemplar representation of the social category Vulcans, as illustrated on the right side of Figure 9.1: The social category of Vulcans is represented by retrieval of information about specific

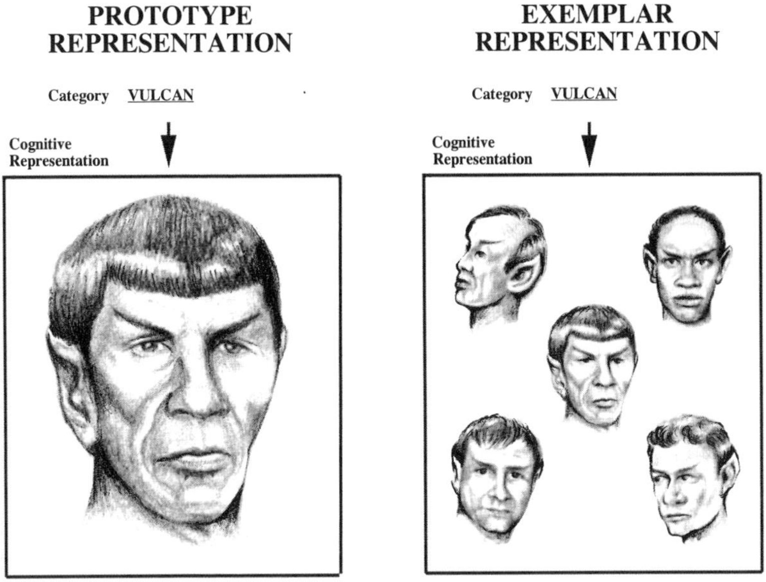

PROTOTYPE REPRESENTATION

EXEMPLAR REPRESENTATION

Category   VULCAN

Category   VULCAN

Cognitive Representation

Cognitive Representation

Figure 9.1. Examples of Prototype (left) and Exemplar (right) Cognitive Representations for the Social Category Vulcans

group exemplars. This exemplar representation is less likely to evoke the various intergroup perception phenomena like ingroup bias, relative heterogeneity, and so on.

Cognitive Representations in Ethnophaulisms. If people really do engage in different modes of cognitive representation of groups as a function of group sizes, one interesting place to observe this effect would be in the use of *ethnophaulisms,* from the Greek roots meaning "a national group" and "to disparage"). These words are the ethnic slurs used to refer to outgroups. The use of ethnophaulisms provides a potent indicator of prototype representation of social groups: To the extent that members of a social category are cognitively represented in a prototype representation mode, information about these people will be processed predominantly in terms of their category membership. In spite of their individuality, category members will be treated primarily as category members, and individual given names will not be as accessible as the labels, the ethnophaulisms, for their category. As suggested by Graumann and Wintermantel's (1989) discussion of ethnic slurs, the use of ethnophaulisms represents a gauge of prototype representation of ethnic groups: "Typing [a member of a social category] by nouns fixates the other person as a *typical* instance of a social category" (p. 192, emphasis added).

Thus, a smaller target ethnic group will be subject to greater prototype representations, as evidenced in the use of ethnophaulisms for that target group. A rather dramatic illustration of this line of reasoning can be found in the works of Shakespeare. Specifically, consider the references to the character Caliban in *The Tempest* and the references to the character Shylock in *The Merchant of Venice*. These two characters epitomize Shakespeare's treatment of the lone representative of some minority target group. When we examine the proportionate use of ethnophaulisms (e.g., "monster" for Caliban; "infidel" for Shylock) in speech as a function of the number of other characters present in each scene, an intriguing pattern emerges. As shown in Figure 9.2, as greater numbers of other people are present in the scene (and the target's proportionate rarity and resultant salience increases), the proportionate use of ethnophaulisms to refer to the minority target increases, $r = .686$, $p = .0017$.[2] The data used here to illustrate the effects of proportionate rarity on the use of ethnophaulisms are admittedly extracted from a play. However, Shakespeare himself admonished us that, "the purpose of playing, whose end, both at the first and now, was and is to hold, as 'twere, a mirror up to nature" (*Hamlet*, Act III, Scene, 2).

Complexity in Ethnophaulisms and Cognitive Representations. The use of ethnophaulisms may serve as evidence for the operation of prototype cognitive representations of the target group. However, the prototype representation evidenced in the use of ethnophaulisms might be expected to occur in varying degrees. One way to gauge the degree of prototype representation in ethnophaulisms is in terms of the complexity in the ethnophaulisms used for an ethnic group. The ethnic group characterized by ethnophaulisms referring to physical traits of members of that group is represented more in a prototype mode (and less in an exemplar mode) than the ethnic group characterized by

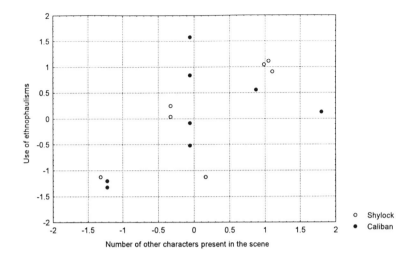

Figure 9.2. The Relation Between Use of Ethnophaulisms and Group Size in Shakespeare's Plays

ethnophaulisms referring to physical traits of members of that group and character traits of members of that group *and* distinctive names of members of that group. Note that this is precisely the approach taken by Brewer, Dull, and Lui (1981), Brewer and Lui (1984), Linville (1982) and Linville, Fischer, and Salovey (1989) in gauging cognitive representations of social groups: Exemplar representation of a group is gauged in terms of more complexity in the sorting of information about that group, whereas prototype representation of a group is gauged in terms of less complexity in the sorting of information about that group.

Following this line of reasoning, Mullen and Johnson (1993) examined complexity in the use of ethnophaulisms as a function of the size of ethnic groups. Specifically, the complexity of the ethnophaulisms used to describe a specific ethnic group was derived from a classification that Allen conducted on his extensive lexicon of over 1,000 ethnophaulisms for ethnic groups in the United States. Allen (1983, pp. 45-73) classified all ethnophaulisms into six types: *physical traits, personal traits, personal names, food habits, group names,* and *other* (miscellaneous). In accord with the procedures followed by Brewer and Lui (1984) and Linville (1982), Scott's H statistic was derived for the ethnophaulisms used to characterize each group. Scott's H statistic (Scott, Osgood, & Peterson, 1979) is a gauge of category complexity that takes into account both the number of categories and the size of each category.[3] In the present context, a small Scott's H would be obtained when a given set of ethno-phaulisms is categorized into a few categories and most of those ethnophaulisms are placed into one of those categories. This repre-sents relatively low complexity and is indicative of relatively extreme prototype representation for that group. A large Scott's H would be obtained when a given set of ethnophaulisms is categorized into a large number of equal-sized categories. This represents relatively high complexity and is indicative of more exemplar representation for that group. The size of each ethnic group was estimated by Allen as the mean size of that group obtained from the 1880, 1910, 1930, and 1970 United States decennial reports (Allen, 1983, Table 4.3). Specifically, Allen (1983, p. 77) defined the size of an ethnic group as the number of first-generation persons of that group determined by mother tongue and country of birth.

The database for Mullen and Johnson's (1993) analyses comprised 30 ethnic groups. These 30 groups represented all of the ethnic groups for which Allen was able to locate ethnophaulisms and to derive group size from the census data. The remaining groups were generally too small to have elicited ethnophaulisms and/or to have been recorded by the census. The Scott's H statistic derived from the ethnophaulisms for each ethnic group was significantly predicted by the size of ethnic group, $r(28) = .526$, $p = .0014$. Thus, there was a significant tendency for smaller groups to be cognitively represented with less complexity in ethnophaulisms. These results could not be dismissed as an artifact of greater prejudice toward smaller groups. That is, relation between smaller group size and more prototype cognitive representation was functionally independent of the effects of prejudice, whereas the relation between cognitive representation and prejudice was substantially re-duced when the effects of group size were partialled out.

Cognitive Representations and Stereotyping. Mullen and Johnson's (1993) analysis of real ethnophaulisms for real ethnic groups lends a degree of ecological validity to their examination of cognitive representations in ethnophaulisms. However, their archival data (like any archival data) carried the possibility of latent confounds. First, the various ethnic groups included in Mullen and Johnson's analyses differed considerably in the semantic content of the ethnophaulisms ascribed to each group. For example, consider two groups of approximately equivalent size, the Italians and the Irish. For Italians, only 13% of their ethnophaulisms referred to personal names and 24% referred to foods; for Irish, 31% referred to personal names, and only 4% referred to foods. The possibility exists that these differences in semantic content may have somehow masked or exaggerated the fundamental link between group size, salience, and cognitive representation. Second, the ethnophaulisms ascribed to specific groups may have varied dramatically in valence. For example, references to personal characteristics (e.g., *paddywhack* for the Irish, alluding to loss of temper and fighting) were often more negative than references to foods (e.g., *potato-eater*). These differences in valence may have somehow masked or exaggerated the fundamental link between group size, salience, and cognitive representation.

Therefore, despite the intriguing patterns revealed in Mullen and Johnson's archival analysis of ethnophaulisms, it seemed important to examine the effects of salience on cognitive representations in ethnophaulisms in a more controlled manner. Specifically, the ethnophaulisms ascribed to novel ethnic groups had to be carefully designed to be matched in terms of semantic content and valence.

Beyond confirming in a more controlled manner the basic effect of group size on cognitive representations that was demonstrated in Mullen and Johnson (1993), it seemed important to examine the links between cognitive representation and stereotypes of ethnic groups. Recall that Mullen and Johnson (1993) reported that the relation between smaller group size and cognitive representation was functionally independent of the effects of prejudice, whereas the relation between cognitive representation and prejudice was substantially reduced when the effects of group size were partialled out. These data were interpreted as indicating that prejudice might be more a consequence than a cause of the effects of group size on cognitive representations. However, once again, the archival nature of Mullen and Johnson's (1993) data leave open alternative possible accounts for these effects (as discussed above). The goal of clarifying the relations between cognitive representations and stereotyping led Mullen and Johnson (1995) to examine complexity in ethnophaulisms in the context of the distinctiveness-based illusory correlation in stereotyping paradigm.

Illusory correlations are erroneous judgments of the relation between two variables. Hamilton and Gifford (1976) introduced the possibility that illusory correlations may be involved in the development of stereotypes. They showed subjects a series of stimulus items, each of which described a member of one of two groups performing either a positive or negative behavior. More of the stimulus items described one of the two groups, and more of the stimulus items described positive behaviors, but the overall proportion of items describing positive and negative behaviors was the same for both groups. Despite the fact that there was no actual correlation between group membership and the performance of a certain type of behavior, subjects overestimated the co-occurrence of the smaller group and the rarer behavior. This illusory correlation effect has been replicated by a number of independent researchers (see Hamilton & Sherman, 1989; Mullen & Johnson, 1990).

Mullen and Johnson's (1995) procedure was modeled after Hamilton and Gifford (1976, Exp. 1) and Mullen and Johnson (1993, Study 2). The experimenter read a description of the experiment as being concerned with the processing and retention of verbal information. Subjects were informed that they would hear about persons that were drawn from two real ethnic groups which would be referred to as Group A and Group B. Further, they were told that in the real world population, Group B is a smaller group than Group A and consequently statements describing members of Group B would occur less frequently in the sentences they would see.

Subjects were presented with 36 standard illusory correlation stimulus sentences (i.e., 16 sentences describing a member of group A performing some positive behavior, 8 group B-positive behavior sentences, 8 group A-negative behavior sentences, and 4 group

B-negative behavior sentences). Next, an ethnophaulism response sheet and a corresponding sheet of small stickers were distributed to subjects. Historically dated ethnophaulisms were selected which would not be recognizeable to contemporary subjects as referring to any specific ethnic group; each ethnophaulism was printed onto small (22 mm × 11 mm) stickers, with a brief explanation or translation printed beneath the ethnophaulism itself (e.g., "JACK (a common name)"; "ALGEREEN (coarse or obscene)"). The 11 ethnophaulisms for group A and the 11 ethnophaulisms for group B were selected to be equivalent in terms of semantic content, valence, the number of syllables, and the length of the ethnophaulism words. Subjects were told about ethnophaulisms and ethnic slurs, and that the stickers contained the ethnophaulisms that have been used in the past for one of the groups they just read about, and our interest was in studying how people think about these things. Subjects were asked to place the stickers on the page so that the ethnophaulisms that were most central to their idea of that ethnic group were placed close to the label (e.g., GROUP A) in the center of the large box, and the ethnophaulisms that were similar to one another were placed close together in the same cluster. When subjects completed this ethnophaulism sorting task for one group, they then received the response sheet and stickers for the remaining group, and completed the ethnophaulism sorting task for the remaining group.

After completing the sorting task, subjects completed an estimation measure of illusory correlation. Specifically, one item indicated that in the sentences they just read, there were 24 statements describing group A, and asked them to estimate how many of those 24 described a member of group A having performed some undesirable behavior. A second item indicated that they had read 12 statements describing group B, and asked them to estimate the number of statements describing a member of group B having performed some undesirable behavior.

The mean Scott's H for the smaller group B ($M = 2.31$) was significantly smaller than the mean Scott's H for the larger group A ($M = 2.43$), $F(1,25) = 4.65$, $p = .0205$. Thus, consistent with the reasoning developed in Mullen (1991) and with the data reported in

Mullen and Johnson (1993), the smaller ethnic group does appear to be subject to greater prototype cognitive representation, as evidenced in less complexity in the ethnophaulisms used to characterize that group.

Each subject's responses on the estimation task were used to construct 2×2 contingency tables representing the number of positive and negative behaviors for each of the two groups. A ϕ coefficient indicating the extent of judged covariation was derived for each of these individual contingency tables. The ϕ coefficients were transformed into Z_{Fisher} scores (scaled so that a positive Z_{Fisher} represented the association between "small group and negative behavior"), and the $\overline{Z}_{Fisher}$ score was tested against zero. A $\overline{Z}_{Fisher}$ of zero would indicate that the subjects accurately judged no correlation between group membership and behavior type. The $\overline{Z}_{Fisher} = 0.177$ was significantly different from zero, $t(25) = 3.406$, $p = .00112$, indicating that a significant illusory correlation effect was obtained. This supports previous findings on illusory correlation and indicates that the specific paradigm used in the present study was creating an illusory correlation effect comparable to that found in previous studies in this area.

The Z_{Fisher} transform of the ϕ coefficient derived from the estimation task provides a single numerical gauge of *illusory correlation*: As this number gets bigger, subjects are overestimating more negative behaviors for the smaller group. An analogous index was obtained for *cognitive representation* by subtracting each subject's Scott's H for the smaller group B from each subject's Scott's H for the larger group A: As this number gets bigger, subjects are engaging in more extreme prototype representation of the smaller group relative to the larger group. The correlation between these two indices reveals that cognitive representation was a significant predictor of illusory correlation, $r(24) = .341$, $p = .0440$, such that more extreme prototype representation of the smaller group predicted more extreme subsequent estimation of negative behaviors for the smaller group.

It is interesting to note that in a second study reported in Mullen and Johnson (1995), positive behaviors, rather than negative behaviors, were distinctive in the illusory correlation stimulus materials. The results of this second study demonstrated that the smaller group still elicited more extreme prototype representation: the mean Scott's H for the smaller group B ($M = 2.01$) was significantly smaller than the mean Scott's H for the larger group A ($M = 2.15$), $F(1,33) = 4.47$, $p = .0211$. In addition, the $\overline{Z}_{Fisher} = 0.083$ was significantly different from zero, $t(33) = 2.283$, $p = .0145$, indicating that a significant illusory correlation effect was still obtained even though the distinctive behaviors were now positive. Finally, the correlation between these two indices reveals that cognitive representation was a significant predictor of illusory correlation, $r(32) = .251$, $p = .0305$, such that more extreme prototype representation of the smaller group predicted more extreme subsequent estimation of positive behaviors for the smaller group. Thus, more extreme proto-type representation of the smaller ethnic group is not dependent upon negative affective valence toward the group, or some underlying assumption that "small groups are bad."

Alternative Contributions to Salience. One issue that is often raised in discussions of Mullen's (1991) formulation of the phenome-nology of being in a group is that many ingroup-outgroup categori-zations of approximately equal size still render prototype repre-sentations of the groups (e.g., males vs. females). Holding aside the possibility that such social categories can be made salient by virtue of situation specific proportionate group sizes (e.g., Mullen, 1983; Taylor, 1981), this concern highlights a more fundamental issue: While the phenomenology of being in a group perspective emphasizes relative group sizes as a common and robust means of enhancing the salience of one group over another, the fundamental mechanism in this perspective is *salience*. Accordingly, the group which is made salient by any means should be subject to greater prototype repre-sentation, even if it is not in a proportionate minority.

Fortunately, successful operationalizations of salience other than proportionate group size can be identified. For example, Sanbon-matsu, Sherman, and Hamilton (1987) reported an illusory correla-tion between membership in a specific group and distinctive (i.e., rare) behaviors when subjects were instructed to pay particular attention to the members of that group. Following this line of reasoning, a third study was conducted by Mullen and Johnson (1995) to examine the effect of salience on cognitive representations and stereotyping of groups of equal size. Even though the two groups were of equal size, if one of the groups was made more salient for some subjects by verbal instruction, then the group to which subjects were led to pay more attention should stimulate more prototype representation than the other group. In turn, these differences in cognitive representation should predict the stereotyping of these groups.

The results of this study confirmed the basic patterns reported in Mullen and Johnson (1993). The more distinctive ethnic groups were subject to greater prototype cognitive representations: the mean Scott's H for the more distinctive group B ($M = 2.21$) was significantly smaller than the mean Scott's H for the less distinctive group A ($M = 2.40$), $t(52) = 2.259$, $p = .0141$. These results also replicated the basic illusory correlation effect of overestimating negative events for the more distinctive group: the $\overline{Z}_{Fisher} = 0.143$ was significantly different from zero, $t(27) = 3.621$, $p = .00060$, indicating that a significant illusory correlation effect was still obtained even though the distinctiveness of the group was defined by verbal instructions rather than by relative size. Finally, the correlation between these two indices reveals that cognitive representation was once again a significant predictor of illusory correlation, $r(26) = .394$, $p = .0189$, such that more extreme prototype representation of the more distinctive group predicted more extreme subsequent estimation of negative behaviors for the more distinctive group.

The Validity of Complexity Approaches to Operationalizing Cognitive Representations. The foregoing studies are all based on the assumption that variation in complexity is a valid means of operationalizing modes of cognitive representations. For example, in the first epigram presented at the beginning of this article it would seem that Pope employed more prototype representation for women than for men, insofar as men are sorted according to "various" passions but women are sorted according to only two passions. In terms of Scott's H, the sorting of women into two categories or clusters renders a Scott's H = 1.000, whereas the sorting of men into three clusters (i.e., conservatively allowing "various" to be represented by three) renders a higher Scott's H = 1.585. This operationalization of cognitive representation conveys that less complexity (lower Scott's H) in the sorting of information about a group is indicative of greater prototype representation of the group.

Thus, Scott's H has been proposed as an operationalization of prototype-exemplar cognitive representation (e.g., Brewer & Lui, 1984; Linville, 1982; Linville et al., 1989). Despite this apparent conventional acceptance, the fact remains that there has been no empirical data employed to confirm or disconfirm the validity of categorical complexity and Scott's H as an operationalization of prototype-exemplar representation of social groups. Therefore, it seems important to determine whether Scott's H varies as a function of experimental manipulations of cognitive representation.

Another way to gauge the type of cognitive representation used for a social group is in terms of the dimensional complexity in the sorting of information about that group. Note that this is analogous to the approach taken by Foster and White (1982), and Funk, Horowitz, Lipshitz, and Young (1976) in gauging cognitive representations of social groups: The similarities or distances between exemplars of the group are subjected to analyses using "goodness of fit" indices derived from Multidimensional Scaling (MDS) such as Stress2, a gauge of dimensional complexity. Exemplar representation of a group is inferred from a poorer fit (higher Stress2) of an n-dimensional space to the geometric configuration of exemplars, whereas prototype representation of a group is inferred from a better fit (lower Stress2) of an n-dimensional space to the geometric configuration of exemplars.[4]

For example, in the second epigram presented earlier, it would seem that Calhoun employed more prototype representation for women than for men, insofar as women's newsworthiness can be represented by only two dimensions (marriage and death) whereas men's newsworthiness was by inference more multidimensional. In terms of Stress2 derived for a two-dimensional solution, the location of women's newsworthiness along two orthogonal dimensions would render a Stress2 approaching zero whereas the location of men's newsworthiness along these two dimensions would render a Stress2 approaching one. This operationalization of cognitive representation conveys that less complexity (lower Stress2) in the sorting of information about a group is indicative of greater prototype representation of the group.

Previous uses of MDS in stereotyping and intergroup perception research have been designed to elucidate the cognitive representation of an array of multiple target groups, where each exemplar is a particular group (e.g., Foster & White, 1982; Funk et al., 1976). In the present effort, MDS will be used to elucidate the cognitive representation of a single specific target group, where each exemplar is a particular member of the group. While Scott's H and categorical complexity has been proposed as an operationalization of prototype-exemplar cognitive representation of specific target groups (e.g., Brewer et al., 1981; Brewer & Lui, 1984; Mullen & Johnson, 1993, 1995), Stress2 and dimensional complexity has never been considered in this regard. Therefore, it seemed useful to determine whether Stress2 varies as a function of experimental manipulations of cognitive representation.

A possible consequence of variation in prototype-exemplar representation is variation in attention to specific features or attributes of exemplars: Prototype representations are presumed to increase attention to specific features that exemplars have in common, whereas exemplar representations are presumed to increase attention to specific features that distinguish exemplars from one another. For example, consider a teacher who has identical twins in her class: The teacher who employs a prototype representation for this social category ("the twins") will focus on the features that the exemplars share in common (e.g., "the twins are atheletic," "the twins are mischievous"). Alternatively, the teacher who employs an exemplar representation for this social category will focus on the features that distinguish between the exemplars (e.g., "Jon is good at math, Ron is good at spelling").[5] Thus, if Scott's H and Stress2 serve as valid indicators of cognitive representations, then increases in attention to distinguishing features for members of a social group should be predicted by increases in both Scott's H and Stress2.

Therefore, Rozell and Mullen (1995) undertook a study in an effort to examine the construct validity of complexity operationalizations of cognitive representation. A set of 15 stick people were modeled after the stimulus materials presented in Kraus et al. (1993). Specifically, these stick people varied on two dimensions: Body size (fat, normal, thin), and arm location (low, normal, high). The total group of 15 was comprised of three exemplars of each of five types of stick people (fat-low, normal-normal, normal-high, thin-normal, thin-high). Each stick person was printed onto a small (22 mm × 11 mm) sticker. The response sheet for the stick person sorting task contained a large (195 mm × 170 mm) printed box, in the center of which was printed a small (34 mm × 8 mm) label box (i.e., GROUP).

The procedure was modelled after Kraus et al. (1993) and Mullen and Johnson (1993, 1995). The stick person response sheet and the corresponding sheet of small stickers were distributed to subjects. Subjects were told that the stickers contained the members of a specific social group, and our interest was in studying how people think about these things. Subjects were asked to place the stickers on the page so that the stickers that were most central to their idea of that group were placed close to the label (i.e., GROUP) in the center of the large box and the stickers that were similar to one another were placed close together in the same cluster. An example of the stick people stickers sorted onto a response sheet is presented in Figure 9.3. After completing the sorting task, subjects were asked to write one sentence describing the strategy they followed in sorting the stickers.

Subjects completed this task in one of three conditions. A *control condition* (*n* = 22) performed the task just as described above. A *prototype instruction condition* (*n* = 33) received an instructional set designed to emphasize attention to common features and memory of the typical group member. This instructional set was derived from Medin's (1989; Medin et al., 1984) characterization of prototype models as representing a category in terms of the central tendency of the category members, and in terms of the average or typical attributes. These subjects in the prototype instruction condition first received the following instructions:

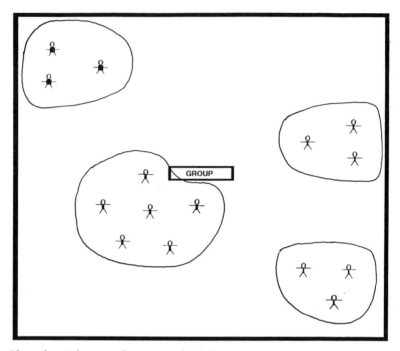

Place the stickers on the page in the following way:

- The stickers that are more central to your impressions of this group should be placed near to the GROUP box in the center of the page. The stickers that are less central to your impression of this group should be placed far from that central box.

- The stickers that are related to one another should be placed near to one another in a "cluster"; the stickers that are different from one another should be placed far from one another in different clusters.

- Use as many or as few clusters as you need. A cluster can contain only one sticker, or it can contain several stickers. A given sticker can only belong to one cluster.

- When all of the stickers have been placed on the page, draw a circle around each separate cluster of stickers that go together in your impression of this group.

Figure 9.3. An Example of the Stick People Sticker Task

In performing this task, pay attention to what the members of this group have in common. Try to keep in mind what the typical group member looks like.

An exemplar instruction condition ($n = 27$) received an instructional set designed to emphasize attention to distinguishing features and memory of each group member. This instructional set was derived from Medin's (1989; Medin et al., 1984) characterization of exemplar models as representing a category in terms of the retrieval of information about specific category members rather than on summary information about typical attributes. These subjects in the exemplar instruction condition first received the following instructions:

In performing this task, pay attention to the differences between the members of this group. Try to keep in mind what each of these group members looks like.

It should be recognized that these instructional sets do not emphasize or even mention the clustering of exemplars into more or fewer categories (categorical complexity). And these instructional sets do *not* emphasize or even mention the configuring of exemplars along more or fewer dimensions (dimensional complexity). Rather, these instructional sets merely direct subjects to cognitively represent the group in terms of the typical group member and common attributes (prototype representation) *or* in terms of retrieval of information about specific group members (exemplar representation).

Scott's H statistic was derived for each subject's sorting of the 15 group members. A one-way ANOVA of Scott's H revealed a significant condition effect, $F(2,79) = 3.205$, $p = .0460$. A significant *a priori* contrast across conditions, $F(1,79) = 6.037$, $p = .00810$, confirmed the predicted pattern of results: The mean Scott's H for the group was lowest in the prototype condition ($M = 1.711$), moderate in the control condition ($M = 1.889$), and highest in the exemplar condition ($M = 1.970$). Thus, consistent with previous uses of this approach (e.g., Brewer & Lui, 1984; Linville et al., 1989; Mullen & Johnson, 1993, 1995), the prototype instructions appeared to render a significant decrease in categorical complexity, whereas the exemplar instructions appeared to render a significant increase in categorical complexity.

A metric MDS analysis was performed on each subject's placement of the stickers on the page and an index of the goodness of fit was derived for each subject. Specifically, the euclidean distances between each pair of the 15 group members were determined, and a two- dimensional metric MDS solution was applied to each subject's matrix of distances. In the present context, a Stress2 approaching 0.000 would be obtained when all 15 stickers are placed directly along two orthogonal dimensions (e.g., in the shape of an "X"). This Stress2 = 0.000 represents relatively low dimensional complexity such that two dimensions adequately account for the subject's placement of the stickers on the page, and is indicative of relatively extreme prototype representation for that group. A Stress2 approaching 1.000 would be obtained when the 15 stickers are placed in a configuration that less clearly defines a two-dimensional space. This Stress2 = 1.000 represents relatively high dimensional complexity such that two dimensions do not adequately account for the subject's placement of the stickers on the page, and is indicative of relatively extreme exemplar representation of that group.

A one-way ANOVA of Stress2 revealed a significant condition effect, $F(2,79) = 6.938$, $p = .0017$. A significant *a priori* contrast across conditions, $F(1,79) = 6.950$, $p = .00504$, partially confirmed the predicted pattern of results: The mean Stress2 for the group was lowest in the prototype condition ($M = 0.614$), and higher in the exemplar condition ($M = 0.692$). However, the mean Stress2 was highest in the control condition ($M = 0.724$). It should be noted that the Stress2 for the prototype condition was significantly different from that for the control condition ($t(79) = 3.492$, $p = .00039$) and that for the exemplar condition ($t(79) = 2.626$, $p = .00519$), whereas the exemplar condition and the control condition did not significantly differ ($t(79) = 0.973$, $p = .1668$). Thus, while the exemplar instructions did not seem to render any significant change in the degree of dimensional complexity, the prototype instructions did render a significant decrease in dimensional complexity.

The sentences that subjects wrote to describe their sticker sorting strategies were analyzed for references to distinguishing features. Specifically, tabulations were made for a subject's mentioning of: size/shape of body; location of arms; location of legs; thickness of neck; and placement of head. A one-way ANOVA of the number of features mentioned revealed a marginally significant condition effect, $F(2,79) = 2.924$ $p = .0595$. A significant a priori contrast across conditions, $F(1,79) = 5.049$, $p = .0137$, confirmed the predicted pattern of results: The mean number of distinguishing features was lowest in the prototype condition ($M = 0.79$), moderate in the control condition ($M = 0.82$), and highest in the exemplar condition ($M = 1.30$). This lends additional credence to the assumption that the prototype and exemplar instructional sets were in fact engaging these distinct modes of cognitive representation.

In addition, the Scott's H derived from the sticker sorting task was a significant predictor of the subsequent number of distinguishing features mentioned, $r(80) = .194$, $p = .0405$: The lower the degree of categorical complexity (as represented by a lower Scott's H), the less attention paid to distinguishing features. Similarly, the Stress2 derived from the sticker sorting task was a significant predictor of the subsequent number of distinguishing features mentioned, $r(80) = .196$, $p = .0392$: The lower the degree of dimensional complexity (as represented by lower Stress2), the less attention paid to distinguishing features.

CONCLUSIONS

The results from Rozell and Mullen's (1995) validation study confirm the use of complexity operationalizations such as Scott's H and Stress2 as indicators of prototype-exemplar cognitive representations. Scott's H and Stress2 decreased when instructions were designed to engage prototype representation, and Scott's H increased when instructions were designed to engage exemplar representation. Moreover, variations in these complexity operationalizations predicted subsequent attention to distinguishing features for members of that group. In sum, Scott's H, and to a somewhat lesser extent

Stress2, varied as expected as a function of experimental manipulations of cognitive representation, and both complexity measures predicted a theoretical correlate of cognitive representation. One puzzle in these data is the fact that Scott's H and Stress2 evidenced slightly different patterns across the experimental conditions: Both complexity operationalizations decreased as predicted in the prototype instruction condition. However, while Scott's H increased as predicted in the exemplar instruction condition, Stress2 was essentially unaffected. Dimensional complexity thus seemed less responsive than categorical complexity to the experimental manipulations of exemplar cognitive representations.

Nonetheless, Stress2 does seem to capture some facet of cognitive representations. This is evidenced by the significant correlation between Stress2 and Scott's H ($r(80) = .296$, $p = .0035$). Moreover, Stress2 was, like Scott's H, a significant predictor of attention to distinguishing features. Thus, dimensional complexity (as operationalized by Stress2) may be a good indicator of cognitive representations, it's just that categorical complexity (as operationalized by Scott's H) seems to be even better. This lends more credence to future uses of Scott's H as an operationalization of prototype-exemplar cognitive representation (see Mullen & Johnson, 1993, 1995).

It is interesting to consider intergroup conflict interventions based upon these results. For example, consider the effects of the verbal instructions employed in this procedure: The prototype instructions decreased attention to distinguishing features, whereas the exemplar instructions increased attention to distinguishing features. In other words, instructions to process information about a target group with prototype representations is likely to exaggerate some of the common consequences of intergroup perception (e.g., ingroup bias, relative heterogeneity, etc.). Alternatively, instructions to process information about a target group with exemplar representations may mitigate some of these common consequences of intergroup perception. However, these common consequences of intergroup perception are notoriously intractable in real world settings. Instilling exemplar cognitive representations for real target groups via instructions may be desirable but very difficult.

There is an intriguing alternative to merely exhorting people to engage in exemplar representation of target groups. The present data show that the strategic engagement of exemplar representation for social groups does lead to greater *categorical* complexity in the cognitive representation of those social groups. It is possible that the reverse logic may also hold: that is, encouraging people to represent a target group with greater categorical complexity might in turn lead to greater exemplar representation for that group. For example, referring once again to the epigrams, Pope might have developed a more generous portrayal of women if he had been encouraged to consider women in terms of those ruled by the love of pleasure and those ruled by the love of sway and those ruled by the love of math and those ruled by the love of medicine, and so on.

It should be recognized that the present data indicate that the strategic engagement of exemplar representation for social groups does *not* lead to more *dimensional* complexity in the cognitive representation of those social groups. Therefore, encouraging people to represent a target group with greater dimensional complexity would not be likely to lead to greater exemplar representation for that group. For example, referring once again to the epigrams, Calhoun might not have developed any more generous portrayal of women if he had been encouraged to consider women's newsworthiness in terms of the dimensions of marriage and death and wealth and strength, and so on. Future research might be directed toward pursuing the link between interventions designed to increase categorical or dimensional complexity employed for target groups and subsequent exemplar representation of those groups.

At a broader level, the present results speak to current discussions about modes of cognitive representation of social groups. Consistent with the phenomenology of being in a group perspective discussed by Mullen (1991), the results of these studies confirm the basic tendency for smaller groups to be cognitively represented with more extreme prototype representations.

These results illustrate the paradox of the non-prototypical exemplar of the minority group, as discussed by Mullen (1991): The non-prototypical exemplar (e.g., in Study 1 of Mullen & Johnson

[1995]), instances of a member of group B engaging in a positive behavior) has the greatest potential to ameliorate the negative stereotype of the minority group, but this non-prototypical exemplar is seldom successful in doing so. The prototype representation of the smaller group (evidenced in Mullen & Johnson, 1993, 1995) makes it less likely that the non-prototypical exemplar will be deeply and accurately processed. And this inaccurate processing of the non-prototypical exemplar is consistent with greater inaccuracies in the handling of that type of exemplar, and the longer decision latencies required to render accurate retrieval of that exemplar (evidenced in Johnson & Mullen, 1994).

This reasoning is similar to the patterns reported by Forgas (1983). Subjects in this earlier research evidenced superior processing of prototype-consistent information for high-salience social subgroups and superior processing of prototype-inconsistent information for low-salience social subgroups. Similarly, Mullen, Johnson, and Anthony (1994) used the category verification paradigm employed by Smith and Zárate (1990) to study exemplar and prototype representations of social groups. In two studies, Mullen et al. (1995) found that prototype representations predominated for smaller groups and exemplar representations predominated for larger groups. Moreover, nonprototypical exemplars for the smaller group were seen as least representative of any social group, and were subject to the minimal amount of attentional processing. Thus, paradoxically, the stimulus events which have the highest potential informational capacity to change stereotypes of minority groups are unlikely to be effective: The cognitive representation of the group engendered by the salience of that minority ethnic group precludes the accurate handling of information about those prototype-disconfirming exemplars. The interplay between relative group size, salience, and cognitive representations remains one of the most intriguing puzzles of the phenomenology of being in a group.

Notes

1. A considerable amount of research (e.g., Medin et al., 1984; Mullen et al., 1994; Schul & Burnstein, 1990; Smith & Zárate, 1990) converges on the tendency

for people to use prototype representations when those prototypes are primed or made easily accessible. The data presented in Mullen (1991) and Mullen et al. (1994) suggest that the salience afforded the smaller group by its relative rarity is what primes or evokes the prototype representation for that group.

2. Another obvious instance of the minority target character in Shakespeare is of course the troubled Moor, Othello. However, there was no variation whatsoever in references to Othello when he was present in the scene. Apparently, his status as leader and his prowess as soldier combined to lead all other characters to refer to him with respect and deference in his presence.

3. Scott's H statistic was calculated as follows:

$$H = \log_2 N - (\textstyle\sum n_i \log2 \, n_i)/N$$

where N = total number of ethnophaulisms, and n_i = number of ethnophaulisms in category or cluster i. See Scott et al. (1979) for a presentation of this index; see Brewer and Lui (1984), and Linville (1982) for applications of this index to prototype-exemplar representations of social groups; and, see Brewer (1988, 1993), Carpenter (1993), Linville and Fischer (1993), and Messick and Mackie (1989) for recent discussions of prototype and exemplar representations of social groups that cite these earlier applications.

4. Stress2 is a goodness of fit index (actually a *poorness* of fit index insofar as Stress2 increases when the original geometric configuration of exemplars is not adequately accounted for by an n-dimensional space). Stress2 is calculated as follows:

$$\text{Stress2} = \left[\textstyle\sum (d_{ij} - \delta_{ij})^2 / \sum (d_{ij} - d)^2 \right]^{1/2}$$

where d_{ij} = original distance between exemplars i and j (e.g., stickers in a sticker sorting task), δij = distance between exemplars i and j estimated from n-dimensional solution, and d = mean original distance between all exemplars). See Coxon (1982), Davison (1982) and Weinberg (1991) for presentations of MDS and Stress2; and, see Foster and White (1982), and Funk et al. (1976) for applications of MDS to the cognitive representation of social groups.

A few things should be made explicit about the present application of MDS to cognitive representations of social groups. Given the nature of the static two-dimensional requirements of the sticker-sorting task (see below), metric MDS with euclidean distances was performed, examining the fit of a two-dimensional model. Moreover, it should be recognized that alternative good-(poor-)ness of fit indices (such as Stress1 and ϕ) were also pursued in the present data. For example, Stress1 and ϕ evidenced a very high correlation with Stress2 in the present data ($r(80)$ = .958 and $r(80)$ = .907, respectively), and the analyses reported below rendered equivalent results when conducted upon Stress1 and ϕ. Some authors (e.g., Coxon, 1982) argue that Stress2 should always be chosen over Stress1, although in the present data there seemed to be no practicable difference in results.

5. We would like to thank Steve Neuberg for suggesting this intriguing possibility.

10

The Contact Hypothesis
The Role of a Common Ingroup Identity on Reducing Intergroup Bias Among Majority and Minority Group Members

SAMUEL L. GAERTNER
MARY C. RUST
JOHN F. DOVIDIO
BETTY A. BACHMAN
PHYLLIS A. ANASTASIO

F or the past 40 years, the "contact hypothesis" (Allport, 1954; Amir, 1969; Cook, 1985) has represented a promising and popular strategy for reducing intergroup bias and conflict. It

AUTHORS' NOTE: Preparation of this chapter was facilitated by a grant from the National Institutes of Mental Health (Grant RO1MH48721) to Samuel Gaertner and John Dovidio. We thank Stephen Worchel and Lowell Gaertner for their thoughtful suggestions on an earlier version of the manuscript. Requests for reprints should be sent to Samuel L. Gaertner, Department of Psychology, University of Delaware, Newark, DE 19716, or via e-mail to Gaertner@strauss.udel.edu.

proposes that intergroup contact under *certain prerequisite conditions* promotes the development of more harmonious intergroup relations. Among these specific conditions are equal status between the groups (optimally within and outside of the contact setting), cooperative intergroup interaction, opportunities for personal acquaintance between outgroup members, and norms within and outside of the contact setting that support egalitarian intergroup interaction (Cook, 1985). Research within laboratory and field settings generally supports the efficacy of the list of prerequisite conditions for achieving improved intergroup relations (Blanchard, Weigel, & Cook, 1975; Cook, 1969, 1985; Deutsch & Collins, 1951; Green, Adams, & Turner, 1988; Stephan, 1978; Weigel, Wiser, & Cook, 1975).

Structurally, however, the contact hypothesis has represented a list of loosely connected, diverse conditions rather than a unifying conceptual framework that explains *how* these prerequisite features achieve their effects. This is problematic because political and socioeconomic circumstances often preclude introducing these features into many contact settings. In the absence of an explanatory framework, it is not clear what alternatives to substitute for these specific conditions.

Recently, researchers have developed more theoretically unifying approaches (Brewer & Miller, 1984; Gaertner, Dovidio, Anastasio, Bachman, & Rust, 1993; Islam & Hewstone, 1993; Miller, Brewer, & Edwards, 1985; Stephan & Stephan, 1984, 1985). Each of these perspectives suggests that the conditions for successful intergroup contact influence the ways that people process social information about outgroup members. Stephan and Stephan (1984, 1985) proposed that these features contribute to the elimination of ignorance about outgroup members and consequently to reduced feelings of intergroup anxiety. With reduced feelings of anxiety, the perceptual field becomes broader and impressions of outgroup members can become more accurate, less polarized, and more favorable (see Islam & Hewstone, 1993). Brewer and Miller (1984) proposed a decategorization model in which the conditions specified by the contact hypothesis are presumed to reduce the tendency to categorize other people as ingroup *and* outgroup members and induce more differentiated, personalized interactions. The resulting individualized impressions of outgroup members then challenge the validity of category-based stereotypes and thereby cause perceivers to abandon them.

The research reported in this chapter examines an additional approach: the common ingroup identity model (Gaertner et al., 1993). This approach recognizes the importance of social categorization for promoting intergroup bias and proposes that the conditions for successful contact, in part, transform members' cognitive representations of the memberships from separate groups to one more inclusive group. That is, equal status, cooperative interaction, interpersonal interaction, and supportive norms reduce bias because they alter members' cognitive representations of the memberships from "us" and "them" to a more inclusive "we" (see Brown & Turner, 1981; Doise, 1978; Feshbach & Singer, 1957; Hornstein, 1976; Worchel, Axsom, Ferris, Samaha, & Schweitzer, 1978). Thus, circumstances that induce a common ingroup identity extend the cognitive and motivational processes that produce positive feelings toward ingroup members (Brewer, 1979) to former outgroup members. In application, a common ingroup identity may be achieved by increasing the salience of existing common superordinate group memberships or by introducing factors (e.g., common tasks or fate) that are perceived to be shared by the memberships. Allport (1954) was aware of the benefits of a common ingroup identity, though he regarded it as a catalyst rather than as a product of the conditions of contact.

> To be maximally effective, contact and acquaintance programs should lead to a sense of equality in social status, should occur in ordinary purposeful pursuits, avoid artificiality, and if possible enjoy the sanction of the community in which they occur. While it may help somewhat to place members of different ethnic groups side by side on a job, the gain is greater if these members regard themselves as part of a *team*. (p. 489, italics added)

In addition, Sherif and Sherif (1969, pp. 268-269) recognized the capacity of intergroup cooperation to facilitate the development of a common superordinate entity, but this was conceived to be a long-term rather than an initial consequence of this activity.

The common ingroup identity model proposes that conditions of contact such as cooperative interdependence, equal status, supportive norms, and degree of interaction can influence cognitive representations of the aggregate in three ways. These factors can influence the extent to which members of different groups perceive that they share a *common ingroup identity,* represent *separate individuals* rather than two groups, or continue to have completely *separate group* identities. Each of these representations has different implications for intergroup bias. The separate individuals and the one-group representations are both hypothesized to reduce intergroup bias—but in different ways. Changing the representation of the aggregate from two groups to separate individuals is expected to reduce bias primarily because the orientation toward ingroup members becomes less positive (Brewer, 1979; Turner, 1985). Changing the representation from two groups to one group, however, should reduce intergroup bias by producing more positive feelings toward former outgroup members.

The development of a common ingroup identity does not necessarily require each group to forsake its subgroup identity completely. For example, it is possible for people to conceive of two groups (e.g., offensive and defensive football squads) as operating interdependently within the context of a superordinate identity. Furthermore, in many contexts, forsaking the original subgroup identity would be impossible or undesirable. Thus, if members of different groups maintained their earlier identities but conceived of themselves, for example, as though they were members of different groups but all playing on the same *team,* the intergroup consequences should be somewhat different than if members maintained a one-group representation in which the original group boundaries were more completely degraded.

Earlier laboratory work has produced evidence that is supportive of the common ingroup identity model. One study directly investigated how categorization and cognitive representations influence intergroup bias. Gaertner, Mann, Murrell, and Dovidio (1989) induced the members of two three-person laboratory-formed groups to conceive of the total six-person aggregate as one group, two groups, or as separate individuals (i.e., no groups) by systematically varying factors within the contact situation such as the spatial arrangement of the members (i.e., integrated, segregated, or separated seating pattern) and the nature of the interdependence among the participants. Dependent variables included ratings of subjects' representations of the aggregate (one group, two groups, or separate individuals) as well as evaluation ratings.

In terms of reducing bias, the one-group and the separate individuals conditions each had lower levels of bias compared to the two-groups condition. Furthermore, the one-group and the separate individuals reduced bias in different ways—as we expected. In the one-group condition, bias was reduced primarily by enhancing the evaluations of former outgroup members, whereas in the separate individuals condition, bias was reduced largely by decreasing the attractiveness of former ingroup members. Thus, as specified by Turner, Hogg, Oakes, Reicher, and Wetherell's (1987) self-categorization theory, "the attractiveness of an individual is not constant, but varies with ingroup membership" (p. 60).

More directly related to the conditions for successful intergroup contact, a second laboratory study (Gaertner, Mann, Dovidio, Murrell, & Pomare, 1990) supported the view that the causal relations between intergroup cooperation and reduced bias are mediated by transformations in members' representations of the aggregate from two groups to one group, as proposed by the model. In this study, two separate three-person groups were brought into contact under circumstances designed to vary independently the members' *representations* of the aggregate (one group or two groups) and the presence or absence of intergroup *cooperative interaction*.

When the groups were induced to conceive of themselves as one group rather than two groups by factors (e.g., seating arrangement, the utilization of the groups' earlier names or the assignment of a new group name to represent the six participants) *independent of cooperation,* bias in evaluative ratings was reduced. This finding supported the assumed causal relationship between members' representations and intergroup bias. Also consistent with our framework, when the groups initially conceived of themselves as two groups, the introduction of cooperative interaction increased the extent to which members rated the aggregate as one group and decreased bias in evaluative ratings. As expected, reduced bias following cooperation was due primarily to enhanced favorable evaluations of outgroup members (see Dovidio, Gaertner, Isen, & Lowrance, 1995). Furthermore, members' perceptions of the aggregate mediated the relation between cooperative interaction and reduced bias. Cooperation increased perceptions of one group, which in turn related to lower bias.

The purposes of the current study (see also Gaertner, Rust, Dovidio, Bachman, & Anastasio, 1994) are to conceptually replicate our laboratory work on the common ingroup identity model in a more naturalistic setting and to extend our previous work by (a) examining how affective reactions predict favorability of responses in intergroup situations, (b) considering the role of dual identities (i.e., two groups on the same team or a minority subgroup in addition to a superordinate common ingroup identity, for example, a Japanese American) as an independent factor reducing bias, and, for this volume in particular, by (c) exploring how majority (i.e., Caucasian) and ethnic minority group status may influence relevant features of the model.

In the present research, a survey was administered to students attending a multicultural high school in which Black, Chinese, Hispanic, Japanese, Jewish, Korean, Vietnamese, and Caucasian (Italian, Polish, German, etc.) students were represented. The survey asked students to rate their degree of agreement with items that measured their impressions of the school's intergroup climate along dimensions proposed by the contact hypothesis (i.e., equal status, cooperative interaction, interpersonal interaction, and supportive norms). The items tapping these specific dimensions were modifications of a subset of items developed by Green et al. (1988) to measure a school's climate relating to Black and White students. Green et al. (1988) found strong positive associations between students' perceptions of favorable conditions of contact and the proportions of interracial friendships, the extent of cafeteria racial integration, and teachers' perceptions of the effectiveness of desegregation. In addition to items measuring the conditions of contact, we included items to measure students' perceptions of the student body as being one group, on the same team, different groups, or separate individuals. In our framework, these perceptions represent the proposed mediators of the relationship between the conditions of contact and students' inter-group attitudes. Finally, we included items to measure students' intergroup affect and attitudes.

There is converging support for the idea that overall attitudinal favorability toward groups and social distance preferences for these groups are strongly determined by affect (Stangor, Sullivan, & Ford, 1991; see also Abelson, Kinder, Peters, & Fiske, 1982, for an examination of these issues in a political context). Therefore, we included affect and favorability items similar to those used by Stangor et al. (1991) and Abelson et al. (1982). These items permit feelings about and overall attitudes toward several groups to be evaluated in a minimum amount of time. One set of items asked about students' affective responses to each of the groups (e.g., How often do Koreans make you feel good?). The other measure asked about each student's overall attitudinal favorability toward *each* of the ethnic, racial, and nationality groups.

With respect to replicating our laboratory research in a natural setting, we expected that mediation analysis (Baron & Kenny, 1986; Judd & Kenny, 1981) would reveal that students' perceptions of the student body as one group or as separate groups would mediate the relation between the conditions of contact and the affective reactions toward these groups as well as students' overall attitudinal favorability toward them. With regard to the determining role of affect on overall attitudinal favorability, as suggested by Stangor et al. (1991; see also Abelson et al., 1982), we expected that mediation analysis would also reveal that affective reactions would predict overall attitudinal favorability toward each group. This possibility is consistent with Stephan and Stephan's (1984, 1985) emphasis on the role that feelings of intergroup anxiety play in determining favorability of intergroup attitudes.

In addition to examining whether transformations in students' representations of the student body mediate the relationship between the conditions of contact and intergroup attitudes, the current study affords an opportunity to extend our previous research by examining the value of a dual identity on the reduction of intergroup bias. If perceiving a common, more inclusive group identity with members of other groups increases positive feelings toward them, then students who identify themselves as American in addition to one of the other minority group identities (e.g., Japanese, Korean, or other—for example, Polish) should have lower degrees of bias overall than students who do not additionally describe themselves with the more inclusive American identity. Although other explanations would of course be plausible (e.g., differences in citizenship status or in assimilation), this result would be consistent with the idea that a cognitive representation in which the subgroup and superordinate identities are salient simultaneously reduces bias toward other groups within the superordinate entity. Similarly, a representation involving two subgroups within a more inclusive superordinate identity (i.e., members of different groups playing on the same team) should be associated with reduced levels of intergroup bias toward others within the superordinate boundary.

The diversity of the student body also permits the current study to examine whether majority and ethnic minority group membership relates to students' perceptions and intergroup attitudes and to the pattern of mediation proposed by the model. Although there is no substantive reason to expect the pattern of mediation to be different for majority and minority students, there are reasons to expect these groups to differ in terms of the favorability of their perceptions of the conditions of contact, their representations of the student body, and in their levels of intergroup bias. Because groups with power and status usually have greater control over intergroup contact conditions, they are more likely to emphasize its positive qualities relative to those with less control. Supportive of these ideas, Islam and Hewstone's (1993) richly detailed study involving university students in Bangladesh reported that the Muslim majority students relative to the Hindu minority students maintained more favorable qualitative perceptions of the conditions of contact, lower levels of intergroup anxiety (see Stephan & Stephan, 1984, 1985), and lower degrees of intergroup bias. In the United States, African Americans perceive less favorable contact (i.e., more conflict) between the social classes (Davis & Smith, 1991) and less equal opportunity for minorities (Kluegel & Smith, 1982) than do White Americans. Furthermore, several studies report that members of majority groups express lower degrees of ingroup bias than minority group members (e.g., Brewer, Manzi, & Shaw, 1993; Gerard & Hoyt, 1974; Mummendey & Simon, 1989; Sachdev & Bourhis, 1991).

Additional research links the increased level of ingroup bias among minority group members to the relatively higher salience of their minority group social identities (see Brewer & Miller, 1984), which is attributable, in part, to the increased self-attention that occurs as the proportion of ingroup membership decreases relative to outgroup membership (Mullen, 1983, 1987). Therefore, when a superordinate identity is available to members of various groups, minority groups may identify less with the superordinate entity than the majority group because of the relative salience of their own group identities. Therefore, in the current study, we expect minority status to be associated with less favorable impressions of the conditions of contact, weaker endorsement of the superordinate representations of the student body, and higher levels of intergroup bias. Two factors could contribute to the higher bias of minority group members. First, as suggested by the work on group size and relative group salience (Mullen, 1983, 1987), bias for minorities may reflect, in part, more positive feelings for ingroup members by minority group than by the majority group. Second, as suggested by the common ingroup identity model (Gaertner et al., 1993), because minorities would be less likely to identify with a superordinate entity than the majority, bias among minorities may reflect less positive feelings toward outgroup members. Nevertheless, given the limitations of this study, we would be unable to determine whether any observed differences between majority and minority students were due to the purely perceptual consequences of being in a numerical minority or majority or to factors associated with possible socioeconomic status or cultural differences between these groups.

In summary, the present research conceptually attempts to replicate the laboratory work on the mediating role of cognitive representations of the aggregate and to extend our previous work by (a) examining how affective responses predict overall attitudinal favorability of intergroup responses (Abelson et al., 1982; Stangor et al., 1991), (b) considering the role of the dual identity (i.e., students identifying themselves as both an American and as a member of an ethnic minority group) on cognitive and affective consequences of intergroup contact, and (c) examining the role of students' majority and minority group status on features pertaining to the common ingroup identity model.

METHOD

Subjects

There were 1,357 students attending a multicultural high school in the northeastern United States that participated in the survey. The sample very closely approximated the school's diversity: 1.6% Black, 1.6% Chinese, 3.7% Hispanic, 4.4% Japanese, 18.0% Korean, 0.9% Vietnamese, and 68.9% Caucasian (about one fifth of whom are Jewish).

Procedure

A survey was administered as a preliminary assessment related to a series of diversity workshops sponsored by the school district. Instructions on the survey stated that participation was voluntary and that students were free to refuse to answer any or all questions. Each student received a computer scan form and a copy of the survey containing 90 items. The first several items asked for demographic information. Among these questions, students were asked to indicate which racial, ethnic, and nationality groups they were members of by indicating "Yes" and "No" as often as each group applied to them: American, Black, Chinese, Hispanic, Japanese, Korean, Jewish, Vietnamese, White, and other(s) _____ (to be indicated on the back of the scan form). Next, the survey asked students to rate their degree of agreement (1-5) with 17 items that inquired about their perceptions of the school's intergroup climate along dimensions specified by the contact hypothesis. These specific items were modifications of those (with the highest factor loadings) developed by Green et al. (1988). Our modifications increased the suitability of these items for use with a more racially and ethnically diverse student body. Our items measured students' perceptions of *equal status* (e.g., "All students at this school are treated equally"), *cooperative interdependence* (e.g., "The different groups of students at this school have important things to offer each other"), *the degree of association and interaction* (e.g., "I talk to students from groups other than my own only when I have to"), and *supportive norms* (e.g., "The principal and assistant principals encourage students to make friends with students from different groups").

We also included four items designed to measure the proposed mediators that involved the extent (1 = Strongly disagree; 5 = Strongly agree) of students' perceptions of the student body as *One Group* ("Despite the different groups at school, there is frequently the sense that we are all just one group"), *Two Groups* ("At school, it usually feels as though we belong to different groups"), and *Separate Individuals* ("At school, it usually feels as though we are individuals and not members of a particular group"). For purposes of exploration, a fourth item, *On the Same Team*, was included to recognize the existence of different groups within the context of a common, superordinate entity ("Although there are different groups of students at this school, it feels as though we are all playing on the same team"). Indeed, the distinction between the one-group and the same-team items is very subtle. We assumed that if these items are perceived to tap different types of superordinate ingroup identities, then in the planned regression analyses (in which they would be entered simultaneously), they would have independent effects.

Finally, two indicators of students' attitudes toward ingroup and outgroup members were measured. First, an adaptation of the "feelings thermometer" used routinely in survey research (Abelson et al., 1982) asked students to indicate their overall favorability (1 = Extremely unfavorable; 5 = Neutral; 9 = Extremely favorable) toward each of the racial, ethnic, and nationality groups represented in the sample. The (1-9) scan form did not easily permit us to use the 100-point scale usually associated with this attitudinal indicator, but this procedure enabled subjects to rate the large number of social groups easily and in a reasonable period of time. Second, as indicators of students' affective reactions to their own group and also about each of the other groups, they rated the extent (1 = Never; 9 = Always) to which each group, "because of things they have done or things that you know about them, usually make[s] you feel" *good, bad, uneasy,* or *respectful.*

RESULTS

Assessing Intergroup Contact

An initial factor analysis with varimax rotation was performed on the students' ratings of the school's conditions of intergroup contact and their perceptions of the student body (as one group, on the same team, different groups, or separate individuals). This analysis yielded four factors (with eigen values of at least 1.00) that very closely approximated the factor structure of the Green et al. (1988) measures for the conditions of contact: equal status, cooperative interdependence, degree of interaction, and supportive norms. A fifth factor (eigen value = 1.18) was composed of items that measured students' representations of the student body (i.e., the proposed mediators). Thus, our modifications to Green et al.'s (1988) items did not alter the utility of these items to tap the same dimensions of contact in our more diverse sample. Also, there is support for the idea that the items developed in our laboratory relating to students' perceptions of the student body (as one group, on the same team, different groups, or as separate individuals) cluster together and have some phenomenological coherence in this multicultural setting.

The items that loaded highest on each of the four dimensions of contact (see Table 10.1) were averaged together to form four separate indexes of contact. The mean scores on each of these indexes (which could range from 1 to 5) suggested that students perceived the conditions of contact to be moderately, but not strongly, favorable: Interdependence (mean = 3.44), Interaction (mean = 3.80), Equal status (mean = 3.21), and Supportive norms (mean = 4.01). The averages of these four separate indexes of contact were averaged together to create a single Conditions of Contact$_{\text{Index}}$ measure (Cronbach's alpha = .61; mean = 3.62).

TABLE 10.1
Items Representing the Conditions of Contact$_{Index}$

Factor Loading	
	Equal Status
.66	Teachers at this school are fair to all groups of students.
.64	All students at this school are treated equally.
.63	Teachers from different groups are treated fairly by the principal and assistant principals.
.61	Teachers from different groups are treated fairly by the students at this school.
	Interaction
.65	I often go through a whole school day and never say more than a few words to a student from a group different from my own.
.65	My friends would think badly of me if I ate lunch with people from a different group than my own.
.50	I talk to students from groups other than my own only when I have to.
	Interdependence
.65	After students from different groups get to know each other, they find they have a lot in common.
.63	Students from different groups in this school need each other.
.63	The different groups of students at this school have important things to offer each other.
	Supportive Norms
.73	The principal and assistant principals encourage students to make friends with students from different groups.
−.69	Teachers do not encourage students to make friends with students of different groups.
.61	This is a school in which everybody is encouraged to be friends.

Perceptions of the Aggregate

Students' ratings of their perceptions of the aggregate (in order of descending magnitude) were generally near the midpoint of the scale: Different Groups = 3.19; Same Team = 3.11; Separate Individuals = 3.02; One Group = 2.69. A series of comparisons between these ratings revealed that (with the exception of the difference between ratings of Same Team and Different Groups, $t(1338) = -1.47$, $p = ns$) they were all reliably different from one another (with probability levels of .03 or smaller). Furthermore, consistent with the factor analysis, these different ratings were reliably (p < .001) and moderately correlated with one another (with rs ranging from –.31 for the relation between One Group and Different Groups to .44 for One Group and Same Team). The moderate correlation between the One Group and the Same Team items suggests that students perceived these as related but not identical concepts. The results of subsequent regression analyses confirmed that these two representations have similar but independent consequences.

Affective Reactions and Attitudinal Favorability

Ingroup and outgroup affective reactions indexes (which could range from 1-9) were constructed for each student by averaging across the four affective ratings (reverse scoring the "bad" and "uneasy" items) so that a high score reflects positive reactions. The Ingroup Affective Reactions$_{Index}$ (Cronbach's alpha = .62) represented the average of each student's ratings of his or her own group (e.g., Korean students' ratings of how Koreans make them feel). The Outgroups Affective Reactions$_{Index}$ (Cronbach's alpha = .76) was composed of the average of (e.g., for Korean) students' ratings of how people from each of the other groups (i.e., Blacks, Caucasians, Chinese, Hispanics, Japanese, Jewish, and Vietnamese) made them feel on each of the four affective descriptors. Similar ingroup and outgroup favorability scores were constructed from each student's (1-9) favorability ratings of each group.

The affective reactions indexes revealed that although feelings about outgroup members overall were somewhat positive (mean = 5.92), affective reactions to ingroup members were even more positive (mean = 6.90), t (1183) = 21.85, p < .001.[1] Likewise, students' overall attitudinal favorability ratings were higher for ingroup members (mean = 7.24) than for outgroup members (mean = 5.87), t (1199) = 23.25, p < .001.[2] The issue we address next is whether students' intergroup biases are related to their ratings of the contact conditions and, if so, whether their perceptions about the student body being one group, on the same team, or members of different groups mediate the relationship between the conditions of contact and intergroup bias.

Tests of Mediation

The multiple regression mediation analysis (Baron & Kenny, 1986; Judd & Kenny, 1981) uses a series of regression analyses to establish mediation. The first analysis tests whether the conditions of contact (i.e., the Conditions of Contact$_{Index}$)[3] predict the measures of bias (i.e., the difference between ingroup and outgroup ratings). This would be similar to a main effect for the independent variable in an analysis of variance within an experimental design. The second analysis examines whether these conditions of contact also influence the proposed mediators (i.e., students' representations of the aggregate as one group, on the same team, different groups, and separate individuals). The third analysis considers the antecedent conditions and the proposed mediators simultaneously and tests whether one or more of the proposed mediators relate to bias over and above the effects of the other variables. Also in this third analysis, the effects of contact on bias, independent of the mediators, should be weaker than before; with complete mediation, the conditions of contact would no longer relate directly to bias.

The results of separate mediation analyses performed on the measures of bias involving affective reactions and overall attitudinal favorability conceptually extend our laboratory work and support the idea that perceptions of contact reduce intergroup bias, at least in part because they transform students' cognitive representations of the aggregate from separate groups to a more inclusive, superordinate group. First, we present the mediation analyses for affective reactions and attitudinal favorability separately. Then, considering the possibility that overall attitudinal favorability toward ingroups and outgroups is strongly determined by affective reactions toward them (Stangor et al., 1991), we consider the Affective Reactions$_{Index}$ and overall favorability measures jointly within the framework of the common ingroup identity model.

Supportive of the contact hypothesis, when bias in affective reactions (i.e., Ingroup$_{Index}$ – Outgroup$_{Index}$) was regressed on the Conditions of Contact$_{Index}$ (see Figure 10.1), the results (prior to entering the proposed cognitive mediators) revealed that students

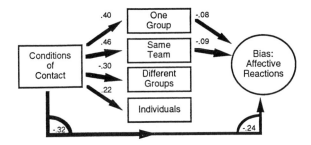

Figure 10.1. Mediation Analysis: Perceptions of the Conditions of Contact
and Bias in Affective Reactions

NOTE: Bold arrows indicate statistically significant standardized betas.

who perceived the conditions of contact to be more favorable had
lower ingroup-outgroup biases in affective reactions (beta = −.32).
Also, consistent with our laboratory work, the ratings of the conditions of contact were also related to the students' cognitive representations of the aggregate. Specifically, when the ratings of these
representations were regressed on the Conditions of Contact$_{\text{Index}}$, the
results indicated (see Figure 10.1) that as the conditions of contact
were rated more favorably, students were *more* likely to perceive the
student body as feeling like one group (beta = .40), as on the same
team (beta = .46), and as separate individuals (beta = .22), but the
less likely they were to perceive it as different groups (beta = −.30).
Thus far, these regression analyses show that the conditions of
contact relate to the measure of intergroup bias and also to the
proposed mediators, as we expected, but they have not yet fully
addressed the issue of mediation. Indeed, mediation was revealed by
the results of the third equation, in which the bias in Affective
Reactions$_{\text{Index}}$ was regressed on the perceptions of the Conditions of
Contact$_{\text{Index}}$ together with each of the four potential mediators (R^2 =
.12, $p < .001$). Supportive of the common ingroup identity model,
Figure 10.1 reveals that in this final equation, perceptions of the
student body as one group (beta = −.08) and on the same team (beta =
−.09) each reliably and independently related to bias. As perceptions

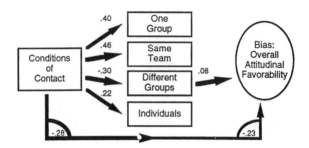

Figure 10.2. Mediation Analysis: Perceptions of the Conditions of Contact
and Bias in Overall Attitudinal Favorability
NOTE: Bold arrows indicate statistically significant standardized betas.

of the common ingroup identities of one group and on the same team increased, bias decreased. Also, the Conditions of Contact$_{Index}$ (beta = −.24) did not relate quite as strongly to bias as it did when the proposed mediators were not considered (beta = −.32), t (1166) = 109.90, $p < .001$.[4] Entering the mediators after the Conditions of Contact$_{Index}$ resulted in an R_2 change of .02 (2%), $p < .0001$.

A similar mediation analysis performed on the bias in Overall Attitudinal Favorability (Ingroup − Outgroup) yielded findings that were also generally supportive of our framework; nevertheless, the pattern of findings was somewhat different than for the affective reactions measure. As indicated in Figure 10.2, supportive of the contact hypothesis, the conditions of contact related to bias in Overall Attitudinal Favorability ratings (beta = −.28). As the conditions of contact were perceived to be more favorable, bias was lower. Furthermore, in the last equation ($R^2 = .086$, $p < .001$) when bias in Overall Attitudinal Favorability plus the proposed mediators were regressed on the Conditions of Contact$_{Index}$, the perception of the student body as different groups (beta = .08) was the only mediator that related reliably and independently to bias. Furthermore, the conditions of contact continued to relate to bias in Overall Attitudinal Favorability toward ingroups and outgroups (beta = −.23) but more weakly than when the proposed mediators were not considered (beta = −.28), t (1178) = −131.00, $p < .001$, an effect consistent

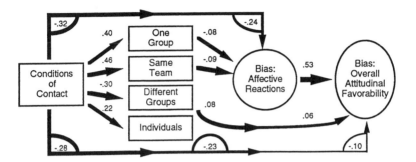

Figure 10.3. Mediation Analysis: Perceptions of the Conditions of Contact and Bias in Affective Reactions and Overall Attitudinal Favorability

NOTE: Bold arrows indicate statistically significant standardized betas.

with mediation. Entering the mediators after the Conditions of Contact$_{Index}$ resulted in an R_2 change of .012 (1.2%), $p < .004$.

These findings are important in several ways. First, they offer support for the common ingroup identity framework in a complex, multicultural setting. Second, the fact that both common ingroup identity representation items (i.e., One Group and On the Same Team) each related independently to bias in affective reactions is consistent with the idea that these items do measure somewhat different aspects of a common ingroup identity. Third, whereas the common ingroup identity representations of One Group and On the Same Team each mediated the relation between the Conditions of Contact and the Affective Reactions measure, the perception of the student body as Different Groups mediated the relation between Conditions of Contact and bias in Overall Attitudinal Favorability. Although the Affective Reactions and Overall Favorability measures of bias were highly related ($r = .572$, $p < .001$), they appear to be determined by a somewhat different pattern of mediation. This seems consistent with an implication of Stangor et al. (1991) that affective reactions and overall attitudinal favorability are not merely synonymous with one another and with the finding that affective reactions are strong determinants of overall attitudinal favorability. Figure 10.3 attempts to integrate these ideas within the framework of the common ingroup identity model.

Figure 10.3, which very speculatively combines portions of Figures 10.1 and 10.2, also shows a path from bias in Affective Reactions$_{Index}$ to bias in Overall Attitudinal Favorability. A fourth equation was executed that regressed bias in Overall Attitudinal Favorability on bias in Affective Reactions$_{Index}$ together with the proposed mediators and also the Conditions of Contact$_{Index}$ ($R^2 = .34$, $p < .0001$). In this last analysis, it appears that bias in Affective Reactions (beta = .53), perceptions of the student body as Different Groups (beta = .06), and the Conditions of Contact (beta = −.10) each have reliable effects on students' bias in Overall Attitudinal Favorability.

In terms of an overall picture, one way of interpreting these findings is that conditions of contact influence students' affective reactions and overall attitudinal favorability toward different groups, directly, as well as in part, through mediation by cognitive representations relating to a common ingroup identity. Overall attitudinal favorability is also determined by affective reactions. Last, Figure 10.3 suggests that the relation between Conditions of Contact and Attitudinal Favorability is mediated by students' representations of the aggregate and by affective reactions. These findings are consistent with the results of Stangor et al. (1991) and generally supportive of the common ingroup identity model.

Although the One Group and the On the Same Team items did have independent effects involving bias in Affective Reactions, we cannot be certain of how students interpreted the meaning of these items. In particular, it is not clear that the positive results for being On the Same Team reflected the value of a cognitive representation in which the subgroup and the superordinate group identities are salient simultaneously. In the next section, however, we provide some support for the value of this dual identity, as well as some evidence pertaining to how students may have interpreted the On the Same Team item.

A Superordinate ("American") Identity

The core assumption of our theoretical model is that sharing a superordinate ingroup identity with members of other groups decreases intergroup bias toward them. Although the previous mediational analyses offered support for this position, the current study provides an additional opportunity to examine this idea. In particular, we can examine the proposed value of a cognitive representation in which the subgroup and superordinate identities are salient simultaneously. Specifically, we hypothesized that students who identified themselves as American, in addition to using another, minority subgroup identity (i.e., Black, Jewish, Korean, or other—for example, Irish), would have *lower* degrees of bias than students who identified themselves only with a minority group designation (i.e., for whom the American superordinate identity was not relevant or salient).[5]

Supportive of this hypothesis, a one-way analysis of variance involving students' intergroup bias on the Affective Reactions$_{Index}$ revealed that bias among students who identified themselves with both a minority subgroup and an American superordinate identity (mean = .88) was lower compared to those students who only claimed a minority group identity (mean = 1.16), $F (1,616) = 4.69, p < .03$. A similar analysis involving bias in Overall Attitudinal Favorability, however, was not supportive of this hypothesis, $F (1,622) = 0.94, p = ns$. Thus, as reflected by the mediation analyses presented earlier, support for the value of a superordinate identity is obtained on the affective reactions measure but not directly for overall attitudinal favorability.

Additional analyses involving the ratings of the different cognitive representations of the students who used a minority self-designation and who did or did not claim a superordinate American identity revealed some relatively strong evidence that the item, "Although there are different groups of students at this school, it feels as though we are all playing on the same team," was interpreted to mean that both subgroup and superordinate identities were salient simultaneously. Among these self-identified minority students who actually differed in their personal use of a superordinate identity, there were no differences in their ratings of the student body as one group, different groups, or separate individuals. The only item that revealed a difference between these groups was playing On the Same Team. Consistent with the interpretation we assumed students would reach, this item was rated more strongly by students who actually used a superordinate and subgroup minority identity (mean = 3.22) than by those who only used a minority group identity (mean = 3.01), $F (1,699) = 4.33, p < .04$. These findings, together with the earlier regression analyses in which the One Group and the On the Same Team items had similar but independent effects, give us additional confidence that these items have similar but somewhat different meanings regarding the extent to which subgroup identities may be salient within a superordinate common ingroup identity. In the next section, we compare the perceptions and intergroup attitudes of the majority of students, who identified themselves as Caucasian (i.e., 68.9% of the respondents), with the minority of students, who identified themselves using one of the other racial or ethnic groups and did not identify themselves as Caucasian.

Majority and Minority Group Status

There were theoretically consistent differences between the majority and minority group students in perceptions of contact, group representations, and bias, but the patterns of mediation for these groups were basically equivalent. Consistent with Islam and Hewstone's (1993) findings relating to perceptions of contact, majority group students had more favorable impressions of the Conditions of Contact$_{Index}$ (mean = 3.68) relative to minority group students (mean = 3.49), $F (1,1320) = 33.67, p < .001$. Reliable differences between majority and minority group members were obtained for the separate dimensions of contact (i.e., equal status, interaction, egalitarian norms) but not for the dimension of cooperative interdependence between the groups (means = 3.44 and 3.45). It was expected that if minority group status increases the salience of members' social identities, then minority group students should less strongly endorse the superordinate representations of the student body (i.e., One Group or On the Same Team) relative to majority students. Partially consistent with this hypothesis, minority students less strongly endorsed the superordinate group item (On the Same Team) than majority group students (mean = 3.00 vs. 3.16), $F (1,1320) = 4.56, p < .03$, and tended to have weaker One Group representations (means = 2.67 and 2.70). Also consistent with an increased salience of a minority group social identity, minority students had weaker Separate Individuals representations of the student body (mean = 2.94) relative to majority group students (mean = 3.07), $F (1,1320) = 4.27$, $p < .04$, and tended to have somewhat stronger Separate Groups representations (means = 3.24 and 3.16).

If minority relative to majority group students have less favorable impressions of the conditions of contact and weaker representations of the aggregate as a superordinate entity, they would be expected also to have *higher* degrees of intergroup bias. Analysis of the bias in Affective Reactions$_{Index}$ supports this hypothesis. Minority group students had higher degrees of bias in affective reactions (mean = 1.15) relative to majority group students (mean = 0.92). Earlier we suggested that the greater bias by minority group members could be due either to more positive feelings toward ingroup members (see Mullen, 1983) or to less favorable feelings toward outgroup members (see Gaertner et al., 1993). In the current study, bias in affective reactions was mainly due to responses to the outgroup: Minority groups' affective reactions to outgroups (mean = 5.75) were less favorable than the majority group's (mean = 6.00), $F (1,1179) = 5.09$, $p < .02$; there were no differences for ingroup members (means = 6.91 and 6.92). Similar comparisons involving the bias in Overall Favorability did not yield reliable differences between minority group (mean = 1.26) and majority group students (mean = 1.42), $F (1,1195) = 1.31$, $p = ns$. Contrary to expectations relating to group size and ingroup salience, majority group members showed more overall favorability to ingroup members (mean = 7.34) than did minority group members (mean = 7.04), $F (1,1195) = 4.89$, $p < .03$, but they also tended to have more favorable evaluations of outgroup members (means = 5.92 vs. 5.78).

Although majority and minority group status related to overall differences in perceptions of the contact conditions, group representations, and bias in affective reactions, *the patterns of mediation* were basically equivalent, as expected. Multiple regression mediation analyses conducted separately for the majority and minority students on bias in Affective Reactions$_{Index}$ and bias in Overall Favorability measures indicated high degrees of similarity in the patterns of mediation. For example, the analyses depicted in Figure 10.1, conducted separately for majority and minority groups, indicated that Conditions of Contact$_{Index}$ (for each group separately) predicted bias in Affective Reactions$_{Index}$ before consideration of the mediators (betas = $-.29$ and $-.35$). The more favorably majority and minority students perceived the conditions of contact, the lower their bias. Also, the more favorably each group perceived the conditions of contact, the more likely they were to perceive the student body as feeling like One Group (betas = $.39$ and $.34$), On the Same Team (betas = $.45$ and $.44$), Separate Individuals (betas = $.26$ and $.05$ [ns]), and less like Different Groups (betas = $-.32$ and $-.22$). Also, consistent with the idea that cognitive representations of the student body mediate the relation between the Conditions of Contact$_{Index}$ and bias in Affective Reactions$_{Index}$, when the cognitive representations were considered with the Conditions of Contact$_{Index}$ for majority and minority groups separately ($R^2 = .07$ and $.13$), the relations between bias in Affective Feelings$_{Index}$ and each of the superordinate group representations of One Group (betas = $-.07$ and $-.09$ [ns]) and On the Same Team (betas = $-.10$ and $-.06$ [ns]) were of equivalent magnitude for these groups, although the betas were not reliable for the sizable minority sample ($n = 314$). In addition, the Conditions of Contact$_{Index}$ related to bias in Affective Feelings$_{Index}$ (betas = $-.22$ and $-.28$) and, consistent with mediation, more weakly than before. In general, the patterns of mediation for majority and minority group students were fundamentally similar.

DISCUSSION

The overall analyses involving students' perceptions of the conditions of intergroup contact in this study's multicultural setting offer continued support for the utility of the contact hypothesis as a strategic framework for reducing intergroup bias for both majority and minority group students. The more favorably students perceived the conditions of contact, the lower their intergroup bias in affective reactions and overall attitudinal favorability. In addition, the mediation analyses conceptually extend our laboratory work and support the idea that the conditions of contact reduce bias, *in part,* because they transform students' cognitive representations from "us" and "them" to a more inclusive "we." Also, because our bias measure is relevant to a variety of ingroups and outgroups rather than to the dynamics of any specific ingroup-outgroup relationship, our conclusions can relate to more general frameworks of intergroup relations.

A Common Ingroup in a Natural Context

This study offers support for the common ingroup identity model in a natural context, where groups are real, contact is frequent, and intergroup attitudes are rich and complexly determined. In view of the inherently larger degree of ambiguity in establishing directions of causality, conclusions derived from a purely correlational design are less certain than those derived from an experiment. In this regard, a more complete picture probably involves dynamic, bidirectional relationships between the variables represented in the analysis. Thus, it is conceivable that group representations influence bias and that bias further influences group representations as well as the conditions of contact. Nevertheless, it is reassuring that these survey results parallel those obtained in our laboratory experiments. In addition, the results that minority relative to majority group students have less favorable impressions of the contact conditions at school, less strongly endorse a superordinate group representation of the student body (i.e., "on the same team"), and have higher levels of intergroup bias in affective reactions are consistent with earlier studies conducted in both laboratory and naturalistic contexts. This pattern of differences for majority and minority students, however, is also supportive of our theoretical framework. When conditions of contact are perceived to be less favorable and the superordinate representations of the aggregate are weaker, higher degrees of bias would be expected, due primarily to less positive feelings toward outgroup members.

In this complex natural setting, however, the representational mediators accounted for a reliable but rather modest 2% of the variance for bias in affective reactions and a reliable and even smaller

1.2% of the variance for bias in overall attitudinal favorability. Fortunately, our sample size provided the lens (i.e., statistical power) necessary to magnify the visibility of these very modest but reliable effects. The two models depicted in Figures 10.1 and 10.2, which include the conditions of contact and the representational mediators, accounted for 12% of the variance in affective reactions and 8.6% of the variance in attitudinal favorability, respectively. The model depicted in Figure 10.3 accounted for 34% of the variance for overall attitudinal favorability, but 25% of that variance is attributable to affective reactions, which is a dependent variable within the structure of the contact hypothesis and the common ingroup identity model. It would be irresponsible to fail to acknowledge that there is still a large amount of variance in intergroup attitudes that these combined frameworks cannot yet explain. Also, it would be irresponsible to fail to put the results of this study in more balanced perspective.

In this survey study, variability in the proposed antecedent conditions of contact was based primarily on variability in students' subjective impressions of the same basic *objective* reality; except for idiosyncratic differences in experience (occasioned in part by students' majority or minority group status), objective reality remained fairly constant. There was no purposeful, systematic manipulation of the objective conditions of contact across students. Thus, except for the space provided by the variability in these impressions, there was not much opportunity for the contact hypothesis and our proposed mediators to exert their full potential impact. In contrast, in our laboratory study (Gaertner et al., 1990) in which we systematically varied the objective conditions of contact (i.e., cooperation), our full model accounted for 48% of the variance in intergroup bias and the representational mediators a very hearty 22% for themselves. How much variability these combined frameworks could explain in an *experimental* design in a natural setting is yet to be determined. Nevertheless, in view of the purely subjective basis for subjects' perceptions of contact in the current study, we view these modest findings as very encouraging, but we also recognize the need for further theoretical development.

We believe that the integration presented in Figure 10.3 represents a promising advancement. It suggests that the relation between the conditions of contact and changes in intergroup attitudinal favorability is mediated by students' cognitive representations of the aggregate and by their intergroup affective reactions. Stephan and Stephan's (1984, 1985) ideas about the processes by which reduced intergroup anxiety broadens the perceptual field and increases the accuracy of intergroup perceptions contributes substantively to understanding the causal connection between affective reactions and overall attitudinal favorability obtained in the current findings as well as the findings by Stangor et al. (1991).

Representations and the Reduction of Bias

From the perspective of the common ingroup identity model, only the Different Groups representation seemed to play a direct role in mediating the conditions of contact and overall attitudinal favorability. The cognitive representations denoting a common ingroup identity (i.e., One Group and On the Same Team), however, seemed to influence overall attitudinal favorability indirectly by mediating the relation between the conditions of contact and intergroup affective reactions. Similarly, when a superordinate American and minority subgroup identities were salient simultaneously, only bias in affective reactions but not overall attitudinal favorability was influenced directly by this more inclusive ingroup representation. Thus, this between-groups comparison conceptually replicates the results of the mediation analyses.

In addition, the reduced bias in affective reactions associated with the ratings of On the Same Team as well as with the dual (superordinate American and subgroup) identities are supportive of our suggestion that the development of a common ingroup identity does not necessarily require each group to forsake its subgroup identity completely. This increases our confidence that the common ingroup identity model is applicable in real, complex intergroup settings in which group identities are important and would not be relinquished easily.

We acknowledge, however, that the dual identities examined in the present study may represent a range of underlying processes and influences, whose full assessment was beyond the scope of this investigation. For example, the development of a dual identity of minorities that involved the American superordinate group likely reflected individual differences in the opportunity and motivation for assimilation. It may also involve, perhaps relatedly, attempts to ameliorate perceived status differentials between the minority group and the majority group. Previous research has demonstrated that intergroup bias is a function of the status between groups, the legitimacy of the status, and the salience of group identity (Ellemers, Wilke, & van Knippenberg, 1993; Mullen, Brown, & Smith, 1992). In the current study, the utilization of a dual identity by members of ethnic minority groups was associated with reduced bias but perhaps also with perceptions of reduced status differentials between these minority students and majority students. Also, it is possible that the impact of a dual identity is moderated by the extent to which the components of the dual identity are imposed or voluntarily adopted, permanent or temporary, or functional or dysfunctional considering the situational context. For example, in the context of a corporate merger, the salience of the earlier subgroup identities may threaten the primary goal of the merger, that is, for two organizations to become one (see Gaertner, Dovidio, & Bachman, in press). However, in the multiethnic high school setting, the salience of subgroup ethnic identities would not necessarily threaten the goals of the superordinate organization. Further investigation of these parameters and processes associated with a dual identity would thus provide important conceptual and practical information about intergroup contact, identity, and the reduction of intergroup bias.

The processes involved in the development of a dual identity have direct implications for the generalization of the benefits of positive intergroup contact. In many contexts, expecting people to abandon their subgroup identities would not only be impossible or undesirable but also could be potentially detrimental to the generalization of any benefits to members of the outgroup not specifically included within the recategorized representation (see Hewstone & Brown, 1986). If earlier group identities were completely degraded, the associative links between former outgroup members who are present and outgroup members who are not present would be severed (see Rothbart & John, 1985). Rather, generalization of benefits to additional outgroup members may be more likely to occur when the revised superordinate representation and the earlier group identities are salient simultaneously (i.e., the perception of two subgroups within one group; see Gaertner et al., 1993). Thus, one direction for our future research is to examine the benefits of the dual identity for purposes of generalization. Also, our future research will further explore the external validity of the general framework by assessing the model's potential for reducing subtle types of interracial bias, such as aversive racism (Gaertner & Dovidio, 1986; Murrell, Betz, Dovidio, Gaertner, & Drout, 1993), as well as the more traditional, overt forms of bias (Dovidio & Gaertner, 1986).

We further note that bias can be reduced by decategorization strategies, such as individuation of outgroup members (Wilder, 1986) or personalized interaction (Brewer & Miller, 1984), that degrade group boundaries and weaken the salience of group identity, as well as by recategorization that enhances perceptions of a common ingroup identity. The finding that Separate Individuals representations did not mediate the reduction of bias does not imply that recategorization is necessarily superior to these decategorization strategies. First, the Separate Individuals representation is not synonymous with outgroup individuation in the work by Wilder (see Wilder, 1986). A Separate Individuals representation in the context of our work implies the decategorization of ingroup members as well as outgroup members. The reduction in salience of one's ingroup identity may in itself have important consequences in intergroup relations (Brewer, in press).

Second, it is possible that decategorization and recategorization strategies may be effective in different types of contexts. Individuation, for instance, might be primarily effective in situations in which individual members of the outgroup are indeed substantially different and discernible from one another in ways that challenge assumptions of outgroup homogeneity (Wilder, 1978). Stereotyping may further be undermined by exposure to individual outgroup members who possess a range of different characteristics that disconfirm group stereotypes (Crocker & Weber, 1983). Personalization may be primarily effective under nonthreatening circumstances that permit the inter-action to become interpersonally and socially focused rather than intergroup oriented and task oriented (Miller et al., 1985) and reveal similarities among members of the different groups.

In contrast, the recategorization may be more effective for reduc-ing bias in circumstances of active conflict in which direct and unstructured interaction among members could escalate intergroup tensions (Sherif & Sherif, 1969). Furthermore, even in situations in which there is no overt animosity, inducing a one-group repre-sentation may be more desirable when members' stereotypes of one another are reasonably accurate or, as is often the case with interac-tions between members of high and low status groups, the situation can be controlled or manipulated to reinforce existing stereotypes. Under these conditions, interaction with outgroup members as indi-viduals would not introduce substantially new information about them, and the information that is exchanged would likely strengthen stereotyping and intergroup categorization.

Moreover, recategorization and decategorization can be comple-mentary rather than competing processes in the reduction of inter-group bias. For instance, recategorization may be used as the initial strategy. The one-group representation capitalizes on the strong inclination of people to categorize persons and objects as a means of simplifying their experience (Rosch, 1975). In contrast, a decategori-zation approach opposes this tendency and thus may meet with more initial resistance and result in less stable consequences. The more positive evaluations of former outgroup members resulting from the one-group approach could then initiate a sequence of further interac-tions that increasingly can improve intergroup relations. For example, perceptions of belonging to a common ingroup, and the consequent more positive feelings toward former outgroup members, could increase the likelihood of cooperative interaction among the members. Coop-erative interaction strengthens the common group boundary and further enhances attraction to the members (Gaertner et al., 1990).

Recategorization may also provide a fertile context for person-alization and individuation to occur. A one-group representation may facilitate the exchange of more intimate, self-disclosing information with former outgroup members that could serve to personalize or individuate members' representations of one another (see Miller et al., 1985). This process, in turn, can enhance ingroup identity by increasing feelings of intimacy, closeness, and cohesiveness among the members. Thus, recategorization and decategorization do not necessarily constitute mutually exclusive approaches but may be orchestrated to produce a comprehensive and overall strategy for improving intergroup relations.

CONCLUSION

The current study has offered modest support for the contact hypothesis, the common ingroup identity model, and the relation between cognitive representations, affective reactions, and overall intergroup attitudinal favorability. The conditions of intergroup contact appear to achieve their effects through several different direct and indirect pathways. Conceptualizing these pathways within a unifying explanatory framework theoretically will help to identify the shared and unique contributions of variables that would otherwise be assessed independently. Pragmatically, we hope that this approach will also help to identify alternatives that can be introduced when particular conditions of contact cannot be fully implemented.

Notes

1. The number of subjects and consequently the degrees of freedom vary somewhat across analyses due to instances of missing data.

2. In general, males seemed somewhat more biased than females, but only weakly. In terms of bias on the affective reactions indexes for ingroups and outgroups, the difference (Ingroup − Outgroup) for male subjects (mean = 1.05) was slightly, but not reliably, greater than for female subjects (mean = .92), $F(1,1178) = 2.064$, $p = ns$. The overall attitudinal favorability index, however, revealed that males (1.52) were reliably more biased than females (1.26), $F(1,1194) = 5.076$, $p < .024$. Nevertheless, there were no reliable differences between male and female subjects in overall favorability for ingroup members (7.36 vs. 7.15, respectively, $F(1,1185) = 2.865$, $p = ns$), nor did males relative to females have lower overall favorability for outgroup members (5.84 vs. 5.90, $F(1,1201) = 0.302$, $p = ns$). Thus, the sex

difference for bias in overall favorability was due to males having slightly, but not reliably, more favorable feelings for ingroup members than females, and by males having slightly, but not reliably, less favorable feelings for outgroup members relative to females.

3. Similar regression analyses were conducted using the emergent factor scores to represent the four conditions of contact (see Table 10.1). These analyses generated nearly identical results to those reported using the Conditions of Contact$_{Index}$. To simplify the presentation of the findings overall and especially to simplify Figures 10.1, 10.2, and 10.3, we chose to present the findings using the Conditions of Contact$_{Index}$ rather than the four separate factors representing the conditions of contact.

4. We thank Suzanne Mannes for suggesting the strategy to test this difference that basically notes the R^2 change when the variable is entered alone and after the mediators are entered in the last equation. To evaluate this change, partial correlation coefficients are used in accordance with the formula in Cohen and Cohen (1975, p. 53).

5. Students who identified themselves as American and also as Caucasian were not selected for this analysis unless they also included some other subgroup classification, for example, Jewish. To have included these students would have simply reduced the comparison to one primarily between minority and majority group students.

11

Emphasizing the Social Nature of Groups in a Developmental Framework

STEPHEN WORCHEL

The history of research on groups has reached the century mark, dating back to Triplett's (1897) examination of social facilitation. Now seems to be a good time to pause, reflect, and review the meandering paths carved by social psychologists' efforts to understand group behavior. Many of the "classic" studies along that path had a number of common features. The group was viewed as a dynamic social system; subjects were placed into face-to-face situations with other members. Behavior was examined over extended periods of time, and investigators traced changes that occurred in interaction patterns, often describing rather than carefully measuring interactions. For example, Sherif, Harvey, White, Hood, and Sherif (1961) observed campers as they engaged in a series

AUTHOR'S NOTE: I would like to thank Dawna Coutant, Leah Worchel, Frankie Wong, Judy Ouellette, William Webb, Michelle Grossman, Hank Rothgerber, Eric Day, and a number of undergraduate students for their work in this program. The research was supported by a grant from the Texas Coordinating Board of Higher Education (Advanced Research Program).

261

of competitive, and later, cooperative encounters over the course of a summer. The investigators found that competition created intergroup hostility and that *repeated* cooperative efforts to obtain superordinate goals reduced this hostility. Lewin, Lippitt, and White (1939) found that laissez-faire leadership style invited considerable ingroup scapegoating when the laissez-faire leader followed an autocratic leader. Festinger, Schachter, and Back (1950) showed that proximity led to the development of friendships in a housing project over several months. Festinger, Riecken, and Schachter (1956) observed that Mrs. Keech and her band of followers sought converts to their group only after their prophecy about the world's end proved false. And Schachter (1951) found that members of a small group were most accepting of a fellow member who began by deviating from group opinion but later switched his position to a conforming one. The list could go on, but the point is that these early studies viewed group behavior as a social process that developed and changed over time. Indeed, groups were defined as social units that involved face-to-face interaction in which a member influenced and was, in turn, influenced by other members.

The focus of this research was on the group rather than on isolated behaviors. When the investigators described behaviors, they placed these behaviors in the context of the group. Groups were presented as dynamic units, often changing, and in order to capture the group, one had to take this change into account. The group was a system, and individual activities were interrelated properties of the group. Sherif et al. (1961), for example, argued that competition led to intergroup hostility, *and* this hostility, in turn, increased the level of competition. Likewise, intergroup competition led members to favor their own group in evaluating group performance, *and* the biased evaluations increased intergroup competition and hostility. Although cause and effect were identified, it was acknowledged that effects could also be causes. There was a crudeness in the methodology, a lack of precision in the definition of the behaviors being studied, and, based on current standards, too little attention was given to identifying underlying processes. In fact, it is unlikely that any of these classic studies would be accepted in major social psychology journals if they were submitted today because of these flaws. Yet reading that literature paints a vivid picture of groups as active systems, much like beehives. These early studies continue to incite new research and ideas.

More recent approaches have taken a very different view of group dynamics. Behaviors that occur within groups are extracted from the group context and subjected to microscopic examination. These behaviors are described as "effects," endpoints in the causal chain. The concern, in many cases, is on the cognitive processes involved rather than on social interaction or group dynamics. For example, several investigators have noted that individuals perceive more diversity in the ingroup than in the outgroup. This observation has been dubbed the "magnification of diversity *effect*" (Goethals & Darley, 1977), the "outgroup homogeneity *effect*" (Jones, Wood, & Quattrone, 1981), or the "relative heterogeneity *effect*" (Mullen & Hu, 1989). Research has examined the conditions under which this perceptual effect is produced and the cognitive processing involved (see Mullen, 1991). Turning to another example, recent minority influence research (Crano, 1989; Nemeth, 1992) has focused on the type of thinking created by hearing the minority's opinion. There is relatively little concern with the impact of the minority on the dynamics of the group or on group factors that influence the power of the minority. Perhaps the cruelest blow of all has been unintentionally dealt by work on social identity and social categorization that has aptly named its paradigm the "minimal group paradigm" (Haslam & Turner, 1992; Tajfel & Turner, 1986). The "group" in this research exists only as a category or as an assignment to a noninteractive set of individuals. One can read many accounts of current group research procedures without ever finding an actual group of subjects (see Mullen & Goethals, 1987). Subjects are examined as individuals, whereas the group lurks outside the room or only in the minds of the subjects.

Whereas the early approaches could be characterized as inclusive, many current approaches are often reductionistic. Rather than studying the body (the group) and the interaction between members, these approaches focus on specific organs (behaviors, effects) and the underlying mechanisms or causes (often cognitive in nature) involved. The methodology is precise, and the results are often illuminating and provocative. But one is left wondering what has been learned about groups. It is easy to understand the basis for Steiner's (1974) question "Where has the group gone in group research?" The situation is reminiscent of the story of the blind men describing an elephant. Each grabs a part of the beast and paints a vivid picture of that part. But the descriptions of the parts never yield a portrait of the whole elephant. For example, although we may develop an appreciation for the conditions that lead to social loafing, it is unclear how loafing affects other group characteristics such as cohesiveness, leadership, or structure.

Finally, we can characterize much present research on group behavior as resembling a snapshot, measuring a behavior at a single point of time. Changes in behavior or the group over time are rarely discussed or measured. The studies typically employ between-subject designs rather than repeated measures of the same subject or group. On the other hand, the earlier work often adopted a longitudinal view, describing change within groups or individuals across the period of the study. One got the impression of watching a motion picture rather than examining a photo album.

The point of this comparison is not to suggest that one approach is superior to another or to wish for a return to the "good old days." Rather, what is needed now is a more balanced approach, one that builds on the past while including the new. Just as the early research was predominated by the observation and description of groups without the careful analysis of specific actions, the pendulum of current research emphasis has swung too far in the opposite direction. There has been too little concern with presenting groups as dynamic bodies that develop and change over time and with describing the impact of actions (effects) as they influence and are influenced by the context in which they occur. Groups often become schema, representations in the mind, that serve as a fixed stage for the performance of a variety of behaviors and thoughts. As a result, much of group research sheds little light on the dynamics of group behavior, and many potentially important group variables are overlooked.

My aim in this paper is to push the pendulum more toward the middle ground that relates individual behavior to group dynamics. As a starting point in this effort, I argue that group change and development are the causal agents for many social and cognitive activities and that these activities can be profitably examined in the group context. The foundation of this approach is the position that groups undergo constant but predictable change, and this change can be identified and related to interpersonal behaviors and individuals' cognitive processes that occur within the group setting. In order to demonstrate this position, I will present a model of group development and research derived from that model.

The approach is not new. There have been several efforts to describe group development (Bales & Strodtbeck, 1951; LaCoursiere, 1979; Mullen, 1987; Tuckman, 1965). Tuckman's (Tuckman, 1965; Tuckman & Jensen, 1977) model is the most widely referenced of these models of group development. Tuckman argued that small groups develop through a series of stages, each characterized by a specific focus or theme. Basing much of his model on observations of T-groups, therapy groups, and small work groups, Tuckman proposed a linear progression of stages from beginning to end: forming, storming, norming, performing, and adjourning. Moreland and Levine (1988, 1992a) recently resurrected the development banner, suggesting that individuals go through a series of relationships with their group, and each phase of the relationship is characterized by different behaviors and perceptions of the group. Although the models of group and member development are somewhat different, each presentation is accompanied by a common plea that these developmental issues be included in research designs.

Despite these pleas, however, research on groups and on cognitive representation of group behaviors has largely ignored these developmental perspectives. An anonymous reviewer of an earlier draft of this chapter offered two suggestions to explain the blind spot research has had for these variables. First, he or she argued that many investigators believe that developmental factors are unimportant or have only a minor impact on group behaviors. Second, the reviewer suggested that conducting group research, especially group development research, is more difficult and requires greater resources (time and subjects). The methods of study are often less precise and likely to receive a hostile reception at journals whose hallmark is protecting current methodological rigor. To these observations, I would like to add a third reason. Because the aim of many of the models of group development was description, many of them do not easily lend themselves to forming specific hypotheses. And if hypotheses are formed, they must be tested on long-term groups as they go through a complete cycle from beginning to death (ending). Although these points may explain the lack of attention, I would argue that their end result is a menu of research that fails to capture the true essence of the dynamic group.

MODEL OF GROUP DEVELOPMENT

In an effort to address the reluctance to conduct group-based research, I have been involved in a program designed to construct a model of group development that would give rise to specific testable hypotheses and to undertake empirical research that demonstrates the importance and viability of considering group development issues. I have also been interested in using the research program to examine both cognitive and interactive behavior within the same paradigm. The model and methodology for developing the model have been described in detail elsewhere (Worchel, in press; Worchel, Coutant-Sassic, & Grossman, 1992; Worchel, Coutant-Sassic, & Wong, 1993) so I will present only a brief summary here.

I began by examining accounts (in newspapers, magazines, books, and proceedings and minutes of organizations) of a wide variety of groups (from small work and therapy groups to social movements) and comparing my observations of group development with earlier works. A number of differences between the model that resulted from my efforts and previous models were easily recognizable. First, there was some disagreement about the specific stages of development and content of those stages. Second, and probably more important, much of the early work (e.g., LaCoursiere, 1979; Tuckman, 1965) involved examinations of groups that were formed for a specific purpose and had definite termination points. Whereas some groups, such as T-groups or single-task groups, fit this model, many other groups do not. I found that in many, if not most cases, groups existed over extended periods of time, although membership in the group changed frequently. For example, the Dallas Cowboys (football team) have a long history, although no member of the 1993 team was a member of the team in 1975. One is reminded of the early Sherif (1936) study that showed how group norms persisted even after all the members of the group that developed the norm had departed the group. Increasing the scope of the groups involved in my study led to two conclusions. First, when examining group development, it is important to examine group formation and member inclusion issues. The formation of groups and the decisions people make to join a group impact both the nature of the group and its longevity and vitality. There are surprisingly few studies that examine how people decide to unite and form a group or how the reasons one has for joining a group affect subsequent behavior and group development. Indeed, most social psychology studies begin with groups that are already formed or ones that are created by the experimenter. The dynamics of a group may well be influenced by the formation process. Second, and most important in the present discussion, is the recognition that group development occurs through repeatable cycles rather than, or in addition to, the linear model offered by previous investigators. Groups, even those that have a defined beginning and ending, progress through cycles that are repeated several times throughout the life of the group. Therefore, it is possible to study developmental stages in groups over the life of the group *and* during segments of the group's life.

Taking these points under consideration, Figure 11.1 presents the basic model of group development, which was constructed from observations of ongoing groups and accounts by others of groups. I begin with Stage I, the Stage of Discontent, because this period often creates the foundation for group formation. Focusing attention on this period allows the examination of the formation process. It is important to recognize, however, that although many groups are created from this foundation, other groups may be created by external forces (e.g., the laboratory group) or by the other factors (individual or situational) that bring people together (e.g., therapy groups).

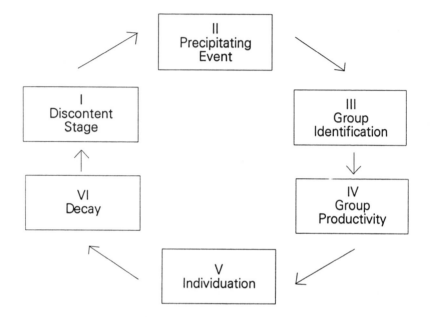

Figure 11.1. Preliminary Model of Group Formation and Development
SOURCE: From Worchel, Coutant-Sassic, and Grossman (1992).

I include this stage in the model to emphasize the need to examine group formation issues.

In the cases in which discontent serves as the foundation of a group, this stage is characterized by feelings of alienation. In many cases, members have withdrawn from group activity; they feel helpless to influence the group. Participation in group activities (e.g., elections, parties, group discussions) declines, and the group is dominated by a few members. Vandalism, passive aggression, and other forms of noninstrumental aggression may be high. At this point, the group is not a major part of the individual's social identity (Tajfel & Turner, 1986). It often takes a Precipitating Event (Stage II) to move the group from this stage. The incident may be relatively minor and unplanned, such as the rumor of the mistreatment of a group member, or it may be more dramatic (e.g., a riot) and, in some cases, staged. In small groups, the incident may be an emotional outburst or attack by a single member. Regardless of the specific nature of the event, it represents the dissatisfaction with the group, identifies a common ground or purpose for disaffected members, initiates contact between group members, and offers some hope that a union of these members can gain control either by taking over the group or forming a new independent group.

Group Identification (Stage III) occurs as the members focus on defining the group and determining its membership. The boundaries of the group are clearly defined and closed to new members (see Festinger, Riecken, & Schachter, 1956). Members become concerned with demonstrating that they belong in and are committed to the group. Conformity is high, and there is a reluctance to draw distinctions between members. The norm of equality dominates the group either in the treatment of group members or in the division of group resources. The members may adopt a common mode of dress; a mascot, flag, slogan, or other symbol may be identified. Groupthink (Janis, 1972, 1982) is common, as members seek to maintain high cohesiveness. Conflict with outgroups will not be avoided; in fact, it may be invited as a way of clearly identifying the group boundary. Leadership is centralized and strong. Members are in a high state of excitement, easily influenced through peripheral channels of processing (Petty & Cacioppo, 1986). The group identity and its impact on the individual's social identity are salient issues. By way of comparison, we can view this period of identification as incorporating features of Tuckman's forming, storming, and norming activities. However, the focus of the storming and norming revolves around group identity and uniformity. Finally, it is important to recognize that we are dealing with the group establishing its identity. Just as Tajfel and Turner (1986) argue that individuals strive to establish their social identity, so, too, are groups concerned with creating a clear group identity. In fact, the individual's quest for a clear social identity may be facilitated by the establishment of the ingroup's identity.

As identity becomes clear, groups turn attention to Group Productivity (Stage IV). The group identifies goals and initiates planning for how to achieve those goals. The group remains salient, but processing of information revolves around productivity issues. Members begin to make distinctions between each other on the basis of skills, motivation, and intelligence, attributes that influence group productivity. Leadership is task oriented. The group assumes a more analytical tone, and central processing of information predominates (Petty & Cacioppo, 1986). New members who can aid productivity are cautiously invited into the group, but they are often given marginal status until they "prove" themselves. The group becomes less antagonistic toward outgroups, but social comparison on productivity dimensions remains prevalent. This stage involves both norming and performing, in Tuckman's terms.

Efforts aimed at facilitating group productivity create the atmosphere for the group to enter the Individuation stage (Stage V). During the Individuation stage, distinctions are drawn between group members based on skills and ability. In addition, productivity often results in a pool of group resources that can be divided between members. The members demand recognition for their contributions to the group, often requesting resources be divided on the basis of equity rather than equality. They magnify the differences between themselves and other group members. Uniforms may be shed as members attempt to "stand out" from the crowd. Increased personal freedom is requested. Solutions to social dilemmas become individually based and, consequently, less group oriented. The group takes a decidedly more cooperative stance toward outgroups as members seek to learn about the outgroups and explore opportunities for themselves in these outgroups. The threat of defection becomes a bargaining tool. The group remains a focal point, but the nature of this focus now involves the individual's relation with the group.

The group next enters a period of Decay (Stage VI) as increasing attention is paid to personal needs and the group becomes less salient. Members become preoccupied with meeting their needs, and open conflict and competition within the group increases. Members blame their group and other members for failures rather than blaming the outgroup. There is a rapid turnover in leadership as the group insists that leaders have less power, thereby making the leaders less effective. Subgroups form and compete for power. Individuals hoard resources and expend minimal effort in group activities. Some members will defect to other groups, carrying with them a bitterness toward their old group. And the group drifts into a new Period of Discontent (Stage I).

I have searched to identify the hand that moves groups from one stage to another, and my analysis uncovered several suspects. Surprisingly, one of the triggers appears to be success, the group achieving the goal of a stage. For example, groups move from Group Productivity to Individuation when they have reached their productivity goal. Often the attainment of this goal results in rewards or material gain, and as the members try to determine how to divide the spoils, individuals step forward to make their claim by stressing their unique contributions (in other words, individuating themselves). Failure can also move a group from one stage to another. A group that fails to reach a production goal becomes the scene of individuating efforts as members attempt to demonstrate that they were not the cause of the failed effort. Finally, time, or possibly boredom, pushes the group into another stage. Members may become irritated when they feel the group is "spinning its wheels" at trying to establish an identity (Stage III) and clamor for the group to move on to finding a task (Stage IV). When the trigger is a negative one, such as failure or boredom, the following stage is often characterized by conflict and that stage is often brief.

This description of groups has several differences from the models offered by other investigators. There are differences in the specific stages that are postulated to comprise group development, although there is a great deal of overlap in identifying behaviors, issues of salience, and the processing of information that occurs during group development. According to the present model, the cycle can be interrupted and the group can return to an earlier stage of development. For example, a threat to the existence of the group may force the group back into the Identification stage, motivating members to protect the independence of their group and reestablish its identity. Indeed, crafty leaders often invite or manufacture outside threats to move the group's attention back to identity issues and consolidate the leader's position of power.

In concluding the description of the model, several points should be made. It is important to recognize that I am suggesting that the natural life of groups is characterized by constant change. The change is often orderly and predictable. Indeed, members may also experience change and development, but that change occurs within a backdrop of group change. And as the group moves through the developmental cycle, different pressures are brought to bear on individual members that influence their behavior. Finally, although individual members may have somewhat differing perceptions of the focus of the group, the model is not one of group member perceptions. Rather, the stages are identified by activities that define the group focus at any point in time. This position does not ignore the possibility of differing individual perceptions of the group or the possibility that wide variance in the perceptions may hinder group development. These issues, however, are not of central concern to the model.

PROGRAM OF RESEARCH

The present model argues that the stage of group development has a dramatic impact on the members' behavior and that the influence can only be examined by studying people in the group setting. The model lends itself to specific predictions, and I have identified and tested some of these predictions both in laboratory and field settings. In some cases, I have begun by focusing on established effects and examining how group development impacts these "effects." The groups in my studies met together once or twice a week for several weeks (3-6 weeks). This ensured that they perceived themselves as a group and had the opportunity for face-to-face interactions.

Group Perceptions

For example, there have been several demonstrations that people view the members of their own group as being more heterogeneous than those of the outgroup (Jones et al., 1981; Linville & Jones, 1980; Park & Rothbart, 1982). The typical paradigm in which these results are found involves asking individuals in clearly defined categories (e.g., men/women, dance majors/physics majors, Princeton students/Rutgers students) to describe their ingroup and the outgroup. In most cases, the groups (categories) are well established and the individual has been a member of the group for some time. Explanations for the effect involve information processing; individuals have more information and experience with their own group. From the standpoint of the present model, this tendency to view the ingroup as heterogeneous is influenced by developmental factors rather than being a stable "effect" that occurs at all times. The model argues that group perceptions are guided by functional considerations rather than information-processing characteristics. According to the model, individuals are motivated to perceive the ingroup as homogeneous during the early identification stages but as heterogeneous during the later phases of the group. The perception of homogeneity enhances the cohesiveness within the group and facilitates group identity. Viewing the ingroup as heterogeneous in the later stages makes it easier for the individual to leave the group or establish his or her distinctiveness.

I have completed several studies that support the developmental influence on ingroup/outgroup perceptions, indicating that perceptions of the homogeneity of the ingroup and outgroup change during the life of the group. In one study (Worchel et al., 1992), subjects were divided into two groups at the beginning of the experiment and the two groups competed on a number of tasks. Subjects who were asked to rate the two groups either prior to or after the first competitive task indicated that their group was more homogeneous than the competing outgroup. However, subjects who were asked to make these ratings after several competitive tasks perceived the outgroup as being more homogeneous than the ingroup. In all cases, subjects had little interaction with either ingroup or outgroup members, so familiarity was an unlikely explanation for the results.

Another interesting finding involved subjects' perceptions of themselves. Several investigators (Cantor, 1981; Turner, Hogg, Oakes, Reicher, & Wetherell, 1987) have suggested that individuals see themselves as the prototypical group member, and comparisons are made against this prototype. In the present study, subjects did perceive themselves as the "typical" or "average" group member in the early stages of the group. However, later in the session, subjects did not rate themselves as being the average or typical group member.

The developmental influences on group and individual perceptions have been replicated in field research investigating students' ratings of the student bodies at their university and a rival university.

This foray into the area of intergroup perceptions has taken me, admittedly through the back door, into one of the inner sanctuaries of cognitive social psychology: stereotypes. Surprisingly, the road leading to the present day study of stereotypes has followed a path similar to that involving the study of groups. Initially, Katz and Braly (1933) conceived stereotypes as perceptions held by one group of another group. They measured stereotypes by identifying a target group (Italians, Germans, etc.) and determining the percentage of members of a perceiving group that identified a specific trait (artistic, lazy, etc.) as characterizing the target group. A characteristic was considered part of the stereotype if a large number of the perceiving group included the trait in their description of the target group. In other words, there was a shared dimension to the stereotype. However, as the study of stereotypes matured, the stereotype was increasingly defined as a collection of attributes that an individual believed to characterize members of a social group (Oakes, Haslam, & Turner, 1994). Research on the topic focused on how individuals processed the information about the target group. The shared, or social, quality of the stereotype was given a more minor role.

However, my examination of group perceptions suggested that a stereotype is a multidimensional concept involving both individual and shared components. I (Worchel & Rothgerber, in press) argued that stereotypes include content (defining traits), a statement of the category or subcategory (target group), an indication of the perception of the degree of homogeneity of the target group, an interpretation of the specific trait, and an indication of the salience or weighting the perceiver gives the trait within the constellation of traits that define the target group. Furthermore, some of the components of stereotypes are more deeply rooted within the perceiving group whereas others are more strongly based within the individual (see Figure 11.2). In other words, the ingroup has a stronger role in defining the substance of some of the dimensions than other dimensions. For example, I have found that the *content* of a stereotype is

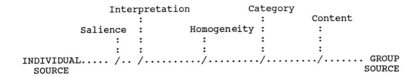

Figure 11.2. The Roots of the Components of Stereotypes

often defined by the perceiving group. Groups often dictate and teach members the content of their perception of outgroups. Members may demonstrate their identification with the ingroup by faithfully adopting (and when required, reciting) this content. On the other hand, the *interpretation* and *salience* of specific traits are most often left to the individual. In this sense, the content of stereotypes is much like a group belief (Bar-Tal, 1989); the group dictates the content and expects loyal members to adopt this position. The dimensions of *categorization* and *homogeneity* of the target group are shaped by more equal contributions from the ingroup and the individual. Given these differences, I argue that within the perceiving group, there is more variability between group members on the interpretation and salience dimensions than on content. My studies on the perceptions of college students found that there is wide agreement on the traits that describe a rival college but significantly less agreement on the homogeneity of the rival group and on the interpretation and salience of the traits. For example, most (87% of the sample) Texas A&M students indicated that the term *drinks alcohol heavily* applied to University of Texas students, but there was considerable disagreement as to whether this was a "bad" or "central" characteristic of the students and what percentage of University of Texas students actually drank heavily.

Based on this multidimensional/social model of a stereotype, I argued that some dimensions of stereotypes are most likely to change when the relationship between groups changes, whereas others are most affected by individual experience. For example, an individual is most likely to change the content of a stereotype when the relationship between ingroup and target group changes (e.g., goes from cooperative to competitive) or the individual receives information about the target group that is shared by all or most ingroup members.

However, changes in the unique personal experience with target group members are most likely to affect interpretation and salience of the traits while the content remains constant. For example, a personal encounter with an emotionally expressive Vulcan is unlikely to change one's stereotype of Vulcans as emotionally reserved. However, the experience may lead the individual to decide that well-traveled Vulcans are not emotionally void (homogeneity), that Vulcans only hide their emotions so as not to attract attention (interpretation), or that emotional reservedness is not among the most important traits defining Vulcans (salience).

Finally, and most directly related to the model, changes within the ingroup, such as developmental maturation, will result in most evident changes in perceptions of homogeneity of the target group or the development of subcategories. Returning to Worchel et al. (1992), we found that although developmental changes in groups affected members' perceptions of outgroup homogeneity, it did not have much of an impact on the traits assigned to the outgroup (content). An untested prediction is that greatest agreement between members of a group on the content dimension of a stereotype will be found during the early stages of identification. As the group matures and individuation takes place, there will be less agreement between members on the description of outgroups. We might also expect that events such as threats to the ingroup's identity will result in an increase in agreement between group members of the content of stereotypes. This analysis paints stereotypes with both social (group) and individual strokes and gives the concept a more dynamic character than many existing approaches. The position argues that events, including developmental changes, within the perceiving group will influence some dimensions of the stereotype. Indeed, individuals may demonstrate their individuality by openly stating that they do not agree with the stereotypes held by most ingroup members. Initial support for my view of stereotypes comes from my research on the perceptions of a rival university held by students and from the changes in the various components of these perceptions that result from changes in the relationship between the two universities, changes in the position of the student within his or her ingroup, and changes in the individual's interactions with members of the target group. Clearly, there is need for more supporting data before adopting this approach, but the initial data argue that the social nature of stereotypes must be included to understand how stereotypes are formed and changed.

Intergroup Relations

Moving to another issue, a basic position of social identity theory (Tajfel & Turner, 1986) is that people will discriminate against the outgroup and favor the ingroup. We might extend this reasoning to suggest that people want cooperative relations with the ingroup members but competitive relations with outgroup members. If this "effect" is universal, it would present problems for the current model, which suggests that the desire for positive interaction with the outgroup should increase over time whereas intragroup competition will characterize later phases of group development. In order to examine this prediction, my associates and I (Worchel et al., 1993) asked subjects to indicate their preferred mode of interaction with both the ingroup and outgroup several times during a 6-week period in which these laboratory groups met. As can be seen in Figure 11.3, subjects' preference for cooperative ingroup interactions and competitive outgroup relations changed over time so that by the group's end, the preferred patterns of interaction were reversed.

Changing the focus from perceptions and desires to behaviors, this research program has examined developmental effects on a variety of behaviors. I have examined minority influence, group and individual productivity, conformity, acceptance of new members, and intergroup aggression within a group development framework. For example, Grossman, Coutant, and Worchel (1993) found that groups are most productive during the middle stages of the group's life, although they are least cohesive at this point. Many of these studies are in the pilot or preliminary stage, but in each case, results suggest that group development plays a major impact in determining not only the magnitude of these effects but also the direction of them.

At this point in my research, I do not think it would be premature to draw a number of conclusions relating to my earlier discussion.

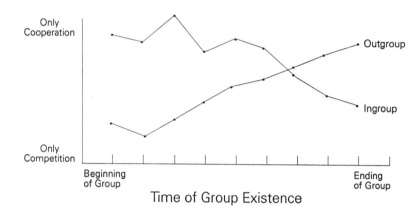

Figure 11.3. Desired Interaction With Ingroup and Outgroup Members
as a Function of Group Development

SOURCE: From Worchel, Coutant-Sassic, and Wong (1993). Reprinted by permission.

First, the failure to consider developmental and time issues in much of the previous research is an unfortunate oversight. These variables have a major impact on social thinking and social behavior in groups. Indeed, group development may be the causal factor for many of these dependent variables. Second, in order to truly study the effects of these developmental factors, it is important to do so in the context of a group that involves social interaction and changing group focuses. It is difficult to conceive how these developmental factors can be captured in a paradigm that merely asks subjects to imagine a group or their membership in a group. The individual motivation and the impact of social interaction that unfolds over time simply cannot be captured outside the group. Along similar lines, I would argue that it is also difficult to study the impact of group development in a collection of strangers who are brought into the laboratory to work simultaneously on a task. This collection is an aggregate, not a group, and aggregates are unlikely to experience the same developmental patterns as groups, even laboratory groups. Finally, the present research suggests that caution must be exercised in identifying behavior and, especially, thought processes as "effects." These "effects" may be transitory states that are dynamic and changing as the group situation changes.

Furthermore, an "effect" may actually be a causal factor for other behaviors. For example, my research suggested that a high level of conformity may actually be a trigger that moves a group from concerns with identification into the Group Productivity stage (Stage IV). At the very least, these effects take on meaning from the group context in which they occur. Removing them from the group situation eliminates the opportunity to determine a host of possible causal conditions and to determine the meaning of these thoughts and behaviors.

A COMMENT ON METHODOLOGY

It has been suggested that one of the reasons for the lack of research on group development is that the research requires significant resources and time. Because most of the models of group development, including the present one, are drawn from long-term groups, it is assumed that the research must examine groups over a long period of time. Indeed, there is a need for this type of research. However, the assumption that this approach is the only way to include developmental variables is mistaken. Few of the models take an explicit position that group development can only occur over weeks or months. In fact, the present model suggests that even in long-term groups there are repeated cycles of the developmental stages. Hence, groups can be studied over shorter periods of time (e.g., a 2-hour laboratory session) if there are efforts to follow development during this time. Gersick (1989), for example, argues that group productivity will be highest during the middle periods of a group's life. She has found support for this position in natural groups over long periods of time as well as in short-term groups. Regardless of the time frame in the study, groups are most productive during their midlife. What seems to be important from a research standpoint is that, regardless of the time period, efforts be made to ensure that subjects feel that they are part of a group and that they have the opportunity to act within the group context.

A second methodological issue concerns the basic nature of the acceptable research paradigm. To a large extent, experimental social psychology is increasingly defined by its research paradigm rather than by the subject matter of the research. The accepted paradigm is one that sets up carefully controlled situations, manipulates a few independent variables, and collects a limited number of supposedly uncontaminated measures. This method is most appropriate in a variety of situations, especially when specific hypotheses regarding cause and effect are being examined. However, this method should not be the only one in the arsenal of research designs. Introductory psychology students learn that an important aim of science is *description*. Careful descriptions of events provide valuable data for understanding human behavior and developing new hypotheses and predictions. The models of group development are descriptive models; they attempt to describe changes in the group over time and allow for specific predictions of the effect of these changes. Given the nature of the beast, descriptive research is not only acceptable, it is vital to understanding group change.

In the research program, I routinely take videotapes of group sessions in addition to collecting specific measures of behavior. The tapes provide a rich reminder of the dynamic nature of group. The tapes are used to help identify the stage of development a group may be in at a certain period of time. Features such as the topic of conversation (identity oriented, product oriented, individual or group oriented), the amount and distribution of participation, and the degree of affect being expressed at a point of time are observed. Analysis of the tapes not only allows for matching topics of group concern with specific behaviors and thought processes (collected during the session), but it helps to identify what types of "triggers" move a group from one stage to another. A major issue for all models of group development is to describe the event or events that move the group through the stages. The videotapes are such a valuable source of data that I am struck with how little they are used in group research in social psychology.

The tapes of group interaction are easy to collect, and although analysis is time consuming, there are many alternative means of analyses. In my initial efforts, analysis involves a simple description of events in terms of nature and number. A more involved approach has been suggested by Gottman's (1981) time series analysis, which not only describes events but also identifies causal series of behaviors. A related methodology is offered by investigators (Robinson, 1988; Wheeler, Reis, & Nezlek, 1983) who use diary entries to identify behavior series. The point is not that descriptive methods should replace the more accepted experimental paradigms; we are not involved in an either-or situation. Rather, descriptive methods should be used to complement experimental methodologies.

The tapes depict ongoing social interaction. This is the grist of group dynamics. Designs that do not include such interaction opportunities forfeit the chance to examine group dynamics. The dynamics of groups are not only important for investigations of overt behavior, but there is a definite need to relate behavior and group development to social thinking. The processing of information can best be understood by placing it in the context of individual group-based behavior. In my own research, I have the opportunity to measure ingroup and outgroup perceptions at various time periods *and* then examine tapes of the groups to determine the social interaction that immediately preceded the perceptions. Therefore, the need to capture social interaction does not preclude social cognition research. It does, however, argue that such research can benefit by employing a group interaction situation.

CONCLUSION

My goal has not been to belittle the contributions of group and cognitive research. Rather, I hope to sound the clarion that there are alternative and complementary approaches that can be used in concert with present research paradigms. My model of group development is not complete; it stands as a skeleton in need of flesh. For example, it is important to better identify what events "push" a group from one stage to another. More attention needs to be given to developing specific measures that identify the stages. But incomplete as the model is, work on it has demonstrated the importance of including a developmental perspective in studying group behavior. Likewise, the studies have emphasized the importance of studying social interaction within the group context. Extracting a behavior or cognitive process and examining it in isolation can be very illuminating. But it is vital to take the next step: Replace that behavior or process into the group context and examine it as part of an ongoing system of social interaction. The present model offers one opportunity to develop specific predictions about the relationship between behaviors, cognition, and the stages of group development.

Having been involved in a program of research studying groups over time, I agree with the reviewer's position that group research can consume enormous amounts of time and resources. However, this effort is necessary to understand and describe group dynamics. There is also an advantage that such studies can be used to examine a variety of behaviors and thought processes within the same design. Finally, I'd like to make a closing pitch that social psychologists employ their talents to include description in their quivers of methodologies. Careful description is necessary not only to set the table for developing more analytical research but also to reconnect these analytical efforts back to the human context from which they were spawned.

Part

IV

A Look to the Future
of Social Cognition Research

12

"Social" Cognition and *Social* Cognition
From the Subjective to the Intersubjective

WILLIAM ICKES
RICHARD GONZALEZ

This volume showcases research that brings together two major traditions in social psychology: the study of social cognition and the study of groups. Although the notion of merging these two traditions is certainly not new (it dates at least as far back as LeBon's [1895/1896] classic work on the group mind), the recent interplay has been fruitful, and it is fair to say that both traditions have benefited. And although it is informative to look at what has already been accomplished, as the other chapters in this volume have done, our task is to look at what remains to be accomplished. The interplay between social cognition and group research holds considerable promise, and we present our view of the direction that future research should take.

The starting point for our analysis is the observation that two research strategies, or "paradigms" (Kuhn, 1962), can be used to link the study of social cognition with the study of dyadic and group processes. The first paradigm focuses on the subjective experience of the individual, whereas the second paradigm focuses on the intersubjective experience of the members of a dyad or a larger group. Consistent with its epistemological assumptions, the first paradigm relies on a methodology in which subjects are tested individually in studies designed to ensure the conceptual and statistical *independence* of each subject's cognitions and behavior from those of the other subjects tested. In contrast, consistent with its epistemological assumptions, the second paradigm relies on a methodology in which subjects are tested together in studies designed not only to permit the *interdependence* of their cognitions and behavior but also to examine these patterns of interdependence as phenomena of fundamental importance to the study of social cognition.

Because of the first paradigm's emphasis on the subjective experience of the individual, some of the social cognition researchers who work within its framework can be characterized as "doing cognitive psychology with social stimuli." A representative example is the study by Srull, Lichtenstein, and Rothbart (1985), who tested models of associative memory using people as their stimulus materials. In contrast, because of the second paradigm's emphasis on the intersubjective experience of dyad or group members, some of the social cognition researchers who work within its framework can be characterized as "doing social psychology with cognitive stimuli." Representative examples here include Sherif's (1935) use of the autokinetic effect to study the development of social norms, and Asch's (1955, 1956) use of the perception of line length to study conformity.

To date, much of the work on social cognition has been done by researchers who, guided by the first paradigm, conduct studies of the subjective experience of individuals in contexts that are intended to restrict opportunities for any genuinely interdependent involvement with others. On the other hand, relatively little work has been done by researchers who, guided by the second paradigm, conduct studies of the intersubjective experience of dyad and group members in contexts that are intended to provide opportunities for interdependent involvement. As a convenient shorthand, we will characterize the first type of research as "social" cognition, with quotation marks indicating that—because of the subject's independence and separation from others—the modifier is of limited or even questionable applicability. In contrast, we will characterize the second type of research as *social* cognition, with italics indicating that—because of the subject's interdependence and involvement with others—the modifier is both essential and defining.

LIMITATIONS OF THE "SOCIAL" COGNITION PARADIGM

The limitations of the "social" cognition paradigm become evident when one attempts to define social cognitive phenomena by positing the necessary and sufficient conditions for such phenomena. In our discussion of this issue, we first examine the necessary and sufficient conditions for cognitive phenomena in general and then examine the necessary and sufficient conditions for the more restricted set of distinctively *social* cognitive phenomena.

An analysis of necessary and sufficient conditions for cognitive phenomena has been made by several cognitive psychologists. These authors have concluded that attempts to define mental experience as "information processing" are inadequate according to the necessary and sufficient criterion. For example, D. R. Griffin (1984) contended that "any serious attention to conscious thoughts or subjective feelings" is "conspicuously absent from most of contemporary cognitive psychology." He then went on to criticize cognitive psychology for its naive belief that conscious experience is "nothing but" information processing. "Information processing is doubtless a necessary condition for mental experience, but is it sufficient? Human minds do more than process information; they think and feel. We experience beliefs, desires, fears, expectations, and many other subjective mental states" (p. 457).

Similarly, when the eminent cognitive psychologist Ulric Neisser (1980) was invited to comment on the papers presented at a major research symposium on "Social Knowing," his criticisms focused on "the extraordinarily narrow perspective from which scholars in this field approach their work." According to Neisser,

They see little need to investigate "social knowing" as it actually occurs in the world, or even to read what others have discovered about it, because (I think) they are not very interested in "social knowing" anyway. . . . Productive scientific activity, like perceptual activity, involves exploration as well as observation and thought; what must be explored are the phenomena as they actually occur. (p. 603)

We interpret Neisser's criticism as doing more than questioning the external validity of the work on social knowing. Instead, it suggests what we believe to be a more profound point: that, because some of the most central and fundamental processes of social knowing operate only within the intersubjective context in which they naturally occur, attempts to study them outside of this context may eliminate the very occurrence of these processes. In other words, if the most central and fundamental phenomena and processes of social cognition are intersubjective, attempts to study them as if they were entirely subjective will necessarily fail to capture what is most genuinely *social* about social cognition.

Markus and Zajonc (1985) have noted that, throughout the history of social psychology, "many . . . authors, such as Mead (1934), Merleau-Ponty (1945), Asch (1952), and Heider (1958b)" (p. 213) have identified reciprocity as a fundamental element that distinguishes object perception from social (i.e., interpersonal) perception. In the case of object perception, the object we perceive is merely a percept, whereas in the case of interpersonal perception, the object we perceive—another human being—perceives us back! Moreover, our mutual recognition that the other person perceives us back adds an even more profound dynamic to interpersonal perception, making it not only reciprocal but intersubjective as well (Mead, 1934; Sartre, 1943). This conclusion was underscored by Markus and Zajonc (1985) at the end of their chapter on cognitive social psychology in *The Handbook of Social Psychology* when they stated that "the properties of social perception and social cognition that make them distinct are reciprocity and intersubjectivity" (p. 213).

Unfortunately, these distinctive elements of social cognition—though acknowledged for decades by major theorists in the field—have generally been ignored for decades by researchers who have attempted to use subjectivist, single-subject paradigms to study what are more appropriately construed as intersubjective phenomena. For various reasons, not least of which are the statistical and methodological difficulties of studying intersubjective phenomena, researchers have attempted to force the problems of social cognition to fit within the single-subject designs and methodological frameworks of mainstream cognitive psychology. In doing so, they have repeatedly failed to acknowledge that the most genuinely *social*-cognitive phenomena are intersubjective rather than subjective. However, as Ickes, Stinson, Bissonnette, and Garcia (1990) have noted,

> If the study of *subjective* phenomena involving or occurring within a single conscious mind is the domain of mainstream cognitive psychology, it follows logically that the study of *intersubjective* phenomena involving or occurring between at least two conscious minds is the proper domain of cognitive social psychology. (p. 730)

We agree with the theoretically compelling but paradigmatically unpopular view that the most genuinely *social*-cognitive phenomena are intersubjective rather than subjective. In fact, we propose that intersubjectivity is the element that is both necessary and sufficient to distinguish cognitive phenomena that are uniquely and distinctively *social* from cognitive phenomena that do not warrant this special qualifying adjective. We further propose that these uniquely social, intersubjective phenomena can be characterized as those involving some form of interdependence between the contents and processes of at least two conscious minds (Ickes, Bissonnette, Garcia, & Stinson, 1990).

Given this definition, it is not difficult to argue that the study of intersubjective phenomena is paradigmatically unpopular because intersubjective phenomena are clearly *not* the most frequently studied phenomena in cognitive social psychology (Ickes, Tooke, Stinson, Baker, & Bissonnette, 1988). In most studies of social cognition, researchers have not inquired how the contents and processes of one mind are interdependent with those of another. Instead, using as their models the studies conducted in traditional cognitive psychology, they have inquired how the contents and processes of individual minds tested "one at a time" are related to "social" stimulus materials whose features and contents have been predetermined by the experimenter. As a consequence, the field of "mainstream" social cognition is, to a large extent, one whose "preoccupation with social information processing" (Swann, 1984, p. 458) has cast the social perceiver in the role of "a hermit, isolated from the social environment" and has relegated other people to the status of experimental "stimuli" or perceptual "targets" (Fiske & Taylor, 1984, p. 416). It is, to a large extent, a field based on the paradoxical assumption that the best way to study social cognition is to first remove it from the social interaction context in which it naturally occurs.

The irony here should be obvious. By attempting to study social cognition outside of its natural context, researchers have severely limited the chances that any genuinely *social* processes can affect their subjects' cognitive activities (Fiske & Goodwin, 1994; Levine, Resnick, & Higgins, 1993). In addition, they have virtually eliminated the possibility of studying those intersubjective phenomena that various writers have argued are the ones that make *social* cognition a unique and distinctive field of research.

"SOCIAL" COGNITION VERSUS *SOCIAL* COGNITION

We have been writing so far as if the distinction between "social" cognition and *social* cognition was clear-cut and obvious. Because that may be assuming a bit too much, it is important that we be more specific about the nature of this distinction and what it entails. Consider, therefore, the following range of hypothetical research scenarios.

> *Scenario 1:* A subject named Ann sits alone in a cubicle. In the upper portion of a TV monitor, she sees one view of a complex, three-dimensional figure. In the lower portion, she sees three similar-looking figures, labeled A, B, and C. She has 15 seconds to decide which of these three figures—if rotated in space to the appropriate orientation—would match the figure at the top of the screen.

Scenario 2: A subject named Ann sits alone in a cubicle. In the upper portion of a TV monitor, she sees a profile drawing of a human face. In the lower portion, she sees ¾ views of three similar-looking faces, labeled A, B, and C. Her task is the same as that of the subject in Scenario 1.

Scenario 3: A subject named Ann sits alone in a cubicle. In the upper portion of a TV monitor, she sees a digitized photograph of a human face. On some trials, the face is male; on other trials it is female; on some trials black, on others white. On a subsequent day, she returns to the cubicle and views a similar set of faces. When each face is presented, she has 15 seconds to decide if the face is "old" (one she saw during the first session) or "new" (one she is seeing now for the first time).

Scenario 4: A subject named Ann sits alone in a cubicle. In the upper portion of a TV monitor, she sees a digitized photograph of a human face—in this trial, that of a black male. In the lower portion of the screen, one line indicates "Name: Carl, Age 22," and a second line contains the descriptive adjective "Athletic." Later, she is shown the same faces again without any other identifying information and is asked to match each face with one of the descriptive adjectives that appear on a list she has been given.

Scenario 5: A subject named Ann sits alone in a cubicle. As in Scenario 4, she sees the video display of Carl and is told that she will be working on a task with him later in the session. Before that happens, however, she is asked to provide her "first impression" of Carl by rating him on a series of bipolar adjective scales.

Scenario 6: A subject named Ann sits alone in a cubicle and interacts via closed-circuit television with Carl, a young black man who tells her that he is also an introductory psychology student participating in the experiment for course credit. In fact, Carl is an experimental confederate. His behavior has been carefully preprogrammed so that he will interact with Ann in a way that is as identical as possible to the way that a white male confederate, also named Carl, would interact with her if she had been randomly assigned to the other condition of the experiment. Following her 5-minute interaction with Carl, Ann is asked to provide her "first impression" of him by rating him on a series of bipolar adjective scales.

Scenario 7: A subject named Ann sits in a waiting room with another subject named Carl, a young black man. The 5-minute

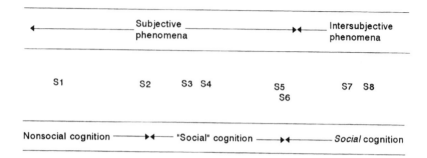

Figure 12.1. Ordering of the Hypothetical Research Scenarios on Two Theoretical Dimensions

interaction they have while waiting for the experiment to begin is spontaneous and unstructured. Following this interaction, the experimenter escorts Ann and Carl to separate cubicles, where they are each asked to rate (a) the quality of their interaction, (b) their own personality, and (c) their partner's personality on a series of bipolar adjective scales.

Scenario 8: A subject named Ann sits in a waiting room with another subject named Carl, a young black man. The 5-minute interaction they have while waiting for the experiment to begin is spontaneous and unstructured. It is also covertly recorded on videotape for subsequent analysis. Later, Ann and Carl will be asked to sign a release form giving their permission for the videotape to be used as data. They will also be asked to view a copy of the tape in separate cubicles, pausing the tape each time they remember having had a specific thought or feeling during the original interaction. During each of these pauses, they record the content of the thought or feeling on a standardized coding form.

In Figure 12.1, we have ordered these eight scenarios from left to right and have also attempted to locate them with respect to the two dimensions depicted at the top and bottom of the figure. The dimension at the top contrasts subjective phenomena with intersubjective phenomena, whereas the dimension at the bottom contrasts nonsocial cognition, "social" cognition, and *social* cognition.

As indicated by its location with respect to the top dimension of Figure 12.1, Scenario 1 involves the study of subjective rather than intersubjective phenomena. It is a study of cognition, rather than perception, because it requires a complex, comparative judgment of the extent to which each of the three "test" stimuli match the "standard" stimulus. Most people would agree that, because of the nature of its stimulus materials and the kinds of research questions that could be tested, Scenario 1 would fall within the nonsocial range of the bottom dimension of Figure 12.1. It probably would not take much to give Scenario 1 a more "social" flavor—by adding, for example, a social facilitation manipulation in which an observer or coactor sits next to Ann during the task. However, by our definition, such a situation would still not fall under the heading of *social* cognition until there is evidence of intersubjectivity in the responses of the subject and the coparticipant.

Scenario 2 resembles Scenario 1 in many respects, the most obvious difference being that drawings of human faces are used as stimuli instead of drawings of more abstract three-dimensional figures. Scenario 2's stimuli are therefore nominally "social," but whether Scenario 2 qualifies as a study of "social" cognition, as opposed to nonsocial cognition, may depend on whether the Scenario 2 study yields substantially different results from the Scenario 1 study. If Scenarios 1 and 2 lead to similar results, we might be inclined to conclude that the subjective phenomena being assessed under Scenario 2 are essentially the same ones being assessed under Scenario 1 and that nonsocial (object) perception, rather than "social" (person) perception, is being investigated in both studies. On the other hand, whereas different results would seem to imply the influence of a social process that is unique to Scenario 2, this outcome could also occur because different cognitive processes might be involved in the two scenarios. In any event, Scenario 2 provides a familiar example of what we mean by "doing cognitive psychology with social stimuli."

Scenario 3 presents the subject with photographic images of real human faces rather than drawings of faces. In addition, it provides a within-subject variation of the gender (female vs. male) and the racial/ethnic background (Black vs. White) of these stimulus faces. Because Scenario 3 uses a recognition task to study memory, it is clearly a study of cognition. But is it also a study of "social" cognition?

We think it is, in that the subject's history of social stereotyping and selective interaction are likely to influence the results. It is not a study of *social* cognition, however, because it lacks the distinctive feature of intersubjectivity (see Figure 12.1).

By the same reasoning, Scenario 4 also represents a traditional "social" cognition study; it therefore warrants no additional comment here. Scenario 5, on the other hand, marks an important transition. Whether or not it is true that Ann will actually meet and work on a task with Carl later in the session, her *belief* that this will happen adds an intersubjective dimension and dynamic to what is still a subjective experience. Although genuine intersubjectivity has not come into play, Ann's anticipated interaction with Carl invokes and implicates this feature in *an imagined or fantasized relationship*. This imagined relationship is clearly subjective rather than intersubjective, as the location of Scenario 5, with respect to the top dimension of Figure 12.1, reveals. At the same time, however, it requires that we locate Scenario 5 very near the fine line that divides "social" cognition from *social* cognition, as its alignment with the bottom dimension of Figure 12.1 indicates.

Does Scenario 6 qualify as a study of *social*—as opposed to "social"—cognition? In this case, Ann and Carl interact via closed-circuit television, and Carl must coordinate at least his speaking turns with Ann in order to sustain her illusion that their interaction is spontaneous when, in reality, his "side" of it is largely predetermined. Scenario 6 represents a borderline example of *social* cognition. The fact that the interaction occurs via television is irrelevant in this regard. What *is* relevant is that Carl's highly scripted and inflexible behavior constrains the degree and type of intersubjectivity that can occur. In Scenario 6, intersubjectivity is at best constrained and at worst disrupted and distorted by Carl's confederate role. In fact, the better Carl plays his role, the greater the constraints on intersubjectivity—a trade-off that should be quite familiar to researchers who are willing to sacrifice "mundane reality" (Carlsmith, Ellsworth, & Aronson, 1976) for the sake of a less ambiguous causal inference.

Although Scenario 6 can be located on the fine line dividing "social" cognition from *social* cognition, it fails to qualify as a study of intersubjective phenomena (see Figure 12.1). The reason is that, of the two interactants in Scenario 6, only Ann is treated as a subject in the research and only her impressions are recorded. Because intersubjective phenomena are those involving some form of interdependence between the contents and processes of at least two conscious minds (Ickes et al., 1988; Ickes, Stinson, et al., 1990), they cannot be investigated in research paradigms in which the thoughts and feelings of only a single subject are assessed, even if that subject has just participated in some form of social interaction.

This brings us, finally, to Scenarios 7 and 8. Both of these scenarios represent examples of what we mean by *social* cognition research in which intersubjective, as well as subjective, phenomena can be investigated. From a conceptual standpoint, they qualify as studies of *social* cognition because the distinctive feature of intersubjectivity is clearly represented in each. From an operational standpoint, they permit the study of intersubjective as well as subjective phenomena because the perceptions, thoughts, and feelings of both participants are assessed. Although these two scenarios focus on the relatively simple case of a dyadic interaction, the dynamics of interdependence can be studied in groups of three or more members as well. It should be evident, however, that these processes become more complex as the group size increases.

INTERSUBJECTIVITY AND INTERSUBJECTIVE PHENOMENA

Consistent with Asch (1952), we propose two necessary conditions for operationally defining an intersubjective (i.e., *social*-cognitive) phenomenon. First, the cognitive responses of at least two interacting individuals must be measured. Second, these responses must be found to be interdependent. These two conditions can be interpreted as clarifying what Asch (1952) meant when he said that "psychological interaction requires a minimum of mutuality" (p. 164).

We will discuss each of the two necessary conditions in turn, asking "How do researchers assess cognitive responses?" and "How do researchers show that these cognitive responses are interdependent?" Before doing so, however, we should begin by clarifying what we mean by the qualifying phrase "at least two interacting individuals." This qualifier obviously limits the domain of intersubjective phenomena to contexts in which the cognitive responses of at least two individuals are assessed. Thus, the following analysis applies to both dyadic and group research. The "interaction" of these individuals is broadly defined; it is not restricted to face-to-face encounters but can include communicative exchanges by telephone, written correspondence, and a variety of other means as well. On the other hand, our definition of interaction must rule out cases in which people experience similar cognitive responses by chance or coincidence. For example, when two people watch the same movie at the same time in different cities, they are not "interacting" even though they may be experiencing very similar cognitive responses to the movie at the same point in time (see Asch, 1952, who made a similar point).

Assessing Cognitive Responses

The assessment of cognitive responses is not a trivial task. Several researchers have developed new and remarkably reliable methods for assessing cognitive responses. Examples include the detailed method used by Pennington and Hastie (1986) to characterize a juror's idiosyncratic story regarding a criminal case, the meticulous work of Ericsson and Simon (1984) in the development of protocol analysis, and the various "thought-listing" techniques developed by researchers such as Brock (1967), Greenwald (1968), Cacioppo and Petty (1981), and Ickes, Bissonnette, et al. (1990); see also Ickes, Robertson, Tooke, and Teng (1986). Researchers might also consider the use of old standbys such as George Kelly's "rep test" (Fransella & Bannister, 1977). However, when interpreting the results obtained with such techniques, one must always be cautious about the degree to which subjects have access to their own internal states (Nisbett & Wilson, 1977).

These techniques share the common goal of assessing an individual's subjective interpretation or "construal" of some stimulus object, event, or circumstance (Ross & Nisbett, 1991). In other words, it is the subjective response to the stimulus that is the focus of study rather than the characteristics of the objective stimulus. For example, in contrast to the prevailing view at the time, Greenwald (1968) suggested that persuasion should be understood from the perspective of how the individual interprets a message rather than the perspective of the objective content of the message.

The first condition for operationally defining an intersubjective phenomenon—measuring the cognitive responses of at least two interacting individuals—can, and probably should, be generalized to include more than *cognitive* responses in the most restrictive sense of that term. A broader view would incorporate other types of responses for which interaction-based interdependence can also be assessed, such as emotions, actions, and motivations. An example of measuring both thoughts *and* feelings for the purpose of assessing intersubjectivity can be found in two studies reported by Ickes et al. (1988). Similarly, in their volume *Close Relationships,* Kelley et al. (1983) distinguish a number of "events" that can be used to describe responses to interaction; these events include thoughts, actions, reactions, and feelings. However, because the present chapter is primarily concerned with the topic of "social" (versus *social*) cognition, our discussion is focused on cognitive responses.

Assessing the Interdependence of Cognitive Responses

Because the term *interdependence* has been misused and overused in the research literature, we need to clarify what we mean by it. Quite simply, we mean that each individual's cognitive responses are influenced by the interaction in which he or she is a participant. In particular, we focus on the most basic and essential aspect of interdependence: whether there is convergence or divergence in the cognitive responses of the participants as a function of their interaction.

As an illustration of what we mean by the convergence and divergence of cognitive responses, consider a relatively common occurrence during airplane travel. A stranger sits next to you and attempts to strike up a conversation. After a few minutes, it becomes evident that you both share a love of contemporary short fiction. The remainder of the flight is filled with a stimulating discussion in which you both reminisce fondly about the gentle humor of Tobias Wolff, shake your heads over the grim stoicism of Raymond Carver, and laugh at the surreal detachment of Frederick Barthelme. This example of convergence in cognitive responses illustrates what Asch (1952) referred to as a "mutual field" (see Newcomb, Turner, & Converse, 1965) and what contemporary psycholinguists call "common ground" (Clark, 1985).

Now consider a different person sitting next to you on the plane. This person persistently takes stabs at starting a conversation. When asked what you do for a living, you reluctantly reply, "I'm a social psychologist." The stranger then makes the comment you have grown to detest ("You're probably analyzing me") and goes on to talk nonstop for the next half hour, pestering you with comments about pop-psychology and self-help books and asking you for your advice on parenting skills and your help in dealing with an obstinate father-in-law. In contrast to the previous scenario, you are not at all interested in this case in trying to find "common ground" or a "mutual field." Instead, you are trying to figure out how to politely convey to this stranger your complete lack of interest in engaging in a discussion (e.g., you blatantly open your briefcase and take out the stack of manuscripts you brought along to review). Thus, your own cognitive responses are diverging with respect to those of the stranger— you are not attempting to find "common ground" but to stake out a private cognitive space of your own.

A simple statistical index of the degree of convergence/divergence in the responses of dyad or group members is the intraclass correlation. Introduced by K. Pearson (1901) as an index of association when dyad members are indistinguishable (e.g., in research on identical twins, it is arbitrary to designate one twin's score as the X variable and the other twin's score as the Y variable, and different designations lead to different Pearson correlation values), the intraclass correlation has grown in popularity among researchers in the area of group processes and interpersonal relations (see Kenny, 1988). The logic underlying the intraclass correlation is that it compares the variability between dyads (or groups) to the variability within dyads (or groups).

In the domain of interpersonal processes, the variance associated with dyad or group membership is treated as a random effect; hence, the intraclass correlation is the random effects analog of R^2 (see Hays, 1988). As it is typically used, the intraclass correlation applies to only one dependent variable. However, generalizations of the intraclass correlation to more than one variable also exist and can be used, for example, to assess the convergence between one partner's anxiety and the other partner's rating of relationship satisfaction (Griffin & Gonzalez, 1995; Kenny & La Voie, 1985).

A more basic index than the intraclass correlation is the difference between the sums of squares between dyads (or groups) and the sums of squares within dyads (or groups). Convergence can be inferred if the sums of squares between groups is greater than the sums of squares within groups, whereas divergence can be inferred if the sums of squares between groups is less than the sums of squares within groups. We call this index CONDIV—an abbreviation of convergence and divergence (see Robinson, 1957). Both the intraclass correlation and the CONDIV index can be used for any size group, even groups of unequal sizes.

The CONDIV index can be given a straightforward interpretation if it is normalized by dividing it by the total sums of squares. Using the relationship that R^2 is equal to the ratio of sums of squares between groups to the total sums of squares, it can be shown that the normalized CONDIV index is linearly related to R^2 (i.e., $2R^2 - 1$). Thus, an $R^2 > 0.50$ implies convergence, whereas an $R^2 < .50$ implies divergence. Because of familiarity with the meaning of R^2, some researchers might prefer to use the normalized CONDIV index rather than the intraclass correlation. In contrast to the intraclass correlation, which can be negative and therefore uninterpretable as a variance or R^2 estimate, the normalized CONDIV index can never be out of bounds. On the other hand, the normalized CONDIV index does not carry the interpretation of an adjusted estimate of the association in the population—an interpretation that can be applied to the intraclass correlation.

Note that these two indexes of convergence/divergence (the intraclass correlation and CONDIV) do not assess change over time. Comparisons of variability over time as a function of interaction have been made by various researchers (Bieri, 1953; Kelley et al., 1983), but they are not the focus of the current discussion. Instead, we define convergence/divergence as the effect of group membership that either makes the responses of the group members more uniform (convergence) or drives them further apart (divergence). We regard this "unifying versus polarizing" effect of group membership as being a phenomenon of widespread and fundamental interest to interpersonal process researchers. Effects based on cross-temporal comparisons of interdependence are arguably just as important, however. If one is willing to do the painstaking work required to study dynamic interaction processes as they unfold over time, statistical techniques for analyzing these dynamic processes are currently available (see Gardner & Griffin, 1989; Gottman & Roy, 1990).

We focus on measures of convergence and divergence because we are concerned, at a fundamental level, with the conceptually analogous notions of consensus, similarity, and reciprocity. The intraclass correlation and the CONDIV index reach their maximum value when the members of a dyad or group respond identically, that is, when they are in perfect agreement, display the same level of behavior, or match each other's previous response. (Note that this consensus, similarity, or reciprocity displayed by the individuals *within* a group conveys the clearest implication regarding group influence when there are also substantial differences *between* the groups.) Other formulations tap a more general covariation or correspondence of the dyad or group members' responses. For example, Kenny and Acitelli (1994) review a correlational technique that assesses the degree to which members in a couple covary; with this technique, a correlation of 1.00 can be obtained in situations in which identical, matched responses do not occur but the responses of one individual are linearly related to those of the other (and when, in the Kenny & Acitelli formulation, the correlation is controlled for mean response).

We should also note that our use of the term *interdependent* differs from that of Thibaut and Kelley (1959). These authors have proposed that in domains involving exchange and coordination problems, outcomes can be interdependent (as, for example, when the members of a married couple derive more pleasure from watching a movie if they see it together rather than alone). On the other hand, in a volume of which Kelley was one of the editors, Berscheid and Peplau (1983) use the term *interdependence* in a manner similar to its use here: " 'interdependence' in the sense that a change in one person causes a change in the other and vice versa" (p. 12).

Research Examples

Our two necessary conditions for operationally defining an intersubjective phenomenon—the assessment of the cognitive responses of two or more interactants and the assessment of the interdependence of those responses—are neither highly stringent nor highly restrictive. Consequently, it should come as no surprise that the available literature provides several examples of participants' cognitive responses either converging or diverging as a function of their interaction in dyads or in larger groups. What may be surprising—to some, if not to others—is that these examples have been provided more often by researchers interested in group processes and interpersonal relations than by researchers interested in what is ostensibly "mainstream" social cognition. As Ickes, Stinson, et al. (1990) have noted,

> Group dynamics researchers have for some time studied intersubjective phenomena under headings such as brainstorming (Diehl & Stroebe, 1987; Street, 1974), group decision making (Janis & Mann, 1977; Miller, 1989; Stasser, Kerr, & Davis, 1989), groupthink (Janis, 1972; McCauley, 1989), group polarization (Moscovici & Zavalloni, 1969; Myers, 1982; Myers & Lamm, 1976), group socialization (Moreland & Levine, 1982, 1989), and majority and minority influence (Latane & Wolfe, 1981; Maass, West, & Cialdini, 1987; Moscovici & Mugny, 1983; Nemeth, 1986). (p. 730)

Most of these intersubjective phenomena are characterized by a general convergence of the participants' cognitive responses as a function of their membership and interaction in the group. Particularly salient examples of this convergent influence were provided by studies of group decision making and groupthink—areas of research focusing on interaction contexts in which achieving a unified consensus is often assumed to be the preeminent value. However, some of these intersubjective phenomena may be characterized by a general divergence of the participants' cognitive responses as a function of their membership and interaction in the group (e.g, group polarization) or by a divergence of the larger group into factions whose members subsequently converge to adopt the appropriate subgroup mentality (e.g., majority and minority group influence).

More recently, interpersonal relations researchers have also begun to study a wide range of intersubjective phenomena. A general research paradigm for studying such phenomena has been developed by Ickes and his colleagues, who have extended the unstructured dyadic interaction paradigm (Ickes, 1982, 1983) to assess dyad members' subjective thoughts and feelings in addition to their overt behavior (Ickes et al., 1986; Ickes, Stinson, et al., 1990; Ickes & Tooke, 1988). To date, this paradigm has been used to explore a number of different aspects of naturalistic social cognition. These include empathic accuracy (Ickes, 1993; Ickes, Stinson, et al., 1990; Marangoni, Garcia, Ickes, & Teng, 1995; Stinson & Ickes, 1992), dyadic intersubjectivity (Ickes et al., 1988), and metaperspective talking (Fletcher & Fitness, 1990; Frable, Blackstone, & Scherbaum, 1990; Ickes et al., 1986). They also include (a) thought/feeling correlates of the interactants' traits and dispositions, (b) thought/feeling correlates of behavioral measures of interactional involvement, and (c) thought/feeling correlates of perceptions of interaction quality and liking for partner (Ickes et al., 1986).

The methodological power of the unstructured dyadic interaction paradigm represents only one advance in the study of *social* cognition. The past decade has seen the development of powerful new statistical models for investigating intersubjective phenomena such as consensus and meta-accuracy in person perception (e.g., Gonzalez & Griffin, in press; Griffin & Gonzalez, 1995; Kenny, 1994; Kenny & Albright, 1987; Malloy & Albright, 1990) and "coorientation" and "shared meaning" effects (Chaplin & Panter,

1993; Kenny & Kashy, 1994). Techniques for studying both within- and between-dyad interdependence have also proven useful in identifying *emergent* social phenomena—for example, that mutual gaze is more than the "coincident looking" defined by the joint probability of the participants' individual gazing behavior (Bissonnette, 1992). These methodological and statistical innovations have been further complemented by creative theoretical models such as Wegner, Giuliano, and Hertel's (1985) analysis of transactive memory and other forms of cognitive interdependence in close relationships.

"SOCIAL" COGNITION AND *SOCIAL* COGNITION

In summary, there are—and historically have been—two major paradigms for the study of social cognition: the subjective, "social" cognition paradigm and the intersubjective, *social* cognition paradigm. The first (subjectivist) paradigm is the same one that mainstream cognitive psychologists have used for nearly a century, differing only in relatively minor respects such as the use of ostensibly "social" stimulus materials. In contrast, the second (intersubjectivist) paradigm developed during the past half century out of the persistent attempts by researchers interested in group dynamics and interpersonal relations to study real social interactions as naturalistically as possible despite all of the statistical and methodological problems involved. Although both paradigms have been used for several decades, the two lines of research they have spawned have proceeded along relatively parallel tracks. Researchers in the first tradition have seldom acknowledged the work of their counterparts in the second tradition. Worse yet, they have typically failed to appreciate that the second tradition offers the greater potential for studying those intersubjective phenomena that theorists from Mead (1934) to Markus and Zajonc (1985) have held to be the most central and distinctive phenomena in the domain of social cognition.

This lack of appreciation is destined to change. As we have noted above, such change is already evident on three fronts:

1. In the development of *new statistical models* that are designed to deal appropriately with the interdependence in the responses of dyad or group members (e.g., Griffin & Gonzalez, 1995; Kashy, 1992; Kenny, 1988, 1994; Kenny, Hallmark, Sullivan, & Kashy, 1993; Kenny & La Voie, 1985; Kraemer & Jacklin, 1979; Mendoza & Graziano, 1982; Thomas & Martin, 1976).

2. In the development of *new procedural models* that are suited to the study of intersubjective phenomena (e.g., Ickes et al., 1986; Ickes et al., 1988; Ickes, Stinson, et al., 1990; Kenny, 1994; Levenson & Ruef, 1992).

3. In the development of *new theoretical models* that begin by assuming the reality of intersubjective phenomena and go on to speculate creatively about the dynamic processes from which these phenomena derive and through which they affect a range of personal and interpersonal outcomes (e.g., Buck & Ginsburg, in press; Duck, 1994; Ickes et al., 1988; Kenny & DePaulo, 1993; Wegner, 1987; Wegner et al., 1985; see also Larson & Christensen, 1993).

Contrasting the Two Paradigms

To help promote the growing recognition that the field of social cognition includes two Kuhnian paradigms that differ substantially in their assumptions about what the core phenomena of social cognition are and how they should be studied, we have summarized the essential differences between the two paradigms in Table 12.1. These points of difference, which necessarily overlap each other to some degree, are useful in making explicit the contrasting theoretical, methodological, and statistical assumptions that distinguish the two paradigms.

Contrasting Theoretical Assumptions. As the first two points of comparison in Table 12.1 reveal, implicit in the "social" cognition and *social* cognition paradigms are strikingly different theoretical views about the nature of social cognition. The first paradigm views social cognition as the subjective reactions of a single individual to a preprogrammed, ostensibly "social," stimulus. In contrast, the second paradigm views social cognition as the subjective reactions of at least two individuals to their interaction experience *and* as the shared, intersubjective meaning that these individuals jointly construct

TABLE 12.1
Essential Differences Between the Two Paradigms

The *"Social" Cognition Paradigm*	The Social *Cognition Paradigm*
1. Views social cognition as the subjective reactions of a single individual to a preprogrammed "social" stimulus event.	1. Views social cognition as the subjective reactions of at least two individuals to their interaction experience *and* as the shared, intersubjective meaning that they jointly construct through their interaction behavior.
2. Is inherently limited to the study of subjective phenomena in that phenomena can be observed and assessed only at the individual level.	2. Can be used to study both subjective and intersubjective phenomena in that phenomena can be observed and assessed both at the individual level and at the dyad or group level.
3. Subjects are tested individually using single-subject designs and data-analytic models that assume that each subject's cognitive responses are statistically independent from those of other subjects.	3. Subjects are tested together, using dyadic or group designs and data-analytic models that assume that each subject's cognitive responses are statistically interdependent with those of the other dyad or group members.
4. The subject can interact only with people (i.e., experimenters or confederates) whose behavior is constrained by an experimental script and ideally does not vary from one subject to the next within the same experimental condition. Mutual influence should, ideally, not occur.	4. The subject can interact with one or more other subjects in a relatively naturalistic way that makes it possible for the behavior of each subject to influence the behavior of every other subject within his or her dyad or group. Mutual influence should occur.
5. The statistical interdependence of the subjects' cognitive responses is typically viewed as an undesirable statistical artifact. Such interdependence, if it cannot be avoided by design, is typically regarded as "nuisance variance" that the researcher must attempt to eliminate or control for in the data analyses.	5. The statistical interdependence of the subjects' cognitive responses is typically viewed with great interest, as potential evidence of an intersubjective phenomenon. The variance associated with this interdependence is therefore regarded as "effect variance," not as "error" or nuisance variance.

through their interaction behavior (Ickes et al., 1988; Schutz, 1970; Wegner et al., 1985). Consistent with these opposing views, the first paradigm is limited to the study of subjective phenomena occurring at the individual level of analysis, whereas the second can address both subjective and intersubjective phenomena occurring both at the individual level and at the dyad or group level. As a consequence, researchers who use the first paradigm should find it difficult to produce any evidence of emergent, intersubjective phenomena, however intrigued they might be by the possibility that such phenomena exist. In contrast, researchers who use the second paradigm should find it relatively easy to study such intersubjective phenomena and to begin the long-term task of documenting and analyzing their different forms, origins, dynamics, and consequences.

Contrasting Methodological Assumptions. As the next two points of comparison in Table 12.1 reveal, the "social" cognition and *social* cognition paradigms also display striking differences in their respective methodologies. In the "social" cognition paradigm, subjects are tested individually and can interact only with people (i.e., experimenters or confederates) whose behavior is constrained by an experimental script. In the *social* cognition paradigm, subjects are tested together—in dyads or in larger groups—and can interact with each other in a relatively naturalistic way that allows genuine mutual influence to occur. Ideally, at least, mutual influence should *not* occur in the "social" cognition paradigm; indeed, any evidence that the subject's behavior has altered the behavior of the experimenters, the confederates, or the other subjects is typically regarded as a serious methodological problem or design flaw.

Contrasting Statistical Assumptions. As the third and fifth points of comparison in Table 12.1 reveal, the "social" cognition and *social* cognition paradigms reflect different statistical assumptions as well. The "social" cognition paradigm uses data-analytic models that assume that each subject's cognitive responses are statistically independent from those of other subjects. If this assumption is violated, the resulting interdependence in the subjects' responses is typically viewed as an undesirable statistical artifact—that is, as "nuisance variance" that the researcher must attempt to eliminate or control for in the data analyses. In contrast, the *social* cognition paradigm uses data-analytic models that assume that each subject's cognitive responses are statistically interdependent with those of the other subjects in their dyad or group. Indeed, any empirical evidence of such interdependence is typically viewed with great interest, as potential evidence of an intersubjective phenomenon.

TOWARD AN EMERGING DIALECTIC

The essential point of this chapter is a simple one: that, by neglecting the study of intersubjective phenomena and concentrating instead on the more traditional study of subjective phenomena, social cognition researchers have failed to address some of the most central, vital, and defining issues in their field. In making this point, we do not want to be misinterpreted as suggesting that all "social" cognition research is bad, whereas all *social* cognition research is good, or that the latter should completely supplant the former. On the contrary, we have learned much, and will continue to learn much more, from research in both domains, and we expect that they will continue to coexist as alternative paradigms for the study of human social cognition. We have been using the word *paradigms* here in the sense intended by Kuhn (1962)—organizing perspectives for the conduct of research in a given area that implicate different philosophical, theoretical, and methodological views of which problems are important and how they should be addressed. Consistent with Kuhn's (1962) analysis, we expect that the *social* cognition paradigm will serve as a dialectical antithesis to the thesis provided by the "social" cognition paradigm, with a consequent sharpening of the issues and enrichment of theory in both domains.

We also expect, however, that the dialectical challenge presented by the *social* cognition paradigm will accelerate the kind of dissatisfaction with "social" cognition research that has led Zajonc to offer the following opinion:

Social psychology is stagnant. It's right now borrowing concepts from cognitive science whose promise is uncertain. Straight cognition has done nothing but remain in people's heads. . . . A gang in Los Angeles choosing to take some chains and guns and go in the street shooting up some others is not going to be understood by the analysis of encoding, storage, and retrieval processes! This emphasis on social cognition has gone too far. (quoted in Aron & Aron, 1989, p. 86)

There is no guarantee, of course, that the *social* cognition paradigm will be any more successful than the "social" cognition paradigm in helping us to understand the causes of urban violence. On the other hand, it does at least promise to move the focus of our research efforts outside of individual minds and into the intersubjective space in which these minds attempt—and often fail—to meet. And it puts the emphasis on the first word in the phrase "social cognition"—where we think it belongs.

Part

V

Discussion of the Chapters

13

What *Is* Social About
Social Cognition Research?

JUDITH L. NYE
AARON M. BROWER

What *is* social about social cognition research? We would argue that there is plenty—provided one looks in the right places. When we began looking several years ago, we found that a number of researchers pursued programs of research that explored social cognitive phenomena in interaction situations. The research presented on these pages is a sampling of the efforts of some of these researchers. We hope you have enjoyed reading about their efforts.

In our own reading of the chapters, we noted that several common themes emerge in the work that is presented here. First and most obvious, to varying degrees all of the chapters involve research that combines social-cognitive processes and small group situations. Many of the chapters also acknowledge the complex nature of social interaction situations and the fact that the social thinker is usually well prepared to meet the cognitive challenge that these situations provide. The research presented here also points out the central role that the group plays in the social thinker's construction of self and that the social thinker often does not bother to distinguish the boundaries between the self and the group. Finally, several chapters note the pivotal role that group success can play in the life of the group and in the subsequent perceptions of the group members. These common themes are discussed in detail in the sections that follow.

SOCIAL THINKING AND THE GROUP SITUATION

In their own way, all of these authors have brought together social thinking and groups research. Perhaps the most explicit attempt to combine the two areas in this volume is offered by Moreland, Argote, and Krishnan (Chapter 3) in their contribution to the literature on Wegner's (1987) concept of transactive memory systems. These memory systems involve more than simply a collection of the knowledge possessed by individual members of the group. They also include an awareness among group members of who knows what within the group. This shared recognition of expertise offers potential benefits for the group. From their research on work groups, Moreland and his associates have found that group performance improves as group members spend more time together and learn to make better use of each member's unique expertise. A second chapter that explicitly addresses socially shared cognitions in groups is by Wittenbaum and Stasser (Chapter 1), who point out that groups are often called on to serve as information-processing units. Conventional wisdom suggests that groups usually make decisions superior to those of individuals, a belief that accounts for the large number of decision-making groups, such as juries and boards of directors, who make critical decisions in our world. According to Wittenbaum and Stasser, these deliberative groups operate under distributed information systems in which information relevant to group decisions varies in the degree to which it is shared by group members. Interestingly, groups tend to show a bias in their information processing, discussing information that group members already share to the detriment of information that is not shared by everyone. The authors discuss this bias in the context of Stasser's collective information sampling model (CIS; Stasser & Titus, 1987), which attempts to account for how information is managed in small groups.

Miles Patterson (Chapter 4) offers an integrative model tying together what he considers to be the interdependent processes of interaction behavior and person perception. His model addresses the complexities of group interaction situations in which individuals often experience conflicting demands on their attention: They must concentrate on their own behavior within the group while at the same time interpreting the behavior of other group members. Patterson suggests that the individual must accomplish this dual role of actor-perceiver with only finite cognitive resources to draw on. His model explains why we may experience difficulty in securing an accurate "reading" of an acquaintance when we are focused on our own cumbersome impression management tasks.

Stephen Worchel (Chapter 11) offers his own model of group development as an example of how groups research and social cognition research can be united. He reminds us that to fully appreciate the social forces driving social cognitions and behavior in groups, we must be aware of temporal influences on group processes. In his chapter, Worchel briefly describes his model of the developmental processes that groups typically experience over time and then goes on to relate the research he has pursued to test the model empirically.

Thus, the chapters in this volume were included for their efforts to join social thinking and group processes. However, by no means do they represent the only research that does so. Both Fiske and Goodwin (Introduction) and Ickes and Gonzalez (Chapter 12) review the work of a number of other researchers who asked the question "What's social about social cognition?" in their own research. The fact is that combining research on social interaction and cognition is nothing new to social psychology. The literature provides ample evidence that social psychologists have been keenly aware of the impact of cognitions on social processes. For example, Gordon Allport (1954) outlined the cognitive mechanisms leading to intergroup prejudice, and the very name "groupthink" betrays Irving Janis's (1972, 1982) thoughts on the link between groups and cognition. More recently, the edited work

Perspectives on Socially Shared Cognition (Resnick, Levine, & Teasley, 1991) presents a significant body of research that links social interaction and social-cognitive processes. In short, our knowledge is growing about what's social about social cognition.

THE COMPLEX NATURE OF SOCIAL INTERACTIONS

A second theme common to these chapters is that they acknowledge the complex nature of social interactions and the sophisticated cognitive methods the social thinker uses to cope with this complexity. Turning first to the complex nature of social interactions, researchers are discovering that even slight shifts in the social environment can make all the difference. For example, Mullen, Rozell, and Johnson (Chapter 9) demonstrate how factors as simple as group size can affect how ingroups and outgroups are represented in the mind of the social thinker. Worchel's (Chapter 11) group development theory suggests that as groups change over time, group members' perceptions of ingroup and outgroup members, and their habits of interacting, change in predictable patterns. The cyclical nature of his model acknowledges that groups do not necessarily end. Although individual group members might change over time, the group often endures, continuing to cycle through its stages (e.g., families, sports teams, academic departments).

Wittenbaum and Stasser (Chapter 1) point out the multitude of factors that can influence how effective a group is in sharing information between members, including time constraints, the expertise and status of individual members, the nature of the group task, and the degree to which group members cooperate with each other. These factors can profoundly affect a group's ability to function. Addressing the complicated nature of the clinical setting, Johnson and Neimeyer (Chapter 7) call on Kenny's (Kenny & La Voie, 1984) social relations model to explain the complex interplay of individual differences and reciprocal perceptions that occur between clients and their therapist in group psychotherapy. The interactions that evolve in this setting, and the group members' interpretations of them, can have significant bearing on the success of the therapy.

Despite the dynamic nature of any interaction situation, the social thinker is usually prepared to meet the demands of these complex social situations, as several chapters point out. In most group interactions, individuals do more than simply sit back to perceive the changing situation; they actively contribute to the unfolding patterns of interaction, bringing their social skills and social cognition capabilities to bear on the task at hand. Moreland, Argote, and Krishnan (Chapter 3), for example, reveal that work groups respond to the complexity of their task by pooling their knowledge, routinely calling on the members with the greatest expertise for a given component of the group task.

Interestingly, as part of their active processing, social thinkers tend to simplify their social world by perceiving it in terms of structured information (categories) rather than as arbitrary or unpredictable attributes (Rosch, 1978). For example, people show a tendency to distinguish between ingroups and outgroups (Stephan, 1985). Evidence suggests that much of our understanding of our social world is rooted in our capacity to break it up into understandable chunks through categorization. This simplification process allows us to manage complex social information quickly and efficiently (Rosch, 1978).

The common ingroup identity model (Gaertner, Rust, Dovidio, Bachman, & Anastasio, Chapter 10) is one theory that capitalizes on the impact of categorization processes on subsequent social thinking. Based on the principles underlying the contact hypothesis (Allport, 1954; Cook, 1985), this model attempts to explain the cognitive mechanisms that contribute to the reduction of prejudice between groups. Gaertner and his associates state that bringing groups together under Cook's (1985) contact conditions encourages group members to change their thinking from " 'us' and 'them' to a more inclusive 'we.' " Thus, such contact may shift cognitive representations from thinking that facilitates prejudice to thinking that gives rise to more positive affective reactions and general attitudes toward the other group.

Although categorization processes play an important role in making the world understandable, Nye and Simonetta (Chapter 6) find that the social thinker employs other information in his or her processing as well. They test the assumptions of Lord's information-processing model (Lord & Maher, 1991) on followers' perceptions of leadership. Lord suggests that followers use a combination of recognition-based and inference-based processes when evaluating the talents of their leaders. Nye and Simonetta, however, find evidence that inference-based processes may override the influence of recognition-based processes.

All of these authors recognize that the social thinker lives in a puzzlingly complex social world in which the rules and the rhythms of groups change constantly, often requiring a great deal of cognitive effort. Viewing social interaction in this light, it is astonishing that we ever feel at ease when in the presence of others and that many of us spend our lives actively seeking the company of other people. Yet as Fritz Heider (1958b) pointed out, humans are amazingly proficient social beings. The social thinker is capable of deliberate, well-considered cognitions as well as more pragmatic "good-enough" cognitions—knowing intuitively when each is called for in interaction situations (Fiske, 1993b; Fiske & Taylor, 1991).

FINDING THE SELF IN THE SOCIAL ENVIRONMENT

Several chapters present evidence that the social thinker's construction of personal identity is an inherently social process. This argument is made most eloquently by Oyserman and Packer (Chapter 8):

> Identity is both highly *personal,* an individually crafted achievement, and also a social *construction* or culturally assigned social representation. . . . Identity is always both "outside in" and "inside out." It is the way we are defined by other people and the way we define ourselves through our actions and symbolic interactions. (p. 200; italics added)

Johnson and Neimeyer (Chapter 7), for example, report findings that members change their self-perceptions in accordance with how other group members see them. In fact, over the life of a group, members' perceptions converge on how they see one another and themselves— group roles become clearer and more consensual over time. Patterson

(Chapter 4) also reports that members use scripts that the group develops for itself in order to cognitively rely on one another in their processing of group information and information about themselves while in their group. Patterson argued that the group situation—that true social situations—very easily overwhelm us cognitively. We therefore look for ways to "cut corners" in our cognitive processing. Placing oneself in the social context of the group is one way to do so.

Oyserman and Packer (Chapter 8) argue persuasively that our selves are defined and understood through three levels of "social fields": the here-and-now situation (where we think of ourselves in ways consistent with the specific social interaction we are in), the social context within which the situation is embedded (whether the interaction takes place at home, at school, at work, at play), and the cultural/political/historical epoch we are in (living, as we do, in the last decade of the 20th century rather than during another time).

Viewed in this way, it is difficult to argue for what is not social about the concept of self. Because any meaning we give to ourselves or our behaviors must be tied to social interaction and socially derived constructs and perceptions, even biological attributes and functions have meaning to us based on social forces. One can think about how body weight and physical size or bodily functions such as burping, bleeding, and sweating have been viewed during different ages and times in our history. We might be able to argue that our height is genetically, and not socially, determined, but we cannot argue that the meaning to ourselves and others of our height is anything other than social. And then again, because height is considered an attractive attribute in society, David Buss (1994) would argue that we select for it in our mates—which means that even the makeup of the gene pool is socially influenced.

EGO BOUNDARIES' EXTENT TO
THE BOUNDARIES OF THE GROUP

Several authors note that in groups that are meaningful to the social thinker—that is, groups to which the members feel some sense of connection and attachment—a phenomenon exists whereby their "ego boundary" or "self-interest" extends to the boundaries of the group. Forsyth and Kelley (Chapter 5) call this a "sociocentric" focus that group members use to replace their egocentric focus. Members who have this sociocentric bias then tend to cognitively shade their judgments in ways that are group serving (vs. self-serving). It is as if their self, or ego, *is* served through the group. The authors found that when groups were successful, members felt that they were receiving valid feedback, that their group successes were more important, that they were more committed to one another, that their membership in the group was more important, and that the degree of consensus in their group was high. In general, success in the group caused members to blur the cognitive distinction between themselves and their group, attaching their personal experiences to their group experiences and vice versa. As Forsyth and Kelley put it, "group members' sense of self-worth prospers when their groups are well respected or admired by others" (p. 109).

Oyserman and Packer (Chapter 8) report a similar finding: The processes used to define one's self are those found embedded in the reference group to which one belongs. Furthermore, one's sense of personal identity changes based on the group one is in. Adolescents, for example, define themselves consistently with their friends when they are with them, consistently with school expectations when in the classroom, and consistently with their family when with their family.

Congruent with this view, self-categorization theory (Turner, 1985) points out that when individuals categorize themselves as members of a given group, they essentially consider themselves to be interchangeable with the other members of their group. Haslam, McGarty, and Turner (Chapter 2) argue that this interchangeability of self and group explains why we are more likely to be persuaded by members of our own group than by outgroup members. Their research suggests that we tend to believe that ingroup members are more credible and relevant sources of information than outgroup members are. Therefore, we listen to them and are more readily persuaded by them.

The chapter by Johnson and Neimeyer (Chapter 7) reveals this "ego-boundary-extending-to-the-group-boundary" effect in another way. In their studies, they found that perceptual "sets" developed in two ways: between self-perceptions and others' perceptions of the self (i.e., over time, group members' perceptions of us become more similar to our self-perceptions) and among perceptions of others (i.e., over time, members' perceptions of others in the group converge). Their research reveals that group members develop shared schemas for roles and norms that arise from the group interactions themselves (vs. being "carried in" by members).

In general, it would seem that when we feel "connected" to a group, we use the same social-cognitive strategies of protection, motivation, and information processing for others in our group as we would for ourselves. Being connected, then, may mean that others begin to see us through our eyes, and we begin to see ourselves through the eyes of these others. Being connected may literally mean creating and sharing with others in our groups the social-cognitive structures used to process information about ourselves, others, and our environments.

THE PERSUASIVE NATURE OF GROUP OUTCOMES

Several authors found that, as the old proverb promises, "nothing succeeds like success." They report that social cognition within groups can be profoundly affected by the success or failure of their groups. Both Forsyth and Kelley (Chapter 5) and Nye and Simonetta (Chapter 6) manipulated group outcomes, telling groups that they either succeeded or failed at their tasks. Their findings were clear: This manipulation affected virtually all judgments that members made—about themselves, other members, and their leaders. Not surprisingly, groups who were successful judged themselves, others, and their leaders more favorably and more generously. Nye and Simonetta point out the implications that such an outcome bias holds for group leaders: Leaders who bring about positive group outcomes for their followers are valued, regardless of the actual quality or nature of their leadership.

Worchel (Chapter 11) also acknowledges the pivotal role that group success can play in group development. He suggests that the act of successfully achieving group goals is sufficient to push groups from the Group Production Stage (Stage IV) to the Individuation Stage (Stage V). In the Individuation Stage, group members step forward to claim their rewards for contributing to the groups' success. In fact, group success can put the group at considerable risk for disbanding, because group members who believe they made the greatest contribution to group success will often consider leaving for a more prestigious group. Worchel also points out that even before groups meet their goals, success impacts on intrapersonal processes within the group. New group members discover that they must first "prove" themselves by making substantial contributions to the group before being fully accepted into the membership.

Several social-cognitive features are at work here in the nothing-succeeds-like-success process. When one changes one's perceptions based on outcomes, one uses tried-and-true information-processing principles in which the end justifies the means. This tendency is particularly easy to see when the outcome is manipulated and therefore has no basis in factual outcome differences—in this case, the processes of schema-based judgments and Lord's (Lord & Maher, 1991) inference-based processing are clearest.

The cause and effect of cognition-based processing is more difficult to tease apart from fact-based processing when outcomes are naturally occurring, such as when real groups are in real competition. In other words, do we judge a leader (or other members) more positively because the group was successful, or was the group successful because of a superior leader (or other members)? But although it may be difficult to tease apart the "factual" from the "cognitive" under these situations, there remains no doubt that success matters and may matter above all else. This is, in fact, the topic of Lord's (Lord & Maher, 1991) work on inference-based cognitive processes, in which he finds that whether successes are real or imagined, they bias subsequent judgments. Nothing else seems to matter, with all other information cast aside.

VARIED RESEARCH METHODOLOGIES

Most of this discussion has addressed the similarities between the chapters presented in this volume. One area in which they differ is in the methodologies they employ to explore social cognition processes. Mullen, Rozell, and Johnson (Chapter 9) borrow from the fine-grained methods of cognitive psychology to study prototype and exemplar representations in the minds of subjects. Moreland, Argote, and Krishnan (Chapter 3) involve participants in an absorbing group task (constructing an AM radio set) as they investigate the transactive memory systems of work groups. Worchel (Chapter 11) commits to the longer-term practice of repeatedly putting groups through their paces to explore temporal effects on group processes. Gaertner, Rust, Dovidio, Bachman, and Anastasio (Chapter 10) survey students in a multiracial high school for their patterns of categorizing ingroups and outgroups. These researchers may employ a variety of methods within their own programs of research as well. For example, Gaertner and his associates report on their success in extending their empirical tests of the common ingroup identity model from the laboratory to the field.

This diversity of methods is appropriate given the assortment of research and statistical methods currently available (Aronson, Brewer, & Carlsmith, 1985; Markus & Zajonc, 1985; McGrath, 1984). As social researchers expand their efforts to study social cognition in true interaction situations, they need to allow themselves greater latitude in their choice of methodologies. Ickes and Gonzalez (Chapter 12) create a continuum of methods that allows us to link research that can be characterized as "doing cognitive psychology with social stimuli" with research that can be characterized as "doing social psychology with cognitive stimuli" (p. 286). Worchel (Chapter 11) suggests that we practice greater balance in our choices of methodologies to study group processes, moving away from exclusive reliance on experimentation. He reminds us that employing a greater variety of methods will provide a richer overall picture of social processes.

The chapters in this book raise one final point worth noting for discussion: whether cognitive and social psychology have always looked at two sides of the same coin. We will close this final chapter with this discussion.

IS SOCIAL PSYCHOLOGY INHERENTLY COGNITIVE, AND IS COGNITIVE PSYCHOLOGY INHERENTLY SOCIAL?

Fiske and Taylor (1991) have made the claim that "social psychology has always been cognitive" (p. 13), an argument that is consistent with what we have been discussing—that whenever meaning or interpretation come into play, cognitive processes are inherent. Moreover, one might turn their statement around to claim that cognitive psychology has always been social, again along the lines we have argued—that social forces are inherent to any meaning and perception that humans generate. It is beyond the scope of this discussion chapter to debate these premises fully. We simply offer them here to highlight processes that appear consistent between the two fields of social cognition and group dynamics.

The debate over whether social processes and cognitive processes are inherently similar could be argued by looking at whether one believes in a basic "constructionist" or "native" premise to human thought, feeling, and behavior. If one takes a constructionist view, then one believes that we *create* our thoughts, feelings, and behaviors (based on experience, learning, and memory) for each interaction or situation we face. If one takes a native view, then one believes that we express a thought, feeling, or behavior that comes from an innate repertoire of such expressions (based, again, of course on experience, learning, and memory). Note that we recognize that experience, learning, and memory are influences in both positions—we are trying not to create "straw men" here. Instead, we wish to point out that the difference in these views has to do with primacy and centrality. From a constructionist perspective, the central processes are those of meaning making, information retrieval and storage, knowledge utilization, and how processes change over time (both in our own lifetimes and over the history of human existence). From a native perspective, what is central is how we are "hard-wired" for perception and response, what qualities people "have," and what processes have remained the same over time. (See Cantor, 1990, for a parallel framing of a similar debate—"having" versus "doing" in personality and cognitive psychology.)

If this is a valid way to represent this debate, then the chapters in this book present evidence that argues for the inherent inseparability of what is cognitive and what is social. It might not be overstating this position too strongly to say that if social and cognitive processes exist that are truly independent, they exert only minor influence on how we live. These independent processes would act in the background, or indirectly through the various paths where cognitive and social processes interact, blend, and enhance one another. The *social-cognitive* processes are the ones that exert powerful influences over our behavior—over who we are and how we act in the world.

So do we now know what is truly social about social cognition? Can the entire history of social psychology be said to be focused on this question? Maybe—even arguably. But several obstacles stand in the way of a complete answer. Imagine how complex a study would have to be to capture the true complexity of social interaction. It would have to monitor the subtle thoughts and feelings of each person in the interaction and the myriad of behaviors exhibited (both conscious and unconscious). It would have to monitor the almost countless cues in the environment, those transmitted among the participants and those simply "out there." It would have to take the histories of the participants into account, the histories of their upbringings, and the histories of their interactions to understand the text and subtext of their interactions. It would have to take into account the cultural, political, economic, and sociological climate in which the interaction took place. And it would have to put the interaction into a historical context.

This is the holy grail of psychology and what might have brought us to this field and keeps us toiling away at it—to understand and describe the wondrous cacophony of our social world. Our humble hope is that this volume is a step in that direction.

References

Abelson, R. P., Kinder, D. R., Peters, M. D., & Fiske, S. T. (1982). Affective and semantic components in political person perception. *Journal of Personality and Social Psychology, 42,* 619-630.

Aiken, L. S., & West, S. G. (1991). *Multiple regression: Testing and interpreting interactions.* Newbury Park, CA: Sage.

Alexander, P. C., Neimeyer, R. A., & Follette, V. M. (1991). Group therapy for women sexually abused as children: A controlled study and investigation of individual differences. *Journal of Interpersonal Violence, 6,* 219-231.

Alexander, P. C., Neimeyer, R. A., Follette, V. M., Moore, M. K., & Harter, S. H. (1989). A comparison of group treatments of women sexually abused as children. *Journal of Consulting and Clinical Psychology, 57,* 479-483.

Allen, I. L. (1983). *The language of ethnic conflict: Social organization and lexical culture.* New York: Columbia University Press.

Allen, R. L., Thornton, M. C., & Watkins, S. C. (in press). An African American racial belief system and social structural relationships: A test of invariance. *National Journal of Sociology.*

Allison, S. T., & Messick, D. M. (1985). The group attribution error. *Journal of Experimental Social Psychology, 21,* 563-579.

Allport, G. W. (1954). *The nature of prejudice.* Reading, MA: Addison-Wesley.

Amaro, H. (1995). Love, sex, and power: Considering women's realities in HIV prevention. *American Psychologist, 50,* 437-447.

Amir, Y. (1969). Contact hypothesis in ethnic relations. *Psychological Bulletin, 71,* 319-342.

Ancona, D. G., & Caldwell, D. F. (1992). Bridging the boundary: External activity and performance in organizational teams. *Administrative Science Quarterly, 37,* 634-665.

Anderson, L. P. (1991). Acculturative stress: A theory of relevance to black Americans. *Clinical Psychology Review, 11,* 685-702.

Anderson, N. H. (1981). *Foundations of information integration theory.* New York: Academic Press.

Anthony, T., Copper, C., & Mullen, B. (1992). Cross-racial facial identification: A social cognitive integration. *Personality and Social Psychology Bulletin, 18,* 296-301.

Argote, L. (1993). Group and organizational learning curves: Individual, system, and environmental components. *British Journal of Social Psychology, 32,* 31-51.

Argote, L., Insko, C. A., Yovetich, N., & Romero, A. A. (1995). Group learning curves: The effects of turnover and task complexity on group performance. *Journal of Applied Social Psychology, 25,* 512-529.

Argote, L., Turner, M. E., & Fichman, M. (1988). To centralize or not to centralize: The effects of uncertainty and threat on group structure and performance. *Organizational Behavior, 42,* 1-17.

Argyle, M., & Dean, J. (1965). Eye-contact, distance and affiliation. *Sociometry, 28,* 289-304.

Aron, A., & Aron, E. N. (1989). *The heart of social psychology.* Lexington, MA: Lexington Books.

Aronson, E., Brewer, M., & Carlsmith, J. M. (1985). Experimentation in social psychology. In G. Lindzey & E. Aronson (Eds.), *The handbook of social psychology: Vol. 1* (3rd ed., pp. 441-486). New York: Random House.

Aronson, J., Cooper, J., & Blanton, H. (1995). From dissonance to disidentification: Selectivity in the self-affirmation process. *Journal of Personality and Social Psychology, 68*(6), 986-996.

Asante, M. K. (1987). *The Afrocentric idea.* Philadelphia, PA: Temple University Press.

Asante, M. K. (1988). *Afrocentricity.* Trenton, NJ: African World Press.

Asch, S. E. (1940). Studies in the principles of judgments and attitudes: II. Determination of judgments by group and by ego standards. *Journal of Social Psychology, 12,* 433-465.

Asch, S. E. (1951). Effects of group pressure upon the modification and distortion of judgments. In H. Guetzkow (Ed.), *Groups, leadership and men* (pp. 177-190). Pittsburg, PA: Carnegie.

Asch, S. E. (1952). *Social psychology* (2nd ed.). Englewood Cliffs, NJ: Prentice Hall.

Asch, S. E. (1955, November). Opinions and social pressure. *Scientific American,* pp. 31-35.

Asch, S. E. (1956). Studies of independence and conformity: 1. A minority of one against unanimous majority. *Psychological Monographs, 70* (9, Whole No. 416).

Asch, S. E., Block, H., & Hertzman, M. (1938). Studies in the principles of judgments and attitudes: I. Two basic principles of judgment. *Journal of Psychology, 5,* 219-251.

Bachman, J. G., Johnson, L. D., & O'Malley, P. M. (1982). *Monitoring the future: Questionnaire responses from the nation's high school seniors.* Ann Arbor: University of Michigan, Institute for Social Research.

Bales, R., & Strodtbeck, F. (1951). Phases in group problem-solving. *Journal of Abnormal and Social Psychology, 46,* 485-495.

Bales, R. F., Cohen, S. F., & Williamson, S. A. (1979). *SYMLOG: A system for the multiple level observation of groups.* New York: Free Press.

Bargh, J. A. (1989). Conditional automaticity: Varieties of automatic influence in social perception and cognition. In J. S. Uleman & J. A. Bargh (Eds.), *Unintended thought* (pp. 3-51). New York: Guilford.

Bargh, J. A., & Raymond, P. (1995). Nonconscious sources of sexual harassment and the misuse of power. *Journal of Social Issues, 51,* 85-96.

Barker, R. G. (1968). *Ecological psychology: Concepts and methods for studying the environment of human behavior.* Stanford, CA: Stanford University Press.

Baron, J., & Hershey, J. C. (1988). Outcome bias in decision evaluation. *Journal of Personality and Social Psychology, 54,* 569-579.

Baron, R. M., & Kenny, D. A. (1986). The moderator-mediator variable distinction in social psychological research: Conceptual, strategic, and statistical considerations. *Journal of Personality and Social Psychology, 51,* 1173-1182.

Bar-Tal, D. (1989). *Group beliefs.* New York: Springer-Verlag.

Bartol, K. M., & Butterfield, D. A. (1976). Sex effects in evaluating leaders. *Journal of Applied Psychology, 61,* 446-454.

Bass, B. M. (1981). *Stogdill's handbook of leadership: A survey of theory and research.* New York: Free Press.

Becker, H. S. (1963). *Outsiders: Studies in the sociology of deviance.* New York: Free Press.

Bem, D. J. (1972). Self-perception theory. In L. Berkowitz (Ed.), *Advances in experimental social psychology* (Vol. 6, pp. 1-62). New York: Academic Press.

Benjamin, L. S. (1974). Structural analysis of social behavior. *Psychological Review, 81,* 392-425.

Berger, J., Fisek, M. H., Norman, R. Z., & Zelditch, M., Jr. (1977). *Status characteristics and social interaction.* New York: Elsevier.

Berger, J., Rosenholtz, S. J., & Zelditch, M. (1980). Status organizing processes. *Annual Review of Sociology, 6,* 479-508.

Berry, D. S. (1990). The perceiver as naive scientist or the scientist as naive perceiver? An ecological view of social knowledge acquisition. *Contemporary Social Psychology, 14,* 145-153.

Berry, D. S., & McArthur, L. Z. (1985). Some components and consequences of a babyface. *Journal of Personality and Social Psychology, 48,* 312-323.

Berscheid, E., & Peplau, L. A. (1983). The emerging science of relationships. In H. H. Kelley, E. Berscheid, A. Christensen, J. H. Harvey, T. L. Huston, G. Levinger, E. McClintock, L. A. Peplau, & D. R. Peterson (Eds.), *Close relationships* (pp. 1-19). New York: Freeman.

Bieri, J. (1953). Changes in interpersonal perceptions following social interaction. *Journal of Abnormal and Social Psychology, 48,* 61-66.

Bissonnette, V. L. (1992). *Interdependence in dyadic gazing.* Unpublished doctoral dissertation, University of Texas at Arlington.

Blanchard, F. A., Weigel, R. H., & Cook, S. W. (1975). The effect of relative competence of group members upon interpersonal attraction in cooperating interracial groups. *Journal of Personality and Social Psychology, 32,* 519-530.

Bodenhausen, G. V., Gaelick, L., & Wyer, R. S., Jr. (1987). Affective and cognitive factors in intragroup and intergroup communication. In C. Hendrick (Ed.), *Group processes and intergroup relations: Review of personality and social psychology* (Vol. 9, pp. 137-166). Newbury Park, CA: Sage.

Borgida, E., Rudman, L. A., & Manteufel, L. (1995). On the courtroom use and misuse of gender stereotyping research. *Journal of Social Issues, 51,* 181-192.

Bottger, P. C. (1984). Expertise and airtime as bases of actual and perceived influence in problem-solving groups. *Journal of Applied Psychology, 69,* 214-221.

Bourdieu, P. (1990). *The logic of practice* (R. Nice, Trans.). Cambridge: Polity. (Original work published 1980)

Braver, S., Linder, D., Corwin, T., & Cialdini, R. B. (1977). Some conditions that affect admissions of attitude change. *Journal of Personality and Social Psychology, 13,* 565-576.

Brawley, L. R. (1984). Unintentional egocentric biases in attributions. *Journal of Sport Psychology, 6,* 264-278.

Brewer, M. B. (1979). Ingroup bias in the minimal intergroup situation: A cognitive-motivational analysis. *Psychological Bulletin, 86,* 307-324.

Brewer, M. B. (1988). A dual process model of impression formation. In T. K. Srull & R. S. Wyer, Jr. (Eds.), *Advances in social cognition* (Vol. 1, pp. 1-36). Hillsdale, NJ: Lawrence Erlbaum.

Brewer, M. B. (1991). The social self: On being the same and different at the same time. *Personality and Social Psychology Bulletin, 17,* 475-482.

Brewer, M. B. (1993). Social identity, distinctiveness, and ingroup homogeneity. *Social Cognition, 11,* 150-164.

Brewer, M. B. (in press). In-group favoritism: The subtle side of intergroup discrimination. In D. M. Messick & A. E. Tenbrunsel (Eds.), *Behavioral research and business ethics.* New York: Russell Sage.

Brewer, M. B., Dull, V., & Lui, L. (1981). Perceptions of the elderly: Stereotypes as prototypes. *Journal of Personality and Social Psychology, 41,* 656-670.

Brewer, M. B., & Lui, L. (1984). Categorization of the elderly by the elderly: Effects of perceiver's category membership. *Personality and Social Psychology Bulletin, 10,* 585-595.

Brewer, M. B., Manzi, J. M., & Shaw, J. S. (1993). In-group identification as a function of depersonalization, distinctiveness, and status. *Psychological Science, 4,* 88-92.

Brewer, M. B., & Miller, N. (1984). Beyond the contact hypothesis: Theoretical perspectives on desegregation. In N. Miller & M. B. Brewer (Eds.), *Groups in contact: The psychology of desegregation* (pp. 281-302). Orlando, FL: Academic Press.

Briggs, G. E., & Naylor, J. C. (1965). Team versus individual training, training task fidelity, and task organization effects on transfer performance by three-man crews. *Journal of Applied Psychology, 49,* 387-391.

Brock, T. C. (1967). Communication discrepancy and intent to persuade as determinants of counterargument production. *Journal of Experimental Social Psychology, 3,* 269-309.

Brown, B. B., & Lohr, N. (1987). Peer group affiliation and adolescent self-esteem: Integration of ego-identity and symbolic-interaction theories. *Journal of Personality and Social Psychology, 52,* 47-55.

Brown, R. J., & Turner, J. C. (1981). Interpersonal and intergroup behavior. In J. C. Turner & H. Giles (Eds.), *Intergroup behavior* (pp. 33-64). Chicago: University of Chicago Press.

Brown, S. M. (1979). Male versus female leaders: A comparison of empirical studies. *Sex Roles, 5,* 595-611.

Brown, V., & Geis, F. L. (1984). Turning lead into gold: Evaluations of men and women leaders and the alchemy of social consensus. *Journal of Personality and Social Psychology, 46,* 811-824.

Browne, A., & Finkelhor, D. (1986). Impact of child sexual abuse: A review of the research. *Psychological Bulletin, 22,* 66-77.

Bruner, J. S., & Tagiuri, R. (1954). The perception of people. In G. Lindzey (Ed.), *Handbook of social psychology* (Vol. 2, pp. 634-654). Reading, MA: Addison-Wesley.

Brunswik, E. (1956). *Perception and the representative design of psychological experiments* (2nd ed.). Berkeley: University of California Press.

Buck, R., & Ginsburg, B. (in press). Communicative genes and the evolution of empathy. In W. Ickes (Ed.), *Empathic accuracy.* New York: Guilford.

Burgoon, J. K. (1978). A communication model of personal space violations: Explication and an initial test. *Human Communication Research, 4,* 129-142.

Burgoon, J. K., Dillman, L., & Stern, L. (1993). Adaptation in dyadic interaction: Defining and operationalizing patterns of reciprocity and compensation. *Communication Theory, 3,* 295-316.

Burnstein, E., & Vinokur, A. (1977). Persuasive argumentation and social comparison as determinants of attitude polarization. *Journal of Experimental Social Psychology, 13,* 315-332.

Buss, D. M. (1994). *The evolution of desire: Strategies of human mating.* New York: Basic Books.

Butterfield, D. A., & Bartol, K. M. (1977). Evaluators of leader behavior: A missing element in leadership theory. In J. G. Hunt & L. L. Larson (Eds.), *Leadership: The cutting edge* (pp. 167-188). Carbondale: Southern Illinois University Press.

Byron, G. G. (1881). The two Foscari. In *The poetical works of Lord Byron.* London: Frederick Warne.

Cacioppo, J. T., & Petty, R. E. (1981). Social psychology procedures for cognitive response assessment: The thought-listing technique. In T. Merluzzi, C. Glass, & M. Genest (Eds.), *Cognitive assessment* (pp. 309-342). New York: Guilford.

Calder, B. J. (1977). An attribution theory of leadership. In B. M. Staw & G. R. Salancik (Eds.), *New directions in organizational behavior* (pp. 179-204). Chicago: St. Claire Press.

Calhoun, A. W. (1918). *Social history of the American family.* Cleveland, OH: Arthur H. Clark.

Campbell, D. T. (1958). Common fate, similarity, and other indices of the status of aggregates of persons as social entities. *Behavioral Science, 3,* 14-25.

Cannon-Bowers, J. A. (1993). Shared mental models in expert team decision making. In N. J. Castellan (Ed.), *Individual and group decision making* (pp. 221-246). Hillsdale, NJ: Lawrence Erlbaum.

Cantor, N. (1981). A cognitive-social approach to personality. In N. Cantor & J. F. Kihlstrom (Eds.), *Personality, cognition, and social interaction.* Hillsdale, NJ: Lawrence Erlbaum.

Cantor, N. (1990). From thought to behavior: "Having" and "doing" in the study of personality and cognition. *American Psychologist, 45,* 735-750.

Cantor, N. (1994). Life task problem solving: Situational affordances and personal needs. *Personality and Social Psychology Bulletin, 20,* 235-243.

Cantor, N., Norem, J. K., Niedenthal, P. M., Langston, C. A., & Brower, A. (1987). Life tasks, self-concept ideals, and cognitive strategies in a life transition. *Journal of Personality and Social Psychology, 53,* 1178-1191.

Cantor, N., & Zirkel, S. (1990). Personality, cognition, and purposive behavior. In L. A. Pervin (Ed.), *Handbook of personality theory and research* (pp. 135-164). New York: Guilford.

Cappella, J. N., & Greene, J. O. (1982). A discrepancy-arousal explanation of mutual influence in expressive behavior for adult and infant-adult interaction. *Communication Monographs, 49,* 89-114.

Carlsmith, J. M., Ellsworth, P. C., & Aronson, E. (1976). *Methods of research in social psychology.* Reading, MA: Addison-Wesley.

Carnoy, M., & Levin, H. M. (1985). *Schooling and work in the democratic state.* Stanford, CA: Stanford University Press.

Carpenter, S. (1993). Organization of ingroup and outgroup information: The influence of gender role orientation. *Social Cognition, 11,* 70-91.

Cernkovich, S. A., & Giordano, P. C. (1992). School bonding, race and delinquency. *Criminology, 30,* 261-291.

Chaiken, S. (1980). Heuristic versus systematic information processing and the use of source versus message cues in persuasion. *Journal of Personality and Social Psychology, 39,* 752-756.

Chaiken, S. (1987). The heuristic model of persuasion. In M. P. Zanna, J. M. Olson, & C. P. Herman (Eds.), *Social influence: The Ontario symposium* (Vol. 5, pp. 3-40). Hillsdale, NJ: Lawrence Erlbaum.

Chaiken, S., & Stangor, C. (1987). Attitudes and attitude change. In M. R. Rosenweig & L. W. Porter (Eds.), *Annual review of psychology* (Vol. 38, pp. 575-630). Palo Alto, CA: Annual Reviews, Inc.

Chaplin, W. F., John, O. P., & Goldberg, L. R. (1988). Conceptions of states and traits: Dimensional attributes with ideals as prototypes. *Journal of Personality and Social Psychology, 54,* 541-557.

Chaplin, W. F., & Panter, A. T. (1993). Shared meaning and the convergence among observers' personality descriptions. *Journal of Personality, 61,* 553-586.

Charters, W. W., & Newcomb, T. M. (1952). Some attitudinal effects of experimentally increased salience of a membership group. In G. E. Swanson, T. M. Newcomb, & E. L. Hartley (Eds.), *Readings in social psychology* (pp. 415-420). New York: Holt.

Cialdini, R. B. (1989). Indirect tactics of image management. In R. A. Giacalone & P. Rosenfeld (Eds.), *Impression management in the organization* (pp. 45-56). Hillsdale, NJ: Lawrence Erlbaum.

Cialdini, R. B., Borden, R. J., Thorne, A., Walker, M. R., Freeman, S., & Sloan, L. R. (1976). Basking in reflected glory: Three (football) field studies. *Journal of Personality and Social Psychology, 34,* 366-375.

Clark, H. H. (1985). Language use and language users. In G. Lindzey & E. Aronson (Eds.), *Handbook of social psychology* (3rd ed., pp. 179-231). New York: Random House.

Clark, H. H., & Brennan, S. E. (1991). Grounding in communication. In L. B. Resnick, J. M. Levine, & S. D. Teasley (Eds.), *Perspectives on socially shared cognition* (pp. 127-149). Washington, DC: American Psychological Association.

Clark, N. K., & Stephenson, G. M. (1989). Group remembering. In P. Paulus (Ed.), *Psychology of group influence* (2nd ed., pp. 357-391). Hillsdale, NJ: Lawrence Erlbaum.

Cohen, J., & Cohen, P. (1975). *Applied multiple regression/correlational analysis for the behavioral sciences.* Hillsdale, NJ: Lawrence Erlbaum.

Cohen, J., & Cohen, P. (1983). *Applied multiple regression/correlation analysis for the behavioral sciences* (2nd ed.). Hillsdale, NJ: Lawrence Erlbaum.

Cook, K. S. (Ed.). (1987). *Social exchange theory.* Newbury Park, CA: Sage.

Cook, S. W. (1969). Motives in a conceptual analysis of attitude-related behavior. In W. J. Arnold & D. Levine (Eds.), *Nebraska symposium on motivation* (Vol. 18, pp. 179-236). Lincoln: University of Nebraska Press.

Cook, S. W. (1985). Experimenting on social issues: The case of school desegregation. *American Psychologist, 40,* 452-460.

Courtois, C. (1988). *Healing the incest wound.* New York: Norton.

Cox, V. C., Paulus, P. B., & McCain, G. (1984). Prison crowding research: The relevance for prison housing standards and a general approach regarding crowding phenomena. *American Psychologist, 39,* 1148-1160.

Coxon, A. P. M. (1982). *The user's guide to multidimensional scaling.* Exeter, NH: Heineman.

Crane, J. (1991). Effects of neighborhoods on dropping out of school and teenage childbearing. In C. Jencks & P. E. Peterson (Eds.), *The urban underclass* (pp. 299-320). Washington, DC: Brookings Institution.

Crano, W. (1989, June). *Judgmental subjectivity/objectivity and minority influence.* Paper presented at the third workshop on Minority Influence, Perugia, Italy.

Crocker, J., & Luhtanen, R. (1990). Collective self-esteem and ingroup bias. *Journal of Personality and Social Psychology, 58,* 60-67.

Crocker, J., & Weber, R. (1983). Cognitive processes in the revision of stereotypic beliefs. *Journal of Personality and Social Psychology, 44,* 55-66.

Cronbach, L. J. (1955). Processes affecting scores on "understanding of others" and "assumed similarity." *Psychological Bulletin, 52,* 177-193.

Cronbach, L. J. (1958). Proposals leading to analytic treatment of social perception scores. In R. Tagiuri & L. Petrullo (Eds.), *Person perception and interpersonal behavior* (pp. 353-379). Stanford, CA: Stanford University Press.

Curry, C., Trew, K., Turner, I., & Hunter, J. (1994). The effect of life domains on girls' possible selves. *Adolescence, 29*(113), 133-150.

Daly, S. (1978). Behavioral correlates of social anxiety. *British Journal of Social and Clinical Psychology, 17,* 117-120.

Dashiell, J. F. (1935). Experimental studies of the influence of social situations on the behavior of individual human adults. In C. Murchison (Ed.), *A handbook of social psychology* (pp. 1097-1158). Worcester, MA: Clark University Press.

David, B., & Turner, J. C. (1992, July). *Studies in self-categorization and minority conversion.* Paper presented at the symposium on Minority Influence at the Joint EAESP/SESP meeting, Leuven/Louvain-la-Neuve, Belgium.

David, B., & Turner, J. C. (in press). Studies in self-categorization and minority conversion: Is being a member of the outgroup an advantage? *British Journal of Social Psychology.*

Davis, J. A., & Smith, T. W. (1991). *General social surveys, 1972-1991: Cumulative codebook.* Chicago: National Opinion Research Center.

Davison, M. L. (1982). *Multidimensional scaling.* New York: John Wiley.

Day, R. D. (1992). The transition to first intercourse among racially and culturally diverse youth. *Journal of Marriage and the Family, 54,* 749-762.

Deaux, K. (1984). From individual differences to social categories: Analysis of a decade's research on gender. *American Psychologist, 39,* 105-116.

Deaux, K. (1993). Reconstructing social identity. *Personality and Social Psychology Bulletin, 19,* 4-12.

Deaux, K. (1995). How basic can you be? The evolution of research on gender stereotypes. *Journal of Social Issues, 51,* 11-20.

Deaux, K., & Major, B. (1987). Putting gender into context: An interactive model of gender-related behavior. *Psychological Review, 94,* 369-389.

de la Haye, A. (1991). Problems and procedures: A typology of paradigms in interpersonal cognition. *European Bulletin of Cognitive Psychology, 11,* 279-304.

Deprét, E. F., & Fiske, S. T. (1993). Social cognition and power: Some cognitive consequences of social structure as a source of control deprivation. In G. Weary, F. Gleicher, & K. Marsh (Eds.), *Control motivation and social cognition* (pp. 176-202). New York: Springer-Verlag.

Derogatis, L. R. (1983). *SCL-90-R: Administration, scoring and procedures manual* (2nd ed.). Towson, MD: Clinical Psychometric Research.

Deutsch, M., & Collins, M. (1951). *Interracial housing: A psychological evaluation of a social experiment.* Minneapolis: University of Minnesota Press.

Deutsch, M., & Gerard, H. B. (1955). A study of normative and informational social influences upon individual judgment. *Journal of Abnormal and Social Psychology, 51,* 629-636.

Devadas, R., & Argote, L. (1995, May). *Organizational learning curves: The effects of turnover and work group structure.* Paper presented at the annual meeting of the Midwestern Psychological Association, Chicago.

Diehl, M., & Stroebe, W. (1987). Productivity loss in brainstorming groups: Toward the solution of a riddle. *Journal of Personality and Social Psychology, 53,* 497-509.

Dijker, A. J., & Fiske, S. T. (1993). *Nonreactive measurement of whites' emotional responses to blacks.* Unpublished manuscript, University of Massachusetts, Amherst.

Doise, W. (1978). *Groups and individuals: Explanations in social psychology.* Cambridge, UK: Cambridge University Press.

Dole, A. A. (1995). Why not drop "race" as a term? *American Psychologist, 50,* 40-41.

Doosje, B., Spears, R., Haslam, S. A., Koomen, W., & Oakes, P. J. (1995). *The effect of comparative context on central tendency and variability judgments and the evaluation of group characteristics.* Unpublished manuscript, University of Amsterdam.

Dovidio, J. F., Brown, C. E., Heltman, K., Ellyson, S. L., & Keating, C. F. (1988). Power displays between women and men in discussions of gender-linked tasks: A multichannel study. *Journal of Personality and Social Psychology, 55,* 580-587.

Dovidio, J. F., & Gaertner, S. L. (1986). Prejudice, discrimination and racism: Historical trends and contemporary approaches. In J. F. Dovidio & S. L. Gaertner (Eds.), *Prejudice, discrimination, and racism* (pp. 1-34). Orlando, FL: Academic Press.

Dovidio, J. F., Gaertner, S. L., Isen, A. M., & Lowrance, R. (1995). Group representations and intergroup bias: Positive affect, similarity and group size. *Personality and Social Psychology Bulletin, 21*(6), 856-865.

Duane, D. (1988). *Spock's world.* New York: Pocket Books.

Duck, S. W. (1977). Inquiry, hypothesis, and the quest for validation. In S. Duck (Ed.), *Theory and practice in interpersonal attraction* (pp. 379-404). New York: Academic Press.

Duck, S. W. (1994). *Meaningful relationships.* Thousand Oaks, CA: Sage.

Dustin, D. S. (1966). Member reactions to team performance. *Journal of Social Psychology, 69,* 237-243.

Dyer, J. L. (1985). *Annotated bibliography and state-of-the-art review of the field of team training as it relates to military teams.* Fort Benning, GA: Army Research Institute for the Behavioral and Social Sciences.

Eagly, A. H. (1983). Gender and social influence: A social psychological analysis. *American Psychologist, 38,* 971-981.

Eagly, A. H. (1995). The science and politics of comparing women and men. *American Psychologist, 50,* 145-158.

Eden, D., & Leviatan, V. (1975). Implicit leadership theory as a determinant of the factor structure underlying supervisory behavior scales. *Journal of Applied Psychology, 60,* 736-741.

Eisenman, R. (1995). Why psychologists should study race. *American Psychologist, 50,* 42-43.

Ellemers, N., Wilke, H., & van Knippenberg, A. (1993). Effects of the legitimacy of low group or individual status on individual and collective status-enhancement strategies. *Journal of Personality and Social Psychology, 64,* 766-778.

Engel, B. T. (1992, May). *Group structure and the sharing of information during decision making.* Paper presented at the annual meeting of the Midwestern Psychological Association, Chicago.

Erez, M., & Earley, P. C. (1993). *Culture, self-identity, and work.* New York: Oxford University Press.

Ericsson, K. A., & Simon, H. A. (1984). *Protocol analysis.* Cambridge: Massachusetts Institute of Technology Press.

Fajans, J. (1985). The person in social context: The social character of baining "psychology." In G. White & J. Kirkpatrick (Eds.), *Person, self and experience: Exploring pacific ethnopsychologies* (pp. 367-397). Berkeley: University of California Press.

Farr, R. M. (1987). Social representations: A French tradition of research. *Journal for the Theory of Social Behaviour, 17,* 343-369.

Feshbach, F., & Singer, R. (1957). The effects of personal and shared threats upon social prejudice. *Journal of Abnormal and Social Psychology, 54,* 411-416.

Festinger, L. (1947). The role of group belongingness in a voting situation. *Human Relations, 1,* 154-180.

Festinger, L. (1950). Informal social communication. *Psychological Review, 57,* 271-282.

Festinger, L. (1954). A theory of social comparison processes. *Human Relations, 7,* 117-140.

Festinger, L., Riecken, H. W., & Schachter, S. (1956). *When prophecy fails.* Minneapolis: University of Minnesota Press.

Festinger, L., Schachter, S., & Back, K. (1950). *Social pressures in informal groups: A study of a housing community.* Stanford, CA: Stanford University Press.

Fine, G. A. (1979). Small groups and culture creation: The idioculture of Little League baseball teams. *American Sociological Review, 44,* 733-745.

Fine, M. (1995). *Secure times: Constructing white working-class masculinities in the late 20th century.* Manuscript submitted for publication.

Fiske, S. T. (1981). Social cognition and affect. In J. Harvey (Ed.), *Cognition, social behavior, and the environment* (pp. 227-264). Hillsdale, NJ: Lawrence Erlbaum.

Fiske, S. T. (1992). Thinking is for doing: Portraits of social cognition from daguerreotype to laserphoto. *Journal of Personality and Social Psychology, 63,* 877-889.

Fiske, S. T. (1993a). Controlling other people: The impact of power on stereotyping. *American Psychologist, 48,* 621-628.

Fiske, S. T. (1993b). Social cognition and social perception. *Annual Review of Psychology, 44,* 155-194.

Fiske, S. T., Bersoff, D. N., Borgida, E., Deaux, K., & Heilman, M. E. (1993). What constitutes a scientific review? A majority retort to Barrett and Morris. *Law and Human Behavior, 17,* 217-233.

Fiske, S. T., & Neuberg, S. L. (1990). A continuum of impression formation, from category-based to individuating processes: Influences of information and motivation on attention interpretation. In M. P. Zanna (Ed.), *Advances in experimental social psychology* (Vol. 23, pp. 1-74). New York: Academic Press.

Fiske, S. T., & Taylor, S. E. (1984). *Social cognition.* Reading, MA: Addison-Wesley.

Fiske, S. T., & Taylor, S. E. (1991). *Social cognition* (2nd ed.). New York: McGraw-Hill.

Fletcher, G. J. O., & Fitness, J. (1990). Occurrent social cognition in close relationship interaction: The role of proximal and distal variables. *Journal of Personality and Social Psychology, 59,* 464-474.

Forgas, J. P. (1983a). The effects of prototypicality and cultural salience on perceptions of people. *Journal of Research in Personality, 17,* 153-173.

Forgas, J. P. (1983b). What is social about social cognition? *British Journal of Social Psychology, 22,* 129-144.

Forsyth, D. R., Berger, R., & Mitchell, T. (1981). The effects of self-serving vs. other-serving claims of responsibility on attraction and attribution in groups. *Social Psychology Quarterly, 44,* 59-64.

Forsyth, D. R., & Schlenker, B. R. (1977). Attributing the causes of group performance: Effects of performance quality, task importance, and future testing. *Journal of Personality, 45,* 220-236.

Foster, B. L., & White, G. M. (1982). Ethnic identity and perceived distance between ethnic categories. *Human Organization, 41,* 121-130.

Frable, D. E. S., Blackstone, T., & Scherbaum, C. (1990). Marginal and mindful: Deviants in social interactions. *Journal of Personality and Social Psychology, 59,* 140-149.

Fransella, F., & Bannister, D. (1977). *A manual for repertory grid technique.* New York: Academic Press.

Fraser, S. L., & Lord, R. G. (1983). *The effect of stimulus prototypicality on leadership perceptions and behavioral ratings.* Unpublished manuscript, University of Akron.

Freedman-Doan, C., Arbreton, A., Harold, R., & Eccles, J. (1993). Looking forward to adolescence: Mothers' and fathers' expectations for effective and behavioral change. *Journal of Early Adolescence, 13*(4), 472-502.

Fridlund, A. J. (1994). *Human facial expression: An evolutionary view.* San Diego, CA: Academic Press.

Frieze, I. H., Whitley, B. E., Jr., Hanusa, B. H., & McHugh, M. C. (1982). Assessing the theoretical models for sex differences in causal attributions for success and failure. *Sex Roles, 8,* 333-343.

Funder, D. C. (1987). Errors and mistakes: Evaluating the accuracy of social judgment. *Psychological Bulletin, 101,* 75-90.

Funk, S. G., Horowitz, A. D., Lipshitz, R., & Young, F. W. (1976). The perceived structure of American ethnic groups: The use of multidimensional scaling in stereotype research. *Sociometry, 39,* 116-130.

Fussell, S. R., & Krauss, R. M. (1989a). The effects of intended audience on message production and comprehension: Reference in a common ground framework. *Journal of Experimental Social Psychology, 25,* 203-219.

Fussell, S. R., & Krauss, R. M. (1989b). Understanding friends and strangers: The effects of audience design on message comprehension. *European Journal of Social Psychology, 19,* 509-525.

Fussell, S. R., & Krauss, R. M. (1991). Accuracy and bias in estimates of others' knowledge. *European Journal of Social Psychology, 21,* 445-454.

Gaertner, S. L., & Dovidio, J. F. (1986). The aversive form of racism. In J. F. Dovidio & S. L. Gaertner (Eds.), *Prejudice, discrimination, and racism* (pp. 61-89). Orlando, FL: Academic Press.

Gaertner, S. L., Dovidio, J. F., Anastasio, P. A., Bachman, B. A., & Rust, M. C. (1993). The common ingroup identity model: Recategorization and the reduction of intergroup bias. In W. Stroebe & M. Hewstone (Eds.), *The European review of social psychology* (Vol. 4, pp. 1-25). Chichester, UK: Wiley.

Gaertner, S. L., Dovidio, J. F., & Bachman, B. A. (in press). Revisiting the contact hypothesis: The induction of a common ingroup identity. *International Journal of Intercultural Relations.*

Gaertner, S. L., Mann, J. A., Dovidio, J. F., Murrell, A. J., & Pomare, M. (1990). How does cooperation reduce intergroup bias? *Journal of Personality and Social Psychology, 59,* 692-704.

Gaertner, S. L., Mann, J. A., Murrell, A., & Dovidio, J. F. (1989). Reducing intergroup bias: The benefits of recategorization. *Journal of Personality and Social Psychology, 57,* 239-249.

Galambos, J. A., Abelson, R. P., & Black, J. B. (Eds.). (1986). *Knowledge structures.* Hillsdale, NJ: Lawrence Erlbaum.

Gardner, R. C. (1993). Stereotypes as consensual beliefs. In M. P. Zanna & J. M. Olson (Eds.), *The psychology of prejudice: The Ontario symposium* (Vol. 7, pp. 1-31). Hillsdale, NJ: Lawrence Erlbaum.

Gardner, W. L. (1992). Lessons in organizational dramaturgy: The art of impression management. *Organizational Dynamics, 21,* 33-46.

Gardner, W., & Griffin, W. (1989). Methods for the analysis of parallel streams of continuously recorded social behaviors. *Psychological Bulletin, 105,* 446-455.

Geis, F. L. (1983, April). *Gender schemas and achievement: Performance and recognition.* Paper presented at the annual meeting of the Eastern Psychological Association, Philadelphia, PA.

Geis, F. L., Boston, M. B., & Hoffman, N. (1985). Sex of authority role models and achievement by men and women: Leadership performance and recognition. *Journal of Personality and Social Psychology, 49,* 636-653.

Geis, F. L., Carter, M. R., & Butler, D. J. (1982). *Research on seeing and evaluating people.* Newark: University of Delaware.

George, C. E. (1967). Training for coordination within rifle squads. In T. O. Jacobs, J. S. Ward, T. R. Powers, C. E. George, & H. H. McFann (Eds.), *Individual and small-unit training for combat operations* (pp. 21-67). Alexandria, VA: George Washington University Press.

Gerard, H. B., & Hoyt, M. F. (1974). Distinctiveness of social categorization and attitude toward ingroup members. *Journal of Personality and Social Psychology, 27,* 836-842.

Gersick, C. J. G. (1988). Time and transition in work teams: Toward a new model of group development. *Academy of Management Journal, 31,* 9-41.

Gersick, C. J. G. (1989). Marking time: Predictable transitions in task groups. *Academy of Management Journal, 32,* 274-309.

Gersick, C. J., & Hackman, J. R. (1990). Habitual routines in task-performing groups. *Organizational Behavior and Human Decision Processes, 47,* 65-97.

Gibson, J. J. (1979). *The ecological approach to visual perception.* Boston: Houghton Mifflin.

Gigone, D., & Hastie, R. (1993). The common knowledge effect: Information sampling and group judgment. *Journal of Personality and Social Psychology, 65,* 959-974.

Gilbert, D. T., & Krull, D. S. (1988). Seeing less and knowing more: The benefits of perceptual ignorance. *Journal of Personality and Social Psychology, 54,* 193-202.

Gilbert, D. T., Krull, D. S., & Pelham, B. W. (1988). Of thoughts unspoken: Social inference and the self-regulation of behavior. *Journal of Personality and Social Psychology, 55,* 685-694.

Gilbert, D. T., Pelham, B. W., & Krull, D. S. (1988). On cognitive busyness: When person perceivers meet persons perceived. *Journal of Personality and Social Psychology, 55,* 733-740.

Gilovich, T. (1987). Secondhand information and social judgment. *Journal of Experimental Social Psychology, 23,* 59-74.

Giola, D. A., & Sims, H. P. (1985). Self-serving bias and actor-observer differences in organizations: An empirical analysis. *Journal of Applied Social Psychology, 15,* 547-563.

Goethals, G. R. (1987). Theories of group behavior: A commentary. In B. Mullen & G. R. Goethals (Eds.), *Theories of group behavior* (pp. 209-229). New York: Springer-Verlag.

Goethals, G. R., & Darley, J. (1977). Social comparison theory: An attribution approach. In J. Sulls & R. Miller (Eds.), *Social comparison processes: Theoretical and empirical perspectives* (pp. 259-279). Washington, DC: Hemisphere.

Gonzalez, R., & Griffin, D. (in press). On the statistics of interdependence: Treating dyadic data with respect. In S. W. Duck, R. Dindia, W. Ickes, R. M. Milardo, R. Mills, & B. Sarason (Eds.), *Handbook of personal relationships: Theory, research, and interventions* (2nd ed.). Chichester, UK: Wiley.

Goodman, P. S., & Garber, S. (1988). Absenteeism and accidents in a dangerous environment: Empirical analysis of underground coal mines. *Journal of Applied Psychology, 73,* 81-86.

Goodman, P. S., & Leyden, D. P. (1991). Familiarity and group productivity. *Journal of Applied Psychology, 76,* 578-586.

Goodman, P. S., & Shah, S. (1992). Familiarity and work group outcomes. In S. Worchel, W. Wood, & J. A. Simpson (Eds.), *Group process and productivity* (pp. 276-298). Newbury Park, CA: Sage.

Goodwin, S. A., & Fiske, S. T. (1995). *Power and motivated impression formation: How powerholders stereotype by default and by design.* Manuscript submitted for publication, University of Massachusetts at Amherst.

Gottman, J. M. (1981). *Time series analysis: A comprehensive introduction for social scientists.* Cambridge, UK: Cambridge University Press.

Gottman, J. M., & Roy, A. K. (1990). *Sequential analysis: A guide for behavioral researchers.* Cambridge, UK: Cambridge University Press.

Graumann, C. F., & Wintermantel, M. (1989). Discriminatory speech acts: A functional approach. In D. Bar-Tal, C. F. Graumann, A. W. Kruglanski, & W. Stroebe (Eds.), *Stereotyping and prejudice: Changing conceptions* (pp. 183-206). New York: Springer-Verlag.

Green, C. W., Adams, A. M., & Turner, C. W. (1988). Development and validation of the school interracial climate scale. *American Journal of Community Psychology, 16,* 241-259.

Green, S. G., & Mitchell, T. R. (1979). Attributional processes of leaders in leader-member interactions. *Organizational Behavior, 23,* 429-458.

Greenwald, A. G. (1968). Cognitive learning, cognitive response to persuasion, and attitude change. In A. G. Greenwald, T. C. Brock, & T. M. Ostrom (Eds.), *Psychological foundations of attitudes* (pp. 147-170). New York: Academic Press.

Griffin, D. R. (1984). Animal thinking. *American Scientist, 72,* 456-464.

Griffin, D. R., & Gonzalez, R. (1995). *Correlational models for dyadic data.* Unpublished manuscript.

Griffith, J. (1989). The army's new unit personnel replacement system and its relationship to unit cohesion and social support. *Military Psychology, 1,* 17-34.

Grossman, M., Coutant, D., & Worchel, S. (1993). *Group productivity over time.* Unpublished manuscript, Texas A&M University.

Hackman, J. R., & Morris, C. G. (1975). Group tasks, group interaction process, and group performance effectiveness: A review and proposed integration. In L. Berkowitz (Ed.), *Advances in experimental social psychology* (Vol. 8, pp. 45-99). New York: Academic Press.

Hall, E. T. (1966). *The hidden dimension.* New York: Doubleday.

Hall, J. (1971). Decisions, decisions, decisions. *Psychology Today, 5,* 51-54, 86, 88.

Hall, J. A. (1984). *Nonverbal sex differences: Communication accuracy and expressive style.* Baltimore: Johns Hopkins University Press.

Hamilton, D. L., Driscoll, D. M., & Worth, L. T. (1989). Cognitive organization of impressions: Effects of incongruency in complex representations. *Journal of Personality and Social Psychology, 57,* 925-939.

Hamilton, D. L., & Gifford, R. K. (1976). Illusory correlation in interpersonal perception: A cognitive basis of stereotypic judgments. *Journal of Experimental Social Psychology, 12,* 392-407.

Hamilton, D. L., & Sherman, S. J. (1989). Illusory correlations: Implications for stereotype theory and research. In D. Bar-Tal, C. F. Graumann, A. W. Kruglanski, & W. Stroebe (Eds.), *Stereotypes and prejudices: Changing conceptions* (pp. 59-82). New York: Springer-Verlag.

Hanson, R. D. (1980). Common sense attributions. *Journal of Personality and Social Psychology, 39,* 996-1009.

Harre, R., & Gillett, G. (1994). *The discursive mind.* Thousand Oaks, CA: Sage.

Harter, S. (1990). Self and identity development. In S. Feldman & G. Elliott (Eds.), *At the threshold: The developing adolescent* (pp. 352-387). Cambridge, MA: Harvard University Press.

Harter, S. L., Alexander, P. C., & Neimeyer, R. A. (1988). Long-term effects of incestuous child abuse in college women: Social adjustment, social cognition, and family characteristics. *Journal of Consulting and Clinical Psychology, 56,* 5-8.

Harter, S. L., & Neimeyer, R. A. (1995). Long-term effects of child sexual abuse: Toward a constructivist theory of trauma and its treatment. In R. A. Neimeyer & G. J. Neimeyer (Eds.), *Advances in personal construct psychology* (Vol. 3, pp. 227-267). Greenwich, CT: JAI.

Harter, S. L., Neimeyer, R. A., & Alexander, P. C. (1989). Personal construction of family relationships. *International Journal of Personal Construct Psychology, 2,* 123-142.

Harvey, D. (1990). *The condition of postmodernity.* Oxford, UK: Basil Blackwell.

Haslam, S. A. (in press). Stereotyping and social influence: Foundations of stereotype sharedness. In R. Spears, P. J. Oakes, N. Ellemers, & S. A. Haslam (Eds.), *The social psychology of stereotyping and group life.* Oxford, UK: Basil Blackwell.

Haslam, S. A., Oakes, P. J., McGarty, C., Turner, J. C., Reynolds, K., & Eggins, R. (in press). Stereotyping and social influence: The mediation of stereotype applicability and sharedness by the views of ingroup and outgroup members. *British Journal of Social Psychology.*

Haslam, S. A., Oakes, P. J., Turner, J. C., & McGarty, C. (1995). Social categorization and group homogeneity: Changes in the perceived applicability of stereotype content as a function of comparative context and trait favorableness. *British Journal of Social Psychology, 34,* 139-160.

Haslam, S. A., Oakes, P. J., Turner, J. C., & McGarty, C. (1996). Social identity, self-categorization and the perceived homogeneity of ingroups and outgroups: The interaction between social motivation and cognition. In R. M. Sorrentino & E. T. Higgins (Eds.), *Handbook of motivation and social cognition* (Vol. 3). New York: Guilford.

Haslam, S. A., & Turner, J. C. (1992). Context-dependent variation in social stereo-typing 2: The relationship between frame of reference, self-categorization and accentuation. *European Journal of Social Psychology, 22,* 251-278.

Hastie, R. (1986). Experimental evidence on group accuracy. In B. Grofman & G. Owen (Eds.), *Information pooling and group decision making* (pp. 129-157). Greenwich, CT: JAI.

Hastie, R., & Pennington, N. (1991). Cognitive and social processes in decision making. In L. Resnick, J. Levine, & S. Teasley (Eds.), *Perspectives on socially shared cognition* (pp. 308-327). Washington, DC: American Psychological Association.

Hastie, R., Penrod, S. D., & Pennington, N. (1983). *Inside the jury.* Cambridge, MA: Harvard University Press.

Hays, W. L. (1988). *Statistics* (4th ed.). New York: Holt, Rinehart & Winston.

Heider, F. (1958a). Social perception and phenomenal causality. In R. Tagiuri & L. Petrullo (Eds.), *Person perception and interpersonal behavior* (pp. 1-26). Stanford, CA: Stanford University Press.

Heider, F. (1958b). *The psychology of interpersonal relations.* New York: John Wiley.

Henggeler, S. W. (1991). Multidimensional causal models of delinquent behavior and their implications for treatment. In R. Cohen & A. Siegel (Eds.), *Context and development* (pp. 211-231). Hillsdale, NJ: Lawrence Erlbaum.

Hewstone, M., & Brown, R. J. (1986). Contact is not enough: An intergroup perspective on the "contact hypothesis." In M. Hewstone & R. J. Brown (Eds.), *Contact and conflict in intergroup encounters* (pp. 1-44). Oxford, UK: Basil Blackwell.

Higgins, E. T., & Bargh, J. A. (1987). Social cognition and social perception. In M. R. Rosenweig & L. Porter (Eds.), *Annual review of psychology* (Vol. 38, pp. 369-425). Palo Alto, CA: Annual Reviews, Inc.

Higgins, E. T., & Sorrentino, R. M. (Eds.). (1990). *Handbook of motivation and cognition: Foundations of social behavior* (Vol. 2). New York: Guilford.

Hilton, J. L., & Darley, J. M. (1991). The effects of interaction goals on person perception. In M. P. Zanna (Ed.), *Advances in experimental social psychology* (Vol. 24, pp. 235-267). New York: Academic Press.

Hinsz, V. B. (1990). Cognitive and consensus processes in group recognition memory performance. *Journal of Personality and Social Psychology, 59,* 705-718.

Hirt, E. R., Zillmann, D., Erickson, G. A., & Kennedy, C. (1992). Costs and benefits of allegiance: Changes in fans' self-ascribed competencies after team victory versus defeat. *Journal of Personality and Social Psychology, 63,* 724-738.

Hogan, D. P. (1989). Institutional perspectives on the life course: Challenges and strategies. In D. I. Kertzer & K. W. Schaie (Eds.), *Age structuring in comparative perspective* (pp. 95-105). Hillsdale, NJ: Lawrence Erlbaum.

Hogg, M. A., & Abrams, D. (1988). *Social identifications: A social psychology of intergroup relations and group processes.* London: Routledge.

Hogg, M. A., & Turner, J. C. (1987). Social identity and conformity: A theory of referent informational influence. In W. Doise & S. Moscovici (Eds.), *Current issues in European social psychology* (Vol. 2, pp. 139-182). Cambridge, UK: Cambridge University Press.

Hogg, M. A., Turner, J. C., & Davidson, B. (1990). Polarized norms and social frames of reference: A test of the self-categorization theory of group polarization. *Basic and Applied Social Psychology, 11,* 77-100.

Holland, D., & Quinn, N. (1987). *Cultural models in language and thought.* Cambridge, UK: Cambridge University Press.

Hollander, E. P. (1958). Conformity, status, and idiosyncrasy credit. *Psychological Review, 65,* 117-127.

Hollander, E. P. (1964). *Leaders, groups, and influence.* New York: Oxford University Press.

Hollander, E. P. (1985). Leadership and power. In G. Lindzey & E. Aronson (Eds.), *Handbook of social psychology* (Vol. 2, 3rd ed., pp. 485-537). New York: Random House.

Hollingshead, A. B. (1993). Information, influence, and technology in group decision making. *Dissertation Abstracts International, 54*(05), 2809B.

Hornstein, H. A. (1976). *Cruelty and kindness: A new look at aggression and altruism.* Englewood Cliffs, NJ: Prentice Hall.

Humphrey, M. S., & Revelle, W. (1984). Personality, motivation, and performance: A theory of the relationship between individual differences and information processing. *Psychological Review, 91,* 153-184.

Hunter, J. A., Stringer, M., & Coleman, J. T. (1993). Social explanations and self-esteem in Northern Ireland. *Journal of Social Psychology, 133,* 643-650.

Hutchins, E. (1991). The social organization of distributed cognition. In L. B. Resnick, J. M. Levine, & S. D. Teasley (Eds.), *Perspectives on socially shared cognition* (pp. 283-307). Washington, DC: American Psychological Association.

Ickes, W. (1982). A basic paradigm for the study of personality, roles, and social behavior. In W. Ickes & E. S. Knowles (Eds.), *Personality, roles, and social behavior* (pp. 305-341). New York: Springer-Verlag.

Ickes, W. (1983). A basic paradigm for the study of unstructured dyadic interaction. In H. Reis (Ed.), *New directions for methodology of social and behavioral science* (pp. 5-21). San Francisco: Jossey-Bass.

Ickes, W. (1993). Empathic accuracy. *Journal of Personality, 61,* 587-610.

Ickes, W., Bissonnette, V., Garcia, S., & Stinson, L. (1990). Implementing and using the dyadic interaction paradigm. In C. Hendrick & M. Clark (Eds.), *Review of personality and social psychology: Vol. 11. Research methods in personality and social psychology* (pp. 16-44). Newbury Park, CA: Sage.

Ickes, W., Robertson, E., Tooke, W., & Teng, G. (1986). Naturalistic social cognition: Methodology, assessment, and validation. *Journal of Personality and Social Psychology, 51,* 66-82.

Ickes, W., Stinson, L., Bissonnette, V., & Garcia, S. (1990). Naturalistic social cognition: Empathic accuracy in mixed-sex dyads. *Journal of Personality and Social Psychology, 59,* 730-742.

Ickes, W., & Tooke, W. (1988). The observational method: Studying the interaction of minds and bodies. In S. Duck (Ed.), *The handbook of personal relationships: Theory, research and interventions* (pp. 79-97). Chichester, UK: Wiley.

Ickes, W., Tooke, W., Stinson, L., Baker, V. L., & Bissonnette, V. (1988). Naturalistic social cognition: Intersubjectivity in same-sex dyads. *Journal of Nonverbal Behavior, 12,* 58-84.

Ingraham, L. J., & Wright, T. L. (1986). A cautionary note of the interpretation of relationship effects in the social relations model. *Social Psychology Quarterly, 49*, 93-97.

Ingraham, L. J., & Wright, T. L. (1987). A social relations model test of Sullivan's anxiety hypothesis. *Journal of Personality and Social Psychology, 52*, 1212-1218.

Isen, A. M. (1984). Toward understanding the role of affect in cognition. In R. S. Wyer, Jr. & T. K. Srull (Eds.), *Handbook of social cognition* (Vol. 3, pp. 179-236). Hillsdale, NJ: Lawrence Erlbaum.

Islam, M. R., & Hewstone, M. (1993). Dimensions of contact as predictors of intergroup anxiety, perceived outgroup variability and outgroup attitude: An integrative model. *Personality and Social Psychology Bulletin, 19*, 700-710.

Janis, I. L. (1972). *Victims of groupthink: A psychological study of foreign policy decisions and fiascoes*. Boston: Houghton Mifflin.

Janis, I. L. (1982). *Groupthink: Psychological studies of policy decisions and fiascoes* (2nd ed.). Boston: Houghton Mifflin.

Janis, I. L., & Mann, L. (1977). *Decision making: A psychological analysis of conflict, choice, and commitment*. New York: Free Press.

Jessor, R., Donovan, J. E., & Costa, F. M. (1992). *Beyond adolescence*. New York: Cambridge University Press.

Johnson, C., & Mullen, B. (1994). Evidence for the accessibility of paired distinctiveness in distinctiveness-based illusory correlation in stereotyping. *Journal of Personality and Social Psychology, 20*, 65-70.

Johnson, M. E. (1993). *A social relations model analysis of structural analysis of social behavior ratings by a non-clinical sample*. Unpublished manuscript, University of Manitoba, Winnipeg.

Johnson, W. E. (1995). *Socially contextualized paternal identity: Construction of idealized or possible selves among poor, urban adolescent African-American males*. Unpublished manuscript, University of Michigan.

Jones, E. E., & Gerard, H. B. (1967). *Foundations of social psychology*. New York: John Wiley.

Jones, E. E., Wood, G., & Quattrone, G. (1981). Perceived variability of personal characteristics in in-groups and out-groups: The role of knowledge and evaluation. *Personality and Social Psychology Bulletin, 7*, 523-528.

Judd, C. M. (1993, October). *Perceived variability and ethnocentrism: Moving beyond the laboratory*. Paper presented at the Institute for Social Research, University of Michigan, Ann Arbor.

Judd, C. M., & Kenny, D. A. (1981). Process analysis: Estimating mediation in evaluation research. *Review of Educational Research, 55*, 5-54.

Judd, C. M., Ryan, C. S., & Park, B. (1991). Accuracy in the judgment of in-group and out-group variability. *Journal of Personality and Social Psychology, 61*, 366-379.

Jussim, L. (1991). Social perception and social reality: A reflection-construction model. *Psychological Review, 98*, 54-73.

Kahneman, D., & Tversky, A. (1973). On the psychology of prediction. *Psychological Review, 80*, 237-251.

Kaiser, H. F. (1970). A second generation little jiffy. *Psychometrika, 35*, 401-416.

Kaiser, H. F. (1974). An index of factorial simplicity. *Psychometrika, 39*, 31-36.

Karau, S. J., & Kelly, J. R. (1992). The effects of time scarcity and time abundance on group performance quality and interaction process. *Journal of Experimental Social Psychology, 28,* 542-571.

Karau, S. J., & Williams, K. D. (1993). Social loafing: A meta-analytic review and theoretical integration. *Journal of Personality and Social Psychology, 65,* 681-706.

Karoly, P. (1993). Mechanisms of self-regulation: A system view. *Annual Review of Psychology, 44,* 23-52.

Karpf, F. B. (1932). *American social psychology: Its origins, development, and European background.* New York: McGraw-Hill.

Kashy, D. A. (1992). Levels of analysis of social interaction diaries: Separating the effects of person, partner, dyad, and interaction. *Dissertation Abstracts International, 53*(1-B), 608-609.

Katz, D., & Braly, K. (1933). Racial stereotypes of 100 college students. *Journal of Abnormal and Social Psychology, 28,* 280-290.

Katz, I., & Hass, R. G. (1988). Racial ambivalence and American value conflict. *Journal of Personality and Social Psychology, 55,* 893-905.

Katz, R. (1982). The effects of group longevity on project communication and performance. *Administrative Science Quarterly, 27,* 81-104.

Kelley, H. H. (1955). Salience of membership and resistance to change of group-anchored attitudes. *Human Relations, 8,* 275-289.

Kelley, H. H. (1972). Causal schemata and the attribution process. In E. E. Jones, D. E. Kanouse, H. H. Kelley, R. E. Nisbett, S. Valins, & B. Weiner (Eds.), *Attribution: Perceiving the causes of behavior* (pp. 151-174). Morristown, NJ: General Learning Press.

Kelley, H. H. (1973). The processes of causal attribution. *American Psychologist, 28,* 107-127.

Kelley, H. H., Berscheid, E., Christensen, A., Harvey, J. H., Huston, T. L., Levinger, G., McClintock, E., Peplau, L. A., & Peterson, D. R. (1983). Analyzing close relationships. In H. H. Kelley, E. Berscheid, A. Christensen, J. H. Harvey, T. L. Huston, G. Levinger, E. McClintock, L. A. Peplau, & D. R. Peterson (Eds.), *Close relationships* (pp. 20-67). New York: Freeman.

Kelly, C. (1989). Political identity and perceived intragroup homogeneity. *British Journal of Social Psychology, 28,* 239-250.

Kelly, J., Wildman, H. E., & Urey, J. R. (1982). Gender and sex role differences in group decision-making social interactions: A behavioral analysis. *Journal of Applied Social Psychology, 12,* 112-127.

Kelman, H. C. (1961). Processes of opinion change. *Public Opinion Quarterly, 25,* 57-78.

Kenny, D. A. (1988). The analysis of data from two-person relationships. In S. Duck (Ed.), *The handbook of personal relationships: Theory, research, and interventions* (pp. 57-77). Chichester, UK: Wiley.

Kenny, D. A. (1990a). Design and analysis issues in dyadic research. In C. Hendrick & M. S. Clark (Eds.), *Review of personality and social psychology: Research methods in personality and social psychology* (Vol. II, pp. 164-184). Newbury Park, CA: Sage.

Kenny, D. A. (1990b). *SOREMO.* Unpublished manuscript, University of Connecticut, Storrs.

Kenny, D. A. (1991). A general model of consensus and accuracy in interpersonal perception. *Psychological Review, 98,* 155-163.

Kenny, D. A. (1994). *Interpersonal perception: A social relations analysis.* New York: Guilford.

Kenny, D. A., & Acitelli, L. K. (1994). Measuring similarity in couples. *Journal of Family Psychology, 8,* 417-431.

Kenny, D. A., & Albright, L. (1987). Accuracy in interpersonal perception: A social relations analysis. *Psychological Bulletin, 102,* 390-402.

Kenny, D. A., & DePaulo, B. M. (1993). Do people know how others view them? An empirical and theoretical account. *Psychological Bulletin, 114,* 145-161.

Kenny, D. A., Hallmark, B. W., Sullivan, P., & Kashy, D. A. (1993). The analysis of designs in which individuals are in more than one group. *British Journal of Social Psychology, 32,* 173-190.

Kenny, D. A., Horner, C., Kashy, D. A., & Chu, L. (1992). Consensus at zero acquaintance: Replication, behavioral cues, and stability. *Journal of Personality and Social Psychology, 62,* 88-97.

Kenny, D. A., & Kashy, D. A. (1994). Enhanced coorientation in the perception of friends: A social relations analysis. *Journal of Personality and Social Psychology, 67,* 1024-1033.

Kenny, D. A., & La Voie, L. (1984). The social relations model. In L. Berkowitz (Ed.), *Advances in experimental social psychology* (Vol. 18, pp. 142-182). New York: Academic Press.

Kenny, D. A., & La Voie, L. (1985). Separating individual and group effects. *Journal of Personality and Social Psychology, 48,* 339-348.

Kenny, D. A., & Nasby, W. (1980). Splitting the reciprocity correlation. *Journal of Personality and Social Psychology, 38,* 249-256.

Kiesler, D. J. (1983). The 1982 interpersonal circle: A taxonomy for complementarity in human transactions. *Psychological Review, 90,* 185-214.

Kipnis, D. (1984). The use of power in organizations and interpersonal settings. In S. Oskamp (Ed.), *Applied social psychology annual* (Vol. 5, pp. 179-210). Beverly Hills, CA: Sage.

Kirchler, E., & Davis, J. H. (1986). The influence of member status differences and task type on group consensus and member position change. *Journal of Personality and Social Psychology, 51,* 83-91.

Kirchmeyer, C. (1993). Multicultural task groups: An account of the low contribution level of minorities. *Small Group Research, 24,* 127-148.

Klages, L. (1926). *Die psychologischen errungenschaften Nietzsches* [*The psychological achievements of Nietzsche*]. Leipzig: Johann Ambrosius Barth.

Klimoski, R., & Mohammed, S. (1994). Team mental model: Construct or metaphor? *Journal of Management, 20,* 403-437.

Kluegel, J. R., & Smith, E. R. (1982). Whites' beliefs about blacks' opportunities. *American Sociological Review, 47,* 518-532.

Kouzes, J. M., & Posner, B. Z. (1990, January). The credibility factor: What followers expect from their leaders. *Management Review,* pp. 29-33.

Krackhardt, D. (1990). Assessing the political landscape: Structure, cognition, and power in organizations. *Administrative Science Quarterly, 35,* 342-369.

Kraemer, H. C., & Jacklin, C. N. (1979). Statistical analysis of dyadic social behavior. *Psychological Bulletin, 86,* 217-224.

Kraus, S., Ryan, C. S., Judd, C. M., Hastie, R., & Park, B. (1993). Use of mental frequency distributions to represent variability among members of social categories. *Social Cognition, 11,* 22-43.

Krauss, R. M., & Fussell, S. R. (1991). Perspective-taking in communication: Representations of others' knowledge in reference. *Social Cognition, 9,* 2-24.

Kruglanski, A. W. (1990). Motivations for judging and knowing: Implications for causal attribution. In E. T. Higgins & R. M. Sorrentino (Eds.), *Handbook of motivation and cognition: Foundations of social behavior* (Vol. 2, pp. 333-368). New York: Guilford.

Krull, D. S. (1993). Does the grist change the mill? The effect of the perceiver's inferential goal on the process of social inference. *Personality and Social Psychology Bulletin, 19,* 340-348.

Krull, D. S., & Erickson, D. J. (1995). Inferential hopscotch: How people draw social inferences from behavior. *Current Directions in Psychological Science, 4*(2), 35-38.

Kuhn, D. (1995). Microgenetic study of change: What has it told us? *Psychological Science, 6*(3), 133-139.

Kuhn, T. S. (1962). *The structure of scientific revolutions.* Chicago: University of Chicago Press.

LaCoursiere, R. (1979). *The life cycle of groups.* New York: Human Sciences Press.

LaCoursiere, R. (1980). *The life cycle of groups: Group developmental stage theory.* New York: Human Sciences Press.

Lamont, M., & Lareau, A. (1988). Cultural capital. *Sociological Theory, 6,* 153-168.

Langer, E. J. (1989). *Mindfulness.* Reading, MA: Addison-Wesley.

Larson, J. R., Jr. (1982). Cognitive mechanisms mediating the impact of implicit leadership theories of leader behavior on leader behavior ratings. *Organizational Behavior and Human Performance, 29,* 129-140.

Larson, J. R., Jr., & Christensen, C. (1993). Groups as problem-solving units: Toward a new meaning of social cognition. *British Journal of Social Psychology, 32,* 5-30.

Larson, J. R., Jr., Christensen, C., Abbott, A. S., & Franz, T. M. (1995, June). *Diagnosing groups: Charting the flow of information in medical decision-making teams.* Paper presented at the Nags Head International Conference on Organizations, Groups, and Social Networks, Boca Raton, FL.

Larson, J. R., Jr., Foster-Fishman, P. G., & Keys, C. B. (1994). Discussion of shared and unshared information in decision-making groups. *Journal of Personality and Social Psychology, 67,* 446-461.

Larson, J. R., Jr., Lingle, J. H., & Scerbo, M. M. (1984). The impact of performance cues on leader-behavior ratings: The role of selective information availability and probabilistic response bias. *Organizational Behavior and Human Performance, 33,* 323-349.

Latane, B., & Wolfe, S. (1981). The social impact of majorities and minorities. *Psychological Review, 88,* 438-453.

Laughlin, P. R. (1980). Social combination processes of cooperative problem-solving groups on verbal intellective tasks. In M. Fishbein (Ed.), *Progress in social psychology* (Vol. 1, pp. 127-155). Hillsdale, NJ: Lawrence Erlbaum.

Laughlin, P. R., & Sweeney, J. D. (1977). Individual-to-group and group-to-individual transfer in problem solving. *Journal of Experimental Psychology: Human Learning and Memory, 3,* 246-254.

Leary, M. R., & Forsyth, D. R. (1987). Attributions of responsibility for collective endeavors. In C. Hendrick (Ed.), *Review of personality and social psychology: Group processes* (Vol. 8, pp. 167-188). Newbury Park, CA: Sage.

Leavitt, H. (1951). Some effects of certain communication patterns on group performance. *Journal of Abnormal and Social Psychology, 46,* 38-50.

LeBon, G. (1896). *The crowd.* London: T. Fisher Unwin. (Originally published 1895 in French)

Levenson, R. W., & Ruef, A. M. (1992). Empathy: A physiological substrate. *Journal of Personality and Social Psychology, 63,* 234-246.

Levine, J. M., & Moreland, R. L. (1987). Social comparison and outcome evaluation in group contexts. In J. C. Masters & W. P. Smith (Eds.), *Social comparison, social justice, and relative deprivation: Theoretical, empirical, and policy perspectives* (pp. 105-127). Hillsdale, NJ: Lawrence Erlbaum.

Levine, J. M., & Moreland, R. L. (1990). Progress in small group research. *Annual Review of Psychology, 41,* 585-634.

Levine, J. M., & Moreland, R. L. (1991). Culture and socialization in work groups. In L. B. Resnick, J. M. Levine, & S. D. Teasley (Eds.), *Perspectives on socially shared cognition* (pp. 257-279). Washington, DC: American Psychological Association.

Levine, J. M., Resnick, L. B., & Higgins, E. T. (1993). Social foundations of cognition. *Annual Review of Psychology, 44,* 585-612.

Lewin, K. (1935). *Dynamic theory of personality.* New York: McGraw-Hill.

Lewin, K., Lippitt, R., & White, R. (1939). Patterns of aggressive behavior in experimentally created social climates. *Journal of Social Psychology, 10,* 271-299.

Lewis, H. B. (1941). Studies in the principles of judgments and attitudes: IV. The operation of "prestige suggestion." *Journal of Social Psychology, 14,* 229-256.

Leyens, J. P. (1990). Intuitive personality testing: A social approach (The 1989 Jos Jaspars Memorial lecture). In J. Extra, A. van Knippenberg, J. van der Pligt, & M. Poppe (Eds.), *Fundamentele sociale psychologie* (Vol. 4, pp. 3-20). Tilburg, The Netherlands: Tilburg University Press.

Liang, D. W., Moreland, R., & Argote, L. (1995). Group versus individual training and group performance: The mediating role of transactive memory. *Personality and Social Psychology Bulletin, 21,* 384-393.

Libby, R., Trotman, K. T., & Zimmer, I. (1987). Member variation, recognition of expertise, and group performance. *Journal of Applied Psychology, 72,* 81-87.

Lichtenstein, S., Fischhoff, B., & Phillips, L. D. (1982). Calibration of probabilities: The state of the art to 1980. In D. Kahneman, P. Slovic, & A. Tversky (Eds.), *Judgment under uncertainty: Heuristics and biases* (pp. 308-334). New York: Cambridge.

Linville, P. (1982). The complexity-extremity effect and age-based stereotyping. *Journal of Personality and Social Psychology, 42,* 193-211.

Linville, P. W., & Fischer, G. W. (1993). Exemplar and abstraction models of perceived group variability and stereotypicality. *Social Cognition, 11,* 92-125.

Linville, P. W., Fischer, G. W., & Salovey, P. (1989). Perceived distributions of the characteristics of ingroup and outgroup members: Empirical evidence and a computer simulation. *Journal of Personality and Social Psychology, 57,* 165-188.

Linville, P. W., & Jones, E. E. (1980). Polarized appraisals of out-group members. *Journal of Personality and Social Psychology, 38,* 689-703.

Littlepage, G. E., & Silbiger, H. (1992). Recognition of expertise in decision-making groups: Effects of group size and participation patterns. *Small Group Research, 23,* 344-355.

Lord, R. G. (1985). An information processing approach to social perceptions, leadership and behavioral measurement in organizations. In L. L. Cummings & B. M. Staw (Eds.), *Research in organizational behavior* (Vol. 8, pp. 87-128). Greenwich, CT: JAI.

Lord, R. G., Binning, J. F., Rush, M. C., & Thomas, J. C. (1978). The effect of performance cues and leader behavior on questionnaire ratings of leadership behavior. *Organizational Behavior and Human Performance, 21,* 27-39.

Lord, R. G., Foti, R. J., & DeVader, C. L. (1984). A test of leadership categorization theory: Internal structure, information processing, and leadership perceptions. *Organizational Behavior and Human Performance, 34,* 343-378.

Lord, R. G., Foti, R. J., & Phillips, J. S. (1982). A theory of leadership categorization. In H. G. Hunt, U. Sekaran, & C. Schriescheim (Eds.), *Leadership: Beyond establishment views* (pp. 104-121). Carbondale: Southern Illinois University Press.

Lord, R. G., & Maher, K. J. (1990). Perceptions of leadership and their implications in organizations. In J. Carroll (Ed.), *Applied social psychology and organizational settings* (pp. 129-154). Hillsdale, NJ: Lawrence Erlbaum.

Lord, R. G., & Maher, K. J. (1991). *Leadership and information processing: Linking perceptions and performance.* Winchester, MA: Unwin Hyman.

Lord, R. G., Phillips, J. S., & Rush, M. C. (1980). Effects of sex and personality on perceptions of emergent leadership, influence, and social power. *Journal of Applied Psychology, 65,* 176-182.

Lorge, I., & Solomon, H. (1962). Group and individual behavior in free-recall verbal learning. In J. H. Criswell, H. Solomon, & P. Suppes (Eds.), *Mathematical methods in small group processes* (pp. 221-231). Stanford, CA: Stanford University Press.

Luhtanen, R., & Crocker, J. (1992). A collective self-esteem scale: Self-evaluation of one's social identity. *Personality and Social Psychology Bulletin, 18,* 302-318.

Maass, A., Clark, R. D., III, & Haberkorn, G. (1982). The effects of differential ascribed category membership and norms on minority influence. *European Journal of Social Psychology, 12,* 89-104.

Maass, A., West, S. C., & Cialdini, R. B. (1987). Minority influence and conversion. In C. Hendrick (Ed.), *Review of personality and social psychology: Vol. 8. Group processes* (pp. 55-79). Newbury Park, CA: Sage.

Mach, Z. (1993). *Symbols, conflict and identity: Essays in political anthropology.* Albany: State University of New York Press.

Mackie, D. M., Gastardo-Conaco, M., & Skelly, J. J. (1992). Knowledge of the advocated position and the processing of ingroup and outgroup persuasive messages. *Personality and Social Psychology Bulletin, 18,* 145-151.

Mackie, D. M., Worth, L. T., & Asuncion, A. G. (1990). Processing of persuasive ingroup messages. *Journal of Personality and Social Psychology, 58,* 812-822.

Malloy, T. E., & Albright, L. (1990). Interpersonal perception in a social context. *Journal of Personality and Social Psychology, 58,* 419-428.

Malloy, T. E., & Kenny, D. A. (1986). The social relations model: An integrative methodology for personality research. *Journal of Personality and Social Psychology, 50,* 713-719.

Mancuso, J. C., & Shaw, M. L. (1988). *Cognition and personal structure.* New York: Praeger.

Manis, M. (1977). Cognitive social psychology. *Personality and Social Psychology Bulletin, 3,* 550-566.

Marangoni, C., Garcia, S., Ickes, W., & Teng, G. (1995). Empathic accuracy in a clinically relevant setting. *Journal of Personality and Social Psychology, 68,* 854-869.

Marcus, D. K., & Holahan, W. (1994). Interpersonal perception in group therapy: A social relations analysis. *Journal of Consulting and Clinical Psychology, 62,* 776-782.

Marcus, D. K., & Kashy, D. A. (1995). The social relations model: A tool for group psychotherapy research. *Journal of Counseling Psychology, 42,* 383-389.

Markus, H. R. (1977). Self-schemata and processing information about the self. *Journal of Personality and Social Psychology, 35,* 63-78.

Markus, H. R., & Kitayama, S. (1991). Culture and the self: Implications for cognition, emotion, and motivation. *Psychological Review, 98,* 224-253.

Markus, H. R., & Kitayama, S. (1994). The cultural construction of self and emotion: Implications for social behavior. In S. Kitayama & H. R. Markus (Eds.), *Emotion and culture: Empirical studies of mutual influence* (pp. 89-130). Washington, DC: American Psychological Association.

Markus, H. R., & Kunda, Z. (1986). Stability and malleability of the self-concept. *Journal of Personality and Social Psychology, 51,* 858-866.

Markus, H. R., & Wurf, E. (1987). The dynamic self-concept. *Annual Review of Psychology, 38,* 299-337.

Markus, H. R., & Zajonc, R. B. (1985). The cognitive perspective in social psychology. In G. Lindzey & E. Aronson (Eds.), *The handbook of social psychology* (Vol. 1, 3rd ed., pp. 137-230). Hillsdale, NJ: Lawrence Erlbaum.

Martin, J. M., & Martin, E. P. (1985). *The helping tradition in the black family and community.* Silver Springs, MD: National Association of Social Workers.

Martin, R. (1988a). Ingroup and outgroup minorities: Differential impact upon public and private responses. *European Journal of Social Psychology, 18,* 39-52.

Martin, R. (1988b). Minority influence and social categorization. *European Journal of Social Psychology, 18,* 369-373.

Mazur, A. (1985). A biosocial model of status in face-to-face groups. *Social Forces, 64,* 377-402.

McArthur, L. Z., & Baron, R. M. (1983). Toward an ecological theory of social perception. *Psychological Review, 90,* 215-247.

McCauley, C. (1989). The nature of social influence in groupthink: Compliance and internalization. *Journal of Personality and Social Psychology, 57,* 250-260.

McGarty, C., & Turner, J. C. (1992). The effects of categorization on social judgment. *British Journal of Social Psychology, 31,* 147-157.

McGarty, C., Turner, J. C., Hogg, M. A., Davidson, B. S., & Wetherell, M. S. (1992). Group polarization as conformity to the prototypical group member. *British Journal of Social Psychology, 31,* 1-20.

McGarty, C., Turner, J. C., Oakes, P. J., & Haslam, S. A. (1993). The creation of uncertainty in the influence process: The roles of stimulus information and disagreement with similar others. *European Journal of Social Psychology, 23,* 17-38.

McGrath, J. E. (1984). *Groups: Interaction and performance.* Englewood Cliffs, NJ: Prentice Hall.

McGrath, J. E. (1993). The JEMCO Workshop: Description of a longitudinal study. *Small Group Research, 24,* 285-306.

McKeever, C. F., Joseph, S., & McCormack, J. (1993). Memory of Northern Irish Catholics and Protestants for violent incidents and their explanations for the 1981 hunger strike. *Psychological Reports, 73,* 463-466.

Mead, G. H. (1909). Social psychology as a counterpart to physiological psychology. *Psychological Bulletin, 6,* 401-408.

Mead, G. H. (1910). Social consciousness and the consciousness of meaning. *Psychological Bulletin, 7,* 397-405.

Mead, G. H. (1934). *Mind, self, and society.* Chicago: University of Chicago Press.

Medin, D. L. (1989). Concepts and conceptual structure. *American Psychologist, 44*(12), 1469-1481.

Medin, D. L., Altom, M. W., & Murphy, T. D. (1984). Given versus induced category representations: Use of prototype and exemplar information in classification. *Journal of Experimental Psychology: Learning, Memory, and Cognition, 10,* 333-352.

Medow, H., & Zander, A. (1965). Aspirations of group chosen by central and peripheral members. *Journal of Personality and Social Psychology, 1,* 224-228.

Mendoza, J. L., & Graziano, W. G. (1982). The statistical analysis of dyadic social behavior: A multivariate approach. *Psychological Bulletin, 92,* 532-540.

Merleau-Ponty, M. (1945). *Phenomenologie de la perception.* Paris: Gallimard.

Messick, D. M., & Mackie, D. M. (1989). Intergroup relations. *Annual Review of Psychology, 40,* 45-81.

Miller, C. E. (1989). The social psychological effects of group decision rules. In P. B. Paulus (Ed.), *Psychology of group influence* (2nd ed., pp. 327-355). Hillsdale, NJ: Lawrence Erlbaum.

Miller, D. T., & Ross, M. (1975). Self-serving biases in the attribution of causality: Fact or fiction? *Psychological Bulletin, 82,* 213-255.

Miller, L. C., & Kenny, D. A. (1986). Reciprocity of self-disclosure at the individual and dyadic levels: A social relations analysis. *Journal of Personality and Social Psychology, 50,* 713-719.

Miller, N., Brewer, M. B., & Edwards, K. (1985). Cooperative interaction in desegregated settings: A laboratory analog. *Journal of Social Issues, 41,* 63-75.

Miller, R. S., & Schlenker, B. R. (1985). Egotism in group members: Public and private attributions of responsibility for group performance. *Social Psychology Quarterly, 48,* 85-89.

Mischel, W. (1995, August). *Cognitive affective theory of person-environment psychology.* Paper presented at the annual meeting of the American Psychological Association, New York.

Moreland, R. L., Hogg, M. A., & Hains, S. C. (1994). Back to the future: Social psychological research on groups. *Journal of Experimental Social Psychology, 30,* 527-555.

Moreland, R. L., & Levine, J. M. (1982). Group socialization in small groups: Temporal changes in individual-group relations. In L. Berkowitz (Ed.), *Advances in experimental social psychology* (Vol. 15, pp. 137-192). New York: Academic Press.

Moreland, R. L., & Levine, J. M. (1988). Group dynamics over time: Development and socialization in small groups. In J. E. McGrath (Ed.), *The social psychology of time* (pp. 151-181). Newbury Park, CA: Sage.

Moreland, R. L., & Levine, J. M. (1989). Newcomers and oldtimers in small groups. In P. B. Paulus (Ed.), *Psychology of group influence* (2nd ed., pp. 143-186). Hillsdale, NJ: Lawrence Erlbaum.

Moreland, R. L., & Levine, J. M. (1992a). Problem identification by groups. In S. Worchel, W. Wood, & J. A. Simpson (Eds.), *Group process and productivity* (pp. 17-47). Newbury Park, CA: Sage.

Moreland, R. L., & Levine, J. M. (1992b). The composition of small groups. In E. J. Lawler, B. Markovsky, C. Ridgeway, & H. A. Walker (Eds.), *Advances in group processes* (Vol. 9, pp. 237-280). Greenwich, CT: JAI.

Moreland, R. L., & Wingert, M. (1995, May). *Training people to work in groups: The role of transactive memory.* Paper presented at the annual meeting of the Midwestern Psychological Association, Chicago.

Moscovici, S. (1980). Towards a theory of conversion behavior. In L. Berkowitz (Ed.), *Advances in experimental social psychology* (Vol. 13, pp. 209-239). New York: Academic Press.

Moscovici, S. (1993). Toward a social psychology of science. *Journal for the Theory of Social Behaviour, 23*(4), 343-374.

Moscovici, S., & Facheaux, C. (1972). Social influence, conformity bias and the study of active minorities. In L. Berkowitz (Ed.), *Advances in experimental social psychology* (Vol. 6, pp. 149-202). New York: Academic Press.

Moscovici, S., Lage, E., & Naffrechoux, M. (1969). Influence of a consistent minority on responses of a majority in a color perception task. *Sociometry, 32*, 365-380.

Moscovici, S., & Mugny, G. (1983). Minority influence. In P. B. Paulus (Ed.), *Basic group processes* (pp. 41-64). New York: Springer-Verlag.

Moscovici, S., & Zavalloni, M. (1969). The group as a polarizer of attitudes. *Journal of Personality and Social Psychology, 12*, 125-135.

Mugny, G., & Papastamou, S. (1982). Minority influence and psychosocial identity. *European Journal of Social Psychology, 12*, 379-394.

Mullen, B. (1983). Operationalizing the effect of the group on the individual: A self-attention perspective. *Journal of Experimental Social Psychology, 19*, 295-322.

Mullen, B. (1987). Self-attention theory: The effects of group composition on the individual. In B. Mullen & G. R. Goethals (Eds.), *Theories of group behavior* (pp. 125-146). New York: Springer-Verlag.

Mullen, B. (1991). Group composition, salience, and cognitive representation: The phenomenology of being in a group. *Journal of Experimental Social Psychology, 27*, 297-323.

Mullen, B., Anthony, T., Salas, E., & Driskell, J. E. (1994). Group cohesiveness and quality of decision making: An integration of tests of the groupthink hypothesis. *Small Group Research, 25*, 189-204.

Mullen, B., Brown, R., & Smith, C. D. (1992). Ingroup bias as a function of salience, relevance, and status: An integration. *European Journal of Social Psychology, 22,* 103-122.

Mullen, B., & Goethals, G. R. (Eds.). (1987). *Theories of group behavior.* New York: Springer-Verlag.

Mullen, B., & Hu, L. (1989). Perceptions of ingroup and outgroup variability: A meta-analytic integration. *Basic and Applied Social Psychology, 10,* 233-252.

Mullen, B., & Johnson, C. (1990). Distinctiveness-based illusory correlations and stereotyping: A meta-analytic integration. *British Journal of Social Psychology, 29,* 11-28.

Mullen, B., & Johnson, C. (1993). Cognitive representation in ethnophaulisms as a function of group size: The phenomenology of being in a group. *Personality and Social Psychology Bulletin, 19,* 296-304.

Mullen, B., & Johnson, C. (1995). Cognitive representation in ethnophaulisms and illusory correlation in stereotyping. *Personality and Social Psychology Bulletin, 21,* 420-433.

Mullen, B., Johnson, C., & Anthony, T. (1994). Relative group size and cognitive representations of ingroup and outgroup: The phenomenology of being in a group. *Small Group Research, 25,* 250-266.

Mullen, B., & Riordan, C. A. (1988). Self-serving attributions for performance in naturalistic settings: A meta-analytic review. *Journal of Applied Social Psychology, 18,* 3-22.

Mummendey, A., & Simon, B. (1989). The impact of importance of comparison dimension and relative in-group size upon intergroup discrimination. *British Journal of Social Psychology, 28,* 1-16.

Murrell, A. J., Betz, B. L., Dovidio, J. F., Gaertner, S. L., & Drout, C. E. (1993). Aversive racism and resistance to affirmative action: Perceptions of justice are not necessarily color blind. *Basic and Applied Social Psychology, 15,* 71-86.

Myers, D. G. (1982). Polarizing effects of social interaction. In H. Brandstatter, J. H. Davis, & G. Stocker-Kreichgauer (Eds.), *Group decision making* (pp. 125-161). London: Academic Press.

Myers, D. G., & Lamm, H. (1976). The group polarization phenomenon. *Psychological Bulletin, 83,* 602-627.

Mynatt, C., & Sherman, S. J. (1975). Responsibility attribution in groups and individuals: A direct test of the diffusion of responsibility hypothesis. *Journal of Personality and Social Psychology, 32,* 1111-1118.

Neimeyer, G. J., & Neimeyer, R. A. (1981). Functional similarity and interpersonal attraction. *Journal of Research in Personality, 15,* 427-435.

Neimeyer, G. J., & Neimeyer, R. A. (1985). Relational trajectories: A personal construct contribution. *Journal of Social and Personal Relationships, 2,* 325-349.

Neimeyer, G. J., & Neimeyer, R. A. (1986). Personal constructs in relationship deterioration: A longitudinal study. *Social Behavior and Personality, 14,* 253-257.

Neimeyer, R. A. (1988). Clinical guidelines for conducting interpersonal transaction groups. *International Journal of Personal Construct Psychology, 1,* 181-190.

Neimeyer, R. A. (1993). Constructivist approaches to the measurement of meaning. In G. J. Neimeyer (Ed.), *Constructivist assessment* (pp. 58-103). Newbury Park, CA: Sage.

Neimeyer, R. A., Brooks, D. L., & Baker, K. D. (1996). Personal epistemologies and personal relationships. In D. Kalekin Fishman & M. Walker (Eds.), *The construction of group realities* (pp. 127-159). Malabar, FL: Krieger.

Neimeyer, R. A., Harter, S., & Alexander, P. C. (1991). Group perceptions as predictors of outcome in the treatment of incest survivors. *Psychotherapy Research, 1,* 148-158.

Neimeyer, R. A., & Mitchell, K. A. (1988). Similarity and attraction: A longitudinal study. *Journal of Social and Personal Relationships, 5,* 131-148.

Neimeyer, R. A., & Neimeyer, G. J. (1983). Structural similarity in the acquaintance process. *Journal of Social and Clinical Psychology, 1,* 146-154.

Neimeyer, R. A., Neimeyer, G. J., & Landfield, A. W. (1983). Conceptual differentiation, integration, and empathic prediction. *Journal of Personality, 51,* 185-191.

Neisser, U. (1980). On "social knowing." *Personality and Social Psychology Bulletin, 6,* 601-605.

Neisser, U. (1992, June). *Distinct systems for "where" and "what": Reconciling the ecological and representational views of perception.* Paper presented at the annual meeting of the American Psychology Society, San Diego, CA.

Nelson, L. J., & Miller, D. T. (1995). The distinctiveness effect in social categorization: You are what makes you unusual. *Psychological Science, 6,* 246-249.

Nemeth, C. J. (1986). Differential contributions of majority and minority influence. *Psychological Review, 93,* 23-32.

Nemeth, C. J. (1992). Minority dissent as a stimulant to group performance. In S. Worchel, W. Wood, & J. A. Simpson (Eds.), *Group process and productivity* (pp. 95-111). Newbury Park, CA: Sage.

Nemeth, C. J., & Kwan, J. (1985). Originality of word associations as a function of majority vs. minority influence. *Social Psychology Quarterly, 48,* 277-282.

Nemeth, C. J., & Wachtler, J. (1983). Creative problem solving as a result of majority vs. minority influence. *European Journal of Social Psychology, 2,* 65-79.

Nemeth, C. J., Wachtler, J., & Endicott, J. (1977). Increasing the size of the minority: Some gains and some losses. *European Journal of Social Psychology, 7,* 15-27.

Neuberg, S. L., & Fiske, S. T. (1987). Motivational influences on impression formation: Outcome dependency, accuracy-driven attention, and individuating processes. *Journal of Personality and Social Psychology, 53,* 431-444.

Newcomb, T., Turner, R., & Converse, P. (1965). *Social psychology: The study of human interaction.* New York: Holt, Rinehart & Winston.

Nisbett, R., & Wilson, T. B. (1977). Telling more than we can know: Verbal reports on mental processes. *Psychological Review, 84,* 231-259.

Norvell, N., & Forsyth, D. R. (1984). The impact of inhibiting or facilitating causal factors on group members' reactions after success and failure. *Social Psychology Quarterly, 47,* 293-297.

Nuttin, J. (1984). *Motivation, planning, and action.* Leuven, Belgium: Leuven University Press.

Nye, J. L., & Brower, A. (Eds.). (1994). Social cognition in small groups [Special issue]. *Small Group Research, 25*(2).

Nye, J. L., & Forsyth, D. R. (1991). The effects of prototype-based biases on leadership appraisals: A test of leadership categorization theory. *Small Group Research, 22,* 360-379.

Oakes, P. J. (1987). The salience of social categories. In J. C. Turner, M. A. Hogg, P. J. Oakes, S. D. Reicher, & M. S. Wetherell (Eds.), *Rediscovering the social group: A self-categorization theory* (pp. 117-141). Oxford, UK: Basil Blackwell.

Oakes, P. J., Haslam, S. A., Morrison, B., & Grace, D. (1995). Becoming an ingroup: Re-examining the impact of familiarity on perceptions of group homogeneity. *Social Psychology Quarterly, 58,* 52-61.

Oakes, P. J., Haslam, S. A., & Turner, J. C. (1994). *Stereotyping and social reality.* Oxford, UK: Basil Blackwell.

Oakes, P. J., & Turner, J. C. (1990). Is limited information processing capacity the cause of social stereotyping? *European Review of Social Psychology, 1,* 112-135.

Oates, J. C. (1995, May). American gothic. *The New Yorker,* pp. 35-36.

Oberle, J. (1990). Teamwork in the cockpit. *Training, 27*(2), 34-38.

Ochs, E., & Schieffelin, B. B. (1983). *Acquiring conversational competence.* Boston: Routledge & Kegan Paul.

Oddou, G. R. (1987). Rock climbing, rappelling, and sailing: Effective management and organization development tools? *Consultation: An International Journal, 6,* 145-157.

Ogbu, J. U. (1991). Minority coping responses and school experience. *Journal of Psychohistory, 18,* 433-456.

Orlinsky, D. E., & Howard, K. L. (1986). Process and outcome in psychotherapy. In S. L. Garfield & A. E. Bergin (Eds.), *Handbook of psychotherapy and behavior change* (3rd ed., pp. 311-384). New York: John Wiley.

Orr, J. E. (1990). Sharing knowledge, celebrating identity: War stories and community memory among service technicians. In D. S. Middleton & D. Edwards (Eds.), *Collective remembering: Memory in society* (pp. 169-189). Newbury Park, CA: Sage.

Oyserman, D. (1993). The lens of personhood. *Journal of Personality and Social Psychology, 65*(5), 993-1009.

Oyserman, D., & Burks, J. (1995). *Social identities vs. possible selves in early adolescence: My future vs. our common fate.* Manuscript submitted for publication.

Oyserman, D., Gant, L., & Ager, J. (1995). A socially contextualized model of African American identity: School persistence and possible selves. *Journal of Personality and Social Psychology, 69*(6), 1216-1232.

Oyserman, D., & Markus, H. R. (1990). Possible selves and delinquency. *Journal of Personality and Social Psychology, 59,* 112-125.

Oyserman, D., & Markus, H. R. (1993). The sociocultural self. In J. Suls (Ed.), *Psychological perspectives on the self* (Vol. 4, pp. 187-220). Hillsdale, NJ: Lawrence Erlbaum.

Oyserman, D., & Saltz, E. (1993). Competence, delinquency, and attempts to attain possible selves. *Journal of Personality and Social Psychology, 65,* 360-374.

Park, B., & Rothbart, M. (1982). Perception of out-group homogeneity and levels of social categorization: Memory for the subordinate attributes of ingroup and outgroup members. *Journal of Personality and Social Psychology, 42,* 1051-1068.

Parks, C. D. (1991). Effects of decision rule and task importance on willingness to share "unique" information. *Dissertation Abstracts International, 52*(07), 3948B.

Pastor, J., McCormick, J., & Fine, M. (in press). Makin' homes: An urban girl thing. In B. Leadbeater & N. Way (Eds.), *Urban adolescent female development.* New York: New York University Press.

Patterson, M. L. (1976). An arousal model of interpersonal intimacy. *Psychological Review, 83,* 237-252.

Patterson, M. L. (1977). Interpersonal distance, affect, and equilibrium theory. *Journal of Social Psychology, 101,* 205-214.

Patterson, M. L. (1982). A sequential functional model of nonverbal exchange. *Psychological Review, 89,* 231-249.

Patterson, M. L. (1983). *Nonverbal behavior: A functional perspective.* New York: Springer-Verlag.

Patterson, M. L. (1991). A functional approach to nonverbal exchange. In R. S. Feldman & B. Rime (Eds.), *Fundamentals of nonverbal behavior* (pp. 458-495). Cambridge, UK: Cambridge University Press.

Patterson, M. L. (1994). Strategic functions of nonverbal exchange. In J. A. Daly & J. M. Wiemann (Eds.), *Strategic interpersonal communication* (pp. 273-293). Hillsdale, NJ: Lawrence Erlbaum.

Patterson, M. L. (1995). A parallel process model of nonverbal communication. *Journal of Nonverbal Behavior, 19,* 3-29.

Patterson, M. L., Churchill, M. E., Farag, F., & Borden, E. (1991/1992). Impression management, cognitive demand, and interpersonal sensitivity. *Current Psychology, 10,* 263-271.

Paulus, P. B., & Nagar, D. (1989). Environmental influences on groups. In P. B. Paulus (Ed.), *Psychology of group influence* (pp. 111-140). Hillsdale, NJ: Lawrence Erlbaum.

Pearson, K. (1901). Mathematical contributions to the theory of evolution, part IX. On the principle of homotyposis and its relation to heredity, to the variability of the individual, and to that of the race. *Philosophical Transactions of the Royal Society of London, 197*(Series A), 285-379.

Pennington, N., & Hastie, R. (1986). Evidence evaluation in complex decision making. *Journal of Personality and Social Psychology, 51,* 242-258.

Pennington, N., & Hastie, R. (1991). A cognitive theory of juror decision making: The story model. *Cardozo Law Review, 13,* 5001-5039.

Pepitone, A. (1981). Lessons from the history of social psychology. *American Psychologist, 36,* 972-985.

Perlmutter, H. V., & De Montmollin, G. (1952). Group learning of nonsense syllables. *Journal of Abnormal and Social Psychology, 47,* 762-769.

Petty, R. E., & Cacioppo, J. T. (1981). *Attitudes and persuasion: Classic and contemporary approaches.* Dubuque, IA: William C. Brown.

Petty, R. E., & Cacioppo, J. T. (1986). The elaboration likelihood model of persuasion. In L. Berkowitz (Ed.), *Advances in experimental social psychology* (Vol. 19, pp. 123-205). New York: Academic Press.

Pfeffer, J. (1977). The ambiguity of leadership. *Academy of Management Review, 12,* 104-112.

Phillips, J. S. (1984). The accuracy of leadership ratings: A cognitive categorization perspective. *Organizational Behavior and Human Performance, 33,* 125-138.

Phillips, J. S., & Lord, R. G. (1981). Causal attributions and perceptions of leadership. *Organizational Behavior and Human Performance, 28,* 143-163.

Phillips, J. S., & Lord, R. G. (1982). Schematic information processing and perceptions of leadership in problem-solving groups. *Journal of Applied Psychology, 67,* 486-492.

Piliavin, J. A., & Martin, R. R. (1978). The effects of sex composition of groups on style of social interaction. *Sex Roles, 4,* 281-296.

Pope, A. (1735). To Mrs. M. Blount. In *A select collection of poems.* New London, CT: Springers.

Pugh, M. D., & Wahrman, R. (1983). Neutralizing sexism in mixed-sex groups: Do women have to be better than men? *American Journal of Sociology, 88,* 746-762.

Radner, R. (1986). Information pooling and decentralized decision making. In B. Grofman & G. Owen (Eds.), *Information pooling and group decision making* (pp. 195-217). Greenwich, CT: JAI.

Redstrom, V., Kelley, K. N., Forsyth, D. R., & Noel, J. G. (1986, April). *The impact of causal attributions on affect.* Paper presented at the annual meeting of the Eastern Psychological Association, New York.

Reno, R. R., & Kenny, D. A. (1992). Effects of self-consciousness and social anxiety on self-disclosure among unacquainted individuals: An application of the social relations model. *Journal of Personality, 60,* 79-94.

Rentsch, J. R. (1990). Climate and culture: Interaction and qualitative differences in organizational meanings. *Journal of Applied Psychology, 75,* 668-681.

Resnick, L. B., Levine, J. M., & Teasley, S. D. (Eds.). (1991). *Perspectives on socially shared cognition.* Washington, DC: American Psychological Association.

Rhee, E., Uleman, J., Lee, K., & Roman, R. (1995). Spontaneous self-descriptions and ethnic identities in individualistic and collectivistic cultures. *Journal of Personality and Social Psychology, 69,* 142-152.

Ridgeway, C. (1991). The social construction of status value: Gender and other nominal characteristics. *Social Forces, 70,* 367-386.

Ridgeway, C. L., & Diekema, D. (1992). Are gender differences status differences? In C. L. Ridgeway (Ed.), *Gender, interaction, and inequality* (pp. 157-180). New York: Springer-Verlag.

Riemer, J. W. (1977). Becoming a journeyman electrician: Some implicit indicators in the apprenticeship process. *Sociology of Work and Occupations, 4,* 87-98.

Ritts, V., & Patterson, M. L. (in press). Effects of social anxiety and action identification on impressions and thoughts in interaction. *Journal of Social and Clinical Psychology.*

Roback, A. A. (1944). *A dictionary of slurs.* Cambridge: Sci-Art.

Roberts, J. E., & McCready, V. (1987). Different clinical perspectives of good and poor therapy sessions. *Journal of Speech and Hearing Research, 30,* 335-342.

Robinson, J. P. (1988). Time diary evidence about the social psychology of everyday life. In J. E. McGrath (Ed.), *The social psychology of time.* Newbury Park, CA: Sage.

Robinson, W. S. (1957). The statistical measurement of agreement. *American Sociology Review, 22,* 17-25.

Rogoff, B. (in press). Transitions in children's participation in sociocultural activities. In A. Sameroff & M. Haith (Eds.), *Reason and responsibility: The passage through childhood.* Chicago: University of Chicago Press.

Rosch, E. (1975). Cognitive representation of semantic categories. *Journal of Experimental Psychology: General, 104,* 192-233.

Rosch, E. (1978). Principles of categorization. In E. Rosch & B. B. Lloyd (Eds.), *Cognition and categorization* (pp. 27-48). Hillsdale, NJ: Lawrence Erlbaum.

Rosenthal, R. (1974). *On the social psychology of the self-fulfilling prophecy: Further evidence for pygmalion effects and their mediating mechanisms.* New York: M.S.S. Information Corporation Modular Publication.

Ross, E. A. (1908). *Social psychology.* New York: Macmillan.

Ross, L., & Nisbett, R. E. (1991). *The person and the situation: Perspectives of social psychology.* New York: McGraw-Hill.

Ross, M., & Sicoly, F. (1979). Egocentric biases in availability and attribution. *Journal of Personality and Social Psychology, 37,* 322-336.

Rothbart, M., & John, O. P. (1985). Social categorization and behavioral episodes: A cognitive analysis of the effects of intergroup contact. *Journal of Social Issues, 41,* 81-104.

Rozell, D., & Mullen, B. (1995, March). *Dimensional complexity as an operationalization of prototype-exemplar cognitive representation.* Paper presented at the 66th annual meeting of the Eastern Psychological Association, Boston.

Ruble, D. N. (1994). A phase model of transitions: Cognitive and motivational consequences. In M. P. Zanna (Ed.), *Advances in experimental social psychology* (Vol. 26, pp. 163-214). New York: Academic Press.

Ruscher, J. B., Fiske, S. T., Miki, H., & Van Manen, S. (1991). Individuating processes in competition: Interpersonal versus intergroup. *Personality and Social Psychology Bulletin, 17,* 595-605.

Ruscher, J. B., & Hammer, E. D. (1994). Revising disrupted impressions through conversation. *Journal of Personality and Social Psychology, 66,* 530-541.

Rush, M., Thomas, J., & Lord, R. G. (1977). Implicit leadership theory: A potential threat to the internal validity of leader behavior questionnaires. *Organizational Behavior and Human Performance, 20,* 93-110.

Sachdev, F., & Bourhis, R. Y. (1991). Power and status differentials in minority and majority group relations. *European Journal of Social Psychology, 21,* 1-24.

Safran, J. D. (1990). Towards a refinement of cognitive therapy in light of interpersonal theory: I. Theory. *Clinical Psychology Review, 10,* 87-105.

Salancik, G. R., & Pfeffer, J. (1978). A social information processing approach to job attitudes and task design. *Administrative Science Quarterly, 23,* 224-253.

Sanbonmatsu, D. M., Sherman, S. J., & Hamilton, D. L. (1987). Illusory correlation in the perception of individuals and groups. *Social Cognition, 5,* 1-25.

Sanderson, C. A., & Cantor, N. (1995). Social dating goals in late adolescence: Implications for safer sexual activity. *Journal of Personality and Social Psychology, 68*(6), 1121-1134.

Sartre, J.-P. (1943). *L'etre et le neant* [*Being and nothingness*] (H. Barnes, Trans.). Paris: Gallimard.

Schachter, S. (1951). Deviation, rejection, and communication. *Journal of Abnormal and Social Psychology, 46,* 190-207.

Schein, E. (1990). Organizational culture. *American Psychologist, 85,* 109-119.

Schlenker, B. R. (1975). Group members' attributions of responsibility for prior group performance. *Representative Research in Social Psychology, 6,* 96-108.

Schlenker, B. R., & Miller, R. S. (1977a). Egocentrism in groups: Self-serving biases or logical information processing? *Journal of Personality and Social Psychology, 35,* 755-764.

Schlenker, B. R., & Miller, R. S. (1977b). Group cohesiveness as a determinant of egocentric perceptions in cooperative groups. *Human Relations, 30,* 1039-1055.

Schlenker, B. R., Soraci, S., Jr., & McCarthy, B. (1976). Self-esteem and group performance as determinants of egocentric perceptions in cooperative groups. *Human Relations, 29,* 1163-1176.

Schlenker, B. R., Weigold, M. F., & Hallam, J. R. (1990). Self-serving attributions in social context: Effects of self-esteem and social pressure. *Journal of Personality and Social Psychology, 58,* 855-863.

Schneider, B., & Yongsook, L. (1990). A model for academic success: The school and home environment of East Asian students. *Anthropology and Education Quarterly, 21*(4), 358-377.

Schopler, J., & Insko, C. A. (1992). The discontinuity effect in interpersonal and intergroup relations: Generality and mediation. *European Review of Social Psychology, 3,* 121-151.

Schul, Y., & Burnstein, E. (1990). Judging the typicality of an instance: Should the category be accessed first? *Journal of Personality and Social Psychology, 58,* 964-974.

Schutz, A. (1970). *On phenomenology and social relations.* Chicago: University of Chicago Press.

Scott, W. A., Osgood, D. W., & Peterson, C. (1979). *Cognitive structure: Theory and measurement of individual differences.* Washington, DC: Winston.

Shaw, T. A. (1994). The semiotic mediation of identity. *Ethos, 22*(1), 83-119.

Shepperd, J. A. (1993). Productivity loss in performance groups: A motivation analysis. *Psychological Bulletin, 113,* 67-81.

Sherif, C. W., Sherif, M., & Nebergall, R. E. (1965). *Attitude and attitude change: The social judgment-involvement approach.* Philadelphia: Saunders.

Sherif, M. (1935). A study of some social factors in perception. *Archives of Psychology, 27,* 1-60.

Sherif, M. (1936). *The psychology of social norms.* New York: Harper & Row.

Sherif, M., Harvey, O., White, B., Hood, W., & Sherif, C. (1961). *Intergroup conflict and cooperation: The robber's cove experiment.* Norman: University of Oklahoma, Institute of Group Relations.

Sherif, M., & Sherif, C. W. (1969). *Social psychology.* New York: Harper & Row.

Shiffrin, R. M., & Schneider, W. (1977). Controlled and automatic human information processing: Perceptual learning, automatic attending, and a general theory. *Psychological Review, 84,* 127-190.

Shiflett, S. C. (1979). Toward a general model of small group productivity. *Psychological Bulletin, 86,* 67-79.

Showers, C. (1992). The motivational and emotional consequences of considering positive or negative possibilities for an upcoming event. *Journal of Personality and Social Psychology, 63*(3), 474-484.

Shrauger, J. S., & Osberg, T. M. (1981). The relative accuracy of self-predictions and judgments by others in psychological assessment. *Psychological Bulletin, 90,* 322-351.

Shweder, R. A., & Sullivan, M. A. (1990). The semiotic subject of cultural psychology. In L. A. Pervin (Eds.), *Handbook of personality* (pp. 399-416). New York: Guilford.

Silberman, M. (1990). *Active training: A handbook of techniques, designs, case examples, and tips.* Lexington, MA: Lexington Books.

Simon, B. (1992). The perception of ingroup and outgroup homogeneity: Re-introducing the social context. In W. Stroebe & M. Hewstone (Eds.), *European review of social psychology* (Vol. 3, pp. 1-30). Chichester, UK: Wiley.

Simon, B., & Brown, R. J. (1987). Perceived intragroup homogeneity in minority-majority contexts. *Journal of Personality and Social Psychology, 53,* 703-711.

Smith, E. R., & Zárate, M. A. (1990). Exemplar and prototype use in social cognition. *Social Cognition, 8,* 243-262.

Smith, E. R., & Zárate, M. A. (1992). Exemplar-based model of social judgment. *Psychological Review, 99,* 3-21.

Smith, P. B., & Bond, M. H. (1994). *Social psychology across cultures: Analysis and perspectives.* Boston: Allyn & Bacon.

Smith-Lovin, L., & Brody, C. (1989). Interruptions in group discussions: The effects of gender and group composition. *American Sociological Review, 54,* 424-435.

Smith-Lovin, L., Skvoretz, J. V., & Hudson, C. G. (1986). Status and participation in six-person groups: A test of Skvoretz's comparative status model. *Social Forces, 64,* 992-1005.

Sniezek, J. A. (1992). Groups under uncertainty: An examination of confidence in group decision making. *Organizational Behavior and Human Decision Processes, 52,* 124-155.

Snodgrass, S. E. (1985). Women's intuition: The effect of subordinate role on interpersonal sensitivity. *Journal of Personality and Social Psychology, 49,* 146-155.

Snyder, M. (1992). Motivational foundations of behavioral confirmation. In M. P. Zanna (Ed.), *Advances in experimental social psychology* (Vol. 25, pp. 67-114). New York: Academic Press.

Snyder, M., & Swann, W. (1978). Behavioral confirmation in social interaction: From social perception to social reality. *Journal of Experimental Social Psychology, 14,* 148-162.

Sorrentino, R. M., & Higgins, E. T. (Eds.). (1986). *Handbook of motivation and social cognition* (Vol. 1). New York: Guilford.

Sorrentino, R. M., & Higgins, E. T. (Eds.). (1996). *Handbook of motivation and social cognition* (Vol. 3). New York: Guilford.

Spears, R., Lea, M., & Lee, S. (1990). De-individuation and group polarization in computer-mediated communication. *British Journal of Social Psychology, 29,* 121-134.

Srull, T. K., Lichtenstein, M., & Rothbart, M. (1985). Associative storage and retrieval processes in person memory. *Journal of Experimental Psychology: Learning, Memory, and Cognition, 11,* 316-345.

Stangor, C., & Duan, C. (1991). Effects of multiple task demands upon memory for information about social groups. *Journal of Experimental Social Psychology, 27,* 357-378.

Stangor, C., & Ford, T. E. (1992). Accuracy and expectancy-confirming processing orientations and the development of prejudice and stereotypes. In W. Stroebe & M. Hewstone (Eds.), *European review of social psychology* (Vol. 3, pp. 57-89). New York: John Wiley.

Stangor, C., & Lange, J. (1993). Mental representations of social groups: Advances in understanding stereotypes and stereotyping. In M. P. Zanna (Ed.), *Advances in experimental social psychology* (Vol. 23, pp. 357-416). New York: Academic Press.

Stangor, C., & McMillan, D. (1992). Memory for expectancy-congruent and expectancy-incongruent information: A review of the social and social developmental literatures. *Psychological Bulletin, 111,* 42-61.

Stangor, C., Sullivan, L. A., & Ford, T. E. (1991). Affective and cognitive determinants of prejudice. *Social Cognition, 9,* 359-380.

Stasser, G. (1988). Computer simulation as a research tool: The DISCUSS model of group decision making. *Journal of Experimental Social Psychology, 24,* 393-422.

Stasser, G. (1992). Pooling of unshared information during group discussion. In S. Worchel, W. Wood, & J. Simpson (Eds.), *Group process and productivity* (pp. 48-57). Newbury Park, CA: Sage.

Stasser, G., Kerr, N. L., & Davis, J. H. (1989). Influence processes and consensus models in decision-making groups. In P. B. Paulus (Ed.), *Psychology of group influence* (2nd ed., pp. 279-326). Hillsdale, NJ: Lawrence Erlbaum.

Stasser, G., & Stewart, D. (1992). Discovery of hidden profiles by decision-making groups: Solving a problem versus making a judgment. *Journal of Personality and Social Psychology, 63,* 426-434.

Stasser, G., Stewart, D. D., & Wittenbaum, G. M. (1995). Expert roles and information exchange during discussion: The importance of knowing who knows what. *Journal of Experimental Social Psychology, 31,* 244-265.

Stasser, G., & Taylor, L. A. (1991). Speaking turns in face-to-face discussions. *Journal of Personality and Social Psychology, 60,* 675-684.

Stasser, G., Taylor, L. A., & Hanna, C. (1989). Information sampling in structured and unstructured discussions of three- and six-person groups. *Journal of Personality and Social Psychology, 57,* 67-78.

Stasser, G., & Titus, W. (1985). Pooling of unshared information in group decision making: Biased information sampling during discussion. *Journal of Personality and Social Psychology, 48,* 1467-1478.

Stasser, G., & Titus, W. (1987). Effects of information load and percentage of shared information on the dissemination of unshared information during group discussion. *Journal of Personality and Social Psychology, 53,* 81-93.

Staw, B. M., Sandelands, L. E., & Dutton, J. E. (1981). Threat-rigidity effects in organizational behavior: A multi-level analysis. *Administrative Science Quarterly, 26,* 501-524.

Steele, C., Spencer, S., & Aronson, J. (1995, August). *Inhibiting the expression of intelligence: The role of stereotype vulnerability.* Paper presented at the annual meeting of the American Psychological Association, New York.

Steiner, I. D. (1972). *Group process and productivity.* New York: Academic Press.

Steiner, I. D. (1974). Whatever happened to the group in social psychology? *Journal of Experimental Social Psychology, 10,* 94-108.

Steiner, I. D. (1986). Paradigms and groups. In L. Berkowitz (Ed.), *Advances in experimental social psychology* (Vol. 19, pp. 251-289). New York: Academic Press.

Stephan, W. G. (1978). School desegregation: An evaluation of predictions made in Brown v. Board of Education. *Psychological Bulletin, 85,* 217-238.

Stephan, W. G. (1985). Intergroup relations. In G. Lindzey & E. Aronson (Eds.), *The handbook of social psychology: Vol. 2* (3rd ed., pp. 599-658). New York: Random House.

Stephan, W. G., & Stephan, C. W. (1984). The role of ignorance in intergroup relations. In N. Miller & M. B. Brewer (Eds.), *Groups in contact: The psychology of desegregation* (pp. 229-257). Orlando, FL: Academic Press.

Stephan, W. G., & Stephan, C. W. (1985). Intergroup anxiety. *Journal of Social Issues, 41,* 157-175.

Stevens, L. E., & Fiske, S. T. (1995). *Forming motivated impressions of a powerholder: Accuracy under task dependency and misperception under evaluation dependency.* Manuscript submitted for publication, University of Massachusetts at Amherst.

Stewart, D. D., & Stasser, G. (1995). Expert role assignment and information sampling during collective recall and decision making. *Journal of Personality and Social Psychology, 69,* 619-628.

Stinson, L., & Ickes, W. (1992). Empathic accuracy in the interactions of male friends versus male strangers. *Journal of Personality and Social Psychology, 62,* 787-797.

Stogdill, R. M. (1963). *Manual for the Leader Behavior Description Questionnaire— Form XII.* Columbus: Ohio State University, Bureau of Business Research.

Street, W. R. (1974). Brainstorming by individuals, coacting and interacting groups. *Journal of Applied Psychology, 59,* 433-436.

Strupp, H. H., & Binder, J. L. (1984). *Psychotherapy in a new key: A guide to time-limited dynamic psychotherapy.* New York: Basic Books.

Stryker, S. (1987). Identity theory: Developments and extensions. In K. Yardley & T. Honess (Eds.), *Self and identity: Psychosocial perspectives* (pp. 89-103). Chichester, UK: Wiley.

Swann, W. B., Jr. (1984). Quest for accuracy in person perception: A matter of pragmatics. *Psychological Review, 91,* 457-477.

Tabachnick, B. G., & Fidell, L. S. (1989). *Using multivariate statistics* (2nd ed.). New York: HarperCollins.

Tajfel, H. (1979). Individuals and groups in social psychology. *British Journal of Social and Clinical Psychology, 18,* 183-190.

Tajfel, H. (1982). Social psychology of intergroup relations. In M. R. Rosenzweig & L. W. Porter (Eds.), *Annual review of psychology* (Vol. 33, pp. 1-39). Palo Alto, CA: Annual Reviews, Inc.

Tajfel, H., & Turner, J. C. (1979). An integrative theory of intergroup conflict. In W. G. Austin & S. Worchel (Eds.), *The social psychology of intergroup relations* (pp. 33-50). Pacific Grove, CA: Brooks/Cole.

Tajfel, H., & Turner, J. C. (1986). The social identity theory of intergroup behavior. In S. Worchel & W. G. Austin (Eds.), *The psychology of intergroup relations* (2nd ed., pp. 7-24). Chicago: Nelson-Hall.

Taylor, C. (1989). *Sources of the self: The makings of the modern identity.* Cambridge, MA: Harvard University Press.

Taylor, D. M., & Tyler, J. K. (1986). Group members' responses to group-serving attributions for success and failure. *Journal of Social Psychology, 126,* 775-781.

Taylor, S. E. (1981a). A categorization approach to stereotyping. In D. L. Hamilton (Ed.), *Cognitive processes in stereotyping and intergroup behavior* (pp. 83-114). Hillsdale, NJ: Lawrence Erlbaum.

Taylor, S. E. (1981b). The interface of cognitive and social psychology. In J. Harvey (Ed.), *Cognition, social behavior, and the environment* (pp. 189-211). Hillsdale, NJ: Lawrence Erlbaum.

Taylor, S. E., & Fiske, S. T. (1978). Salience, attention, and attribution: Top-of-the-head phenomena. In L. Berkowitz (Ed.), *Advances in experimental social psychology* (Vol. 11, pp. 249-288). New York: Academic Press.

Tetlock, P. E. (1992). The impact of accountability on judgment and choice: Toward a social contingency model. In M. P. Zanna (Ed.), *Advances in experimental social psychology* (Vol. 25, pp. 331-376). New York: Academic Press.

Tetlock, P. E., & Levi, A. (1982). Attribution bias: On the inconclusiveness of the cognition-motivation debate. *Journal of Experimental Social Psychology, 18,* 68-88.

Tetlock, P. E., & Manstead, A. S. R. (1985). Impression management versus intrapsychic explanations in social psychology: A useful dichotomy? *Psychological Review, 92,* 59-77.

Tetrault, L. A., Schriesheim, C. A., & Neider, L. L. (1988). Leadership training interventions: A review. *Organization Development Journal, 6,* 77-83.

Thibaut, J., & Kelley, H. (1959). *The social psychology of groups.* New York: John Wiley.

Thomas, E. A. C., & Martin, J. A. (1976). Analyses of parent-infant interaction. *Psychological Review, 83,* 141-158.

Triandis, H. C. (1989). The self and social behavior in differing cultural contexts. *Psychological Review, 96,* 506-520.

Trice, H. M., & Beyer, J. M. (1984). Studying organizational cultures through rites and ceremonials. *Academy of Management Review, 9,* 653-669.

Triplett, N. (1897). The dynamogenic factors in pacemaking and competition. *American Journal of Psychology, 9,* 507-533.

Trope, Y. (1986). Identification and inferential processes in dispositional attribution. *Psychological Review, 93,* 239-257.

Truzzi, M., & Easto, P. (1972). Carnivals, road shows, and freaks. *Trans-Action, 9,* 26-34.

Tuckman, B. W. (1965). Developmental sequence in small groups. *Psychological Bulletin, 63,* 384-399.

Tuckman, B. W., & Jensen, M. A. C. (1977). Stages of small group development revisited. *Group and Organization Studies, 2,* 419-427.

Turner, J. C. (1975). Social comparison and social identity: Some prospects for intergroup behavior. *European Journal of Social Psychology, 5,* 5-34.

Turner, J. C. (1982). Towards a cognitive redefinition of the social group. In H. Tajfel (Ed.), *Social identity and intergroup relations* (pp. 15-40). Cambridge, UK: Cambridge University Press.

Turner, J. C. (1985). Social categorization and the self-concept: A social cognitive theory of group behavior. In E. J. Lawler (Ed.), *Advances in group processes: Theory and research* (Vol. 2, pp. 77-122). Greenwich, CT: JAI.

Turner, J. C. (1987). The analysis of social influence. In J. C. Turner, M. A. Hogg, P. J. Oakes, S. D. Reicher, & M. S. Wetherell (Eds.), *Rediscovering the social group: A self-categorization theory* (pp. 68-88). Oxford, UK: Basil Blackwell.

Turner, J. C. (1991). *Social influence.* Milton Keynes: Open University Press.

Turner, J. C., Hogg, M. A., Oakes, P. J., Reicher, S. D., & Wetherell, M. S. (Eds.). (1987). *Rediscovering the social group: A self-categorization theory.* Oxford, UK: Basil Blackwell.

Turner, J. C., & Oakes, P. J. (1986). The significance of the social identity concept for social psychology with reference to individualism, interactionism, and social influence. *British Journal of Social Psychology, 25,* 237-252.

Turner, J. C., & Oakes, P. J. (1989). Self-categorization theory and social influence. In P. B. Paulus (Ed.), *Psychology of group influence* (2nd ed., pp. 233-275). Hillsdale, NJ: Lawrence Erlbaum.

Turner, J. C., Oakes, P. J., Haslam, S. A., & McGarty, C. A. (1994). Self and collective: Cognition and social context. *Personality and Social Psychology Bulletin, 20,* 454-463.

Turner, J. C., Wetherell, M. S., & Hogg, M. A. (1989). Referent informational influence and group polarization. *British Journal of Social Psychology, 28,* 135-147.

Uleman, J. S., & Bargh, J. A. (Eds.). (1990). *Unintended thought.* New York: Guilford.

Vallacher, R. R., & Wegner, D. M. (1987). What do people think they're doing? Action identification and human behavior. *Psychological Review, 94,* 3-15.

van Knippenberg, A., & Wilke, H. A. M. (1992). Prototypicality of arguments and conformity to ingroup norms. *European Journal of Social Psychology, 22,* 141-155.

Vaught, C., & Smith, D. L. (1980). Incorporation and mechanical solidarity in an underground coal mine. *Sociology of Work and Occupations, 7,* 159-187.

Veroff, J., Sutherland, L., Chadiha, L., & Ortega, R. M. (1993). Newlyweds tell their stories: A narrative method for assessing marital experiences. *Journal of Social and Personal Relationships, 10,* 437-457.

Volpato, C., Maass, A., Mucchi-Faina, A., & Vitti, E. (1990). Minority influence and social categorization. *European Journal of Social Psychology, 20,* 119-132.

Vreven, R., & Nuttin, J. (1976). Frequency perception of successes as a function of results previously obtained by others and by oneself. *Journal of Personality and Social Psychology, 34,* 734-743.

Walsh, J. P., & Ungson, G. R. (1991). Organizational memory. *Academy of Management Review, 16,* 57-91.

Warner, R. M., Kenny, D. A., & Stoto, M. (1979). A new round-robin analysis of variance for social interaction data. *Journal of Personality and Social Psychology, 37,* 1742-1757.

Watson, W. E., Kumar, K., & Michaelsen, L. K. (1993). Cultural diversity's impact on interaction process and performance: Comparing homogeneous and diverse task groups. *Academy of Management Journal, 36,* 590-602.

Watson, W. E., Michaelsen, L. K., & Sharp, W. (1991). Member competence, group interaction, and group decision making: A longitudinal study. *Journal of Applied Psychology, 76,* 803-809.

Wegner, D. M. (1987). Transactive memory: A contemporary analysis of the group mind. In B. Mullen & G. R. Goethals (Eds.), *Theories of group behavior* (pp. 185-208). New York: Springer-Verlag.

Wegner, D. M., Erber, R., & Raymond, P. (1991). Transactive memory in close relationships. *Journal of Personality and Social Psychology, 61,* 923-929.

Wegner, D. M., Giuliano, T., & Hertel, P. T. (1985). Cognitive interdependence in close relationships. In W. J. Ickes (Ed.), *Compatible and incompatible relationships* (pp. 253-276). New York: Springer-Verlag.

Weick, K. E., & Roberts, K. H. (1993). Collective mind in organizations: Heedful interrelating on flight decks. *Administrative Science Quarterly, 38,* 357-381.

Weigel, R. H., Wiser, P. I., & Cook, S. W. (1975). The impact of cooperative learning experiences on cross-ethnic relations and attitudes. *Journal of Social Issues, 31,* 219-244.

Weinberg, S. L. (1991). An introduction to multidimensional scaling. *Measurement and Evaluation in Counseling and Development, 24,* 12-36.

Weingart, L. R. (1992). Impact of group goals, task component complexity, effort, and planning on group performance. *Journal of Applied Psychology, 77,* 682-693.

Weinstein, N. D. (1982). Unrealistic optimism about susceptibility to health problems. *Journal of Behavioral Medicine, 5,* 441-460.

Weissman, M. M., & Paykel, E. S. (1974). *The depressed woman.* Chicago: University of Chicago Press.

Wetherell, M. S. (1987). Social identity and group polarization. In J. C. Turner, M. A. Hogg, P. J. Oakes, S. D. Reicher, & M. S. Wetherell (Eds.), *Rediscovering the social group: A self-categorization theory* (pp. 142-170). Oxford, UK: Basil Blackwell.

Wheeler, L., Reis, H., & Nezlek, J. (1983). Loneliness, social interaction, and sex roles. *Journal of Personality and Social Psychology, 45,* 943-953.

White, G. M. (1992). Ethnopsychology. In T. Schwartz, G. M. White, & C. A. Lutz (Eds.), *New directions in psychological anthropology* (pp. 21-46). Cambridge, UK: Cambridge University Press.

Wicker, A. W. (1969). Attitudes vs. actions: The relationship of verbal and overt behavioral responses to attitude objects. *Journal of Social Issues, 41,* 41-78.

Wicker, A. W. (1979). *An introduction to ecological psychology.* Pacific Grove, CA: Brooks/Cole.

Wilder, D. A. (1978). Reduction of intergroup discrimination through individuation of the outgroup. *Journal of Personality and Social Psychology, 36,* 1361-1374.

Wilder, D. A. (1986). Social categorization: Implications for creation and reduction of intergroup bias. In L. Berkowitz (Ed.), *Advances in experimental social psychology* (Vol. 19, pp. 291-355). New York: Academic Press.

Wilder, D. A. (1990). Some determinants of the persuasive power of ingroups and outgroups: Organization of information and attribution of independence. *Journal of Personality and Social Psychology, 59,* 1202-1213.

Willis, P. (1981). *Learning to labor: How working-class kids get working-class jobs.* New York: Columbia University Press. (Original work published 1977)

Wilson, T. D., & Schooler, J. W. (1991). Thinking too much: Introspection can reduce the quality of preferences and decisions. *Journal of Personality and Social Psychology, 60,* 181-192.

Winter, D. (1992). *Personal construct psychology in clinical practice.* London: Routledge.

Wittenbaum, G. M. (1996). *Information sampling in mixed-sex decision-making groups: The impact of diffuse status and task-relevant cues.* Unpublished doctoral dissertation, Miami University, Oxford, OH.

Wittenbaum, G. M., Stasser, G., & Merry, C. J. (in press). Tacit coordination in anticipation of small group task completion. *Journal of Experimental Social Psychology.*

Wolin, S. J., & Bennett, L. A. (1984). Family rituals. *Family Process, 23,* 401-420.

Wolosin, R. J., Sherman, S. J., & Till, A. (1973). Effects of cooperation and competition on responsibility attribution after success and failure. *Journal of Experimental Social Psychology, 9,* 220-235.

Wood, W., & Karten, S. J. (1986). Sex differences in interaction style as a product of perceived sex differences in competence. *Journal of Personality and Social Psychology, 50,* 341-347.

Worchel, S. (in press). The seasons of a group's life. In J. Deschamps, J. F. Morales, D. Paez, & H. Paicheler (Eds.), *Current perspectives on social identity and social categorization.* Barcelona, Spain: Anthropos.

Worchel, S., Axsom, D., Ferris, F., Samaha, C., & Schweitzer, S. (1978). Factors determining the effect of intergroup cooperation on intergroup attraction. *Journal of Conflict Resolution, 22,* 428-439.

Worchel, S., Coutant, D., & Grossman, M. (1994, July). *Patterns of individual and group performance.* Paper presented at 23rd International Congress of Applied Psychology, Madrid, Spain.

Worchel, S., Coutant-Sassic, D., & Grossman, M. (1992). A developmental approach to group dynamics: A model and illustrative research. In S. Worchel, W. Wood, & J. A. Simpson (Eds.), *Group process and productivity* (pp. 181-202). Newbury Park, CA: Sage.

Worchel, S., Coutant-Sassic, D., & Wong, F. (1993). Toward a more balanced view of conflict: There is a positive side. In S. Worchel & J. A. Simpson (Eds.), *Conflict between people and groups* (pp. 76-92). Chicago: Nelson-Hall.

Worchel, S., & Rothgerber, H. (in press). Changing the stereotype of stereotypes: Emphasizing the social side of the perceptions of groups. In R. Spears, P. Oakes, N. Ellemers, & S. A. Haslam (Eds.), *The social psychology of stereotyping and group life.* Oxford, UK: Basil Blackwell.

Wortman, C. B., Costanzo, P. R., & Witt, T. R. (1973). Effects of anticipated performance on the attribution of causality to self and others. *Journal of Personality and Social Psychology, 27,* 372-381.

Wright, T. L., & Ingraham, L. J. (1986). A social relations model test of the interpersonal circle. *Journal of Personality and Social Psychology, 50,* 1285-1290.

Wright, T. L., Ingraham, L. J., & Blackmer, D. R. (1985). The simultaneous study of individual differences and relationship effects in attraction. *Journal of Personality and Social Psychology, 47,* 1059-1062.

Wyer, R. S. (1988). Social memory and social judgment. In P. R. Solomon, G. R. Goethals, C. M. Kelley, & B. R. Stephens (Eds.), *Memory: Interdisciplinary approaches* (pp. 243-270). New York: Springer-Verlag.

Wyer, R. S., Jr., Budesheim, T. L., & Lambert, A. J. (1990). Cognitive representations of conversations about persons. *Journal of Personality and Social Psychology, 58,* 218-238.

Wyer, R. S., Jr., Lambert, A. J., Budesheim, T. L., & Gruenfeld, D. H. (1992). Theory and research on person impression formation: A look to the future. In L. L.

Martin & A. Tesser (Eds.), *The construction of social judgment* (pp. 3-36). Hillsdale, NJ: Lawrence Erlbaum.

Wyer, R. S., Jr., & Srull, T. K. (1986). Human cognition in its social context. *Psychological Review, 93,* 322-359.

Wyer, R. S., Jr., & Srull, T. K. (1994). *Handbook of social cognition* (2nd ed.). Hillsdale, NJ: Lawrence Erlbaum.

Yalom, L. D. (1985). *The theory and practice of group psychotherapy* (3rd ed.). New York: Basic Books.

Yetton, P. W., & Bottger, P. C. (1982). Individual versus group problem solving: An empirical test of a best-member strategy. *Organizational Behavior and Human Performance, 29,* 307-321.

Zaccaro, S. J., Peterson, C., Walker, S. (1987). Self-serving attributions for individual and group performance. *Social Psychology Quarterly, 50,* 257-263.

Zajonc, R. B. (1980). Cognition and social cognition: A historical perspective. In L. Festinger (Ed.), *Retrospections on social psychology* (pp. 180-204). New York: Oxford University Press.

Zander, A. (1971). *Motives and goals in groups.* New York: Academic Press.

Zander, A. (1985). *The purposes of groups and organizations.* San Francisco: Jossey-Bass.

Zebrowitz, L. A. (1990). *Social perception.* Pacific Grove, CA: Brooks/Cole.

Author Index

364

Subject Index

373

About the Contributors

Phyllis A. Anastasio is a social psychologist interested in changing group stereotypes through intergroup interaction. She is currently Assistant Professor of Psychology at Holy Family College.

Linda Argote received a PhD in Organizational Psychology from the University of Michigan and is currently Professor in the Graduate School of Industrial Administration at Carnegie Mellon University. She has also taught at the Kellogg Graduate School of Management at Northwestern University and in the Department of Industrial Engineering and Engineering Management at Stanford University. Her research and teaching focus on how groups and organizations acquire, retain, and transfer information. She is a Department Editor for *Management Science* and a Senior Editor for *Organization Science*. She also serves on the editorial boards of the *Journal of Organizational Behavior,* the *Journal of Engineering and Technology Management,* and the *Personality and Social Psychology Bulletin.*

Betty A. Bachman is a social psychologist interested in intergroup relations in organizational settings, particularly during mergers and acquisitions. She is currently Assistant Professor of Psychology at Siena College.

Aaron M. Brower received his PhD in 1985 from the University of Michigan and is Associate Professor and Associate Director of the University of Wisconsin-Madison School of Social Work. His current research explores differences between American subcultural groups in their educational attainment and life course decision making and on the roles played by goals and self-appraisals in meeting educational and developmental transitions. He has published widely in professional journals and is the Associate Editor of *Small Group Research*. In addition to coediting *What's Social About Social Cognition?*, he coauthored *Social Cognition and Individual Change* and *Advances in Group Work Research*.

John F. Dovidio is a social psychologist who does research on intergroup relations, prosocial behavior, and interpersonal dominance. He is currently Professor of Psychology at Colgate University.

Susan T. Fiske, PhD, is Distinguished University Professor, Department of Psychology, University of Massachusetts at Amherst. Her federally funded research focuses on motivation and stereotyping, and she is the coauthor, with Shelley E. Taylor, of *Social Cognition* (1984; 2nd ed., 1991). She is also the coeditor, with Daniel Gilbert and Gardner Lindzey, of the forthcoming 4th edition of the *Handbook of Social Psychology*.

Donelson R. Forsyth is Professor of Psychology at Virginia Commonwealth University. He received his PhD in Social Psychology from the University of Florida in 1978. His research interests include individuals' and groups' reactions to performance feedback, self-maintenance, and ethical thought.

Samuel L. Gaertner is a social psychologist who does research on racism and intergroup relations. He is currently Professor of Psychology at the University of Delaware.

Richard Gonzalez, PhD, is Associate Professor of Psychology at the University of Washington. His research interests include decision making, group processes, statistical modeling of data, and psychology and law.

Stephanie A. Goodwin, MS, is finishing the PhD program in personality and social psychology, University of Massachusetts at Amherst, after completing her undergraduate training at the University of Texas at Austin. Her graduate work has also included a year at the University of Louvain at Louvain-la-Neuve, Belgium. Her research interests lie in social cognition, especially stereotyping and power.

S. Alexander Haslam completed his undergraduate degree at the University of St. Andrews in 1985. After that he spent a year at Emory University as a Jones Scholar before completing his PhD as a Commonwealth Scholar at Macquarie University under the supervision of John Turner. After lecturing in the Faculty of Health Sciences at the University of Sydney, he took up a post as a postdoctoral researcher in the Department of Psychology at the Australian National University. He is now a Lecturer in the same department. His primary interests are in the areas of stereotyping, social categorization, and group processes. He is the coeditor (with Craig McGarty) of the forthcoming book *The Message of Social Psychology: Perspectives on Mind in Society* and the coauthor (with Penny Oakes and John Turner) of *Stereotyping and Social Reality* (1994).

William Ickes is completing his PhD as a Commonwealth Scholar at Macquarie University under the supervision of John Turner. After lecturing in the Faculty of Health Sciences at the University of Sydney, he took up a post as a postdoctoral researcher in the Department of Psychology at the Australian National University. He is now a Lecturer in the same department. His primary interests are in the areas of stereotyping, social categorization, and group processes. He is the coeditor (with Craig McGarty) of the forthcoming bookssistant Professor in the Department of Psychology at Hofstra University. His research interests include social cognition and (inter)group perceptions.

Craig Johnson, PhD, is Assistant Professor in the Department of Psychology at Hofstra University. His research interests are in the areas of social cognition and (inter)group processes.

Marianne E. Johnson has served on the faculty of the Department of Psychology at the University of Manitoba since completing her PhD in Clinical Psychology at Vanderbilt University in 1988. In collaboration with Hans Strupp, she has investigated recurrent relationship themes and other aspects of the psychotherapy process and has a particular interest in the use of the social relations model to study group process. She has recently completed training as an analyst at the C. G. Jung Institute in Zurich, Switzerland.

Karl N. Kelley graduated in 1987 with a PhD in Psychology from Virginia Commonwealth University. He is currently Assistant Professor at North Central College. His research interests include attributional and affective reactions following performance feedback and social psychology applied to organizational and education settings.

Ranjani Krishnan is a PhD student in the Katz Graduate School of Business at the University of Pittsburgh. Her research interests include group behavior, employment contracts, and incentive systems in managerial accounting.

Craig McGarty was educated at the University of Adelaide and Macquarie University, receiving his PhD from Macquarie University in 1991 (where he was a tutor from 1985 to 1989). His PhD (supervised by John Turner) was on categorization and the social psychology of judgment. He spent 1990 as a Lecturer in Social Psychology/Social Interaction at the University of Western Sydney, Nepean. In 1991, he moved to the Australian National University as a research associate. Since 1993, he has been a Lecturer in Psychology in the Division of Psychology at the Australian National University. He has worked on a wide variety of topics in experimental social psychology, approached from the perspective of self-categorization theory; his recent work has focused on categorization, social stereotyping and the perception of minorities, and social influence and persuasion. He is the coeditor (with Alex Haslam) of the forthcoming book, *The Message of Social Psychology: Perspectives on Mind in Society.*

Richard L. Moreland received a PhD in Social Psychology at the University of Michigan and is currently Professor of Psychology and Management at the University of Pittsburgh. He is interested in many aspects of small groups, especially the changes that they undergo over time. This interest has led him to study such phenomena as the formation and dissolution of groups, group development, and the socialization of group members. He is an Associate Editor for the *Personality and Social Psychology Bulletin* and serves on the editorial boards of the *Journal of Experimental Social Psychology* and the *Journal of Personality and Social Psychology.*

Brian Mullen, PhD, is Professor in the Department of Psychology at Syracuse University. His research interests include social cognition perspectives on (inter)group phenomena and meta-analysis.

Robert A. Neimeyer, PhD, is Professor in the Department of Psychology, University of Memphis. An active contributor to psychotherapy theory and research, the majority of his work has drawn on concepts and methods in personal construct theory and related constructivist approaches to personality and psychotherapy. He has published 14 books, including *Personal Construct Therapy Casebook* (1987), *Advances in Personal Construct Theory, Vols. 1, 2, & 3* (1990, 1992, 1995), and *Constructivism in Psychotherapy* (1995). He is the coeditor of the *Journal of Constructivist Psychology* and serves on the editorial boards of a number of other journals. In recognition of his scholarly contributions, he was granted the Distinguished Research Award by the University of Memphis in 1990.

Judith L. Nye, PhD, is Associate Professor of Psychology at Monmouth University, New Jersey. Her current research focuses on social cognition group processes, specifically impression formation and the interaction between leaders and followers. Of additional and related interest are the effects of sex role stereotypes on impressions of leaders.

Daphna Oyserman received her PhD in Social Work and Social Psychology from the University of Michigan and taught at the Hebrew University of Jerusalem until 1991 when she joined the Merrill-Palmer Institute (Wayne State University), where she is currently a Research Scientist. Her research interests focus on the interplay between sociocultural context, self-concept, and everyday behaviors. Her research, currently funded by NIMH and the W. T. Grant Foundation, focuses on the interplay between social context, gender and ethnic identity, possible selves, and everyday behaviors, with a particular focus on school persistence, social obligation, coping, and well-being.

Martin J. Packer, PhD, is Associate Professor in the Psychology Department of Duquesne University. His research focuses on children's development in social context, employing an interpretive methodology. He is coauthor, with Richard Addison, of *Entering the Circle: Hermeneutic Investigation in Psychology* (1989).

Miles L. Patterson, PhD, is Professor of Psychology at the University of Missouri-St. Louis. He is the author of two books and more than 50 chapters and scholarly articles on nonverbal communication. From 1986 to 1991, he served as the editor of the *Journal of Nonverbal Behavior.*

Drew Rozell is a graduate student in the Department of Psychology at Syracuse University. His research interests include intergroup perception phenomena, particularly the effects of skin tone on ethnic perceptions.

Mary C. Rust is a graduate student in the social psychology program at the University of Delaware. She is interested in intergroup relations.

Leo G. Simonetta, PhD, is Assistant Professor of Public Administration and Urban Studies at Georgia State University in Atlanta. He is also the Polling Director at the Applied Research Center at that university. His current research interests include group development and the socialization of new group members.

Garold Stasser received his PhD in Social Psychology at the University of Illinois at Urbana-Champaign and is currently Professor of Psychology at Miami University (Ohio). His major scholarly interests include group decision making, information exchange and idea generation during group discussion, and computer simulation of social interaction. He currently serves as a Consulting Editor of the *Journal of Personality and Social Psychology* and the *Journal of Experimental Social Psychology.*

John C. Turner is Professor of Psychology at the Australian National University. He did his BA (1971) and PhD (1975) degrees in Social Psychology in England at the Universities of Sussex and Bristol, respectively. He is a past Visiting Member of the Institute for Advanced Study, Princeton, New Jersey (1982-1983), and has also held appointments at the University of Bristol and Macquarie University in Sydney. He is currently (1994-1996) Dean of the Faculty of Science at the ANU. His research interests are in social identity, intergroup relations, group processes, and social cognition, particularly from the perspective of self-categorization theory. He is coauthor of *Rediscovering the Social Group: A Self-Categorization Theory* (1987) and, more recently, has published *Social Influence* (1991) and, with Penny Oakes and Alex Haslam, *Stereotyping and Social Reality* (1994).

Gwen M. Wittenbaum is Assistant Professor of Communication at Michigan State University and received her PhD in social psychology from Miami University (Ohio). Her research interests lie at the interface between social cognition and small group processes. Recent research has examined the impact of group discussion on social judgment, the effect of member status on information use in decision-making groups, and the influence of task and social information on group coordination. Along with Sandra I. Vaughan and Garold Stasser, she recently completed a chapter on group coordination to appear in the book *Social Psychological Applications to Social Issues: Applications of Theory and Research on Groups*.

Stephen Worchel, PhD, is the McFadden Professor of Liberal Arts at Texas A&M University. His research interests include group dynamics, conflict and conflict resolution, and intergroup behavior. More recently he has become interested in applying research in group dynamics into the areas of ethnic identity and conflict and political processes.